MEN, WOMEN, AND CHAIN SAWS

MEN·WOMEN·AND CHAIN SAWS

GENDER IN THE MODERN HORROR FILM

By Carol J. Clover

PRINCETON UNIVERSITY PRESS • PRINCETON, NEW JERSEY

Published by Princeton University Press, 41 William Street,

Princeton, New Jersey 08540

All Rights Reserved

Library of Congress Cataloging-in-Publication Data

Clover, Carol J., 1940–

Men, women, and chain saws : gender in the modern horror

film / Carol J. Clover.

p. cm.

Includes bibliographical references and index.

ISBN 0-691-04802-9

ISBN 0-691-00620-2 (pbk.)

1. Horror films—History and criticism. 2. Women in motion pictures.

3. Sex role in motion pictures. I. Title.

PC1995.9.H6C53 1992 791.43'616—dc20 91-28571 CIP

This book has been composed in Linotron Palatino

Princeton University Press books are printed on acid-free paper

and meet the guidelines for permanence and durability of the

Committee on Production Guidelines for Book Longevity of the

Council on Library Resources

First Princeton paperback printing, 1993

Printed in the United States of America

20 19 18 17 16

ISBN-13: 978-0-691-00620-8

ISBN-10: 0-691-00620-2

FOR *Greta* AND *Joshua*

CONTENTS

ACKNOWLEDGMENTS

I HAVE, in the course of writing a book in what is for me a new field, racked up a long list of debts both intellectual and spiritual. To Frances Ferguson for so recklessly commissioning "Her Body, Himself" to begin with. To Bill (William Ian) Miller for once again asking the hardest questions, and especially for knowing without asking just how medieval a project this is. To Thomas Laqueur and Kaja Silverman for keeping me on track. To Richard Hutson, Kathleen Moran, and Carolyn Porter—the "movie group"—for criticism and for illuminating debate, traces of which are evident throughout this book. To Sally Gearhart, Walter Herbert, Lynn Hunt, Michael Rogin, Vivian Sobchack, and Linda Williams for helpful readings and suggestions at various points along the way. To Frank Grady and Terry Mulcaire for good movie company and discussion. To the Yuppie Bikers for the larger perspective.

Thanks too to the John Simon Guggenheim Memorial Foundation for the fellowship that enabled me to write a large portion of the book during 1988–1989, and to the University of California at Berkeley for research support.

MEN, WOMEN, AND CHAIN SAWS

Carrie and the Boys

THE HIT HORROR MOVIE of 1976, in fact one of the winners in a horror-happy decade, was *Carrie*.[1] Directed by Brian De Palma and based on a novel by Stephen King, it tells the story, as King sums it up in *Danse Macabre*, of "a girl named Carrie White, the browbeaten daughter of a religious fanatic. Because of her strange clothes and shy mannerisms, Carrie is the butt of every class joke; the social outsider in every situation."[2] Actually, much of the torment Carrie comes in for has to do with menstruation. When she gets her first period in the locker room shower and doesn't know what it is, the other girls scream with laughter and shout "Plug it up! Plug it up!" as they pelt her with tampons and sanitary pads. But the source of her pain soon becomes the source of her power: "She also has a mild telekinetic ability which intensifies after her first menstrual period, and she finally uses this power to 'bring down the house' following a terrible social disaster at her high school prom." The disaster in question is a grim practical joke whereby she is led to believe that she has been elected queen of the senior prom, only to have a bucket of pig's blood dumped down on her at the moment she is crowned. To which she responds with the force of her telekinetic will, causing the gym to go up in flames and her entire high school class with it.

With its prom queens, menstrual periods, tampons, worries about clothes and makeup, *Carrie* would seem on the face of it the most feminine of stories. For author King, it is also a feminist one:

> If *The Stepford Wives* concerns itself with what men want from women, then *Carrie* is largely about how women find their own channels of power, and what men fear about women and women's sexuality . . . which is only to say that, writing the book in 1973 and only out of college three years, I was fully aware of what Women's Liberation implied for me and others of my sex. The book is, in its more adult implications, an uneasy masculine shrinking from a future of female equality. For me, Carrie White is a sadly misused teenager, an example of the sort of person whose spirit is so often

---

[1] The other mainstream horror hit of 1976 was *The Omen*. The low-budget tradition that year produced George Romero's *Martin* and David Lynch's *Eraserhead*.

[2] Stephen King, *Danse Macabre*, p. 171.

broken for good in that pit of man- and woman-eaters that is your normal suburban high school. But she's also Woman, feeling her powers for the first time and, like Samson, pulling down the temple on everyone in sight at the end of the book.[3]

But where exactly is the horror here? If "women's liberation" is the fear, is Carrie its representative monster, and if she is, who is the victim, and who is the hero?

The answer would seem to be that, like Samson, Carrie is all three in turn. Throughout most of the movie she is the victim of monstrous schoolmates and a monstrous mother, but when, at the end, she turns the tables, she herself becomes a kind of monstrous hero—hero insofar as she has risen against and defeated the forces of monstrosity, monster insofar as she has herself become excessive, demonic. She has become, in short, what I shall throughout this book call the female victim-hero (the hero part always understood as implying some degree of monstrosity), whose status in both roles has indeed been enabled by "women's liberation." Feminism, that is, has given a language to her victimization and a new force to the anger that subsidizes her own act of horrific revenge.

But to whom does this tale appeal? King again:

> And one reason for the success of the story in both print and film, I think, lies in this: Carrie's revenge is something that any student who has ever had his gym shorts pulled down in Phys Ed or his glasses thumb-rubbed in study hall could approve of.

Now although the "his" in King's brief analysis of *Carrie*'s popularity may in principle refer to the universal subject, the "any student" in question here looks a lot like an adolescent boy.[4] Pulling gym shorts down and thumb-rubbing glasses are things boys do to each other, not, by and large, things that girls do to each other or that boys do to girls. They are oblique sexual gestures, the one threatening sodomy or damage to the genitals or both, and the other threatening damage to the eyes—a castration of sorts. (Remember that Samson too, whom King invokes as Carrie's analogue, was bound, shorn, and blinded before he managed to bring the temple down.) The boy so threatened and so humiliated, King seems to be saying, is a boy who recognizes himself in a girl who finds herself bleeding from her

---

[3] Ibid., pp. 171–72. See also Vivian Sobchack, "Child/Alien/Father," n. 4).

[4] Fifteen-year-old boys, to be exact. "A film which appealed directly to the fifteen-year-olds that provided the spike point for movie-going audiences—and one with a subtext tailored to match—was the Brian De Palma adaptation of my novel *Carrie*" (King, *Danse Macabre*, p. 12).

crotch in the gym shower, pelted with tampons, and sloshed with pig's blood at the senior prom.

What this "gym shorts and glasses" remark of King's admits, glancingly but unmistakably, is a possibility that film theory, film criticism, cultural studies analysis, movie reviews, and popular political commentary seldom entertain: the possibility that male viewers are quite prepared to identify not just with screen females, but with screen females in the horror-film world, screen females in fear and pain. That identification, the official denial of that identification, and the larger implications of both those things are what this book is about.

What horror, what viewers, and what sort of "identification" exactly? The compass of this book is rather narrow. I concern myself chiefly with American cinematic horror (a category I define somewhat loosely),[5] chiefly with films from the 1970s to the mid-1980s (with some reference back to progenitors), and only with those subgenres in which female figures and/or gender issues loom especially large: slasher films, occult or possession films, and rape-revenge films.[6] I originally planned to concentrate on low or exploitation horror (terms I mean descriptively, not judgmentally), but that proved both impractical and finally intellectually unjustifiable (the traffic between low and high is such that it is unnatural to separate them), and I have accordingly mixed the levels. As the following chapters will suggest, it remains my conviction that innovation trickles upward as often as downward, and that the fiscal conditions of low-budget filmmaking are such that creativity and individual vision can prosper there in ways that they may not in mainstream environments.[7] As I shall pro-

[5] It has not been my concern to define horror or to adhere to the definitions of others (Noël Carroll's in his *Philosophy of Horror*, for example). I have been guided for the most part by video rental store categorizations, which, despite some variation from store to store, seem to capture better than any definition I know what the public senses to be "horror." The tendency to classify a plot as "horror" when it is low budget and "drama" or "suspense" when it is highly produced is a phenomenon I will take up in the following chapters (particularly in connection with rape-revenge movies).

[6] For more historical and generic treatments of horror, see especially Charles Derry, *Dark Dreams*; James B. Twitchell, *Dreadful Pleasures* and *Preposterous Violence*; Andrew Tudor, *Monsters and Mad Scientists*; Carlos Clarens, *An Illustrated History of the Horror Film*; Ivan Butler, *The Horror Film*; Noël Carroll, *The Philosophy of Horror*; and S. S. Prawer, *Caligari's Children*; R.H.W. Dillard, *Horror Films*; David Soren, *The Rise and Fall of the Horror Film*; and William Everson, *Classics of the Horror Film*.

[7] In horror director John Carpenter's blunt terms, "In independent studio work, often you're out for a different purpose, and you can take more chances because you have less money at risk. Whereas, when you're making a big studio film, even a medium one, you're talking about 12 to 15 million dollars—well, the risks have to stop

pose, the independent, low-budget tradition has been central in the manufacture of the new "tough girls" that have loomed so large in horror since the mid-seventies: not only figures like Carrie, whose power somehow derives from their female insides, but the boyish, knife-wielding victim-heroes of slasher films and the grim avengers of their own rapes in films like *Ms. 45* and *I Spit on Your Grave*.

To the question of who watches such films, there is no neat answer. Film audiences are in general less analyzed than television audiences, and because what statistical surveys there are tend to be sponsored by major studios and a fair percentage of horror is (or has been) produced independently, horror audiences are especially understudied. Horror movies tend to be made less on the basis of audience statistics than on the basis of hunch, imitation (hence the proliferation of sequels and rip-offs), and, in higher-budget cases, test audience results. To complicate matters further, many horror films have short theatrical runs, or no theatrical release at all, but return their investment on videocassette rentals, the audience for which is largely hidden from research view.

Still, what formal surveys and informal accounts there are bear out with remarkable consistency Stephen King's presumption that adolescent males hold pride of place. At theater screenings, in any case, the constituencies typically break down, in order of size, as follows: young men, frequently in groups but also solo; male-female couples of various ages (though mostly young); solo "rogue males" (older men of ominous appearance and/or reactions); and adolescent girls in groups.[8] The proportions vary somewhat from subgenre to subgenre and from movie to movie (the more mainstream the film, the more "normal" the audience), but the preponderance of young males appears constant. Certainly boys are the unmistakable target audience of horror fanzines. Nor do videocassette rentals seem to depart significantly from the profile. In the absence of statistics, I have polled some sixty employees of rental outlets (half in the San Francisco area, half elsewhere in the country) about the clientele for certain films (*Texas Chain Saw Massacre*, *I Spit on Your Grave*, *Ms. 45*, *Witchboard*, *Videodrome*, and *The Evil Dead*), and they confirm to a person the young male bias. Three local outlets were generous enough to track for a period of about four weeks the rentals of two low-budget rape-revenge films, *I Spit on Your Grave* and *Ms. 45*. (The reasons

---

because you need to make money back. It's just a fact of life in Hollywood" (Carpenter as quoted in Robert C. Cumbow, *Order in the Universe*, p. 194).

[8] See Bruce A. Austin, *The Film Audience* and "Portrait of a Cult Film Audience." See also Twitchell, *Dreadful Pleasures*, pp. 68–71 and 307; Roger Ebert, "Why Movie Audiences Aren't Safe Any More."

for my interest in those two films in particular will become clear in chapter 3.) Their results were consistent: *Ms. 45* was rented about four times out of five by men, and its renters of both sexes were nearly all under the age of twenty-five; *I Spit on Your Grave*, much the grislier of the two, rented nine times out of ten to male viewers, mostly under the age of twenty-five but occasionally older. (The odd blip reported by one employee of "two women at least thirty" turned out to be friends of mine renting it at my suggestion.) The renter of a videocassette is not necessarily its only watcher, of course, and Berkeley audiences are not all audiences, but the numbers are suggestive, and they do square with the standard profile of theater audiences for horror.

I want to stress, before I pass on to other matters, that the bias of my book is even more extreme than the bias of the overall horror audience. My interest in the male viewer's stake in horror spectatorship is such that I have consigned to virtual invisibility all other members of the audience, despite the fact that their loyalty and engagement can be just as ardent and their stake in the genre just as deserving of attention. One of the surprises of this project has been the number of what I once thought of as unlikely people—middle-aged, middle-class people of both sexes—who have "come out" to me about their secret appetite for so-called exploitation horror, and I have developed a great respect, through conversations not only with them but with teenage fans, for the variety and richness of people's relationship to such texts. A study of horror film audiences per se would take into account the full range of their composition—not to speak of the range of experiences the same movie may offer the "rogue male," the adolescent boy, and the middle-aged woman. This book, however, is not about horror audiences per se any more than it is about horror per se. It is a book that explores the relationship of the "majority viewer" (the younger male) to the female victim-heroes who have become such a conspicuous screen presence in certain sectors of horror. That pairing has much to tell us, I think, about spectatorship in general, not to speak of the politics of representation, the politics of displacement, and the politics of criticism and theory.[9]

"Identification" is the subject of a voluminous theoretical literature. Following Christian Metz, commentators tend to distinguish be-

---

[9] For a succinct summary of the issues involved in studying the masochistic dimension of male spectatorship, see Tania Modleski's "Introduction" to *The Women Who Knew Too Much*, esp. pp. 9–13. I am in full sympathy with Modleski's insistence that discussions of male spectatorship not lose sight of the stakes for women and hope that my book has followed Modleski's example.

tween primary identification (with the camera, wherever it may be and whatever it may be up to) and secondary identification (with the character of empathic choice).[10] Both are fluid, character-identification on the psychoanalytic grounds that competing figures resonate with competing parts of the viewer's psyche (masochistic victim and sadistic monster, for example), and camera-identification on the cinematographic grounds that the camera can entertain different positions with ease—not just character positions, but omniscient ones— and with different degrees of "personality" (the hand-held first-person or subjective camera thought by convention to be the most personal of all). Laura Mulvey has famously maintained that the cinematic gaze (constitutive of primary identification) is not gender-free but is structured by male or masculine perceptions, a fact revealed when the camera's object is a woman. The cinematic apparatus, according to Mulvey, has two ways of looking at a woman, both organized around defending against her "castration" and both of which, therefore, presuppose a male (or masculine) gazer: a sadistic-voyeuristic look, whereby the gazer salves his unpleasure at female lack by seeing the woman punished, and a fetishistic-scopophilic look, whereby the gazer salves his unpleasure by fetishizing the female body in whole or part.[11]

Needless to say, horror movies spend a lot of time looking at women, and in first-person ways that do indeed seem well described by Mulvey's "sadistic-voyeuristic" gaze. But the story does not end there. A standard horror format calls for a variety of positions and character sympathies in the early phases of the story, but, as the plot goes on, a consolidation at both levels (story and cinematography), and in the final phase a fairly tight organization around the functions of victim and hero (which may be collapsed into one figure or, alternatively, split into many). Although the camerawork of *Carrie* repeatedly invites us to take the perspective of Carrie's sadistic tormentors (a familar feature of Brian De Palma's direction), the majority position throughout, and certainly the position that prevails in the final phase, is Carrie's own. (It seems clear on the face of it that involvement in her revenge at the end is contingent on an earlier involvement with her pain.) I shall be arguing throughout this book that by any measure, horror is far more victim-identified than the standard view would have it—which raises questions about film theory's con-

[10] Christian Metz, "The Imaginary Signifier" in *The Imaginary Signifier*. Among the commentaries on identification I shall be citing throughout, one summary, in nontechnical language, stands out as particularly useful: that of John Ellis in *Visible Fictions* (pp. 40–50).

[11] Laura Mulvey, "Visual Pleasure and Narrative Cinema."

ventional assumption that the cinematic apparatus is organized around the experience of a mastering, voyeuristic gaze.

In fact, horror's system of sympathies transcends and preexists any given example. Patrons of a slasher film or a rape-revenge film know more or less what to expect well before the film rolls, and at least one horror director (William Friedkin) has suggested that their emotional engagement with the movie begins while they are standing in line— a proposition that acknowledges the profoundly formulaic nature of the enterprise.[12] And as anyone who sees horror at the right venue (designated mall or downtown matinees) can attest, horror audiences can be startlingly "competent" (in the linguistic sense) and startlingly public about it. As Andrew Britton describes it:

> It became obvious at a very early stage that every spectator knew exactly what the film was going to do at every point, even down to the order in which it would dispose of its various characters, and the screening was accompanied by something in the nature of a running commentary in which each dramatic move was excitedly broadcast some minutes before it was actually made. The film's total predictability did not create boredom or disappointment. On the contrary, the predictability was clearly the main source of pleasure, and the only occasion for disappointment would have been a modulation of the formula, not the repetition of it. Everyone had parted with his or her four bucks in the complete confidence that *Hell Night* was a known quantity, and that it would do nothing essentially different from any of its predecessors. Everyone could guess what would happen, and it did happen. In the course of the evening, art had shrunk to its first cause, and I had the incongruous sense, on coming out, of having been invited to participate in communion.

"This highly ritualised and formulaic character," he concludes, "is the most striking feature of the contemporary entertainment film."[13]

---

[12] Derry, *Dark Dreams*, pp. 123–24. More on this in chapter 4.

[13] Andrew Britton, "Blissing Out," pp. 2–3. Britton here echoes the Frankfurt School critique of mass culture, especially Max Horkheimer and Theodor W. Adorno's arguments in *Dialectic of Enlightenment* (pp. 120–28). It should be noted, however, that the characteristics which prompt Britton's political contempt are by no means peculiar to "Reaganite entertainment"; they are the usual characteristics of orally performed "literature" everywhere: in Western tradition from the Greeks through the late Middle Ages and beyond, and in the Third World, and in pockets of the First and Second, in our own time. Britton's description could very nearly stand as a summary of the aesthetics of oral literature, right down to the phrase "ritualised and formulaic." So too horror's habit of cross-referencing or "intertextuality," which Britton finds solipsistic, narcissistic, hermetic, and banal (and Vera Dika, in her *Games of Terror*, finds "postmodern"); it too is a standard feature of oral cycles. As for the aggressive behavior of horror audiences, it is worth noting that according to historian Lawrence W. Levine,

Although many folklorists disown horror movies as products too mediated by technology, authorial intention, and the profit motive to be seen as folklore in any authentic sense, the fact is that horror movies look like nothing so much as folktales—a set of fixed tale types that generate an endless stream of what are in effect variants: sequels, remakes, and rip-offs.[14] "Basically, sequels mean the same film," observes director John Carpenter, who should know. "That's what people want to see. They want to see the same movie again."[15] Audiences may thrill to the killer's particular shtick (his hockey mask or knife-fingers or whatever) or to the special effect that shows the bloody stump up close—surface effects are the stuff of fanzines—but the structure, functions or subject positions, and narrative moves are as old as the hills.[16] Much of the commentary on horror has concerned itself with mapping the cinematographic moves that are presumed to be constitutive of "identification"; horror movies rub our noses in camerawork. But it is important to remember that in a large or gross or deep-structural sense, the "identifications" of horror are already in place, installed long before the individual movie was even a glint in the director's eye.[17] Camerawork may play with the terms, but it does not set them.

The very fact that the cinematic conventions of horror are so easily and so often parodied would seem to suggest that, individual variation notwithstanding, its basic structures of apperception are fixed and fundamental. The same is true of the stories they tell. Students of folklore or early literature recognize in horror the hallmarks of oral

---

extravagantly participatory audiences (shouting, throwing things) were the norm in all manner of performances (operatic, dramatic, symphonic) until toward the end of the nineteenth century, when they were silenced and "sacralized" (*Highbrow/Lowbrow*).

[14] The most complete folkloric treatments of horror movies to date are Twitchell's *Dreadful Pleasures* and Harold Schechter's *The Bosom Serpent*.

[15] John Carpenter, as quoted by Cumbow in *Order in the Universe*, p. 68.

[16] Interviews with horror filmmakers turn remarkably often on fantasies, dreams, and childhood memories, or mention myths or folktales or legends by way of establishing archetype (note King's reference to Samson), or directly or indirectly reveal a dependence on Freud. Some filmmakers seem quite conscious manipulators, others unwitting purveyors, of the traditions on which their art rests. William Castle is evidently one of the latter: "I get calls from all over the United States, in fact I get letters from all over the world, from students who are studying film and have taken these films and are looking for hidden meanings. It's a very strange thing. I definitely feel that possibly in my unconscious I was trying to say something. . . . Truly, it is possible that deeply buried within my unconsciousness was the feeling of trying to say something" (as quoted in Derry, *Dark Dreams*, p. 112). Others, as I shall suggest in the chapters that follow, are rather more premeditated.

[17] A recent essay by Anne Friedberg reminds us of the psychosexual processes that precondition our cinematic identifications ("A Denial of Difference").

narrative: the free exchange of themes and motifs, the archetypal characters and situations, the accumulation of sequels, remakes, imitations. This is a field in which there is in some sense no original, no real or right text, but only variants; a world in which, therefore, the meaning of the individual example lies outside itself. The "art" of the horror film, like the "art" of pornography, is to a very large extent the art of rendition or performance, and it is understood as such by the competent audience.[18] A particular example may have original features, but its quality as a horror film lies in the way it delivers the cliché. James B. Twitchell rightly recommends an

> ethnological approach, in which the various stories are analyzed as if no one individual telling really mattered. . . . You search for what is stable and repeated; you neglect what is "artistic" and "original." This is why, for me, auteur criticism is quite beside the point in explaining horror. . . . The critic's first job in explaining the fascination of horror is not to fix the images at their every appearance but, instead, to trace their migrations to the audience and, only then, try to understand why they have been crucial enough to pass along.[19]

That auteur criticism is at least partly beside the point is clear from interviews with such figures as John Carpenter (*Halloween, The Fog*)—interviews which would seem to suggest that, like the purveyors of folklore, the makers of film operate more on instinct and formula than conscious understanding. So bewildered was Hitchcock by the unprecedented success of *Psycho* that he approached the Stanford Research Institute about doing a study of the phenomenon.[20]

What makes horror "crucial enough to pass along" is, for critics since Freud, what has made ghost stories and fairy tales crucial enough to pass along: its engagement of repressed fears and desires and its reenactment of the residual conflict surrounding those feelings. Horror films thus respond to interpretation, as Robin Wood puts it, as "at once the personal dreams of their makers and the collective dreams of their audiences—the fusion made possible by the

---

[18] As Morris Dickstein puts it, "The 'art' of horror film is a ludicrous notion since horror, even at its most commercially exploitative, is genuinely subcultural like the wild child that can never be tamed, or the half-human mutant who appeals to our secret fascination with deformity and the grotesque" ("The Aesthetics of Fright," p. 34).

[19] Twitchell, *Dreadful Pleasures*, p. 84.

[20] "I was sufficiently interested in the picture's success to contact Stanford University Research Institute so they could find out why it was such a hit. But when they wanted $75,000 to do the research job, I told them I wasn't *that* curious" (as quoted by Donald Spoto in *The Dark Side of Genius*, p. 457).

shared structures of a common ideology."[21] And just as attacker and attacked are expressions of the same self in nightmares, so they are expressions of the same viewer in horror film. We are both Red Riding Hood *and* the Wolf; the force of the experience, in horror, comes from "knowing" both sides of the story. It is no surprise that the first film to which viewers were not admitted once the theater darkened was *Psycho*. Whether Hitchcock actually meant with this measure to intensify the "sleep" experience is unclear, but the effect both in the short run, in establishing *Psycho* as the ultimate thriller, and in the long run, in altering the cinema-going habits of the nation, is indisputable. In the current understanding, horror is the least interruptible of all film genres, and this fact itself bears witness to the compulsive nature of the stories it tells.

So too horror's cast of characters—or, more properly, its cast of functions or subject positions. Like the low-mythic tradition of which it is a part, horror is organized around functions that are understood to preexist and constitute character. Although a gorilla, a blob, a shark, and a motel attendant are superficially very different entities, they all do more or less the same job, narratively speaking, and they all end up at least temporarily evacuated from the operative universe. Likewise the categories victim and hero, roles no less prefabricated and predictable for their being performed by many or one, tall or short, dark or light, male or female.[22]

In fact, of course, males and females are not evenly distributed over the categories. The functions of monster and hero are far more frequently represented by males and the function of victim far more garishly by females. The fact that female monsters and female heroes, when they do appear, are masculine in dress and behavior (and often even name), and that male victims are shown in feminine postures at the moment of their extremity, would seem to suggest that gender inheres in the function itself—that there is something about the victim function that wants manifestation in a female, and something about the monster and hero functions that wants expression in

---

[21] Robin Wood, "Return of the Repressed," p. 26. Horror itself repeatedly thematizes the dream. The newest wrinkle on the tradition is Wes Craven's *Nightmare on Elm Street*, in which it is the nightmare itself, shared by the teenagers who live on Elm Street, that is fatal. The one girl who survives does so by first refusing to sleep and then, at the same time that she acknowledges her parents' inadequacies, by conquering the feelings that prompt the deadly nightmare. On the workings of literary and cinematic fantasy, see especially Mark Nash, "*Vampyr* and the Fantastic," and Rosemary Jackson, *Fantasy*.

[22] Tudor's *Monsters and Mad Scientists*, which charts the history of horror from 1931 to 1984 by charting the metamorphosis of the functional categories ("threat," "victim," etc.) is in its own way a folkloristic project.

a male. Sex, in this universe, proceeds from gender, not the other way around. A figure does not cry and cower because she is a woman; she is a woman because she cries and cowers. And a figure is not a psychokiller because he is a man; he is a man because he is a psychokiller. Jurij Lotman has suggested that there are really only two "characters" (subject positions or functions) in myth: a mobile, heroic being who crosses boundaries and "penetrates" closed spaces, and an immobile being who personifies that damp, dark space and constitutes that which is to be overcome. Because the latter is so obviously coded feminine, as Teresa de Lauretis notes, the former is perforce masculine.[23] Horror is more complicated, but the general point holds: the perceived nature of the function generates the characters that will represent it, mobile heroism wanting male representatives, and passive dank spaces wanting female ones.

The picture grows even more complicated if we entertain the possibility that these films are informed by not one but two accounts of sexual difference, between which they slide uneasily. According to Thomas Laqueur's history of medical treatises from the Greeks to Freud, sexual difference as we officially know it—the "two-sex" or "two-flesh" model, which construes male and female as "opposite" or *essentially* different from one another (and which therefore underwrites psychoanalytic thought)—has not existed from time immemorial but is a relatively modern construction that sits, in fact, rather lightly on large sectors of the culture.[24] To judge from a rich variety of medical, linguistic, pictorial, and narrative evidence, an earlier world construed the sexes as inside versus outside versions of a single genital/reproductive system, differing in degree of warmth or coolness and hence in degree of value (hot being superior to cool), but essentially the same in form and function, and hence ultimately fungible versions of one another. It is not that the male body has a penis, a female body a vagina, and the one-sex body both. It is that penis and vagina are one and the same organ; if one happens to extrude and the other one to intrude (in an inside-out and upward-extending fashion), they are physiologically identical (and the same words did for both). Likewise, all humans have testes, the male ones

[23] Jurij Lotman, "The Origin of Plot in the Light of Typology," and Teresa de Lauretis, "Desire in Narrative," in her *Alice Doesn't*. De Lauretis's essay is a must-read in this connection. See also her "Violence of Rhetoric" in *Technologies of Gender* and Claude Lévi-Strauss's "Structure and Form."

[24] Thomas Laqueur, *Making Sex*. It has long been recognized that earlier eras had a rather different sense of sexual difference (and hence of homosexuality). The virtue of Laqueur's study of medical treatises is that it provides an explicitly corporeal model against which to read fantasy.

outside and the female ones inside (and again, the same words did for both). So too bodily fluids: the genital fluid that in the coolness of the female is normally red and manifest as menses becomes, in the greater heat of the male, whitish and manifest as semen (and female orgasm, understood as analogous to male ejaculation, was thought necessary for conception). Needless to say, the "one sex" in question was essentially male, women being "inverted, and less perfect, men" possessed of "exactly the same organs but in exactly the wrong places."[25] Or, in another formulation, "the men are men and so are the women."[26] The point here is not that there is no notion of sexual difference, but that the difference was conceived as less a set of absolute opposites than as a system of isomorphic analogues, the superior male set working as a visible map to the invisible and inferior female set. And as Laqueur has shown, a universe in which every part and function of the one was understood to have its counterpart in the other is a universe in which certain conditions could activate menstruation in men or a traveling down of the sexual member in women—eventualities richly attested in early materials. It is a universe, in other words, of slippage and fungibility, in which maleness and femaleness are always tentative and hence only apparent.

Although the one-sex model was displaced by the two-sex one in educated circles in the late eighteenth century,[27] when the female sex was in effect invented as "opposite" to the male, one-sex thinking continued—and continues—to exercise a firm grip on the popular mind. On the human mind in general, if we are to believe Freud's account of the one-sex imaginings that plague the subject as he or she marches toward a two-sex maturity possibly never fully arrived at.[28] The concepts of penis envy, phallic women, and anal menstruation/intercourse/birth are all constructions of one-sex thinking, and in such fantasies as the classic "a child is being beaten," the fantasiz-

---

[25] Ibid., p. 26. The rise of the "two-sex" model in the late eighteenth century marked, in effect, the invention of a separate female sex.

[26] Berkeley Kaite, "The Pornographic Body Double," p. 160.

[27] Why then is something of a puzzle. Laqueur observes that the change was not immediately motivated by any significant medical discovery; moreover, what we now call ovaries continued to be called "testes" for more than a century after the "discovery" of the egg (*Making Sex*, esp. pp. 149–63). In his review of Laqueur's book, Stephen Jay Gould suggests that "this transition is but one manifestation of the greatest intellectual transformation in modern Western thinking"—a transformation that had to do with "our most fundamental ideas about causality and meaning" ("The Birth of the Two-Sex World," p. 11).

[28] Consider, for example, this male analysand's description of intercourse: "It was beautiful. She was very wet. I just slid into her penis" (Arnold M. Cooper, "What Men Fear," p. 127). Leo Rangell ("The Interchangeability of Phallus and Female Genital") cites a variety of such convictions.

ing boy's identifications are so fluid that the question of whether it is in male or female form that he imagines himself being "loved" by his father is, for all practical purposes, moot.[29] (The fantasy of being "beaten," in which beating is understood in sexual terms, is a crucial one in the study of modern horror films, and one to which I shall return in some detail in later chapters.) For Freud, the two-sex theorist par excellence, such thoughts were immature misconceptions bound, should they linger too long, to cause neurosis in the adult. That Freud himself was not free of one-sex reasoning, however, is clear not only from the extraordinary intellectual efforts he found it necessary to expend in constructing the sexes as separate but also— to take just two examples—from his apperception of the clitoris as a "little penis" and from what has been claimed to be his own fantasy of anal procreation.[30]

Its subject matter alone guarantees the cultural conservatism of horror. Stories of werewolves, vampires and other undead, and possession (by incubus, succubus, dybbuk, Satan) are stories that stem from the one-sex era, and for all their updating, they still carry with them, to a greater or lesser degree, a premodern sense of sexual difference. Horror may in fact be the premier repository of one-sex reasoning in our time (science fiction running a close second). The world of horror is in any case one that knows very well that men and women are profoundly different (and that the former are vastly superior to the latter) but one that at the same time repeatedly contemplates mutations and slidings whereby women begin to look a lot like men (slasher films), men are pressured to become like women (possession films), and some people are impossible to tell apart (the figure in *God Told Me To* who is so genitally ambiguous that the doctor did not know what sex to assign, the pubescent girl in *Sleepaway Camp* who turns out to be a boy, the rapist in *The Incubus* whose ejaculate consists of equal parts of semen and menstrual blood, and so on). The one-sex model is echoed not only in horror's bodily constructions, however; it is also echoed in its representation of gender as the definitive category from which sex proceeds as an effect—and in its deep interest in precisely such "proceedings." If such fantasies

[29] Sigmund Freud, " 'A Child Is Being Beaten.' " I present the boy's case here (rather than the girl's) both because it is the one relevant to this chapter and also because it is the one Freud regards as problematic. See chapter 4, below.

[30] Laqueur, *Making Sex*, pp. 233–43; and Wayne Koestenbaum, "Privileging the Anus." The opposite is also true. If, that is, Freud's two-sex story is contaminated by one-sex reasoning, his accounts of one-sex fantasies (penis envy, anal birth, etc.) are contaminated by two-sex logic and thus remain loosely governed by the familiar binary. Laqueur discusses briefly the politics of "representing one sex in a two-sex world" (pp. 122–30).

are regressive by the lights of psychoanalytic theory, they have a long and distinguished pedigree.

The reason that I have appealed not only to psychoanalytic theory but to a cultural-discursive account of one-sex thinking is that it suggests the kind of stories (reports, legends, anecdotes) such thinking has told and can tell—stories that bear a more immediate resemblance to the stories that horror movies tell than do the rather more unmediated or unsublimated or undisplaced scenarios of psychoanalysis, and stories that conjure a level of variation and permutation that go beyond Freud's more synoptic style. Moreover, although some horror scenarios seem written directly out of Freud, and although all horror scenarios may be ultimately amenable to psychoanalysis, many horror scenarios have a pre-Freudian and premodern cast—a quality of "slidingness" that is more immediately apprehensible in the terms of one-sex reasoning than in the oppositional categories of psychoanalysis. Laqueur's observation in "Representing One Sex in a Two Sex World" that "the body with its one elastic sex was far freer to express theatrical gender and the anxieties thereby produced than it would be when it came to be regarded as the foundation of gender" applies as well to a certain inappositeness between the one-sex world of horror movies and the two-sex framework we necessarily use to analyze it.[31] Although the one-sex model and the repertory of one-sex fantasies that underwrite horror movies do not contradict psychoanalysis (psychoanalysis after all both acknowledges one-sex reasoning and seeks to explain it), they do add a dimension—an elaborate and low-mythic quality that is missing in the Freudian account.

Returning to horror: if we assume, in line with one-sex logic, that the sex of a character proceeds from the gender of the function he or she represents, and that the gender of the function proceeds from real-life perceptions of social and bodily differences, then it follows that when we observe a consistent change in the surface male-female configurations of a traditional story-complex, we are probably looking, however obliquely, at a deeper change in the culture. There are in fact some remarkable developments in the sex-gender system of horror since the mid-1970s. Chief among these is the emergence of the girl hero, a development of which Andrew Tudor writes: "It is true, of course, that female protagonists are more significant in the modern genre, and that they are permitted more autonomy and resourcefulness than were the "heroines" of earlier films. The sole survivor of *Halloween*'s rampaging psychotic, for example, or of *Alien*'s

[31] Laqueur, *Making Sex*, p. 125. For examples of "slidings," see esp. pp. 122–29.

salivating monstrosity (both 1979 [sic]), forcefully played by Jamie Lee Curtis and Sigourney Weaver respectively, are afforded a degree of effective participation in the action all but unheard of prior to the seventies." Tudor cautions against taking these strong girls to heart, however. "They and their sisters remain significant exceptions to the continuing pattern of male domination of the genre's central situations. Women have always featured as horror-movie victims, and it is therefore to be expected that they should *seem* more prominent in a period of victim centrality. Whether that implies a new gender-structure for the genre is another matter entirely."[32] Tudor very much underestimates the number of such women in modern horror; at least two genres, rape-revenge and slasher, are organized around them, and to judge from such films as *Aliens, Sleeping with the Enemy,* and *Silence of the Lambs,* the phenomenon has moved to the mainstream. Well taken, however, is his suggestion that the new prominence of women is the structural effect of a greater investment in the victim function. For whatever reason, modern horror seems especially interested in the trials of everyperson, and everyperson is on his or her own in facing the menace, without help from "authorities."

But by Tudor's own account, it is not only in their capacity as victims that these women appear in these films. They are, in fact, protagonists in the full sense: they combine the functions of suffering victim and avenging hero. For reasons on which I shall speculate more fully later, horror cinema has traditionally and on the whole held those functions separate. That they should now be bolted together in the figure of a female is a development that Tudor's structural argument does not account for. Here, I think, we need to take the films, and Stephen King's remarks about women's liberation, at face value. The women's movement has given many things to popular culture, some more savory than others. One of its main donations to horror, I think, is the image of an angry woman—a woman so angry that she can be imagined as a credible perpetrator (I stress "credible") of the kind of violence on which, in the low-mythic universe, the status of full protagonist rests. It is worth remembering that the victim and hero functions are also fused in the so-called action film—but in the person of a male (hence the absence of any women to speak of). Like the tough girls of horror, Rambo and Dirty Harry undergo all manner of indignity before they rise to annihilate their tormentors. Crucial to such films, according to John Ellis, "is the notion of survival through a series of threats of physical mutila-

---

[32] Tudor, *Monsters and Mad Scientists,* p. 127.

tion, to which many characters succumb. It is a phantasy that is characteristic of males."[33] It is a fantasy equally crucial to horror film, the difference being that there it has remarkably often come to be run through the figure of a woman.

But what is to be gained, for the male viewer, by running it through a woman? (Let me put aside for the moment the issue of what "woman" might mean in this formulation.) Or, to pose the question another way, what difference between the action-film and the horror-film experience might account for the latter's preference for a victim-hero in female form? One answer has to do with horror's greater emphasis on the victim part of the story; for although male action films can indeed wallow in suffering, they also wallow in extended frenzies of sadism of a sort exceptional in horror.[34] Another has to do with the nature or quality of the suffering, which is said to be based on castration anxiety in the action film,[35] but which may be a far messier and less wholesome business in horror. So messy and so unwholesome, in fact, that running it through a woman may be the only way it can be run.[36] Here we arrive at the politics of displacement: the use of the woman as a kind of feint, a front through which the boy can simultaneously experience forbidden desires and disavow them on grounds that the visible actor is, after all, a girl. Finally, there is the female body itself, the metaphoric architecture of which, with its enterable but unseeable inner space, has for so long been a fixture in the production of the uncanny.

Conspicuously missing from this analysis is any reference to the male viewer's stake in the sadistic, voyeuristic side of horror—the pleasure he may take in watching, from some safe vantage or other, women screaming, crying, fleeing, cringing, and dying, or indeed the pleasure he may take in the thought of himself as the cause of

[33] Ellis, *Visible Fictions*, p. 44. (Ellis is writing of "war" films in the most general sense.) Action films tend either to reverse the terms sooner than horror films or, more typically, to alternate between the modes throughout. Extremely sustained and suspenseful periods of suffering and fear are more the stuff of horror than the stuff of action.

[34] On male suffering in action cinema, see especially Paul Smith, "Action Movie Hysteria." The subgenre of horror that most closely approximates the suffering-revenge proportions of the male action film is the rape-revenge film—the subject of chapter 3.

[35] So go the standard analyses of the action film; see also Ellis (*Visible Fictions*, p. 44) and Smith, "Action Movie Hysteria."

[36] For a discussion, on the clinical side of psychoanalytic theory, of the ways that what is expressed as castration anxiety may mask anxieties of other kinds, see Cooper, "What Men Fear," and Lane, "The Genital Envy Complex." In the chapters that follow, I shall suggest that the flamboyant castration imagery of horror cinema has similarly been overperceived and underinterrogated.

their torment. I have no doubt that horror cinema offers such pleasures, and in the chapters that follow I will suggest when and why
that dimension emerges and matters. I do not, however, believe that
sadistic voyeurism is the first cause of horror. Nor do I believe that
real-life women and feminist politics have been entirely well served
by the astonishingly insistent claim that horror's satisfactions begin
and end in sadism. As Stephen King's remarks on *Carrie* indicate,
horror's misogyny is a far more complicated matter than the "blood-
lust" formula would have it, and I suspect that the critical insistence
on that formula constitutes its own version of a politics of displacement. If I err, in the chapters that follow, on the side of complication,
it is because I believe that the standard critique of horror as straightforward sadistic misogyny itself needs not only a critical but a political interrogation.

This book began in 1985 when a friend dared me to go see *The Texas
Chain Saw Massacre*. I was familiar with the horror classics and with
stylish or "quality" horror (Hitchcock, De Palma, and the like), but
exploitation horror I had assiduously avoided. Seeing *Texas* was a
jolting experience in more ways than one. It jolted me into questioning for the first time the notion of the "male gaze" and its assumption
of masculine mastery. It also jolted me into wondering about the notion of "exploitation" and the relation of that notion to film theory.
Which led me to a video store the following day to check out three
more movies on the basis of their box covers (screaming women,
poised knives, terrified eyeballs). Some months and several dozen
movies later I was writing an essay that was eventually published in
Representations (1987) and which serves, in revised form, as the first
chapter of this book: "Her Body, Himself." The other chapters were
written between 1988 and 1990, during which time the genre continued, in its own frustratingly protean way, to change before my eyes.
Chapter 3, "Getting Even," forms something of a pair with chapter
1, rape-revenge and slasher films being the premier examples of the
female victim-hero complex. Chapter 2, "Opening Up," offers an unorthodox reading of a genre of which women have traditionally been
at the center, though in no sense as heroes: the possession film. Finally there is chapter 4, "The Eye of Horror," which takes up not a
genre but a thematics and speculates in more theoretical terms on
just what horror's appeal is all about. I did not know, when I began
this project, that it would take me in some of the directions it has: so
deeply into the etiology of sadomasochism, for example, and into issues of male homosexuality. I feel especially tentative on the latter
point, for I am fully aware that gay studies has emerged as a field
related to but also distinct from feminism in the last few years, and

that its discourse has been almost as frustratingly expansive as horror itself.

Like many such stories, mine has something of the character of a conversion narrative. The initial dare took me into a territory I might not otherwise have explored, and against all odds I have ended up something of a fan. Like others before me, I discovered that there are in horror moments and works of great humor, formal brilliance, political intelligence, psychological depth, and above all a kind of kinky creativity that is simply not available in any other stripe of filmmaking; one of the benefits of this project has been the discovery of the unexpected gem. And although I now look forward to catching up on "good" movies, I will never see any kind of movie with quite the same eyes again. To a remarkable extent, horror has come to seem to me not only the form that most obviously trades in the repressed, but itself the repressed of mainstream filmmaking. When I see an Oscar-winning film like *The Accused* or the artful *Alien* and its blockbuster sequel *Aliens* or, more recently, *Sleeping with the Enemy* and *Silence of the Lambs*, and even *Thelma and Louise*, I cannot help thinking of all the low-budget, often harsh and awkward but sometimes deeply energetic films that preceded them by a decade or more—films that said it all, and in flatter terms, and on a shoestring. If mainstream film detains us with niceties of plot, character, motivation, cinematography, pacing, acting, and the like, low or exploitation horror operates at the bottom line, and in so doing reminds us that every movie has a bottom line, no matter how covert or mystified or sublimated it may be.

Certainly I will never again take for granted that audience males identify solely or even mainly with screen males and audience females with screen females. If Carrie, whose story begins and ends with menstrual imagery and seems in general so painfully girlish, is construed by her author as a latter-day variant on Samson, the biblical strong man who overcame all manner of handicap to kill at least six thousand Philistines in one way or another, and if her target audience is any high school boy who has been pantsed or had his glasses messed with, then we are truly in a universe in which the sex of a character is no object. No accident, insofar as it is historically and, above all, politically overdetermined, but also no object—no impediment whatever to the audience's experience of his or her function. That too is one of the bottom-line propositions of horror, a proposition that is easily missed when you watch mainstream cinema but laid bare in exploitation cinema and, once registered, never lets you see any movie "straight" again.

Her Body,
Himself

AT THE BOTTOM of the horror heap lies the slasher (or splatter or shocker or stalker) film: the immensely generative story of a psychokiller who slashes to death a string of mostly female victims, one by one, until he is subdued or killed, usually by the one girl who has survived.[1] Drenched in taboo and encroaching vigorously on the pornographic, the slasher film lies by and large beyond the purview of the respectable (middle-aged, middle-class) audience. It has also lain by and large beyond the purview of respectable criticism. Staples of drive-ins and exploitation houses, where they "rub shoulders with sex pictures and macho action flicks," these are films that are "never even written up."[2] Even commentaries that celebrate "trash" disavow the slasher, usually passing it over in silence or bemoaning it as a degenerate aberration.[3] Film magazine articles on the genre rarely get past technique, special effects, and profits. Newspapers relegate reviews of slashers to the syndicated "Joe Bob Briggs, Drive-In Movie Critic of Grapevine, Texas," whose lowbrow, campy tone ("We're talking two breasts, four quarts of blood, five dead bodies. . . . Joe Bob says check it out")

[1] A longer version of this essay was published under the title "Her Body, Himself: Gender in the Slasher Film" in *Representations* 20 (1987). At that time, the only full-length studies of the slasher or splatter film (very broadly defined) were William Schoell's unhelpful *Stay Out of the Shower* and John McCarty's *Splatter Movies*. Since then, Dika has published *Games of Terror*, a structural analysis with social-political commentary of the slasher (or stalker) film proper. Also since then, of course, the slasher formula itself has, in one guise or another, passed into the mainstream; see the Afterword.

[2] Dickstein, "The Aesthetics of Fright," p. 34.

[3] "Will Rogers said he never met a man he didn't like, and I can truly say the same about the cinema," Harvey R. Greenberg writes in his paean to horror, *The Movies on Your Mind*. His claim does not, however, extend to the "plethora of execrable imitations [of *Psycho*] that debased cinema" (p. 137).

establishes what is deemed the necessary distance between the readership and the movie.[4] There are of course the exceptional cases: critics or social observers who have seen at least some of the films and tried to come to grips with their ethics or aesthetics or both. Just how troubled is their task can be seen from its divergent results. For one critic, *The Texas Chain Saw Massacre* is "the *Gone With the Wind* of meat movies."[5] For another it is a "vile little piece of sick crap . . . nothing but a hysterically paced, slapdash, imbecile concoction of cannibalism, voodoo, astrology, sundry hippie-esque cults, and unrelenting sadistic violence as extreme and hideous as a complete lack of imagination can possibly make it."[6] Writes a third, "[Director Tobe] Hooper's cinematic intelligence becomes more apparent in every viewing, as one gets over the initial traumatizing impact and learns to respect the pervasive felicities of camera placement and movement."[7] The Museum of Modern Art bought the film the same year that at least one country, Sweden, banned it.

Robin Wood's tack is less aesthetic than ethnographic. "However one may shrink from systematic exposure to them [slasher films], however one may deplore the social phenomena and ideological mutations they reflect, their popularity . . . suggests that even if they were uniformly execrable they shouldn't be ignored."[8] We may go a step further and suggest that the qualities that locate the slasher film outside the usual aesthetic system—that indeed render it, along with pornography and low horror in general, the film category "most likely to be betrayed by artistic treatment and lavish production values"[9]—are the very qualities that make it such a transparent source for (sub)cultural attitudes toward sex and gender in particular. Unmediated by otherworldly fantasy, cover plot, bestial transformations, or civilized routine, slasher films present us in startlingly direct terms with a world in which male and female are at desperate odds but in which, at the same time, masculinity and femininity are more states of mind than body. The premise of this chapter, then, is that the slasher film, not despite but exactly because of its crudity and compulsive repetitiveness, gives us a clearer picture of current sexual

---

[4] "Joe Bob Briggs" was evidently invented as a solution to the *Dallas Times Herald*'s problem of "how to cover trashy movies." See Calvin Trillin's "American Chronicles: The Life and Times of Joe Bob Briggs, So Far," *New Yorker*, 22 December 1986, pp. 73–88.

[5] Lew Brighton, "Saturn in Retrograde," p. 27.

[6] Stephen Koch, "Fashions in Pornography," pp. 108–9.

[7] Wood, "Return of the Repressed," p. 30.

[8] Robin Wood, "Beauty Bests the Beast," p. 63.

[9] Dickstein, "The Aesthetics of Fright," p. 34.

attitudes, at least among the segment of the population that forms its erstwhile audience, than do the legitimate products of the better studios.

If popularity alone measures the fitness of a form for study, and if profits and sequels are the measure of popularity, then the slasher qualifies. *Halloween* cost $320,000 to make and within six years had grossed more than $75,000,000; even a highly produced film like *The Shining* has repaid its costs tenfold. *Alien* (a science-fiction/slasher hybrid) and *The Hills Have Eyes* are at Part Two. *The Texas Chain Saw Massacre* and *Psycho* are currently at Part Three. *A Nightmare on Elm Street* and *Halloween* have reached Part Five, and *Friday the Thirteenth* Part Eight. These are better taken as remakes than sequels; although the later part purports to take up where the earlier part left off, in most cases it simply duplicates with only slight variation the plot and circumstances—the formula—of its predecessor. Nor do different titles indicate different plots; *Friday the Thirteenth* is set at summer camp and *Halloween* in town, but the story is much the same, compulsively repeated in those thirteen films and in dozens like them under different names. The popularity of the slasher began to tail off in the mid-eighties, and by the end of the decade the form was largely drained.

But for some twelve years the slasher was the "exploitation" form of choice for junior horror fans. Although girls too went to slasher movies, usually in the company of boyfriends but sometimes in same-sex groups (my impression is that the *Nightmare on Elm Street* series in particular attracted girls in groups), the majority audience, perhaps even more than the audience for horror in general, was largely young and largely male—conspicuously groups of boys who cheer the killer on as he assaults his victims, then reverse their sympathies to cheer the survivor on as she assaults the killer. Young males are also, I shall suggest, the slasher film's implied audience, the object of its address. The question, then, has to do with that particular audience's stake in that particular nightmare; with what in the story is crucial enough to warrant the price of admission, and what the implications are for the current discussion of women and film.

THE SLASHER FILM

The appointed ancestor of the slasher film is Hitchcock's *Psycho* (1960). Its elements are familiar: the killer is the psychotic product of a sick family, but still recognizably human; the victim is a beautiful, sexually active woman; the location is not-home, at a Terrible Place; the weapon is something other than a gun; the attack is registered from the victim's point of view and comes with shocking suddenness. None of these features is original, but the unprecedented success of Hitchcock's particular formulation, above all the sexualization of both motive and action, prompted a flood of imitations and variations. In 1974, however, a film emerged that revised the *Psycho* template to such a degree and in such a way as to make a new phase: *The Texas Chain Saw Massacre* (Tobe Hooper).[10] Together with *Halloween* (John Carpenter, 1978), it engendered a new spate of variations and imitations.

The plot of *Chain Saw* is simple enough. Five young people are driving through Texas in a van; they stop off at an abandoned house and are serially murdered by the psychotic sons of a degenerate local family; the sole survivor is a woman. The horror, of course, lies in the elaboration. Early in the film the group picks up a hitchhiker, but when he starts a fire and slashes Franklin's arm (having already slit open his own hand), they kick him out. The abandoned house they subsequently visit, once the home of Sally and Franklin's grandparents, turns out to be right next door to the house of the hitchhiker and his family: his brother, Leatherface; their father; an aged and only marginally alive grandfather; and their dead grandmother and her dog, whose mummified corpses are ceremonially included in the family gatherings. Three generations of slaughterhouse workers, once proud of their craft but now displaced by machines, have taken up killing and cannibalism as a way of life. Their house is grotesquely decorated with human and animal remains—bones, feathers, hair, skins. The young people drift apart in their exploration of the abandoned house and grounds and are picked off one by one by Leatherface and Hitchhiker. Last is Sally. The others are attacked and killed with dispatch, but Sally must fight for her life, enduring all manner of horrors through the night. At dawn she manages to escape to the highway, where she scrambles into a pickup and is saved.

Likewise the nutshell plot of *Halloween*: a psychotic killer (Michael) stalks a small town on Halloween and kills a string of teenage friends, one after another; only Laurie survives. The twist here is that Michael has escaped from the asylum in which he has been incarcerated since the age of six, when he killed his sister minutes after she and her boyfriend parted following an illicit interlude in her parents' bed. That murder, in flashback, opens the film. It is related entirely in the killer's first person (I-camera), and only after the fact is the

[10] For an account of the ways the "family horror" aspect of the *Psycho* formula has evolved over the decades, see Patricia Erens, "The Stepfather."

identity of the perpetrator revealed. Fifteen years later, Michael escapes his prison and returns to kill Laurie, whom he construes as
another version of his sister (a sequel clarifies that she is in fact his
younger sister, adopted by another family at the time of the earlier
tragedy). But before Michael gets to Laurie, he picks off her high
school friends: Annie, in a car on her way to her boyfriend's; Bob,
going to the kitchen for a beer after sex with Lynda; Lynda, talking
on the phone with Laurie and waiting for Bob to come back with the
beer. At last only Laurie remains. When she hears Lynda squeal and
then go silent on the phone, she leaves her own babysitting house to
go to Lynda's. Here she discovers the three bodies and flees, the
killer in pursuit. The remainder of the film is devoted to the back-
and-forth struggle between Laurie and Michael. Again and again he
bears down on her, and again and again she either eludes him (by
running, hiding, breaking through windows to escape, locking herself in) or strikes back (once with a knitting needle, once with a
hanger). In the end, Dr. Loomis (Michael's psychiatrist in the asylum) rushes in and shoots the killer (though not so fatally as to prevent his return in the sequels.[11]

Before we turn to an inventory of generic components, let us add
a third, later example: *The Texas Chain Saw Massacre II*, from 1986. The
slaughterhouse family (now cutely named the Sawyers) is the same,
though older and, owing to their unprecedented success in the sausage business, richer.[12] When Mr. Sawyer begins to suspect from her
broadcasts that a disk jockey named Stretch knows more than she
should about one of their recent crimes, he dispatches his sons
Leatherface and Chop Top to the radio station late at night. There
they seize the technician and corner Stretch. At the crucial moment,
however, power fails Leatherface's chain saw. As Stretch cowers before him, he presses the now-still blade up along her thigh and

[11] Dika outlines the narrative sequence of the standard "stalker" film as follows. Past
Event: The young community is guilty of a wrongful action; the killer sees an injury,
fault, or death; the killer kills the guilty members of the young community. Present
Event: an event commemorates the past action; the killer's destructive force is reacti-
vated; the killer reidentifies the guilty parties; a member from the old community
warns the young community; the young community pays no heed; the killer stalks
members of the young community; the killer kills members of the young community;
the heroine sees the extent of the murders; the heroine sees the killer; the heroine does
battle with the killer; the heroine kills or subdues the killer; the heroine survives; but
the heroine is not free. See her *Games of Terror*, esp. p. 136.

[12] The evolution of the human-sausage theme is typical of the back-and-forth borrowing in low horror. *Texas Chain Saw Massacre I* hints at it; *Motel Hell* turns it into an
industry ("Farmer Vincent's Smoked Meats: This is It!" proclaims a local billboard);
and *Texas Chain Saw Massacre II* expands it to a statewide chili-tasting contest.

against her crotch, where he holds it unsteadily as he jerks and shudders in what we understand to be orgasm. After that the sons leave. The intrepid Stretch tracks them to their underground lair outside of town. Tumbling down the Texas equivalent of a rabbit hole, Stretch finds herself in the subterranean chambers of the Sawyer operation. Here, amid all the slaughterhouse paraphernalia and within walls that drip with blood, the Sawyers live and work. Like the decrepit mansion of Part One, the residential parts of the establishment are quaintly decorated with human and animal remains. After a long ordeal at the hands of the Sawyers, Stretch manages to scramble up through a culvert and beyond that up onto a nearby pinnacle, where she finds a chain saw and wards off her final assailant. The Texas Ranger, who had followed her to the Sawyers with the intention of saving her and busting the case, evidently perishes in a grenade explosion underground, leaving Stretch the sole survivor.

The spiritual debt of all the post-1974 slasher films to *Psycho* is clear, and it is a rare example that does not pay a visual tribute, however brief, to the ancestor—if not in a shower stabbing, then in a purling drain or the shadow of a knife-wielding hand. No less clear, however, is the fact that the post-1974 examples have, in the usual way of folklore, contemporized not only Hitchcock's terms but also, over time, their own. We have, in short, a cinematic formula with a twenty-six-year history, of which the first phase, from 1960 to 1974, is dominated by a film clearly rooted in the sensibility of the 1950s, while the second phase, bracketed by the two *Texas Chain Saw* films from 1974 and 1986, responds to the values of the late sixties and early seventies. That the formula in its most recent guise may be in decline is suggested by the campy, self-parodying quality of *Texas Chain Saw II*, as well as the emergence, in legitimate theater, of the slasher satire *Buckets of Blood*. Between 1974 and 1986, however, the formula evolved and flourished in ways of some interest to observers of popular culture, above all those concerned with the representation of women in film. To apprehend in specific terms the nature of that mutation, let us, with *Psycho* as the benchmark, survey the genre by component category: killer, locale, weapons, victims, and shock effects.

Killer

The psychiatrist at the end of *Psycho* explains what we already guessed from the action: that Norman Bates had introjected his mother, in life a "clinging, demanding woman," so completely that she constituted his other, controlling self. Not Norman but "the mother half of his mind" killed Marion—*had* to kill Marion—when he (the Norman half) found himself aroused by her. The notion of a killer propelled by psychosexual fury, more particularly a male in gender distress, has proved a durable one, and the progeny of Norman Bates stalk the genre up to the present day. Just as Norman wears his mother's clothes during his acts of violence and is thought, by the screen characters and also, for a while, by the film's spectators, to *be* his mother, so the murderer in the *Psycho*-imitation *Dressed to Kill* (Brian De Palma, 1980), a transvestite psychiatrist, seems until his unveiling to be a woman; like Norman, he must kill women who arouse him sexually. Likewise, in muted form, Hitchhiker, Chop Top, and Leatherface in the *Chain Saw* films: none of the brothers shows overt signs of gender confusion, but their cathexis to the sick family— in which the mother is conspicuously absent but the preserved corpse of the grandmother (answering the treated body of Mrs. Bates in *Psycho*)[13] is conspicuously present—has palpably arrested their development. Both are in their twenties (thirties, in Part Two), but Hitchhiker and Chop Top seem gangly kids and Leatherface jiggles in baby

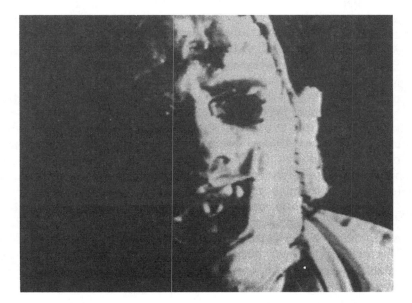

Leatherface in *Texas Chain Saw Massacre.*

[13] And answering to the films of his mother that "Buffalo Bill" (the would-be transsexual psychokiller of *Silence of the Lambs*) compulsively runs for himself every evening. So, in any case, the novel; the film omits the detail, which is also reminiscent of the childhood footage, including shots of his mother's funeral, Mark compulsively screens for himself in *Peeping Tom* (see chapter 4).

fat behind his butcher's apron. Like Norman Bates, whose bedroom still displays his childhood toys, Hitchhiker/Chop Top and Leatherface are permanently locked in childhood. Only when Leatherface "discovers" sex in Part Two does he lose his appetite for murder. In *Motel Hell*, a send-up of modern horror with special reference to *Psycho* and *Chain Saw II*, we are repeatedly confronted with a portrait of the dead mother silently presiding over all manner of cannibalistic and incestuous doings on the part of her adult children. The most recent incarnation of Norman Bates is *Silence of the Lambs'* Buffalo Bill, a mother-fixated would-be transsexual who, having been denied a sex-change operation, is sewing his own woman-suit out of real women's skins.

No less in the grip of boyhood is the killer in *The Eyes of Laura Mars* (1978). The son of a hooker, a hysterical woman absent for days at a time, the killer has up to now put his boyish anger to good use in police work—the film makes much of the irony—but the sight of Laura's violent photographs causes it to be unleashed in full force. The killer in *Hell Night* is the sole member of his family to survive, as a child, a murderous rampage on the part of his father; the experience condemned him to an afterlife as a murderer himself. In *Halloween* the killer *is* a child, at least in the first instance: Michael, who at the age of six is so enraged at his sister (evidently for her sexual relations with her boyfriend, enacted on the parental bed) that he stabs her to death with a kitchen knife. The remainder of the film details his return killing spree at the age of twenty-one, and Dr. Loomis, who has overseen the case in the interim, explains that although Michael's body has attained maturity, his mind remains frozen in infantile fury. In *It's Alive*, the killer is a literal infant, evidently made monstrous through intrauterine apprehension of its parents' ambivalence (early in the pregnancy they considered an abortion).

Even killers whose childhood is not immediately at issue and who display no overt gender confusion are often sexually disturbed. The murderer in *A Nightmare on Elm Sreet* is an undead child molester. The killer in *Slumber Party Massacre* says to a young woman he is about to assault with a power drill: "Pretty. All of you are very pretty. I love you. Takes a lot of love for a person to do this. You know you want it. You want it. Yes." When she grasps the psychodynamics of the situation in the infamous crotch episode of *Texas Chain Saw II*, Stretch tries a desperate gambit: "You're really good, you really are good, you're the best," she repeats; and indeed, immediately after ejaculation Leatherface becomes palpably less interested in his saw. The parodic *Motel Hell* spells it out: "His pecker don't work; you'll see when he takes off his overalls—it's like a shriveled prune," Bruce says of his killer-brother Vincent when he learns of Terry's plans to marry him. Terry never does see, for on her wedding night he attempts (needless to say) not sex but murder. Actual rape is practically nonexistent in the slasher film, evidently on the premise—as the crotch episode suggests—that violence and sex are not concomitants but alternatives, the one as much a substitute for and a prelude to the other as the teenage horror film is a substitute for and a prelude to the "adult" film (or the meat movie a substitute for and prelude to the skin flick).[14] When Sally under torture (*Texas Chain Saw I*) calls out "I'll do anything you want," clearly with sexual intention, her assailants respond only by mimicking her in gross terms; she has profoundly misunderstood the psychology.

Female killers are few and their reasons for killing significantly different from men's. With the possible exception of the murderous mother in *Friday the Thirteenth I*, they show no gender confusion. Nor is their motive overtly psychosexual; their anger derives in most cases not from childhood experience but from specific moments in their adult lives in which they have been abandoned or cheated on by men (*Strait-Jacket, Play Misty for Me, Attack of the 50-Foot Woman*).[15] (Rape-revenge films like *Ms. 45* and *I Spit on Your Grave I* will discuss in chapter 3.) *Friday the Thirteenth I* is a noteworthy anomaly. The killer is revealed as a middle-aged woman whose son, Jason, drowned years earlier as a consequence of negligence on the part of the camp counselors. The anomaly is not sustained in the sequels, however. Here the killer is Jason himself, not dead after all but living in a forest hut. The pattern is a familiar one; his motive is vengeance for the death of his mother, his excessive attachment toward whom is manifested in his enshrining of her severed head. Like Stretch in the crotch episode of *Texas Chain Saw II*, the girl who does final combat with Jason in Part Two sees the shrine, grasps its significance (she's a psych major), and saves herself by repeating in a commanding tone, "I am your mother, Jason; put down the knife." Jason, for his part, begins to see his mother in the girl (I-camera) and obeys her.

[14] Writes Wood: "The release of sexuality in the horror film is always presented as perverted, monstrous, and excessive, both the perversion and the excess being the logical outcome of repressing. Nowhere is this carried further than in *Texas [Chain Saw] Massacre [I]*. Here sexuality is totally perverted from its functions, into sadism, violence, and cannibalism. It is striking that there is no suggestion anywhere that Sally is the object of an overtly sexual threat; she is to be tormented, killed, dismembered, and eaten, but not raped" ("Return of the Repressed," p. 31).
[15] The bias is intact in 1991's two nonhorror examples of female-murderer movies, *Mortal Thoughts* and *Thelma and Louise*. The targets of the former are impossible husbands; of the latter, a would-be rapist and, indirectly, a leering truckdriver (he is not himself murdered, but his eighteen-wheeler is).

In films of the *Psycho* type (*Dressed to Kill, The Eyes of Laura Mars*), the monster is an insider, a man who functions normally in the action until, at the end, his other self is revealed. *Texas Chain Saw* and *Halloween* introduced another sort of monster: one whose only role is that of killer and one whose identity as such is clear from the outset. Norman may have a normal half, but these killer have none. They are emphatic misfits and outsiders. Michael is an escapee from a distant asylum; Jason subsists in the forest; the Sawyer sons live a bloody subterranean existence outside of town. Nor are they clearly seen. We catch sight of them only in glimpses—few and far between in the beginning, more frequent toward the end. They are usually large, sometimes overweight, and often masked. In short, they may be recognizably human, but they are only marginally so, just as they are only marginally visible—to their victims and to us, the spectators. In one key respect, however, the killers are superhuman: their virtual indestructibility. Just as Michael (in *Halloween*) repeatedly rises from blows that would stop a lesser man, so Jason (in the *Friday the Thirteenth* films) survives assault after assault to return in sequel after sequel. It is worth noting that the killers are normally the fixed elements and the victims the changeable ones in any given series.

Terrible Place

The Terrible Place, most often a house or tunnel, in which victims sooner or later find themselves is a venerable element of horror. The Bates mansion is just one in a long list of such venues—a list that continues, in the modern slasher, with the decaying mansion of *Texas Chain Saw I*, the abandoned and haunted mansion of *Hell Night*, the house for sale but unsellable in *Halloween* (also a point of departure for such films as *Rosemary's Baby* and *The Amityville Horror*), and so on. What makes these houses terrible is not just their Victorian decrepitude, but the terrible families—murderous, incestuous, cannibalistic—that occupy them. So the Bates mansion enfolds the history of a mother and son locked in a sick attachment, and so the *Texas Chain Saw* mansion/labyrinth shelters an outlaw brood presided over by the decaying corpse of the grandmother. Jason's forest hut (in the *Friday the Thirteenth* sequels) is no mansion, but it houses another mummified mother (or at least her head), with all the usual candles and dreadful paraphernalia. The terrors of the *Hell Night* mansion stem, we learn, from an early owner's massacre of his children. Into such houses unwitting victims wander in film after film, and it is the conventional task of the genre to register in close detail the victims' dawning understanding, as they survey the visible evidence, of the human crimes and perversions that have transpired there. That perception leads directly to the perception of their own immediate peril.

In *The Texas Chain Saw Massacre II*, horrors unfold in a subterranean labyrinth connected to the world above by channels and a culvert. The family is intact, indeed thrives, but for reasons evidently having to do with the nature of their sausage business has moved residence and slaughterhouse underground. Likewise the second basement of the haunted mansion in *Hell Night*: strewn with decaying bodies and skeletons, lighted with masses of candles. Other tunnels are less familial: the one in *Body Double* that prompts Jake's claustrophobic faint, and the horror house tunnel in *He Knows You're Alone* in which the killer lurks. The morgue episode in the latter film, certain of the hospital scenes in *Halloween II*, and the bottom-cellar scenes from various films may be counted as Terrible Tunnels: dark, exitless, slick with blood, and laced with heating ducts and plumbing pipes. In *Hell Night*, as in *Texas Chain Saw II*, Terrible House (the abandoned mansion) and Terrible Tunnel (the second basement) are one and the same.

The house or tunnel may at first seem a safe haven, but the same walls that promise to keep the killer out quickly become, once the killer penetrates them, the walls that hold the victim in. A phenomenally popular moment in post-1974 slashers is the scene in which the victim locks herself in (a house, room, closet, car) and waits with pounding heart as the killer slashes, hacks, or drills his way in. The action is inevitably seen from the victim's point of view; we stare at the door (wall, car roof) and watch the surface open to first the tip and then the shaft of the weapon. In Hitchcock's *The Birds*, it is the birds' beaks we see penetrating the door. The penetration scene is commonly the film's pivotal moment; if the victim has up to now simply fled, she now has no choice but to fight back.

Weapons

In the hands of the killer, at least, guns have no place in slasher films. Victims sometimes avail themselves of firearms, but like telephones, fire alarms, elevators, doorbells, and car engines, guns fail in a pinch. In some basic sense, the emotional terrain of the slasher film is pretechnological. The preferred weapons of the killer are knives, hammers, axes, ice picks, hypodermic needles, red hot pokers, pitchforks, and the like. Such implements serve well a plot predicated on stealth and the unawareness of later victims that the bodies of their friends are accumulating just yards away. But the use of noisy chain saws and power drills and the nonuse of such relatively silent means as bow and arrow, spear, catapult, and sword[16] would seem to suggest that closeness and tactility are also at issue. The sense is clearer if we include marginal examples like *Jaws* and *The Birds*, as well as related werewolf and vampire genres. Knives and needles, like teeth, beaks, fangs, and claws, are personal extensions of the body that bring attacker and attacked into primitive, animalistic embrace.[17] In the rape-revenge film *I Spit on Your Grave*, the heroine forces her rapist at gunpoint to lower his pants, presumably with the intention of shooting him in the genitals. But she changes her mind and invites him home for what he all too readily supposes will be a voluntary follow-up to an earlier gang rape. Then, as they sit together in a bubble bath, she castrates him with a knife. If we wondered why she gave up the pistol, now we know: all phallic symbols are not equal, and a hands-on knifing answers a hands-on rape in a way that a shooting, even a shooting preceded by a humiliation, does not.

Beyond that, the slasher evinces a fascination with flesh or meat itself as that which is hidden from view. When the hitchhiker in *Texas Chain Saw I* slits open his hand for the thrill, the onlookers recoil in horror—all but Franklin, who seems fascinated by the realization that all that lies between the visible, knowable outside of the body and its secret insides is one thin membrane, protected only by a collective taboo against its violation. It is no surprise that the rise of the slasher film is concomitant with the development of special effects that let us see with our own eyes the "opened" body.

Victims

Where once there was one victim, Marion Crane, there are now many: five in *Texas Chain Saw I*, four in *Halloween*, fourteen in *Friday the Thirteenth III*, and so on. (As Schoell puts it, "other filmmakers figured that the only thing better than one beautiful woman being gruesomely murdered was a whole series of beautiful women being gruesomely murdered.")[18] Where once the victim was an adult, now

---

[16] With the occasional exception: for example, the spear gun used in the sixth killing in *Friday the Thirteenth III*.

[17] Stuart Kaminsky, *American Film Genres*, p. 107.

[18] Schoell, *Stay Out of the Shower*, p. 35. It may be argued that *Blood Feast* (1963), in which a lame Egyptian caterer slaughters one woman after another for their bodily parts (all in the service of Ishtar), provides the serial-murder model (it is the obvious model of *Blood Diner*, and Frank Henenlotter's *Frankenhooker* updates the formula). *Peeping Tom* (1960), in which a photographer seeks out women to photograph and kill (with a camera equipped with a spike) is another important film in the tradition; see

she is typically in her teens (hence the term "teenie-kill pic"). Where once she was female, now she is both girl and boy, though most often and most conspicuously girl. For all this, her essential quality remains the same. Marion is first and foremost a sexual transgressor. The first scenes show her in a hotel room dressing at the end of a lunch hour, asking her lover to marry her. It is, of course, her wish to be made an honest woman of that leads her to abscond with forty thousand dollars, an act that leads her to the Bates motel in Fairvale. In much the way we watched her dress in the opening sequences, we now watch her undress. Moments later, nude in the shower, she dies.

In the slasher film, sexual transgressors of both sexes are scheduled for early destruction. The genre is studded with couples trying to find a place beyond purview of parents and employers where they can have sex, and immediately afterward (or during the act) being killed. The theme enters the tradition with the Lynda-Bob subplot of *Halloween*. Finding themselves alone in a neighborhood house, Lynda and Bob make hasty use of the master bedroom. Afterward, Bob goes downstairs for a beer. In the kitchen he is silently dispatched by the killer, Michael, who then covers himself with a sheet (it *is* Halloween), dons Bob's glasses, and goes upstairs. Supposing the bespectacled ghost in the doorway to be Bob, Lynda jokes, bares her breasts provocatively, and finally, in irritation at "Bob" 's stony silence, dials Laurie on the phone. Now the killer advances, strangling her with the telephone cord, so that what Laurie hears on the other end are squeals she takes to be orgasmic. *Halloween II* takes the scene a step further. Here the victims are a nurse and orderly who have sneaked off for sex in the hospital therapy pool. The watching killer, Michael again, turns up the thermostat and, when the orderly goes to check it, kills him. Michael then approaches the nurse from behind (she thinks it is the orderly) and strokes her neck. Only when he moves his hand toward her bare breast and she turns around and sees him does he kill her.

Postcoital death, above all when the circumstances are illicit, is a staple of the genre. Denise, the English vamp in *Hell Night*, is stabbed to death in bed during Seth's after-sex trip to the bathroom. In *He Knows You're Alone*, the student having the affair with her professor is similarly murdered in bed while the professor is downstairs changing a fuse; the professor himself is stabbed when he returns and discovers the body. The *Friday the Thirteenth* series exploits the device at

---

chapter 4, below. But it is to the scenes (and music) of *Psycho* that slasher films pay homage, even when the plots have gone their own way.

least once per film. Particularly gruesome is the variant in Part Three. Invigorated by sex, the boy is struck by a gymnastic impulse and begins walking on his hands; the killer slices down on his crotch with a machete. Unaware of the fate of her boyfriend, the girl crawls into a hammock after her shower; the killer impales her from below.[19] Brian De Palma's *Dressed to Kill* presents the infamous example of the sexually desperate wife, first seen masturbating in her morning shower during the credit sequence, who lets herself be picked up later that day in a museum by a man with whom she has sex first in a taxi and later in his apartment. On leaving his place in the evening, she is suddenly attacked and killed in the elevator. The cause-and-effect relationship between (illicit) sex and death could hardly be more clearly drawn.

Killing those who seek or engage in unauthorized sex amounts to a generic imperative of the slasher film. It is an imperative that crosses gender lines, affecting males as well as females. The numbers are not equal, and the scenes not equally charged; but the fact remains that in most slasher films after 1978 (following *Halloween*), men and boys who go after "wrong" sex also die. This is not the only way males die; they also die incidentally, as girls do, when they get in the killer's way or try to stop him, or when they stray into proscribed territory. The victims of *Hell Night, Texas Chain Saw*, and the *Friday the Thirteenth* films are, respectively, those who trespass in Garth Manor, those who stumble into the environs of the slaughterhouse family, and those who become counselors at a cursed camp, all without regard to sex. Boys die, in short, not because they are boys, but because they make mistakes.

Some girls die for the same mistakes. Others, however, and always the main ones, die—plot after plot develops the motive—because they are female. Just as Norman Bates's oedipal psychosis is such that only female victims will do, so Michael's sexual anger toward his sister (in the *Halloween* series) drives him to kill her—and after her a string of sister surrogates. In much the same way, the transsexual psychiatrist in *Dressed to Kill* is driven to murder only those women who arouse him and remind him of his hated maleness. In *The Eyes of Laura Mars*, the killer's hatred of his mother drives him to prey on women specifically—with the significant exception of one gay male.

---

[19] This theme too is spoofed in *Motel Hell*. Farmer Vincent's victims are two hookers, a kinky couple looking for same (he puts them in room number 1 of the motel), and Terry and her boyfriend Bo, out for kicks on a motorcycle. When Terry (allowed to survive) wonders aloud why someone would try to kill them, Farmer Vincent answers her by asking pointedly whether they were married. "No," she says, in a tone of resignation, as if accepting the logic.

He Knows You're Alone features a killer who in consequence of an earlier jilting preys exclusively on brides-to-be.

But even in films in which males and females are killed in roughly even numbers, the lingering images are of the latter. The death of a male is nearly always swift; even if the victim grasps what is happening to him, he has no time to react or register terror. He is dispatched and the camera moves on. The death of a male is moreover more likely than the death of a female to be viewed from a distance, or viewed only dimly (because of darkness or fog, for example), or indeed to happen offscreen and not be viewed at all. The murders of women, on the other hand, are filmed at closer range, in more graphic detail, and at greater length. The pair of murders at the therapy pool in *Halloween II* illustrates the standard iconography. We see the orderly in two shots: the first at close range in the control room, just before the stabbing, and the second as he is being stabbed, through the vapors in a medium long shot; the orderly never even sees his assailant. The nurse's death, on the other hand, is shot entirely in medium close-up. The camera studies her face as it registers first her unwitting complicity (as the killer strokes her neck and shoulders from behind), then apprehension, and then, as she faces him, terror; we see the knife plunge into her repeatedly, hear her cries, and watch her blood fill the pool. This cinematic standard has a venerable history, and it remains intact in the slasher film. Indeed, "tits and a scream" are all that is required of actresses auditioning for the role of victim in "Co-Ed Frenzy," the fictive slasher film whose making constitutes the frame story of *Blow-Out*. It is worth noting that none of the auditioners has both in the desired amount, and that the director must resort to the use of doubles: one for the tits, one for the screams.

Final Girl

The image of the distressed female most likely to linger in memory is the image of the one who did not die: the survivor, or Final Girl. She is the one who encounters the mutilated bodies of her friends and perceives the full extent of the preceding horror and of her own peril; who is chased, cornered, wounded; whom we see scream, stagger, fall, rise, and scream again. She is abject terror personified. If her friends knew they were about to die only seconds before the event, the Final Girl lives with the knowledge for long minutes or hours. She alone looks death in the face, but she alone also finds the strength either to stay the killer long enough to be rescued (ending A) or to kill him herself (ending B). But in either case, from 1974 on, the survivor figure has been female. In Schoell's words: "The vast majority of contemporary shockers, whether in the sexist mold or not, feature climaxes in which the women fight back against their attackers—the wandering, humorless psychos who populate these films. They often show more courage and levelheadedness than their cringing male counterparts."[20] Her scene occupies the last ten to twenty minutes (thirty in the case of *Texas Chain Saw I*) and contains the film's emphatic climax.

The sequence first appears in full-blown form (ending A) in *Texas Chain Saw I* with Sally's spirited self-defense and eventual rescue. Her brother and companions were dispatched suddenly and uncomprehending, one by one, but Sally survives the ninth round: long enough to see what has become of her fellows and is in store for her, long enough to meet and even dine with the whole slaughterhouse family, long enough to undergo all manner of torture (including the ancient grandfather's feeble efforts to strike a fatal hammer blow on the temple as they bend her over a washtub), and long enough to bolt and rebolt, be caught and recaught, plead and replead for her life, and eventually escape to the highway. For nearly thirty minutes of screen time—a third of the film—we watch her shriek, run, flinch, jump or fall through windows, sustain injury and mutilation. Her will to survive is astonishing; in the end, bloody and staggering, she finds the highway, Leatherface and Hitchhiker in pursuit. Just as they bear down on her, a truck comes by and crushes Hitchhiker. Minutes later a pickup driver plucks Sally up and saves her from Leatherface. The final shots show us a receding Leatherface from her point of view (the bed of the pickup): standing on the highway, wounded (having gashed open his abdomen during the truck episode) but upright, waving the chain saw crazily over his head.

Halloween's Final Girl is Laurie. Her desperate defense is shorter in duration than Sally's but no less fraught with horror. Limping from a leg wound, she flees to a garden shed and breaks in through the window with a rake. Neighbors hear her screams for help but suspect a Halloween prank and shut the blinds. She gets into her own babysitting house—by throwing a potted plant at a second-story window to rouse the children—just as the killer descends. Minutes later he comes through the window and they grapple; she manages to fell him with a knitting needle and seizes his butcher knife—but drops it when he seems dead. As she goes upstairs to the children, the killer rises, takes the knife, and goes after her. She takes refuge in a closet,

---

[20] Further: "Scenes in which women whimper helplessly and do nothing to defend themselves are ridiculed by the audience, who find it hard to believe that anyone— male or female—would simply allow someone to kill them with nary a protest" (Schoell, *Stay Out of the Shower*, pp. 55–56).

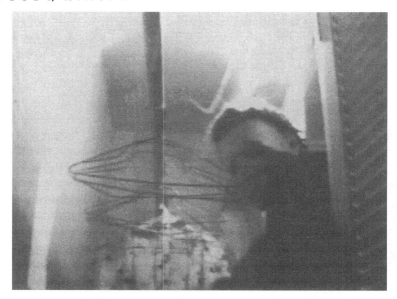

Michael discovers Laurie in the closet (*Halloween*).

lashing the two doorknobs together from the inside. As the killer slashes and stabs at the closet door—we see this from her inside perspective—she bends a hanger into a weapon and, when he breaks the door down, stabs him in the eye. Again thinking him vanquished, she sends the children for the police and sinks down in pain and exhaustion. The killer rises again, but just as he is about to stab her, Dr. Loomis, alerted by the children, rushes in and shoots the killer.

Given the drift in just the four years between *Texas Chain Saw* and *Halloween*—from passive to active defense—it is no surprise that the films following *Halloween* present Final Girls who not only fight back but do so with ferocity and even kill the killer on their own, without help from the outside.[21] Valerie in *Slumber Party Massacre* (a film directed by Amy Jones and scripted by Rita Mae Brown) takes a machete-like weapon to the killer, striking off the bit from his power

[21] There are exceptions, some of them disturbing. In *Splatter University*, Professor Julie Parker is clearly established as a Final Girl from the outset and then killed right at the beginning of what we are led to believe will be the Final Girl sequence (she kicks the killer, a psychotic priest-scholar who keeps his knife sheathed in a crucifix, in the groin and runs for the elevator—only to be cornered and stabbed to death). So meticulously are the conventions observed, and then so grossly violated, that we can only assume sadistic intentionality. This is a film in which (with the exception of an asylum orderly in the preface) only females are killed, and in highly sexual circumstances.

drill, severing his hand, and finally impaling him. Alice assaults and decapitates the killer of *Friday the Thirteenth*. Pursued by the killer in *Hell Night*, Marti pries the gate key from the stiff fingers of a corpse to let herself out of the mansion grounds to safety; when the car will not start, she repairs it on the spot; when the car gets stuck in the roadway, she inside and the killer on top, she frees it in such a way as to cast the killer on the gate's upper spikes. The grittiest of the Final Girls is Nancy of *A Nightmare on Elm Street I*. Aware in advance that the killer will be paying her a visit, she plans an elaborate defense. When he enters the house, she dares him to come at her, then charges him in direct attack. As they struggle, he springs the contraptions she has set so that he is stunned by a swinging sledge hammer, jolted and half-incinerated by an electrical charge, and so on. When he rises yet again, she chases him around the house, bashing him with a chair.[22] In *Texas Chain Saw II*, from 1986, the Final Girl sequence takes mythic measure. Trapped in the underground slaughterhouse, Stretch repeatedly flees, hides, is caught, tortured (at one point forced to don the flayed face of her murdered technician companion), and nearly killed. She escapes with her life chiefly because Leatherface, having developed an affection for her after the crotch episode, is reluctant to ply his chain saw as his father commands. Finally Stretch finds her way out, leaving the Texas Ranger to face certain death below, and clambers up a nearby pinnacle, Chop Top in pursuit. In a crevice near the summit she finds the mummified grandmother, ceremoniously enthroned in an open-air chamber, and on her lap, a functional chain saw. She turns the saw on Chop Top, gashing open his abdomen and tossing him off the precipice. The final scene shows her in extreme long shot, in brilliant sunshine, waving the buzzing chain saw triumphantly overhead. (It is a scene we are invited to compare to the final scene of *Texas Chain Saw I*, in which the wounded Leatherface is shown staggering after the pickup on the highway and waving his chain saw crazily over *his* head.) In Part One the Final Girl, for all her survivor pluck, is, like Red Riding Hood, saved through male agency. In Part Two, however, there is no male agency; the figure so designated, the Texas Ranger, proves so utterly ineffectual that he cannot save himself, much less the girl. The comic ineptitude and failure of would-be "woodsmen" is a repeated theme in the later slasher films. In *Slumber Party Massacre*, the role is played by a woman—though a butch one (the girls' basketball

[22] This film is complicated by the fact that the action is envisaged as a living dream. Nancy finally kills the killer by killing her part of the collective nightmare.

coach). She comes to the slumber party's rescue only to fall victim to the drill herself. But to focus on just who brings the killer down, the Final Girl or a male rescuer, is—as the easy alternation between the two patterns would seem to suggest—to miss the point. The last moment of the Final Girl sequence is finally a footnote to what went before—to the quality of the Final Girl's fight, and more generally to the qualities of character that enable her, of all the characters, to survive what has come to seem unsurvivable.

The Final Girl sequence too is prefigured, if only rudimentarily, in *Psycho*'s final scenes, in which Lila (Marion's sister) is caught reconnoitering in the Bates mansion and nearly killed. Sam (Marion's boyfriend) detains Norman at the motel while Lila snoops about (taking note of Norman's toys). When she perceives Norman's approach, she flees to the basement. Here she encounters the treated corpse of Mrs. Bates and begins screaming in horror. Norman bursts in and is about to strike when Sam enters and grabs him from behind. Like her generic sisters, then, Lila is the spunky inquirer into the Terrible Place: the one who first grasps, however dimly, the past and present danger, the one who looks death in the face, and the one who survives the murderer's last stab.

There the correspondences end, however. The *Psycho* scene turns, after all, on the revelation of Norman's psychotic identity, not on Lila as a character—she enters the film midway and is sketchily drawn—and still less on her self-defense. The Final Girl of the slasher film is presented from the outset as the main character. The practiced viewer distinguishes her from her friends minutes into the film. She is the Girl Scout, the bookworm, the mechanic. Unlike her girlfriends (and Marion Crane) she is not sexually active. Laurie (*Halloween*) is teased because of her fears about dating, and Marti (*Hell Night*) explains to the boy with whom she finds herself sharing a room that they will be using separate beds. Although Stretch (*Texas Chain Saw II*) is hardly virginal, she is not available, either; early in the film she pointedly turns down a date, and we are given to understand that she is, for the present, unattached and even lonely. So too Stevie of Carpenter's *The Fog*, like Stretch a disk jockey; divorced mother and newcomer in town, she is unattached and lonely but declines male attention. The Final Girl is also watchful to the point of paranoia; small signs of danger that her friends ignore, she registers. Above all she is intelligent and resourceful in a pinch. Thus Laurie even at her most desperate, cornered in a closet, has the wit to grab a hanger from the rack and bend it into a weapon; Marti can hot-wire her getaway car, the killer in pursuit; and the psych major of *Friday the Thir-*

A survivor goes after the killer of *Slumber Party Massacre*.

teenth II, on seeing the enshrined head of Mrs. Voorhees, can stop Jason in his tracks by assuming a stridently maternal voice. Finally, although she is always smaller and weaker than the killer, she grapples with him energetically and convincingly.

The Final Girl is boyish, in a word. Just as the killer is not fully masculine, she is not fully feminine—not, in any case, feminine in the ways of her friends. Her smartness, gravity, competence in mechanical and other practical matters, and sexual reluctance set her apart from the other girls and ally her, ironically, with the very boys she fears or rejects, not to speak of the killer himself. Lest we miss the point, it is spelled out in her name: Stevie, Marti, Terry, Laurie, Stretch, Will, Joey, Max. Not only the conception of the hero in *Alien* and *Aliens* but also the surname by which she is called, Ripley, owes a clear debt to slasher tradition.

With the introduction of the Final Girl, then, the *Psycho* formula is radically altered. It is not merely a question of enlarging the figure of Lila but of absorbing into her role, in varying degrees, the functions of Arbogast (investigator) and Sam (rescuer) and restructuring the narrative action from beginning to end around her progress in relation to the killer. In other words, *Psycho*'s detective plot, revolving around a revelation, yields in the modern slasher film to a hero plot, revolving around the main character's struggle with and eventual triumph over evil. But for the femaleness, however qualified, of that main character, the story is a standard one of tale and epic.

Shock

One reason that the shower sequence in *Psycho* has "evoked more study, elicited more comment, and generated more shot-for-shot analysis from a technical viewpoint than any other in the history of cinema" is that it suggests so much but shows so little.[23] Of the forty-odd shots in as many seconds that figure the murder, only a single fleeting one actually shows the body being stabbed. The others present us with a rapid-fire sequence of shots of the knife, of the shower, of Marion's face, arm, and feet, finally the bloody water as it swirls down the drain and dissolves to the image of a large, still eye. The horror resides less in the actual images than in their summary implication.

Although Hitchcock is hardly the first director to prefer the oblique rendition of physical violence, he may, to judge from current examples, be one of the last. For better or worse, the perfection of special effects has made it possible to show maiming and dismemberment in extraordinarily credible detail. The horror genres are the natural repositories of such effects; what can be done is done, and slashers, at the bottom of the category, do it most and worst. Thus we see heads squashed and eyes popped out, faces flayed, limbs dismembered, eyes penetrated by needles in close-up, and so on.

With this new explicitness also comes a new tone. If the horror of *Psycho* was taken seriously, the "horror" of the slasher films is of a rather more complicated sort. Audiences express uproarious disgust ("Gross!") as often as they express fear, and it is clear that the makers of slasher films pursue the combination. More particularly: spectators tend to be silent during the stalking scenes (although they sometime call out warnings to the stalked person), scream out at the first slash, and make loud noises of revulsion at the sight of the bloody stump. The rapid alternation between registers—between something like "real" horror on one hand and a camp, self-parodying horror on the other—is by now one of the most conspicuous characteristics of the tradition. In its cultivation of intentionally outrageous excess, the slasher film intersects with the cult film, a genre devoted to such effects. Just what this self-ironizing relation to taboo signifies, beyond a remarkably competent audience, is unclear—it is yet another aspect of the phenomenon that has lain beyond criticism—but for the time

---

[23] Spoto, *The Dark Side of Genius*, p. 454. See also William Rothman, *Hitchcock*, pp. 246–341.

being it stands as a defining characteristic of the lower genres of popular culture.

THE BODY

On the face of it, the relation between the sexes in slasher films could hardly be clearer. The killer is with few exceptions recognizably human and distinctly male; his fury is unmistakably sexual in both roots and expression; his victims are mostly women, often sexually free and always young and beautiful. Just how essential this victim is to horror is suggested by her historical durability. If the killer has over time been variously figured as shark, fog, gorilla, birds, and slime, the victim is eternally and prototypically the damsel. Cinema hardly invented the pattern. It has simply given visual expression to the abiding proposition that, in Poe's famous formulation, the death of a beautiful woman is the "most poetical topic in the world."[24] As horror director Dario Argento puts it, "I like women, especially beautiful ones. If they have a good face and figure, I would much prefer to watch them being murdered than an ugly girl or man."[25] Brian De Palma elaborates: "Women in peril work better in the suspense genre. It all goes back to the *Perils of Pauline*. . . . If you have a haunted house and you have a woman walking around with a candelabrum, you fear more for her than you would for a husky man."[26] Or Hitchcock, during the filming of *The Birds*: "I always believe in following the advice of the playwright Sardou. He said, 'Torture the women!' The trouble today is that we don't torture women enough."[27] What the directors do not say, but show, is that "Pauline" is at her very most effective in a state of undress, borne down upon by a blatantly phallic murderer, even gurgling orgasmically as she dies. The case could be made that the slasher films available at a given neighborhood video rental outlet recommend themselves to censorship under the Dworkin-MacKinnon guidelines at least as readily as do the hard-core films the next section over, at which that legislation aimed; for if some of the victims are men, the argument goes, most are women, and the women are brutalized in ways that come too close to real life for comfort. But what this line of reasoning does not take into account is the figure of the Final Girl. Because slashers lie for all practical purposes beyond the purview of legiti-

[24] Edgar Allan Poe, "The Philosophy of Composition," p. 55.
[25] Argento as quoted in Schoell, *Stay Out of the Shower*, p. 54.
[26] De Palma as quoted in ibid., p. 41.
[27] Hitchcock as quoted in Spoto, *The Dark Side of Genius*, p. 483.

mate criticism, and to the extent that they have been reviewed at all
have been reviewed on an individual basis, the phenomenon of the
female victim-hero has scarcely been acknowledged.[28]

It is, of course, "on the face of it" that most of the public discussion
of film takes place—from the Dworkin-MacKinnon legislation to Siskel and Ebert's reviews to our own talks with friends on leaving the
movie house. Underlying that discussion is the assumption that the
sexes are what they seem; that screen males represent the Male and
screen females the Female; that this identification along gender lines
authorizes impulses toward violence in males and encourages impulses toward victimization in females. In part because of the massive authority cinema by nature accords the image, even academic
film criticism has been slow—slower than literary criticism—to get
beyond appearances. Film may not appropriate the mind's eye, but
it certainly encroaches on it; the gender characteristics of a screen
figure are a visible and audible given for the duration of the film. To
the extent that the possibility of cross-gender identification has been
entertained, it has been that of the female with the male. Thus some
critics have wondered whether the female viewer, faced with the
screen image of a masochistic/narcissistic female, might not rather
elect to "betray her sex and identify with the masculine point of
view." The reverse question—whether men might not also, on occasion, elect to betray their sex and identify with screen females—has
scarcely been asked, presumably on the assumption that men's interests are well served by the traditional patterns of cinematic representation. For there is the matter of the "male gaze." As E. Ann Kaplan
sums it up, "within the film text itself, men gaze at women, who
become objects of the gaze; the spectator, in turn, is made to identify
with this male gaze, and to objectify the woman on the screen; and
the camera's original 'gaze' comes into play in the very act of filming."[29] But if it is so that all of us, male and female alike, are by these
processes "made to" identify with men and "against" women, how
are we then to explain the appeal to a largely male audience of a film
genre that features a female victim-hero? The slasher film brings us

[28] Cf. Dika's *Games of Terror*, which, although not particularly concerned with the
female heroes of slasher films, does recognize their centrality and does suggest a reason for their emergence at this historical moment. The phenomenon has otherwise
tended to be slighted or denied in treatments of modern horror (Carroll, *The Philosophy
of Horror*; Tudor, *Monsters and Mad Scientists*; Twitchell, *Dreadful Pleasures*). Wood's essay "Beauty Bests the Beast" acknowledges the phenomenon but confines itself to a
few examples.

[29] Silvia Bovenschen, "Is There a Feminine Aesthetic?" p. 114; E. Ann Kaplan,
Women and Film, p. 15. See also Mary Ann Doane, "Misrecognition and Identity."

squarely up against fundamental questions of film analysis: where does the literal end and the figurative begin? how do the two levels interact and what is the significance of the interaction? and to which, in arriving at a political judgment (as we are inclined to do in the case of low horror and pornography in particular), do we assign priority?

A figurative or functional analysis of the slasher begins with the processes of point of view and identification. The male viewer seeking a male character, even a vicious one, with whom to identify in a sustained way has little to hang onto in the standard example. On the good side, the only viable candidates are the boyfriends or schoolmates of the girls. They are for the most part marginal, undeveloped characters. More to the point, they tend to die early in the film. If the traditional horror plot gave the male spectator a last-minute hero with whom to identify, thereby "indulging his vanity as protector of the helpless female,"[30] the slasher eliminates or attenuates that role beyond any such function; indeed, would-be rescuers are not infrequently blown away for their trouble, leaving the girl to fight her own fight. Policemen, fathers, and sheriffs appear only long enough to demonstrate risible incomprehension and incompetence. On the bad side, there is the killer. The killer is often unseen or barely glimpsed, during the first part of the film, and what we do see, when we finally get a good look, hardly invites immediate or conscious empathy. He is commonly masked, fat, deformed, or dressed as a woman. Or "he" *is* a woman: woe to the viewer of *Friday the Thirteenth I* who identifies with the male killer only to discover, in the film's final sequences, that he was not a man at all but a middle-aged mother. In either case, the killer is himself eventually killed or otherwise evacuated from the narrative. No male character of any stature lives to tell the tale.

The one character of stature who does live to tell the tale is in fact the Final Girl. She is introduced at the beginning and is the only character to be developed in any psychological detail. We understand immediately from the attention paid it that hers is the main story line. She is intelligent, watchful, levelheaded; the first character to sense something amiss and the only one to deduce from the accumulating evidence the pattern and extent of the threat; the only one, in other words, whose perspective approaches our own privileged understanding of the situation. We register her horror as she stumbles on the corpses of her friends. Her momentary paralysis in the face of death duplicates those moments of the universal nightmare experi-

[30] Wood, "Beauty Bests the Beast," p. 64.

ence—in which she is the undisputed "I"—on which horror frankly
trades. When she downs the killer, we are triumphant. She is by any
measure the slasher film's hero. This is not to say that our attachment
to her is exclusive and unremitting, only that it adds up, and that in
the closing sequence (which can be quite prolonged) it is very close
to absolute.

An analysis of the camerawork bears this out. Much is made of the
use of the I-camera to represent the killer's point of view. In these
passages—they are usually few and brief, but striking—we see
through his eyes and (on the soundtrack) hear his breathing and
heartbeat. His and our vision is partly obscured by the bushes or
window blinds in the foreground. By such means we are forced, the
logic goes, to identify with the killer. In fact, however, the relation
between camera point of view and the processes of viewer identification is poorly understood; the fact that Steven Spielberg can stage
an attack in *Jaws* from the shark's point of view (underwater, rushing
upward toward the swimmer's flailing legs) or Hitchcock an attack in
The Birds from the bird-eye perspective (from the sky, as they gather
to swoop down on the streets of Bodega) would seem to suggest either that the viewer's identificatory powers are unbelievably elastic
or that point-of-view shots can sometimes be pro forma.[31] It has also
been suggested that the hand-held or similarly unanchored first-person camera works as much to destabilize as to stabilize identification.
I shall return to such matters at some length in chapter 4. For the
moment, let us accept this equation: point of view = identification.
We are linked, in this way, with the killer in the early part of the film,
usually before we have seen him directly and before we have come
to know the Final Girl in any detail. Our closeness to him wanes as
our closeness to the Final Girl waxes—a shift underwritten by story
line as well as camera position. By the end, point of view is hers: we
are in the closet with her, watching with her eyes the knife blade
pierce the door; in the room with her as the killer breaks through the
window and grabs at her; in the car with her as the killer stabs
through the convertible top, and so on. And with her, we become if
not the killer of the killer then the agent of his expulsion from the
narrative vision. If, during the film's course, we shifted our sympathies back and forth and dealt them out to other characters along the

[31] The locus classicus in this connection is the view-from-the-coffin shot in Carl Th.
Dreyer's *Vampyr*, in which the I-camera sees through the eyes of a dead man. See
Nash, "*Vampyr* and the Fantastic," esp. pp. 32–33. The 1987 remake of *The Little Shop
of Horrors* (itself originally a low-budget horror film, made the same year as *Psycho* in
two days) has us see the dentist from the proximate point of view of the patient's
tonsils.

way, we belong in the end to the Final Girl; there is no alternative. When Stretch eviscerates Chop Top at the end of *Texas Chain Saw II*, she is literally the only character left alive, on either side.

Audience response ratifies this design. Observers unanimously stress the readiness of the "live" audience to switch sympathies in midstream, siding now with the killer and now, and finally, with the Final Girl. As Schoell, whose book on shocker films wrestles with its own monster, "the feminists," puts it:

> Social critics make much of the fact that male audience members cheer on the misogynous misfits in these movies as they rape, plunder, and murder their screaming, writhing female victims. Since these same critics walk out of the moviehouse in disgust long before the movie is over, they don't realize that these same men cheer on (with renewed enthusiasm, in fact) the heroines, who are often as strong, sexy, and independent as the [earlier] victims, as they blow away the killer with a shotgun or get him between the eyes with a machete. All of these men are said to be identifying with the maniac, but they enjoy *his* death throes the most of all, and applaud the heroine with admiration.[32]

What filmmakers seem to know better than film critics is that gender is less a wall than a permeable membrane.[33]

No one who has read "Red Riding Hood" to a small boy or attended a viewing of, say, *Deliverance* (an all-male story that women find as gripping as men do)—or, more recently, *Alien* and *Aliens*, with whose space-age female Rambo, herself a Final Girl, male viewers seem to engage with ease—can doubt the phenomenon of cross-gender identification.[34] This fluidity of engaged perspective is in

[32] Schoell, *Stay Out of the Shower*, p. 55. Two points in this paragraph deserve emending. One is the suggestion that rape is common in these films; it is in fact virtually absent, by definition (see note 14 above). The other is the characterization of the Final Girl as "sexy." She may be attractive (though typically less so than her friends), but she is with few exceptions sexually inactive.

[33] Likewise age and social group. Wood is struck by the willingness of the teenage audience to identify "against" itself, with the forces of the enemy of youth. "Watching it [*Texas Chain Saw Massacre I*] recently with a large, half-stoned youth audience, who cheered and applauded every one of Leatherface's outrages against their representatives on the screen, was a terrifying experience" ("Return of the Repressed," p. 32).

[34] "I really appreciate the way audiences respond," Gail Anne Hurd, producer of *Aliens*, is reported to have said. "They buy it. We don't get people, even rednecks, leaving the theater saying 'That was stupid. No woman would do that.' You don't have to be a liberal ERA supporter to root for Ripley"; as reported in the *San Franciso Examiner Datebook*, 10 August 1986, p. 19. *Time* magazine (28 July 1986) suggests that Ripley's maternal impulses (she squares off against the worst aliens of all in her quest to save a little girl) give the audience "a much stronger rooting interest in Ripley, and that gives the picture resonances unusual in a popcorn epic." The drift has gained

keeping with the universal claims of the psychoanalytic model: the threat function and the victim function coexist in the same unconscious, regardless of anatomical sex. But why, if viewers can identify across gender lines and if the root experience of horror is sex blind, are the screen sexes not interchangeable? Why not more and better female killers, and why (in light of the maleness of the majority audience) not Pauls as well as Paulines? The fact that horror film so stubbornly figures the killer as male and the principal as female would seem to suggest that representation itself is at issue—that the sensation of bodily fright derives not exclusively from repressed content, as Freud insisted, but also from the bodily manifestations of that content.

Nor is the gender of the principals as straightforward as it first seems. The killer's phallic purpose, as he thrusts his drill or knife into the trembling bodies of young women, is unmistakable. At the same time, however, his masculinity is severely qualified: he ranges from the virginal or sexually inert to the transvestite or transsexual, and is spiritually divided ("the mother half of his mind") or even equipped with vulva and vagina. Although the killer of *God Told Me To* is represented and taken as a male in the film text, he is revealed, by the doctor who delivered him, to have been sexually ambiguous from birth: "I truly could not tell whether that child was male or female; it was as if the sexual gender had not been determined . . . as if it were being developed."[35] In this respect, slasher killers have much in common with the monsters of classic horror—monsters who, in Linda Williams's formulation, represent not just "an eruption of the normally repressed animal sexual energy of the civilized male" but also the "power and potency of a *non-phallic* sexuality." To the extent that the monster is constructed as feminine, the horror film thus expresses female desire only to show how monstrous it is.[36] The inten-

---

steam since then (and since the original writing of this essay). On the use of "rednecks" as the categorical Other, see chapter 3.

[35] Further: "When she [the mother] referred to the infant as a male, I just went along with it. Wonder how that child turned out—male, female, or something else entirely?" The birth is understood to be parthenogenetic, and the bisexual child, literally equipped with both sets of genitals, is figured as the reborn Christ. See also *Sleepaway Camp*, a film claimed to be especially popular with subteens, in which the mystery killer at the camp turns out to be one of the girl campers, a figure in turn revealed, in a climactic scene in which she is viewed without clothes, to be a boy.

[36] Linda Williams, "When the Woman Looks," p. 90. Williams's emphasis on the phallic leads her to dismiss slasher killers as a "non-specific male killing force" and hence a degeneration in the tradition. "In these films the recognition and affinity between woman and monster of classic horror film gives way to pure identity: she *is* the monster, her mutilated body the only visible horror" (p. 96). This analysis does not do

tion is manifest in *Aliens*, in which the Final Girl, Ripley, is pitted in the climactic scene against the most terrifying "alien" of all: an egg-laying Mother.

Decidedly "intrauterine" in quality is the Terrible Place, dark and often damp, in which the killer lives or lurks and whence he stages his most terrifying attacks. "It often happens," Freud wrote, "that neurotic men declare that they feel there is something uncanny about the female genital organs. This *unheimlich* place, however, is an entrance to the former *Heim* [home] of all human beings, to the place where each of us lived once upon a time and in the beginning. . . . In this case too then, the *unheimlich* is what once was *heimisch*, familiar; the prefix *'un'* [un-] is the token of repression."[37] It is the exceptional film that does not mark as significant the moment that the killer leaps out of the dark recesses of a corridor or cavern at the trespassing victim, usually the Final Girl. Long after the other particulars have faded, the viewer will remember the images of Amy assaulted from the dark halls of a morgue (*He Knows You're Alone*), or Melanie trapped in the attic as the savage birds close in (*The Birds*). In such scenes of convergence the Other is at its bisexual mightiest, the victim at her tiniest, and the component of sadomasochism at its most blatant.

The gender of the Final Girl is likewise compromised from the outset by her masculine interests, her inevitable sexual reluctance, her apartness from other girls, sometimes her name. At the level of the cinematic apparatus, her unfemininity is signaled clearly by her exercise of the "active investigating gaze" normally reserved for males and punished in females when they assume it themselves; tentatively at first and then aggressively, the Final Girl looks *for* the killer, even tracking him to his forest hut or his underground labyrinth, and then *at* him, therewith bringing him, often for the first time, into our vision as well. When, in the final scene, she stops screaming, faces the killer, and reaches for the knife (sledge hammer, scalpel, gun, machete, hanger, knitting needle, chain saw), she addresses the monster on his own terms. To the critics' objection that *Halloween* in effect punished female sexuality, director John Carpenter responded: "They [the critics] completely missed the boat there, I think. Because if you turn it around, the one girl who is the most sexually uptight just keeps stabbing this guy with a long knife. She's the most sexu-

---

justice to the obvious bisexuality (or at least modified masculinity) of slasher killers, nor does it take into account the new strength of the female victim. The slasher film may not, in balance, be more subversive than traditional horror, but it is certainly not less so.

[37] Sigmund Freud, "The 'Uncanny,' " p. 245.

ally frustrated. She's the one that killed him. Not because she's a virgin, but because all that repressed energy starts coming out. She uses all those phallic symbols on the guy. . . . She and the killer have a certain link: sexual repression."[38] For all its perversity, Carpenter's remark does underscore the sense of affinity, even recognition, that attends the final encounter. But the "certain link" that puts killer and Final Girl on terms, at least briefly, is more than "sexual repression." It is also a shared masculinity, materialized in "all those phallic symbols"—and it is also a shared femininity, materialized in what comes next (and what Carpenter, perhaps significantly, fails to mention): the castration, literal or symbolic, of the killer at her hands. The Final Girl has not just manned herself; she specifically unmans an oppressor whose masculinity was in question to begin with.[39] By the time the drama has played itself out, darkness yields to light (typically as day breaks) and the close quarters of the barn (closet, elevator, attic, basement) give way to the open expanse of the yard (field, road, lakescape, cliff). With the Final Girl's appropriation of "all those phallic symbols" comes the dispelling of the "uterine" threat as well. Consider again the paradigmatic ending of *Texas Chain Saw II*. From the underground labyrinth, murky and bloody, in which she faced saw, knife, and hammer, Stretch escapes through a culvert into the open air. She clambers up the jutting rock and with a chain saw takes her stand. When her last assailant comes at her, she slashes open his lower abdomen—the sexual symbolism is all too clear—and flings him off the cliff. Again, the final scene shows her in extreme long shot, standing on the ledge of a pinnacle, drenched in sunlight, buzzing chain saw held overhead.

The tale would indeed seem to be one of sex and parents. The patently erotic threat is easily seen as the materialized projection of the viewer's own incestuous fears and desires. It is this disabling cathexis to one's parents that must be killed and rekilled in the service of sexual autonomy. When the Final Girl stands at last in the light of day with the knife in her hand, she has delivered herself into the adult world. Carpenter's equation of the Final Girl with the killer has more than a grain of truth. The killers of *Psycho*, *The Eyes of Laura Mars*, *Friday the Thirteenth II–VI*, and *Cruising*, among others, are explicitly figured as sons in the psychosexual grip of their mothers (or fathers, in the case of *Cruising*). The difference is between past and present and between failure and success. The Final Girl enacts in the present,

---

[38] John Carpenter interviewed by Todd McCarthy, "Trick or Treat."

[39] See Williams, "When the Woman Looks" for a fuller speculation on castration as the link between woman and killer.

and successfully, the parenticidal struggle that the killer himself enacted unsuccessfully in his own past—a past that constitutes the
film's backstory. She is what the killer once was; he is what she could
become should she fail in her battle for sexual selfhood. "You got the
choice, boy," says the tyrannical father of Leatherface in *Texas Chain
Saw II,* "sex or the saw; you never know about sex, but the saw—the
saw is the family."

The tale is no less one of maleness. If the experience of childhood
can be—is perhaps ideally—enacted in female form, the breaking
away requires the assumption of the phallus. The helpless child is
gendered feminine; the autonomous adult or subject is gendered
masculine; the passage from childhood to adulthood entails a shift
from feminine to masculine. It is the male killer's tragedy that his
incipient femininity is not reversed but completed (castration) and
the Final Girl's victory that her incipient masculinity is not thwarted
but realized (phallicization). When De Palma says that female frailty
is a predicate of the suspense genre, he proposes, in effect, that the
lack of the phallus, for Lacan the privileged signifier of the symbolic
order, is itself simply horrifying, at least in the mind of the male observer. Where pornography (the argument goes) resolves that lack
through a process of fetishization that allows a breast or leg or whole
body to stand in for the missing member, the slasher film resolves it
either through eliminating the woman (earlier victims) or reconstitut-
ing her as masculine (Final Girl). The moment at which the Final Girl
is effectively phallicized is the moment that the plot halts and horror
ceases. Day breaks, and the community returns to its normal order.

Casting psychoanalytic verities in female form has a venerable cinematic history. Ingmar Bergman, for one, has made a career of it.
One immediate practical advantage, by now presumably unconscious on the part of makers as well as viewers, has to do with a
preestablished cinematic "language" for capturing the moves and
moods of the female body and face. The cinematic gaze, we are told,
is male, and just as that gaze "knows" how to fetishize the female
form in pornography (in a way that it does not "know" how to fetishize the male form),[40] so it "knows," in horror, how to track a
woman ascending a staircase in a scary house and how to study her
face from an angle above as she first hears the killer's footfall. A set

---

[40] So traditional film and heterosexual pornography, in any case. Gay male pornography, however, films some male bodies in much the same way that heterosexual pornography films female bodies, and even mainstream cinema has begun to linger over
male torsos and buns in ways that halt the narrative flow (such halting being, for Laura
Mulvey, the hallmark of the fetishizing gaze). See Mulvey, "Visual Pleasure and Narrative Cinema," esp. pp. 11–14.

of conventions we now take for granted simply "sees" males and females differently.

To this cinematic habit may be added the broader range of emotional expression traditionally allowed women. Angry displays of force may belong to the male, but crying, cowering, screaming, fainting, trembling, begging for mercy belong to the female. Abject terror, in short, is gendered feminine, and the more concerned a given film is with that condition—and it is the essence of modern horror—the more likely the femaleness of the victim.[41] It is no accident that male victims in slasher films are killed swiftly or offscreen, and that prolonged struggles, in which the victim has time to contemplate her imminent destruction, inevitably figure females. Only when one encounters the rare expression of abject terror on the part of a male (as in *I Spit on Your Grave*) does one apprehend the full extent of the cinematic double standard in such matters.[42]

It is also the case that gender displacement can provide a kind of identificatory buffer, an emotional remove that permits the majority audience to explore taboo subjects in the relative safety of vicariousness. Just as Bergman came to realize that he could explore castration anxiety more freely via depictions of hurt female bodies (witness the genital mutilation of Karin in *Cries and Whispers*), so the makers of slasher films seem to know that sadomasochistic incest fantasies sit more easily with the male viewer when the visible player is female. It is one thing for that viewer to hear the psychiatrist intone at the end of *Psycho* that Norman as a boy (in the backstory) was abnormally attached to his mother; it would be quite another to see that attachment dramatized in the present, to experience in nightmare form the elaboration of Norman's (the viewer's own) fears and desires. If the former is playable in male form, the latter, it seems, is not.

The Final Girl is, on reflection, a congenial double for the adolescent male. She is feminine enough to act out in a gratifying way, a way unapproved for adult males, the terrors and masochistic pleasures of the underlying fantasy, but not so feminine as to disturb the structures of male competence and sexuality. The question then arises whether the Final Girls of slasher films—Stretch, Stevie, Marti, Will, Terry, Laurie, and Ripley—are not boyish for the same reason that female "victims" in Victorian flagellation literature—"Georgy,"

[41] Tudor's *Monsters and Mad Scientists* charts and speculates on the reasons for the increasing centrality of victimization in horror cinema.

[42] See chapter 3 ("Getting Even") for a comparison of the visual treatment of the (male) rape in *Deliverance* with the (female) rapes in such films as Hitchcock's *Frenzy*, Wes Craven's *Last House on the Left*, and Ingmar Bergman's *The Virgin Spring*.

"Willy"—are boyish: because they are transformed males. The transformation, Steven Marcus writes, "is itself both a defense against and a disavowal of the fantasy it is simultaneously expressing—namely, that a *boy* is being beaten—that is, loved—by another man."[43] What is represented as male-on-female violence, in short, is figuratively speaking male-on-male sex. For Marcus, the literary picture of flagellation, in which *girls* are beaten, is utterly belied by the descriptions (in *My Secret Life*) of real-life episodes in which the persons being beaten are not girls at all but "gentlemen" dressed in women's clothes ("He had a woman's dress on tucked up to his waist, showing his naked rump and thighs. . . . On his head was a woman's cap tied carefully round his face to hide whiskers") and whipped by prostitutes. Reality, Marcus writes, "puts the literature of flagellation out of the running . . . by showing how that literature is a completely distorted and idealized version of what actually happens."[44] Applied to the slasher film, this logic reads the femaleness of the Final Girl (at least up to the point of her transformation) and indeed of the woman victims in general as only apparent, the artifact of heterosexual deflection. It may be through the female body that the body of the audience is sensationalized, but the sensation is an entirely male affair.[45]

At least one director, Hitchcock, explicitly located thrill in the equation victim = audience. So we judge from his marginal jottings in the shooting instructions for the shower scene in *Psycho:* "The slashing. An impression of a knife slashing, as if tearing at the very screen, ripping the film."[46] Not just the body of Marion is to be ruptured, but also the body on the other side of the film and screen: our witnessing body. As Marion is to Norman, the audience of *Psycho* is to Hitchcock; as the audiences of horror film in general are to the directors of

[43] Steven Marcus, *The Other Victorians*, pp. 260–61. Marcus distinguishes two phases in the development of flagellation literature: one in which the figure being beaten is a boy, and the second, in which the figure is a girl. The very shift indicates, at some level, the irrelevance of apparent sex. "The sexual identity of the figure being beaten is remarkably labile. Sometimes he is represented as a boy, sometimes as a girl, sometimes as a combination of the two—a boy dressed as a girl, or the reverse." The girls often have sexually ambiguous names, as well. The beater is a female, but in Marcus's reading a phallic one—muscular, possessed of body hair—representing the father.

[44] Ibid., pp. 125–27.

[45] It could be argued that *The Burning*, a summer-camp slasher movie in which the function of Final Girl is filled not by a female character but by a nerdish male one (who finally finds it in himself to stop cringing and running and fight back, with the result that it is he, not the "normal" boys, who brings the monster down), reveals the essential maleness of the story (and hence supports a reading of the Final Girl as boy in drag). The question remains why the function is so frequently and conspicuously played by a female.

[46] As quoted by Spoto, *The Dark Side of Genius*, p. 431.

those films, female is to male. Hitchcock's "torture the women" then means, simply, torture the audience. De Palma's remarks about female frailty ("Women in peril work better in the suspense genre. . . . you fear more for her than you would for a husky man") likewise contemplate a male-on-"female" relationship between director and viewer. Cinefantastic horror, in short, succeeds in incorporating its spectators as "feminine" and then violating that body—which recoils, shudders, cries out collectively—in ways otherwise imaginable, for males, only in nightmare. The equation is nowhere more plainly put than in David Cronenberg's *Videodrome*. Here the threat is a mind-destroying video signal; the victims, television viewers. Despite the (male) hero's efforts to defend his mental and physical integrity, a deep, vagina-like gash appears on his lower abdomen. Says the media conspirator as he thrusts a videocassette into the victim's gaping wound, "You must open yourself completely to this."

If the slasher film is "on the face of it" a genre with at least a strong female presence, it is in these figurative readings a thoroughly male exercise, one that finally has very little to do with femaleness and very much to do with phallocentrism. Figuratively seen, the Final Girl is a male surrogate in things oedipal, a homoerotic stand-in, the audience incorporate; to the extent she means "girl" at all, it is only for purposes of signifying male lack, and even that meaning is nullified in the final scenes. Our initial question—how to square a female victim-hero with a largely male audience—is not so much answered as it is obviated in these readings. The Final Girl is (apparently) female not despite the maleness of the audience, but precisely because of it. The discourse is wholly masculine, and females figure in it only insofar as they "read" some aspect of male experience. To applaud the Final Girl as a feminist development, as some reviews of *Aliens* have done with Ripley, is, in light of her figurative meaning, a particularly grotesque expression of wishful thinking.[47] She is simply an agreed-upon fiction and the male viewer's use of her as a vehicle for his own sadomasochistic fantasies an act of perhaps timeless dishonesty.

For all their immediate appeal, these figurative readings loosen as many ends as they tie together. The audience, we have said, is pre-

---

[47] This would seem to be the point of the final sequence of Brian De Palma's *Blow-Out*, in which we see the boyfriend of the victim-hero stab the killer to death but later hear the television announce that the woman herself vanquished the killer. The frame plot of the film has to do with the making of a slasher film ("Co-Ed Frenzy"), and it seems clear that De Palma means his ending to stand as a comment on the Final Girl formula of the genre. De Palma's (and indirectly Hitchcock's) insistence that only men can kill men, or protect women from men, deserves a separate essay.

dominantly male; but what about the women in it? Do we dismiss them as male-identified and account for their experience as an "immasculated" act of collusion with the oppressor?[48] This is a strong judgment to apply to large numbers of women; for while it may be that the audience for slasher films is mainly male, this does not mean that there are not also many female viewers who actively like such films, and of course there are also women, however few, who script, direct, and produce them. These facts alone oblige us at least to consider the possibility that female fans find a meaning in the text and image of these films that is less inimical to their own interests than the figurative analysis would have us believe. Or should we conclude that males and females read these films differently in some fundamental sense? Do females respond to the text (the literal) and males the subtext (the figurative)?[49]

Some such notion of differential understanding underlies the homoerotic reading. The silent presupposition of that reading is that male identification with the female cannot be, and that the male viewer/reader who adjoins feminine experience does so only by homosexual conversion. But does female identification with male experience then similarly indicate a lesbian conversion? Or are the processes of patriarchy so one-way that the female can identify with the male directly, but the male can identify with the female only by transsexualizing her? Does the Final Girl mean "girl" to her female viewers and "boy" to her male viewers? If her masculine features qualify her as a transformed boy, do not the feminine features of the killer qualify him as a transformed woman (in which case the homoerotic reading can be maintained only by defining that "woman" as phallic and retransforming her into a male)? Striking though it is, the analogy between the Victorian flagellation story's Georgy and the slasher film's Stretch falters at the moment that Stretch turns on her assailant and unmans him. Are we to suppose that a homoerotic beating fantasy suddenly yields to what folklorists call a lack-liquidated fantasy? Further: is it simply coincidence that this combination tale—trials, then triumph—bears such a marked resemblance to the classic (male) hero story? Does the standard hero story featuring an anatomical female "mean" differently from one featuring an anatomical male?

As Marcus perceived, the relationship between the Georgy stories of flagellation literature and the real-life anecdote of the Victorian gentlemen is a marvelously telling one. In his view, the maleness of

---

[48] The term is Judith Fetterley's. See her *Resisting Reader*.

[49] On the possible variety of responses to a single film, see Norman N. Holland, "I-ing Film."

the latter must prove the essential or functional maleness of the former. What his analysis does not come to full grips with, however, is the clothing the gentleman wears—not that of a child, as Marcus's "childish" reading of the scene contemplates, but explicitly that of a woman.[50] These women's clothes can of course be understood, within the terms of the homoerotic interpretation, as a last-ditch effort on the part of the gentleman to dissociate himself from the (incestuous) homosexuality implicit in his favored sexual practice. But can they not just as well, and far more economically, be explained as part and parcel of a fantasy of literal femaleness? By the same token, cannot the femaleness of the gentleman's literary representatives— the girls of the flagellation stories—be understood as the obvious, even necessary, extension of that man's dress and cap? The same dress and cap, I suggest, haunt the margins of the slasher film. This is not to deny the deflective convenience, for the male spectator (and filmmaker), of a female victim-hero in a context so fraught with taboo; it is only to suggest that the femaleness of this character is also conditioned by a kind of imaginative curiosity about the feminine in and of itself.

So too the psychoanalytic case. These films do indeed seem to pit the child in a struggle, at once terrifying and attractive, with the parental Other, and it is a rare example that does not directly thematize parent-child relations. But if Freud stressed the maternal source of the *Unheimlich*, the Other of our films is decidedly androgynous: female/feminine in aspects of character and place (the "intrauterine" locale) but male in anatomy. Conventional logic may interpret the killer as the phallic mother of the transformed boy (the Final Girl), but the text itself does not compel such a reading. On the contrary, the text at every level presents us with hermaphroditic constructions—constructions that draw attention to themselves and demand to be taken on their own terms.

For if we define the Final Girl as nothing more than a figurative male, what do we then make of the context of the spectacular gender play in which she is emphatically situated? In his essay on the uncanny, Freud rejected out of hand Jentsch's theory that the experience of horror proceeds from intellectual uncertainty (curiosity?)— feelings of confusion, induced by an author or a coincidence, about

---

[50] Marcus contents himself with noting that the scene demonstrates a "confusion of sexual identity." In the literature of flagellation, he adds, "this confused identity is also present, but it is concealed and unacknowledged." But it is precisely the femaleness of the beaten figures that does acknowledge it (Marcus, *The Other Victorians*, p. 127).

who, what, and where one is.[51] One wonders, however, whether
Freud would have been quite so dismissive if, instead of the mixed
materials he used as evidence, he were presented with a coherent
story corpus—forty slashers, say—in which the themes of incest and
separation were relentlessly played out by a female character, and
further in which gender identity was repeatedly thematized as an issue in and of itself. For although the factors we have considered thus
far—the conventions of the male gaze, the feminine constitution of
abject terror, the value for the male viewer of emotional distance
from the taboos in question, the special horror that may inhere, for
the male audience, in phallic lack, the homoerotic deflection—go a
long way in explaining why it is we have Pauline rather than Paul as
our victim-hero, they do not finally account for our strong sense that
gender is simply being fooled with, and that part of the thrill lies
precisely in the resulting "intellectual uncertainty" of sexual identity.

The "play of pronoun function" that underlies and defines the
cinefantastic is nowhere more richly manifested than in the slasher;
if the genre has an aesthetic base, it is exactly that of a visual identity
game.[52] Consider, for example, the now-standard habit of letting us
view the action in the first person long before revealing who or what
the first person *is*. In the opening sequence of *Halloween I*, "we" are
belatedly revealed to ourselves, after committing a murder in the cinematic first person, as a six-year-old boy. The surprise is often within
gender, but it is also, in a striking number of cases, across it. Again,
Friday the Thirteenth I, in which "we" stalk and kill a number of teenagers over the course of an hour of movie time without even knowing who "we" are; we are invited, by conventional expectation and
by glimpses of "our" own bodily parts—a heavily booted foot, a
roughly gloved hand—to suppose that "we" are male, but "we" are
revealed, at film's end, as a woman. If this is the most dramatic case
of pulling out the gender rug, it is by no means the only one. In
Dressed to Kill, we are led to believe, again by means of glimpses, that
"we" are female—only to discover, in the denouement, that "we"
are a male in drag. In *Psycho*, the dame we glimpse holding the knife

[51] Freud, "The 'Uncanny,' " esp. pp. 219–21 and 226–27. For a fine discussion of
Freud's relation to Jentsch's position in this essay, see Françoise Meltzer's "The Uncanny Rendered Canny: Freud's Blind Spot in Reading Hoffman's 'The Sandman.' "

[52] For Jackson (*Fantasy*) and Nash ("*Vampyr* and the Fantastic"), the fantastic depends for its effect on the uncertainty of vision, a profusion of perspectives and a
confusion of subjective and objective. To the extent that film can present "unreal"
combinations of objects and events as "real" through the camera eye, Jackson argues,
the "cinematic process itself might be called fantastic" (p. 31). Nash coins the term
"cinefantastic" to describe the "play of pronoun function" in which horror/fantasy
films in particular engage (esp. p. 37).

with a "visible virility quite obscene in an old lady" is later revealed, after additional gender teasing, to be Norman in his mother's clothes.[53] *Psycho II* plays much the same game. *Cruising* (in which, not accidentally, transvestites play a prominent role) adjusts the terms along heterosexual/homosexual lines. The tease here is whether the originally straight detective assigned to the string of murders in a gay community does or does not succumb to his assumed homosexual identity; the camerawork leaves us increasingly uncertain as to his (our) sexual inclinations, not to speak of his (our) complicity in the crimes. Even at film's end we are not sure who "we" were during several of the first-person sequences.[54]

The gender-identity game, in short, is too patterned and too pervasive in the slasher film to be dismissed as supervenient. It would seem instead to be an integral element of the particular brand of bodily sensation in which the genre trades. Nor is it exclusive to horror. It is directly thematized in comic terms in the "gender-benders" *Tootsie* (in which a man passes himself off as a woman), *All of Me* (in which a woman is literally introjected into a man and affects his speech, movement, and thought), and *Switch*. It is also directly thematized, in the form of bisexual and androgynous figures and relations, in such cult films as *Pink Flamingos* and *The Rocky Horror Picture Show*. (Some version of it is indeed repeatedly enacted on MTV.) It is further thematized (predictably enough, given their bodily concerns) in such pornographic films as *Every Woman Has a Fantasy*, in which a man, in order to gain access to a women's group in which sexual fantasies are discussed, dresses and passes himself off as a woman. (The degree to which "male" pornography in general relies for its effect on cross-gender identification remains an open question; the proposition makes a certain sense of the obligatory lesbian sequences and the phenomenal success of *Behind the Green Door*, to pick just two examples.)[55] All of these films, and others like them, seem to be ask-

---

[53] Raymond Durgnat, *Films and Feelings*, p. 216.

[54] Not a few critics have argued that the ambiguity is the unintentional result of bad filmmaking.

[55] In her review of *Not a Love Story*, Susan Barrowclough writes that the "male spectator takes the part not of the male, but the female. Contrary to the assumption that the male uses pornography to confirm and celebrate his gender's sexual activity and dominance, is the possibility of his pleasure in identifying with a 'feminine' passivity or subordination" (pp. 35–36). Alan Soble seconds the proposal in his *Pornography* (esp. p. 93). Claims porn/sexploitation filmmaker Joe Sarno: "My point of view is more or less always from the woman's point of view; I stress the efficacy of women for themselves. In general, I focus on the female orgasm as much as I can" (as quoted by V. Vale and Andrea Juno, *Incredibly Strange Films*, p. 94). "Male identification with women," Kaja Silverman writes, "has not received the same amount of critical atten-

ing some version of the question: what would it be like to be, or to seem to be, if only temporarily, a woman? Taking exception to the reception of *Tootsie* as a feminist film, Elaine Showalter argues that the success of "Dorothy Michaels" (the Dustin Hoffman character), as far as both plot and audience are concerned, lies in the veiling of masculine power in feminine costume. *Tootsie*'s cross-dressing, she writes,

> is a way of promoting the notion of masculine power while masking it. In psychoanalytic theory, the male transvestite is not a powerless man; according to the psychiatrist Robert Stoller, in *Sex and Gender*, he is a "phallic woman" who can tell himself that "he is, or with practice will become, a better woman than a biological female if he chooses to do so." When it is safe or necessary, the transvestite "gets great pleasure in revealing that he is a male-woman. . . . The pleasure in tricking the unsuspecting into thinking that he is a woman, and then revealing his maleness (e.g., by suddenly dropping his voice) is not so much erotic as it is proof that there is such a thing as a woman with a penis." Dorothy's effectiveness is the literal equivalent of speaking softly and carrying a big stick.[56]

By the same literalistic token, then Stretch's success must lie in the fact that in the end, at least, she "speaks loudly" *even though* she carries *no* "stick." Just as "Dorothy" 's voice slips serve to remind us that her character really is male, so the Final Girl's "tits and scream" serve more or less continuously to remind us that she really is female—even as, and despite the fact that, she in the end acquits herself "like a man."[57] Her chain saw is thus what "Dorothy Michaels" 's skirt is: a figuration of what she *does* and what she *seems*, as opposed to—and the films turn on the opposition—what she *is*. The idea that appearance and behavior do not necessarily indicate sex—indeed, can misindicate sex—is predicated on the understanding that sex is one thing and gender another; in practice, that sex is life, a less-than-interesting given, but that gender is theater. What-

---

tion [as sublimation into professional "showing off" and reversal into scopophilia], although it would seem to be the most potentially destabilizing, at least as far as gender is concerned" (in her discussion of the Great Male Renunciation in "Fragments of a Fashionable Discourse," p. 141 (briefly recapitulated in *The Acoustic Mirror*, pp. 24–27). The most significant development in the consideration of pornographic "identifications" is Linda Williams's 1989 *Hard Core*.

[56] Elaine Showalter, "Critical Cross Dressing," p. 138.

[57] Whatever its other functions, the scene that reveals the Final Girl in a degree of undress serves to underscore her femaleness. As a reviewer remarked of the scene toward the end of *Aliens* (likewise *Alien*), "we have Ripley wandering around clad only in her underwear. A little reminder of her gender, lest we lose sight of it behind all that firepower?" (Christine Schoefer, *East Bay Express*, 5 September 1986, p. 37).

ever else it may be, Stretch's waving of the chain saw is a moment of high drag. Its purpose is not to make us forget that she is a girl but to thrust that fact on us. The moment, it should be added, is also one that openly mocks the literary/cinematic conventions of symbolic representation.

It may be just this theatricalization of gender that makes possible the willingness of the male viewer to submit himself to a brand of spectator experience that Hitchcock designated as "feminine" in 1960 and that has become only more so since then. In classic horror, the "feminization" of the audience is intermittent and ceases early. Our relationship with Marion's body in *Psycho* halts abruptly at the moment of its greatest intensity (slashing, ripping, tearing). The considerable remainder of the film distributes our bruised sympathies among several lesser figures, male and female, in such a way and at such length as to ameliorate the Marion experience and leave us, in the end, more or less recuperated in our presumed masculinity. Like Marion, the Final Girl is the designated victim, the audience incorporate, the slashing, ripping, and tearing of whose body will cause us to flinch and scream out in our seats. But unlike Marion, she does not die. If *Psycho*, like other classic horror films, solves the femininity problem by obliterating the female and replacing her with representatives of the masculine order (mostly but not inevitably males), the modern slasher solves it by regendering the woman. We are, as an audience, in the end "masculinized" by and through the very figure by and through whom we were earlier "feminized." The same body does for both, and that body is female.

The last point is the crucial one: the same *female* body does for both. The Final Girl (1) undergoes agonizing trials, and (2) virtually or actually destroys the antagonist and saves herself. By the lights of folk tradition, she is not a heroine, for whom phase 1 consists in being saved by someone else, but a hero, who rises to the occasion and defeats the adversary with his own wit and hands. Part 1 of the story sits well on the female; it is the heart of heroine stories in general (Red Riding Hood, Pauline), and in some figurative sense, in ways I have elaborated in some detail, it is gendered feminine even when played by a male. Odysseus's position, trapped in the cave of the Cyclops, is not after all so different from Pauline's lashed to the tracks or Sally's tied to a chair in the dining room of the slaughter-house family. The decisive moment, as far as the fixing of gender is concerned, lies in what happens next: those who save themselves are male, and those who are saved by others are female. No matter how "feminine" his experience in phase 1, the traditional hero, if he rises against his adversary and saves himself in phase 2, will be male.

What is remarkable about the slasher film is how close it comes to reversing the priorities. Presumably for the various functional or figurative reasons I have considered in this chapter, phase 1 wants a female: on that point all slashers from *Psycho* on are agreed. Abject fear is still gendered feminine, and the taboo anxieties in which slashers trade are still explored more easily via Pauline than Paul. The slippage comes in phase 2. As if in mute deference to a cultural imperative, slasher films from the seventies bring in a last-minute male, even when he is rendered supernumerary by the Final Girl's sturdy defense. By 1980, however, the male rescuer is either dismissably marginal or dispensed with altogether; not a few films have him rush to the rescue only to be hacked to bits, leaving the Final Girl to save herself after all. At the moment that the Final Girl becomes her own savior, she becomes a hero; and the moment that she becomes a hero is the moment that the male viewer gives up the last pretense of male identification. Abject terror may still be gendered feminine, but the willingness of one immensely popular current genre to re-represent the hero as an anatomical female would seem to suggest that at least one of the traditional marks of heroism, triumphant self-rescue, is no longer strictly gendered masculine.

So too the cinematic apparatus. The classic split between "spectacle and narrative," which "supposes the man's role as the active one of forwarding the story, making things happen," is at least unsettled in the slasher film.[58] When the Final Girl (in films like *Hell Night* and *Texas Chain Saw Massacre II*) assumes the "active investigating gaze," she exactly reverses the look, making a spectacle of the killer and a spectator of herself. Again, it is through the killer's eyes (I-camera) that we saw the Final Girl at the beginning of the film, and through the Final Girl's eyes that we see the killer, often for the first time with any clarity, sometime around the middle of the film and toward the end increasingly. The gaze becomes, at least for a while, female. More to the point, the female exercise of scopic control results not in her annihilation, in the manner of classic cinema, but in her triumph; indeed, her triumph *depends* on her assumption of the gaze.[59]

It is no surprise, in light of these developments, that the Final Girl should show signs of boyishness. Her symbolic phallicization, in the

---

[58] Mulvey, "Visual Pleasure and Narrative Cinema," p. 12.

[59] Of the "woman's film" (in particular *The Two Mrs. Carrolls*), Mary Ann Doane has written: "The woman's exercise of an active investigating gaze can only be simultaneous with her own victimization. The place of her specularization is transformed into the locus of a process of seeing designed to unveil an aggression against itself" (*The Desire to Desire*, p. 136). It must be this expectation of punishment that the slasher plays with and then upends.

last scenes, may or may not proceed at root from the horror of lack on the part of audience and maker. But it certainly proceeds from the need to bring her in line with the epic laws of Western narrative tradition—the very unanimity of which bears witness to the historical importance, in popular culture, of the literal representation of heroism in male form—and it proceeds no less from the need to render the reallocated gaze intelligible to an audience conditioned by the dominant cinematic apparatus.

It is worth noting that the higher genres of horror have traditionally resisted such developments. The idea of a female who outsmarts, much less outfights—or outgazes—her assailant is unthinkable in the films of De Palma and Hitchcock.[60] Although the slasher film's victims may be sexual teases, they are not in addition simpleminded, scheming, physically incompetent, and morally deficient in the manner of these filmmakers' female victims. And however revolting their special effects and sexualized their violence, few slasher murders approach the level of voluptuous sadism that attends the destruction of women in De Palma's films. For reasons on which we can only speculate, femininity is more conventionally elaborated and inexorably punished, and in an emphatically masculine environment, in the higher forms—the forms that *are* written up, and not by Joe Bob Briggs.

That the slasher film speaks deeply and obsessively to male anxieties and desires seems clear—if nothing else from the maleness of the majority audience. And yet these are texts in which the categories masculine and feminine, traditionally embodied in male and female, are collapsed into one and the same character—a character who is anatomically female and one whose point of view the spectator is unambiguously invited, by the usual set of literary-structural and cinematic conventions, to share. The willingness and even eagerness (so we judge from these films' enormous popularity) of the male viewer to throw in his emotional lot, if only temporarily, with not only a woman but a woman in fear and pain, at least in the first instance, would seem to suggest that he has a vicarious stake in that fear and pain. If it is also the case that the act of horror spectatorship is itself registered as a "feminine" experience—that the shock effects induce in the viewer bodily sensations answering the fear and pain of the screen victim—the charge of masochism is underlined. This is not to say that the male viewer does not also have a stake in the sadistic

---

[60] In fact, as Modleski has shown (*The Women Who Knew Too Much*) Hitchcock's relation to women is an ambivalent one. No one has attempted such an analysis of De Palma.

side; narrative structure, cinematic procedures, and audience response all indicate that he shifts back and forth with ease. It is only
to suggest that in the Final Girl sequence his empathy with what the
films define as the female posture is fully engaged, and further, because this sequence is inevitably the central one in any given film,
that the viewing experience hinges on the emotional assumption of
the feminine posture. Kaja Silverman takes it a step further: "I will
hazard the generalization that it is always the victim—the figure who
occupies the passive position—who is really the focus of attention,
and whose subjugation the subject (whether male or female) experiences as a pleasurable repetition of his/her own story," she writes.
"Indeed, I would go so far as to say that the fascination of the sadistic
point of view is merely that it provides the best vantage point from
which to watch the masochistic story unfold."[61]

The slasher is hardly the first genre in the literary and visual arts
to invite identification with the female; one cannot help wondering
more generally whether the historical maintenance of images of
women in fear and pain does not have more to do with male vicarism
than is commonly acknowledged. What distinguishes the slasher,
however, is the absence or untenability of alternative perspectives
and hence the exposed quality of the invitation. As a survey of the
tradition shows, this has not always been the case. The stages of the
Final Girl's evolution—her piecemeal absorption of functions previ-
ously represented in males—can be located in the years following
1978. The fact that the typical patrons of these films are the sons of
marriages contracted in the sixties or even early seventies leads me
to speculate that the dire claims of that era—that the women's movement, the entry of women into the workplace, and the rise of divorce
and woman-headed families would yield massive gender confusion
in the next generation—were not entirely wrong. We preferred, in
the eighties, to speak of the cult of androgyny, but the point is
roughly the same. The fact that we have in the killer a feminine male

---

[61] Kaja Silverman, "Masochism and Subjectivity," p. 5. Needless to say, this is not
the explanation for the girl-hero offered by the industry. *Time* magazine on *Aliens*: "As
Director Cameron says, the endless 'remulching' of the masculine hero by the 'male-
dominated industry' is, if nothing else, commercially shortsighted. 'They choose to
ignore that 50% of the audience is female. And I've been told that it has been proved
demographically that 80% of the time it's women who decide which film to see' " (28
July 1986). It is of course not Cameron who established the female hero of the series
but Ridley Scott (in *Alien*), and it is fair to assume, from his careful manipulation of
the formula, that Scott got her from the slasher film, where she has flourished for some
time with audiences that are heavily male. (Nor is Cameron's claim that even mainstream audiences are 50% female borne out by any audience study I know of.) Cameron's analysis is thus both self-serving and beside the point.

and in the main character a masculine female—parent and everyteen, respectively—would seem, especially in the latter case, to suggest a loosening of the categories, or at least of the category of the feminine.[62] It is not that these films show us gender and sex in free variation; it is that they fix on the irregular combinations, of which the combination masculine female repeatedly prevails over the combination feminine male. The fact that masculine males (boyfriends, fathers, would-be rescuers) are regularly dismissed through ridicule or death or both would seem to suggest that it is not masculinity per se that is being privileged, but masculinity in conjunction with a female body—indeed, as the term victim-hero contemplates, masculinity in conjunction with femininity. For if "masculine" describes the Final Girl some of the time, and in some of her more theatrical moments, it does not do justice to the sense of her character as a whole. She alternates between registers from the outset; before her final struggle she endures the deepest throes of "femininity"; and even during the final struggle she is now weak and now strong, now flees the killer and now charges him, now stabs and is stabbed, now cries out in fear and now shouts in anger. She is a physical female and a characterological androgyne: like her name, not masculine but either/or, both, ambiguous.[63]

Robin Wood speaks of the sense that horror, for him the by-product of cultural crisis and disintegration, is "currently the most important of all American [film] genres and perhaps even the most progressive, even in its overt nihilism."[64] Likewise Vale and Juno say of the "incredibly strange films," mostly low-budget horror, that their volume surveys, "They often present unpopular—even radical—views addressing the social, political, racial, or sexual inequities, hy-

[62] Dika proposes a political-allegorical reading of the Final Girl: "Female (a rarity in the American genre film) and "castrated," she is a symbol for an enfeebled United States, but one that, when roused, is still strong" (*Games of Terror*, p. 138).

[63] If this analysis is correct, we may expect horror films of the future to feature Final Boys as well as Final Girls (Pauls as well as Paulines). Two figures may be incipient examples: Jesse, the pretty boy in *A Nightmare on Elm Street II*, and Ashley, the character who dies last in *The Evil Dead* (1983). Neither quite plays the role, but their names, and in the case of Jesse the characterization, seem to play on the traditions. *Misery* offers an interesting turn on the convention. Here the "feminine" or masochistic position is occupied by a man (one indeed with broken legs) and the position of sadistic, gender-disturbed, serial murderer (who "adores" the object of her attentions in much the way slasher killers sometimes "adore" their female victims) is played by a woman. It is an arrangement that allows for a particularly prolonged and brutal sadistic reversal.

[64] Wood, "Return of the Repressed," p. 28. For the opposite view, based on classic horror in both literary and cinematic manifestations, see Franco Moretti, "The Dialectic of Fear."

Opening Up

IT IS NO WONDER, given the developments of the last twenty years, that horror should worry the nature of the masculine: what it is, what it should and should not be. Traditional masculinity, as we have seen, does not fare well in the slasher film; the man who insists on taking charge, or who believes that logic or appeals to authority can solve the problem, or (above all) who tries to act the hero, is dead meat. But the theme is a side one there—a kind of formulaic throwaway. It is in the realm of the occult that issues of masculinity and male sexuality come under long and hard scrutiny. On the face of it, the occult film is the most "female" of horror genres, telling as it regularly does tales of women or girls in the grip of the supernatural. But behind the female "cover" is always the story of a man in crisis, and that crisis is what the occult film, and this chapter, are about.[1]

The category of the occult film is a vast and untidy one, if indeed it is a category at all. For present purposes it may be defined generally to include all those films—and there are a great many—that have as their central concern human responses to ghostly or satanic doings. Some, like *Witchboard* and its immediate model *The Exorcist*, turn on satanic possession and exorcism. Some (for example, *The Omen*) have Satan already in the world (not having been aborted by

---

[1] Like horror in general, the great majority of occult horror is scripted, and virtually all of it directed and produced, by men, and despite my impression that occult films have a greater share of female viewers than other sorts of horror (there are no reliable statistics), it would seem that the constructed viewer is also male.

an exorcism).[2] Some are concerned more with spirits of the departed (e.g., *Don't Look Now* or *Poltergeist*) than with Satan. In some the possessed entity is not a person but a house—which can be exorcised in much the same way a possessed woman is exorcised ("This house is now clean!" announces the medium Tangina after the exorcism in *Poltergeist*). Some are nominally about satanic possession but focus on the processes of transmission rather than either the condition of possession or the nature of the satanic itself (e.g., *Prince of Darkness*); in their fascination with contagion, these films have much in common, and indeed overlap, with modern vampire, werewolf, and zombie films. Others (e.g., *The Fury, Carrie*) concern themselves with the telepathic and telekinetic powers of certain "gifted" individuals— powers that are at least obliquely tied to dead spirits or Satan or both. Still others play in the register of voodoo or equivalent folk religions (e.g., *The Believers, The Serpent and the Rainbow*). Finally there are the so-called alien possession films, in which, as in *Alien* and *Aliens*, humans are penetrated and colonized by unclean spirits of the space-age kind.

If we cannot reduce this vast range to a single formula or morphology, we can point to some general tendencies. The most obvious of these is the split between two competing systems of explanation— White Science and Black Magic, to use the terminology of *The Serpent and the Rainbow*. White Science refers to Western rational tradition. Its representatives are nearly always white males, typically doctors, and its tools are surgery, drugs, psychotherapy, and other forms of hegemonic science. Black Magic, on the other hand, refers to satanism, voodoo, spiritualism, and folk variants of Roman Catholicism. A world of crosses, holy water, seances, candles, prayer, exorcism, strings of garlic, beheaded chickens, and the like, its inhabitants are blacks, Native Americans, mixed-race peoples (especially Cajun and Creole) and third-world peoples in general, children, old people, priests, Transylvanians—but first and foremost women. (In the few instances in which the representative of White Science is a woman, she is more or less like the pants-wearing, title-bearing Dr. Gene Tuskin—note name—of *The Exorcist II*.[3] When Black Magic is represented by an adult white male, he is likely to be a writer or an English teacher, as in *Salem's Lot*.) The inevitable lesson of the modern occult film is that White Science has its limits, and that if it does not yield, in the extremity, to the wisdom of Black Magic, all is lost. If a woman is possessed by the devil, neurosurgery is not the answer; an exor-

[2] In *The Visitor* (1979), the emissary of Christ, sent from heaven to keep a diabolical child from being born (the mother is host), actually recommends an abortion.

[3] So, for example, the female doctors in *From Beyond, Nightmare on Elm Street III*, and *Hellhole*.

cism is. Before one can provide a supernatural solution, however, one must admit the supernatural nature of the problem.[4] Wherein lies the plot: convincing the White Science person of the necessity and indeed the superiority of Black Magic. The drama of these films thus turns on the process of conversion: the shedding of disbelief, the acceptance of the mystical or irrational. Insofar as the occult film repeatedly elaborates the distinction between White Science and Black Magic in racial, class, and gender terms, it traffics in some of the most basic social tensions of our time.

With the White Science/Black Magic opposition in mind, let us look more closely at two occult films of the possession variety (that is, films which tell of a girl/woman possessed by the devil and of the man/men involved in her exorcism): *The Exorcist* (William Friedkin, 1973) and *Witchboard* (Kevin S. Tenney, 1987). Although the latter is commonly taken as one of the "countless imitations" of the former, both films are better seen as variants in a tradition extending all the way back to the Bible—one of the repeated and explicit points of both Friedkin's film version of *The Exorcist* and the novel by William Peter Blatty on which it is based.[5] And as these two films and dozens like them attest, that tradition is alive and well in modern horror: the possession or exorcism plot, assimilated directly or indirectly and in varying degrees to a psychoanalytic model, is one of the most generative ones of our time. (In its fully secularized form, the exorcism story is not a horror drama at all but a psychological one in which, as in *Ordinary People*, the afflicted person is not possessed but emotionally distressed, the exorcist not a priest but a psychiatrist, and the treatment not incantations but some version of the "talking cure.") What interests me here is not the genre per se, but one of its inform-

[4] According to Tzvetan Todorov, this is "the very heart" of the fantastic. "In a world which is indeed our world, the one we know, a world without devils, sylphides, or vampires, there occurs an event which cannot be explained by the laws of this same familiar world. The person who experiences the event must opt for one of two possible solutions: either he is the victim of an illusion of the senses, of a product of the imagination—and laws of the world then remain what they are; or else the event has indeed taken place, it is an integral part of reality—but then this reality is controlled by laws unknown to us. Either the devil is an illusion, an imaginary being; or else he really exists, precisely like other living beings—with this reservation, that we encounter him infrequently. The fantastic occupies the duration of this uncertainty. Once we choose one answer or the other, we leave the fantastic for a neighboring genre, the uncanny or the marvelous. The fantastic is that hesitation experienced by a person who knows only the laws of nature, confronting an apparently supernatural event" (*The Fantastic*, p. 25).

[5] The novel opens with the passage from Luke 8:27–30 in which Christ encounters a man possessed by the devil ("My name is Legion . . ."), and throughout are interspersed bits of Karras's readings in the history of possession and exorcism.

ing themes or subplots: the charting of a male in crisis.[6] The "opening story," as I shall call it, is by no means exclusive to the possession
film—it crops up all over occult horror—but it is in the possession
film that it typically takes its fullest and most transparent form. Certainly it is at center stage, though in quite different ways, in both *The
Exorcist* and *Witchboard*. Standing at fourteen years' remove from one
another, they attest as well to the theme's evolution during the period of contemporary horror they very nearly bracket.[7]

The Exorcist gets under way when a twelve-year-old girl, Regan, begins to behave strangely. Her concerned mother, an actress, turns to
medicine, and Regan is treated to the full panoply of White Science:
drugs, X-rays, EEG, a lumbar tap, neurosurgery, and psychiatry. All
of this fails, of course, and Regan's condition worsens.[8] Meanwhile,
the Jesuit Father Karras, thanks to the death of his mother and
doubts about his effectiveness as a priest-psychiatrist, is undergoing
something of a crisis in his life and faith. When the medical profession admits defeat, her mother approaches Karras about an exorcism.
By this time there is reason to believe that the diabolical presence has
not only desecrated a statue of the Virgin Mary in the local church
(affixing a penis and elongating the breasts) but also killed a man by
forcing him bodily out of an upper-story window. Karras's first encounter with Regan is worth examining in some detail. I quote here
from the novel:[9]

> In the ticking silence, Karras hesitated, then entered the room slowly,
> almost flinching backward at the pungent stench of moldering excrement
> that hit him in the face like a palpable blast.

[6] For a more inclusive reading of the genre, see Derry, *Dark Dreams*, chapter 3 ("The
Horror of the Demonic").

[7] According to Tudor, "invasive supernature" themes (including demonic possession) underwent a startling boom in the seventies and eighties. See his *Monsters and
Mad Scientists*, pp. 158–84.

[8] For an account of the changing fortunes of science and scientists in horror cinema,
see ibid., passim.

[9] I have made an exception to my "films only" policy in the case of *The Exorcist*
because although Friedkin's direction constantly draws attention to Karras's tormented condition (long pauses, soulful looks, broken-off conversations), it never explains what the trouble is. Friedkin's decision not to render the interior monologues
on which the novel's meaning depends—and in which Regan's meaning for Karras is
revealed—leaves us with a cinematic text that hints and nudges but never tells. Because what is hinted and nudged at is crucial for the tradition at large (not to say for a
coherent understanding of just this film), I have taken recourse to the rather more
transparent novel where Karras's investment is at stake. In so doing, I note that Friedkin himself has noted (Derry, *Dark Dreams*, p. 123) that the first hour of the film—its
exposition—may be "very hard to follow unless you've read the book" and suggest
that the second hour offers some of the same difficulty.

Quickly reining back his revulsion, he closed the door. Then his eyes locked, stunned, on the thing that was Regan, on the creature that was lying on its back in the bed, head propped against a pillow while eyes bulging wide in their hollow sockets shone with mad cunning and burning intelligence, with interest and with spite as they fixed upon his, as they watched him intently, seething in a face shaped into a skeletal, hideous mask of mind-bending malevolence. Karras shifted his gaze to the tangled, thickly matted hair; to the wasted arms and legs; the distended stomach jutting up so grotesquely; then back to the eyes: they were watching him . . . pinning him . . . shifting now to follow as he moved to a desk and chair near the window.[10]

So wasted is "the thing that was Regan" that there is some question as to how much longer it can last. Karras and a renowned colleague, Father Merrin, undertake an exorcism so grueling that it kills Merrin. Karras, in his distress, sees that Regan is about to die and dares the devil to exit her and enter himself instead. At exactly that moment, he falls to his death through the same upper-story window—presumably by the force of the devil's entry—and Regan is cured.

Witchboard's title refers to the Ouija board through which the evil spirit Malfeitor (Portuguese for "evildoer") enters the world and "progressively entraps" a law student named Linda. (The Ouija board is one of several "quotations" from *The Exorcist*. Regan uses the board, and a character worries aloud, "In story after story that I've heard about séances, Ouija boards, *all* of that, they always seem to point to the opening of a door of some sort.")[11] Linda is flanked by two men: her present boyfriend Jim, and her former boyfriend Brandon. Jim, we quickly see, is emotionally disabled: unable to tell Linda he loves her, much less to marry her, hostile to the very thought of religious or spiritual experience, a heavy smoker and drinker, relentless in his sarcastic joking—a man "with ice in his veins," who has not cried since the age of eight, and who lately dropped out of medical school because he could not "*care* enough." Brandon is a rather different sort. He grasps what Jim cannot: that Linda's mounting affliction stems from supernatural causes and that she must be exorcised sooner rather than later. "At first the spirit will be extremely helpful and friendly, so she's lured into using the board more and more," he tries to explain to the derisive Jim. "Pretty soon all she wants to do is use the board. Everything else, like going to classes, becomes unimportant. This is called progressive entrapment. When she reaches this stage, the spirit changes. He starts to frighten and terrorize her, gradually breaking down her resistance. And once

[10] William Peter Blatty, *The Exorcist*, p. 203.
[11] Ibid., p. 76.

that's over, he's able to possess her." Jim sees Linda's decline (she grows increasingly irritable, begins swearing "like a truckdriver," shows all the symptoms of pregnancy, becomes haggard and depressed), but he insists on natural and rational causes. Only after a series of bizarre events and fatal accidents (Jim's work partner and a medium are killed by Malfeitor) does Jim finally acknowledge the reality of the spirit world and join with Brandon in an attempt to stop the demon before it is too late. But Brandon too is killed. In a climactic and emotional scene, Jim embraces Brandon's corpse, weeps dramatically (for the first time since the age of eight), and rushes to save Linda from the final stage of entrapment. He arrives almost too late: Linda is now fully possessed—dressed in Malfeitor's clothes, speaking with his voice, and wielding his murderous hatchet. But after a struggle, during which Linda/Malfeitor pins Jim and forces him finally to say that he loves her, Jim finally manages to damage the board, thus obliterating Malfeitor and reclaiming Linda. The film ends with their wedding.

As the synopses indicate, these are "dual focus" narratives, attention alternating between the story of female possession on one hand and the story of male crisis on the other. The question is how to explain this gendered division of narrative labor—to understand what it is about the male crisis that needs harnessing to a narrative of female hysteria or indeed psychosis. I begin by looking more closely at the female and male stories in turn as they appear not only in *The Exorcist* and *Witchboard* but in other occult films as well.

THE FEMALE STORY

In the language of the film, Linda is the devil's "portal."[12] She and Regan stand in a long line of female portals, from the equally gullible Eve through the professional portals—sibyls and prophetesses—of classical and medieval times to the majority of psychic and New Age channelers of our own day.[13] Certainly the portals of occult

[12] In the climactic struggle, Linda/Malfeitor claims that it is *Jim* who is the intended portal. The action suggests otherwise, and it seems likely that this is just another of the devil's lies. The devil is repeatedly portrayed as a liar. As Father Merrin puts it (in *The Exorcist*), "The demon is a liar, but also mixes lies with the truth."

[13] Marcia Kinder and Beverle Houston report that "the incident on which the novel is said to be based actually involved a boy and that the sex change also introduces the dimension of woman as the weaker vessel" ("Seeing Is Believing," p. 52). It also introduces the more salacious dimension of woman as enterable and fillable.

horror are almost invariably women. Beyond the possession film proper, represented here by *The Exorcist* and *Witchboard*, there is the related and phenomenally popular telekinesis story, also peopled overwhelmingly by females—usually pubescent girls. The typical telekinesis film (*Carrie, Friday the Thirteenth VII, Firestarter, The Fury,* etc.) treads a careful line between supernatural explanations and secular ones. Blatty's novel spells out the former: "In the demoniacal form of possession, for example, the 'demon' may speak in languages unknown to the first personality, or . . . manifest various parapsychic phenomena, telekinesis for example: the movement of objects without application of material force."[14] When Carrie (*Carrie,* 1976) realizes that she has the power to will events, she goes to the library to research "miracles." If she had hoped her abilities qualified her as a saint, however, she is disappointed; she is merely telekinetic. Her fundamentalist mother takes it a step further: "You have Satan's power!" To which Carrie retorts, "It's not Satan's power, it's *me;* when I concentrate, I can move things!" We know better: such is her pain and rage—at her cruel schoolmates and at her awful mother— that she has in fact become the devil's portal. So supernatural and psychosexual intersect: cause a girl enough pain, repress enough of her rage, and—no matter how fundamentally decent she may be— she perforce becomes a witch.[15]

In *The Fury* (1978), the telekinetic figure is doubled in the figures of the adolescent Gillian (a girl) and Robin (a boy), separately captured and trained by paragovernmental agents. The film turns on their struggle to escape their captivity—both physical and mental—and find each other. Here the demonic source of their "psychometric" powers is clear to see—in the figure of the scientist (played by John Cassavetes), whose evil plots and glowing blue eyes (transferred, during the course of the film, to both Gillian and Robin) mark him as Satan-on-earth. Gillian is the standard portal: an adolescent female whose anger at her divorced mother opens her to satanic entry. Robin's maleness seems at first glance to constitute an exception, but as his name suggests, his story is on closer inspection much the same,

[14] Blatty, *The Exorcist*, p. 172. The passage is ostensibly a quotation from a learned treatise.

[15] Kinder and Houston write that, in *The Exorcist*, Blatty and Friedkin "present us with data for a psychological interpretation (divorce, Regan's jealousy of Burke, the father's rejection of Regan, her forthcoming thirteenth birthday, unusual physical contact between mother and daughter); then they reject it in favor of a phenomenological devil" ("Seeing Is Believing," p. 47). As I shall suggest below, it is here as elsewhere not so much a question of exclusion as it is a question of syncretizing; the same way that masculinity is not rejected but modified, made to assimilate to the feminine, so psychology is joined to religion, not cast out in favor of it.

played out in brutal sexual detail not with his actual mother (who is dead) but with an older woman doctor, one of his captors, to whom he is sexually enslaved. His rage at that "mother" finally explodes and he kills her. Satanic possession is gendered feminine, it seems, even when the portal is a male.

Indeed, satanic possession is gendered feminine even when the portal is a car. The prologue to *Christine* (1983) shows us a Plymouth Fury that will come to be called Christine taking her final form on a Detroit assembly line.[16] One auto worker she maims and one she kills. There is no overt explanation for her malevolence, but a shot of the "alley" underneath the car suggests that the evil entered from below. She lives a long life of evil, in any case, killing her owners and attackers and regenerating herself after every smashing. Not even being cubed in a metal compactor and thrown into the car graveyard can do her in; in the final scenes of the film, the cube begins to creak and tremble and the radio to play. (Virtually all satanic films end with a scene that indicates that the force in question is only temporarily laid to rest and that evil will shortly rise again.) Christine's femininity is not a side issue; it is the central one. To Arnie Cunningham, her teen owner, she is more than a car; she is an ersatz sex object—"pure body," as one of his friends puts it in the beginning of the film. Or as the film's heroine, Lee, declares: "This car's a girl!" Through Christine, Arnie himself shows signs of what *Witchboard* called "progressive entrapment." Like Regan (*The Exorcist*) and Linda (*Witchboard*), Arnie grows increasingly foulmouthed, hostile, aggressive—indeed, macho (his swaggering masculinity at the film's end is the exact counterpart of Linda's male voice and clothing and physical hostility). Also like them, he is initially too nice (in his case a nerd at school and a wimp at home), and it appears to be just this "niceness," in combination with the usual repressed rage at his parents, that makes him open to satanic entry. When his high-school friends mispronounce his name as "Cuntingham," they are closer to the mark than they know.

The female may not be the exclusive port of entry for the satanic, but she has been since Eve the favored one. The pattern carries over into films in which Satan has been converted into a poltergeist, space alien, ghost, or marauding monster. *Poltergeist* (1982) opens with the five-year-old Carol Anne's coming into contact with the "TV people": "Hello," she addresses the empty screen (the television has been left on after the family is all asleep). "What do you look like? Talk louder,

[16] For a "secular" reading of *Christine*, see Cumbow's *Order in the Universe*, esp. chapter 10, "Rock and Roll Is Here to Stay."

I can't hear you." And then, after a pause, as if in answer, "Five. Yes. Yes. I don't know. I don't know."[17] She puts her hands on the screen as if she wants in, and it is indeed only a matter of time before she is in fact pulled through it to the "other side." The film turns on the family's fevered efforts to get her back—efforts that involve seeking the services first of the parapsychologist Dr. Lesh and her associates and finally of a midget medium, who performs a version of an exorcism, retrieving Carol Anne from the other side and for the moment, at least, ridding the house of its disturbing spirits: "This house is now clean!" The spirits, we come to know, belong to the dead on whose cemetery—a cemetery never properly relocated—the Cuesta Verde tract development now stands.[18] But even here, among the reasonably roused spirits of the dead, the devil lurks. As the medium explains, Carol Anne was drawn into the television by a figure appearing to be another child—"but to us it is—The Beast!"

What is striking about the gender terms of *Poltergeist* is not merely the receptivity of a young girl to the supernatural, but the fact that its supernatural discourse in general is so emphatically a discourse of females. It is Carol Anne's mother, Diane, who first accepts Carol Anne's account of the "TV people" and figures it must have something to do with the chairs that have begun moving about the kitchen of their own accord. Indeed, Diane immediately sets about domesticating the supernatural occurrences: "It's just another side of nature," she says to her husband Steve, that evening, as she cheerfully demonstrates its workings to him. And of course both the parapsychologist, Dr. Lesh, and the medium are middle-aged women.[19] Dr.

[17] It should be noted that Carol Anne's canary has just died and been ceremoniously buried in the backyard. The "recent loss" trope is so standard as to be a virtual sine qua non of supernatural horror. Usually it is the death or divorce-departure of a parent (*Making Contact, E.T., Carrie, The Fury, The Believers, The Exorcist, The Kindred, Firestarter,* and so on), but it may also be the loss of a child (*The Omen, Don't Look Now*) or the loss of a spouse or lover (*The Entity*). In this way, as in others, supernatural horror is like the European fairy tale, which frequently takes as its point of departure the death of someone near (usually a parent). In the case of horror, the point seems to be that such a loss opens a space for the supernatural, and that immediate survivors are "open" to otherwordly invasion.

[18] In *Poltergeist*, as in a great many horror films, capitalist greed is the first cause of horror. Conspicuous examples are *The Prophecy*, in which the illegal use of mercury by a paper company causes murderous monsters to grow in the forest, and *Alien*, in which the company's quest for specimens outweighs its regard for the lives of its workers.

[19] Possession horror abounds with task-force teams of parapsychologists who set up research stations in the suspicious place in hopes of documenting the supernatural. The theme has been a commonplace ever since *The Haunting* (1963; adapted from Shir-

Lesh's helpers are male, but their knowledge is limited to technical know-how (one is a video man whose business it is to tape the evidence) and scientific explanations; the big picture, and the intuitive moves, are all Dr. Lesh's. Once Carol Anne disappears and the supernatural begins to express itself in earnest, the adult males—Steve and Dr. Lesh's two techs—are shunted aside. The lengthy and hushed conversation, at the heart of the film, about death as the moment at which one walks into and joins a brilliant, ecstatic light, is a conversation conducted by women only. Men are silent auditors, each sitting in darkness in the sides and corners of the room—at the margins of the feminine center, and at the margins of the cinematic frame. The only male privy to the magical feminine is the boy Robbie, again in the typical terms of horror not yet fully gendered masculine.[20] In the same way that women spectators are figured as more open to the image (see chapter 4), so women in general are figured as more open to the supernatural—and perhaps, ultimately, for the same reason.

That gender split is typical. In *Don't Look Now* (1973), Laura and John, parents of a recently drowned child, go to Venice. There Laura falls in with two English spinster-sisters, of whom one, the blind one, is a medium who has been in touch with the dead child. "She's blind—the one who has second sight—she's blind," Laura explains to John. John will have none of it: "It's ridiculous! I'm not going to get involved with two neurotic old women and their mumbo jumbo." Later, at the police station, an officer inspects sketches of those women and remarks: "Age makes women grow to look more like each other. Don't you think that? But men, each becomes quite distinct. Women seem to converge." The seance that follows is an all-woman affair, very much the counterpart of the female-engineered "exorcisms" of *Poltergeist, The Entity, Making Contact*, and a variety of other possession films. (It is also the counterpart of the exorcism in *The Exorcist*, reminding us again that Roman Catholic priests and women are functionally one and the same in horror.) The irony of *Don't Look Now* is that John is himself second-sighted but ignores the signs until too late. In the film's concluding moments he finally turns

---

ley Jackson's *The Haunting of Hill House*). It is noteworthy that the head parapsychologist, a man in *The Haunting*, is now typically female (though not in *E.T.*).

 [20] Like traditional cultures, which tend to divide society into two groups—able-bodied men, and everyone else (boys, old men, and all women)—popular culture tends to regard boys as "unsubjects" who are, as Doane puts it, "denied access to the full subjectivity bestowed on the adult male within patriarchal culture" (*The Desire to Desire*, p. 90). Thus Eliot in *E.T.*, for example, Joey in the derivative *Making Contact*, and Robbie in *Poltergeist*.

and follows the red-caped figure he now thinks may be the ghost of his daughter—only to have the figure turn on him, reveal herself as a crone, and kill him.[21] Only middle-aged women—they who are all alike—survive.

The Omen would seem to be an exception, focusing as it does not on the process of satanic possession but on the product: the diabolical child Damien, orphaned at birth and quickly and secretly adopted by Robert Thorn and presented to his unwitting wife Cathy in place of their own stillborn infant. In fact, however, as suspicions about Damien's nature grow, so do questions about the dead mother, and the possibility of her having served as portal becomes the central issue of the film. Father Brennan (yet another Roman Catholic priest who plies his knowledge of the occult for human and Christian purposes) tries to describe her, but he is cut off in mid-sentence by guards who take him away: "I saw its mother! His mother was a—." It is in any case to that mother's grave, its whereabouts in an Etruscan cemetery discovered only after great trouble, that Mr. Thorn and his photographer friend must eventually betake themselves in the film's climactic scenes. And if the child's real mother never enters the frame, her latter-day surrogates do, in the form of nannies in the devil's service. Again, it is Mrs. Thorn, despite her ignorance of the adoption, and not her husband Robert, who after all arranged it, who first begins to suspect the supernatural nature of the child they are rearing. Thus even *The Omen,* for all its manifest concern with males—Damien, Robert, the photographer, and various Catholic priests—locates the essential mystery with the mother who "was a—."

The mystery rests emphatically with the female in *The Godsend.* In this human version of the cuckoo myth, a nameless pregnant woman with strange eyes and satanic rings on her fingers turns up at a family's house, goes into labor, is delivered of a baby girl, and disappears. The baby girl, whom the family then adopts, has her mother's eyes; she proceeds to kill, over the next few years, not only her four adoptive siblings, but her adoptive mother's unborn fetus (by causing a miscarriage) and her adoptive father's sperm supply (by passing mumps on to him and so sterilizing him). Lest we forget the origin of this "godsend," we are reminded at the film's end, when we spot the satanic mother in a park—again pregnant, and again ingratiating herself with yet another unsuspecting family.

The mispronunciation (in *Christine*) of Arnie Cunningham's name

---

[21] On the problems of sight, first as well as second, in *Don't Look Now,* see Kinder and Houston, "Seeing Is Believing," esp. pp. 52–61.

as "Cuntingham" is apt, for where Satan is, in the world of horror, female genitals are likely to be nearby. The word *vulva* itself is related to *valve*—gate or entry to the body—and so it regularly serves for all manner of spirits, but the unclean one above all, in occult horror. When the seance in *Don't Look Now* stalls, the blind medium turns suddenly to Laura: "Are your legs crossed?" "Why, yes," Laura naively replies. Whatever else those crossed legs may mean, they also signify access blocked; only when she uncrosses them can the seance go forward. Linda's legs (in *Witchboard*) are emphatically uncrossed when, after emerging from a nearly fatal shower (only scalding water came out), she sinks down into a squat, legs conspicuously foregrounded (the camera is near floor-level). A look of horror crosses her face as she contemplates an attacker we do not see—the very image of a woman in standard rape posture—and the scene cuts. The next image shows her dressed in Malfeitor's clothes and speaking in Malfeitor's voice. It is a cut as standard in cinema as in nineteenth-century fiction, and it means very much the same thing. Rosemary (in *Rosemary's Baby*) is impregnated in just such a narrative gap: one sequence shows her growing drowsy and Guy tucking her in; the next her surrealistic dreams; and the next her waking in the morning and Guy's revelation, as he tucks in his shirttails, that he "didn't want to miss baby night. . . . it was kind of fun in a necrophile way." As in *Demon Seed*, the narrative gap is filled out and "colored in" with a medley of disconnected, visually shocking images, "behind" which, as it were, the rape and monstrous impregnation take place. Both cuts, in fact, cut into the woman: in *Rosemary's Baby* into her unconscious psyche as she is impregnated, and in *Demon Seed*, via the camera penis, into the reproductive space itself.

The vagina is quite explicitly the supernatural port of entry in *Deadly Blessing* (1981), in which some demonic Hittite women cause an enormous snake to appear in a bathtub in which Martha is relaxing, thighs apart. The same director has Freddy Kruger's hand make an intercrural appearance in the bathtub as Nancy lies relaxing in *Nightmare on Elm Street*, and Cronenberg's *Shivers* has a bathing woman vaginally penetrated by a parasite that looks like a cross between a penis and a turd. *The Entity* (1983) tells a classic incubus story in which Carla is repeatedly raped by a cold and foul-smelling but invisible being. *It's Alive* gives us a mutant infant in place of the devil, but we understand it to have been deposited, as it were, by an emotionally defective father, and it bursts into its murderous rampage in the delivery room directly from its mother's loins.[22] Just how the car

---

[22] Robin Wood rightly regards the "relationship of *It's Alive* to the Satanist cycle [as]

Christine came to be possessed is not made explicit, but a shot in the opening scene of the ominous "alley" over which she passes on the assembly line invites us to suspect that she was entered the way houses built over graveyards or other supernatural sites (as in *Poltergeist*) are entered: through an unprotected opening on the underside.[23]

But if all women are by nature open, some women are more open than others. "Plug it up! Plug it up!" Carrie's schoolmates call as they toss tampons in a film that is from beginning to end permeated with menstrual references and imagery. When Carrie's mother links menstruation to the supernatural, she articulates one of horror's abiding verities. At the very least, a menstruating woman is a woman "open." Stephen King's idea that menstruation brings with it telekinetic abilities turns up again in *The Fury*, when the doctor warns the female members of the staff to avoid the telekinetic Gillian when they have their "monthlies," for it is then that they are most susceptible to her powers—and indeed, Gillian does real damage to one of her menstruating friends. (One of her first telepathic acts is to "know" of another woman's pregnancy.)[24] When Gillian's male counterpart Robin strikes out at the older female doctor whose sexual servant he has been, he causes her to spin violently and her blood to spatter about the room. Virtually the first line of dialogue in *Audrey Rose*, a reincarnation-possession story, consists of young Ivy's report to her mother that a girlfriend has just gotten her first menstrual period at the age of nine. Ivy herself is approaching her twelfth birthday, and within hours of the "menstrual" conversation with her mother she

more that of intelligent comment than of 'rip off' " ("Gods and Monsters," p. 23). I disagree, however, with the reasons he offers for the child's monstrosity (that it has been irradiated, and that it is "the logical product of the family itself"). The fact that the film as a whole hinges on the issue of parental (above all paternal) acknowledgment suggests that it was the thought of abortion, tendentiously discussed midway during the film, that brought the disaster about. Far from being the "logical product of the family itself," the infant is the logical product of a failed or unwelcoming family; a proper family would never have considered terminating a pregnancy. The film, in short, could hardly be more pro-life or pro-family.

[23] For Cumbow, the close-up V on Christine's grille (the film's opening image and one that recurs throughout) links " 'Victory' with a suggestion of the female genitalia as Christine is compared with passionate lover, treacherous dominatrix, and, finally, all-powerful witch. . . . Christine's violence is, at first, the product of the passion between her and Arnie. Later, it is the wrath of a woman scorned, its key image the Plymouth's grille, a cryptic *vagina dentata*" (*Order in the Universe*, pp. 125 and 131).

[24] King, *Danse Macabre*, p. 171. See the Introduction for a fuller consideration of this point. *The Fury*, written and directed by De Palma in 1978, is obviously dependent on *Carrie*.

begins to exhibit symptoms of possession.[25] (*Ghostbusters* twits the convention when it has the parapsychologist ask three questions of a woman who has experienced paranormal phenomena: whether schizophrenia runs in her family; whether she habitually uses drugs; and whether she is menstruating.) "Menstruation," a British gynecologist once wrote, "is like a red flag outside an auction sale; it shows that something is going on inside."[26] In the world of occult horror, in any case, menstrual blood would seem to have little to do with castration or loss and much to do with powerful things going on behind closed doors.[27]

If the mechanics of Regan's possession (*The Exorcist*) are less explicit, they are no less traditional. Two signs alert us to the presence of the supernatural in the Georgetown house: an eerie growling and cold wind blowing through an ever-open second-floor window in Regan's room. That window proves the rough equivalent of the television screen in *Poltergeist*; try as she might, Regan's mother can never keep it closed, and her fussing over it is one of the film's leitmotivs. Indeed, both of the film's two deaths involve tumbles through that window onto a set of concrete steps on the street below. Lest we miss the point, it is articulated for us by the detective investigating one of those deaths. "Watch out for draughts," he advises when he learns of an open window in the sick girl's room. "A draught in the fall when the house is hot is a magic carpet for bacteria." The draft, we understand, is indeed a magic carpet, but not for bacteria. So severe is the draft during the exorcism itself that the men who perform it are bundled in coats and exhaling steam columns.

[25] Although Mr. Hoover insists on the distinction between reincarnation and possession, it is blurred in the minds of the other characters, and Ivy's symptoms are in many respects much like those of Regan and Linda.

[26] Dr. Matthews Duncan, as quoted by Laqueur (*Making Sex*, pp. 214–15).

[27] Noting the menstrual theme in *Carrie* and *The Exorcist*, Barbara Creed argues that "the horror film's obsession with blood, particularly the bleeding body of woman, where her body is transformed into the 'gaping wound,' suggests that castration anxiety is a central concern of the horror film—particularly the slasher sub-genre" ("Horror and the Monstrous Feminine," p. 52). The slide from possession to slasher effaces the huge difference between the two sensibilities as far as the female body is concerned. The female body in the possession film is indeed a site of abjection (in Kristeva's sense), but as Creed herself notes in another context (p. 63), it is not so absolutely the site of castration, and even the terms of its abjection are not absolute. Sobchack has a quite different tack: "Both *The Exorcist* and *Carrie* seem to me provocatively read in Lacanian terms; lacking both a phallus and the Phallus (or patriarchal law), the female teenagers in these films have no access to the patriarchal Symbolic. Without submission to and acquisition of patriarchal discourse, their pubescent bodies seek expression through Other means—through menstruation. Indeed, the flow contained by the constraints of the Father, their physical and bloody 'rage' is an apocalyptic feminine explosion of the frustrated desire to 'speak' " ("Child/Alien/Father," p. 33 n. 5).

The idea of impregnation by the "pneuma" is ancient and wide-spread in both learned and popular beliefs, and it turns up repeat-edly in occult films in connection with the reproduction/possession complex of ideas. It plays on an equally ancient and widespread as-sociation between the vagina and the throat—an association reflected in the fantasy of the vagina dentata, in the German word for the neck of the uterus, *Mutterhals* ("mother throat"), and in the folk belief that the body is open to the devil both during sneezing (hence "God bless you" or *Gesundheit* as preemptive formulas) and during orgasm.[28] *Poltergeist* draws on the more spiritual version of the tradition when it has Diane Freeling, desperate mother of the girl who has been pulled into the "other side," start up the stairs and suddenly stop and open her mouth wide when a gust of wind hits her face: "She just moved through me. My God! I felt her. I can smell her. It's her, I felt her, it's my baby—she went through my soul!" Her husband Steve gapes, but the female parapsychologist, Dr. Lesh, throws a knowing look. Here the "pneuma" is more spiritual than diabolical, but the general idea is the same; whether through the actual throat or the "mother throat," women gulp things in. In *Prince of Darkness*, as in *The Exorcist*, the pneuma is specifically diabolical: "It just got colder in here. It's suddenly as if—as if—something moved through the room." In that film, however, possession is transmitted by fluids: Susan becomes possessed when some ancient liquid, churning in an urn, flies through the air and lands in her open mouth, and she shares her possession by vomiting into the mouths of her friends. (The sexual possibilities do not go unexploited; when Susan mounts Lisa and leans down to kiss her, Lisa takes it as a lesbian assault—only to find that the kiss turns to mouth-to-mouth transfer of the devil's own liquid.)

Possession via oral penetration is a cliché of recent horror film. In *The Hidden* (1987) and *Night of the Creeps* (1986), swift creatures (like legless rodents) dart into people's mouths, and the possessed person gets relief only by "kissing" the creature into someone else. A num-

[28] See Laqueur, *Making Sex*, esp. pp. 254 and 258. For a literary account of the asso-ciation of throat and vagina among the Greeks, see Nicole Loraux, *Tragic Ways of Killing a Woman*, esp. p. 61 (where the woman is characterized as "caught between two mouths, between two necks"). The connection also figures in Silverman's discussion of cinematic voice: "In classic cinema . . . there is an implied equation of woman's voice with her vagina, each of which is posited as a major port of entry into her sub-jectivity, but which is actually, I would argue, the site at which that subjectivity is introduced into her" (*The Acoustic Mirror*, p. 67). See also Rangell's discussion of the male analysand who displaced the pain of a urethral stone into a neck spasm, both of which he understood in vaginal terms ("The Interchangeability of Phallus and Female Genital," pp. 506–7).

ber of films (*The Kindred*, for example) show snakes, tentacles, or other suchlike forcing their way into terrified women's mouths and throats. A particularly popular scene (in *The Evil Dead*, for example) has one person ingesting the spew of another who in turn, now infected or possessed, goes on to spew on a third, and so on. The fact that the horror in such films resides less in the quality and experience of possession itself than in the geometric progression of its transmission—the processes of contagion—sets them at some distance from the occult film proper. But insofar as they concern themselves with bodies penetrated, invaded, and colonized—bodies convulsed by some alien force—they also attest to an archetypal horror story. And insofar as that story turns on bodily orifices, holes—natural passages to an inner space—it would appear to be a story built around the female body.[29]

But orifices and spaces are themselves not the whole story. I have mentioned in passing the superfluity of reproductive themes in the possession film, and it is now time to consider them in some detail. The spectacular example is, of course, *Rosemary's Baby*. Rosemary's possession comes about because, as a female, she is naturally enterable; but it also takes the very specific form of pregnancy and Satan the very specific form of a growing fetus. When Guy tells Rosemary that he "didn't want to miss baby night," he acknowledges not just an act of "necrophile" penetration, as he puts it the morning after, but impregnation as well. (What distinguishes *Rosemary's Baby* from the run-of-the-mill possession film is the fact that Guy plays a secondary role and that he is not a resister of the supernatural but its first dupe.) *The Visitor* (1979) updates the plot. Here the woman, Barbara, resists the urgings of boyfriend Ray (like Guy, he has sold his soul for success) to marry and produce a son; she suspects there is something odd about her insides, and she does not want to risk another pregnancy. She is righter than she knows. As the Chairman of the Board (for the satanic neighbors of Rosemary have now become a corporate committee) explains, "Barbara is a miracle of nature. She carries in her womb something which transcends the world of everyday reality. She is able to give birth to children of immense powers, both natural and supernatural." When Barbara "refuses intervention," the Chairman announces that they'll "turn to a more efficient method"—the medical implantation of a fetus. Thanks to the agency

[29] "Both male and female physiology lend themselves to the analogy with the vessel which must not pour away or dilute its vital fluids," Mary Douglas writes. "Females are correctly seen as, literally, the entry by which the pure content may be adulterated. Males are treated as pores through which the precious stuff may ooze out and be lost, the whole system being thereby enfeebled" (*Purity and Danger*, p. 126).

of the eponymous visitor, however (an emissary of Christ who announces that "that child must never see the light of day"), the pregnancy is terminated—an abortion in the name of Christianity—and the satanic plot foiled. Even more reproduction-preoccupied is *The Godsend*. Between its opening and closing scenes, both of which show us a mightily pregnant woman ingratiating herself with a family, we are treated to a childbirth (with the woman of the house serving as midwife), an adoption, the murder of four children and the distress of the now childless parents, a miscarriage, and a bizarre sterilization (the satanic child Bonnie, ill with mumps, breathes into her sleeping father's mouth).

In *Witchboard*, too, possession is connected with what at least appears to be pregnancy, and the two conditions are repeatedly linked. "No wonder you're a nervous wreck," Jim tells Linda. "You're not going crazy, you're becoming a mother. Granted, it's almost the same thing." Later, when Brandon tries to convince Jim that Linda is showing all the symptoms of progressive entrapment, Jim responds, "They're also the symptoms of pregnancy." The phantom pregnancy has indeed become a commonplace of the possession film. Even *Prince of Darkness* has one: during the course of an afternoon nap, Kelly swells to nine-month girth—but then suddenly deflates and is left withered and covered with sores. *The Brood*, a marginal case, has a woman bearing her monstrous offspring—the "children of her rage"—from external amniotic sacs hanging from her abdomen.

Even a film like *The Omen*, not about female possession but about the adoption of a satanic child, is haunted by the question of fertility and conception; Robert Thorn undertakes an arduous quest-voyage to a godforsaken corner of Italy to gather information about Damien's real mother—in order to ascertain whether the devil, in fact, was the father. And *Poltergeist*, of course, is a virtual swamp of reproductive themes and images. Young Carol Anne is retrieved from the "other side" when her mother ventures into the fleshy, red sucking pit (Montrelay's "insatiable organ hole") that has emerged in the bedroom; the father holds the safety cord firmly, and in a scene scripted ultimately by Lamaze, he pulls the two of them, now covered with amniotic ooze, back into this life. (*Poltergeist II* reproduces this ultimate birth scene in rather more heavenly terms: girl and mother are "sucked" onto the "other side," where they join the recently deceased grandmother, and must be redelivered into the here and now by father and son.) Finally, there are science fiction films like *Alien/ Aliens* in which penetration per se is a minor matter next to what another era called "consequences": finding oneself corporeal host to things growing inside and eventually bursting forth. (The fact that

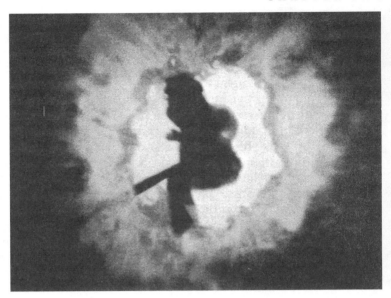

The "rebirth" scene from *Poltergeist*: Carol Anne being reeled in by her father from the Other Side.

the colonized body is in these cases typically male may point up one of the distinguishing features of science fiction.) And of course the governing imagery of both these films, but particularly the latter, is notoriously maternal and uterine. The importance of reproductive themes and images to satanic/possession stories emerges clearly in the comparison with other brands of horror, in which they are by and large absent. Sex, in a variety of forms, looms large in the thematic "field" of the standard slasher, vampire, werewolf, zombie, and even rape-revenge film, but reproduction, when it occurs at all, occurs only in passing (science fiction being, again, a partial and complicated exception). It is the possession film—stories that hinge on psychic breaking and entering—that plunges us repeatedly into a world of menstruation, pregnancy, fetuses, abortion, miscarriage, amniotic fluid, childbirth, breastfeeding.

The female side of the dual focus narrative, then, is a body story with a vengeance. Film after film interrogates what *Beyond Evil* calls the "physical presence" of a woman: forces it to externalize its inner workings, to speak its secrets, to give a material account of itself—in short, to give literal and visible *evidence*.[30] It is remarkable how many

[30] Possession films are in this respect remarkably like those woman's films Doane categorizes as "medical discourse" films. "In the films of the medical discourse, the

of these films in fact put the female body to some sort of formal trial. The most frequent trial, a virtual sine qua non of the genre, is the battery of medical tests, which inevitably come up with a negative result (that is, they produce no organic explanation for the aberrant physical and psychological symptoms). Following that come other sorts of trials. When the medical probing of Regan's body "with alien instrumentation" turns up nothing,[31] her case is submitted to an elaborate church protocol, a series of qualifying questions: does she speak languages she has never heard? how can we be sure she has never heard them? does her voice change quality? is there a manifestation of a new personality? does she show psychokinetic abilities? can she divulge future or hidden events? and so on. Eventually, her

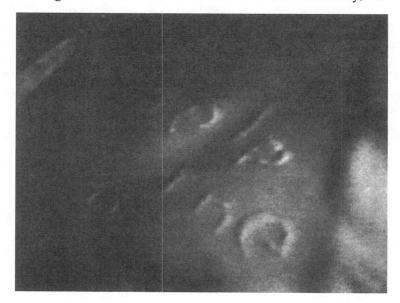

Regan's midriff (*The Exorcist*).

woman is quite clearly the *object* of knowledge, her body the site of a continual examination of symptoms" (*The Desire to Desire*, p. 134; more generally, see chapter 2, "Clinical Eyes: The Medical Discourse"). Silverman is more specific: "Many of the texts which fall into this category . . . focus on the interaction between male doctor and female patient, and they all manifest an intense fascination with a space assumed to be inside the patient's body" (*The Acoustic Mirror*, p. 59). More generally, Silverman's chapter "Body Talk" is concerned with the way the female voice is consigned to interiority in mainstream cinema. What I am suggesting here is that occult horror gives a more conflicted account of the idea of interiority, if not the female interior, and in ways that suggest why it is that higher forms keep harping on it.

[31] Greenberg, *The Movies on Your Mind*, p. 247.

body becomes readable in the most literal sense: the words HELP ME appear on the skin of her midriff, as if written from the inside. (The letter *A*, initial of the demonic spirit, likewise appears on the skin of the possessed Barbara in *Beyond Evil*.) As in the medieval ordeal, skin is made to speak the truth about what it hides.

The most startling trial is surely that of *Audrey Rose* (1977). The film announces its concern with evidence at the outset when the police refuse, for lack of legal grounds, to arrest a man Mr. Templeton has observed watching and following his daughter Ivy. "Honey, there's nothing they [the police] can do unless he draws blood," he reports bitterly to his wife. But as the film's problem takes shape—Ivy shows signs of being host to the troubled soul of a dead girl, one Audrey Rose—it is Mr. Templeton himself who needs evidential "blood." Like the good representative of White Science that he is, he steadfastly refuses to entertain the possibility of reincarnation: "When I die," he tells his wife, who leans toward the mystical explanation, "it's going to be the end of me. No wings, no harps, no pitchforks, nothing. It's done, it's the end, it's finished." Because the possibility of reincarnation raises the question of which man is the real father, Mr. Templeton (father to Ivy) or Mr. Hoover (father to Audrey Rose), the case is submitted to trial.[32] The first phase is played out in the courtroom (Hindu mystics testifying on behalf of reincarnation, Western authorities testifying on behalf of a standard psycho-physiological account), and the second phase in an amphitheater reminiscent of the famed Salpetrière. Now on literal center stage, surrounded by a variety of spectators (judge, jury, lawyers, family, interested outsiders), the eleven-year-old Ivy is placed under hypnosis *explicitly in order* to get her to act *out*, give a visible account of, her occulted self. And so she does, producing the evidential "blood" in the form of a dramatic regression to the moment of death of her earlier-life self.[33] But largely because of the White Science framework in which the trial is played out (the court hypnotist allies himself with Western psychoanalysis and against Eastern reincarnation), in turn the result of Ivy's father's recalcitrant rationalism, the cure ends up killing the patient. A similar but even more extreme "female body" trial is that of *The Entity*, in which a woman who is plagued by an incubus is put on display on more or less the centerline of a high school gym in hopes that her invisible assailant can somehow be apprehended. Raped she is, but for all the efforts to trap "him," the

[32] On issues of paternity in modern horror and s/f, see Sobchack, "Child/Alien/Father" and "Bringing It All Back Home."

[33] Ivy's amphitheatrical "trial" is remarkably like the "talking cure" that is "negotiated with astonishing frequency and openness" in the "woman's film" of the 1940s.

rapist comes and goes without a trace, and the "doctors" in the press box split the verdict. *The Entity*, which claims to be based on a true case, is one of the few possession films that ends with White Science and Black Magic in a draw.

THE MALE STORY

But to say that the foregrounded or spectacle story of the possession film is built around the female body does not mean that the films as a whole are about females only or even mainly—or even, as individual characters, at all. On the contrary, the possession film's psychological interest, its problem, typically resides at least as much in the significant bystander—the boyfriend, husband, doctor, or priest—who attends and struggles to understand as it does in the afflicted person herself. The quandary of the rational male faced with the satanic or its equivalents is a simple one: should he cling to his rational, scientific understanding of human behavior, or should he yield to the irrational? To that quandary the experience of the troubled woman, however theatrical its manifestation, is largely accessory. *Don't Look Now* is first and foremost not about Laura, but about John's slow—too slow, it turns out—acknowledgment of the "other" reality. *Witchboard* is decidedly less about Linda's progressive entrapment than about Jim's painful progress from alienated wise guy to warmhearted groom and his reconciliation with Brandon. *The Exorcist*, for all its focus on Regan's excrescences, turns on Father Karras's tortured relation to his mother, his guilt, his spiritual father (Merrin), his calling. ("There is no indication that Blatty or Friedkin has any feeling for the little girl's helplessness and suffering, or her mother's," wrote Pauline Kael.)[34] *The Unholy* (1988) distinguishes between belief in God and belief in the satanic; a devout Christian, Father Michael dismisses all talk of the satanic as "claptrap" until he experiences its depredations firsthand—a conversion helped along by a woman toward whom he has sexual feeling. Likewise *Beyond Evil* (1980): only when Larry has accepted the reality of the supernatural and the powers of a local "healer"—all of which he initially dismissed—can he set about saving his possessed wife Barbara. Mr.

---

[34] As quoted by Kinder and Houston, "Seeing Is Believing," p. 47. The complaint is a common one; see also Greenberg's remark that "literally nothing is left to one's imagination except the pity and compassion that surely have informed the directorial point of view. Even the doctor's diagnostics are distorted into invasions of Regan's pitiful body with alien instrumentation that parallel the Demon's vicious invasion of her mind" (*The Movies on Your Mind*, p. 247).

Templeton's inability to accept what his wife and everyone else involved finally do accept, the fact that his daughter Ivy is the reincarnation of Audrey Rose, results in her death. *The Omen* turns on Robert Thorn's dawning realization that the child he is raising is inhuman and his eventual decision and efforts to kill it. *It's Alive* tells how the father of a mutant infant first denies his paternity ("It's not my child. . . . I had nothing to do with this. . . . It's no relation to me") but in the process of dealing with the patriarchal authorities is slowly "maternalized": the film's final moments show him not only "owning" his monstrous offspring, but trying to save it. *The Believers* centers on the white cop-psychiatrist Cal's progressive involvement with (black) voodoo cults and his eventual capitulation to the idea that his son is in fact possessed and must be exorcised. As if in mute deference to an archetype, *The Serpent and the Rainbow* includes a Haitian woman for whom "possession is as natural as breathing," but she is very much a bit player to the hero of the piece, the representative of an American pharmaceutical company (White Science) sent to Haiti to acquire a sample of a voodoo drug (Black Magic); initially a doubter, he ends up a believer. *Angel Heart* turns on the self-discovery of Harald Angel, a process that is enacted directly and literally on the bodies of female mediums (a white spiritualist and a Cajun voodoo practitioner, both of whom he "unconsciously" kills). *Poltergeist* distributes its sympathies rather more evenly, but we are repeatedly invited to watch Steve passively watch the women—Diane, the medium, Dr. Lesh—engage the supernatural. There are of course exceptions, chief among them *Rosemary's Baby*, in which the experience of the affected woman herself is the center of attention and the experience of the husband of only passing interest, but the standard scheme puts, or at least seems to put, the female body on the line only in order to put the male psyche on the line.

But a closer look at the male psyches in question, and more to the point the nature of the line on which they are put, suggests that the terms are not that simple—and may indeed be growing less simple all the time. The differences between *The Exorcist* and *Witchboard* point up a drift in sensibility, and it is to these films that we again turn.

As its title suggests, *The Exorcist* is less about the possessed girl than about Father Damien Karras. He is in something of a crisis when the story opens, and his encounter with Regan, together with the death of his mother, drives him to an emotional brink. He is relieved of his duties as counselor and told to rest. The causes of his distress are not spelled out, but the obsessive themes of his interior monologue lead us to some speculations. The most obvious of these is guilt over his mother's death (exacerbated by Regan's habit of speaking in her voice); had he taken proper care of her, visited her more frequently, she would at least have had a happier last few years. Beyond that, there is a kind of internal dialogue, an ongoing argument, between his religious and spiritual self on one hand and his professionally trained medical and psychiatric self on the other. (Much of the novel is spent charting Karras's mental weighing of the alternatives, a quality that does not translate to the screen.) Thus the war between White Science and Black Magic is here played out not only on the usual larger social level (medical profession and the institutional Church versus the occult branch of the church and the superstitions of the household help) but also on the individual and internal level, in the psyche of the exorcist himself. If the idea was that the two systems should be complements or versions of one another (this being why, presumably, the order sent him to "Harvard, Bellevue, Johns Hopkins, places like that"), they are for Karras no longer so. Some unspecified past disappointment caused him to abandon his once-passionate faith and turn from explanations involving God and the devil to explanations like hysteria or schizophrenia. Until he meets Regan.

Karras's spiritual anguish—his alternation between the desire to believe in the Christian explanation for Regan's condition and his rational inclination to believe in the psychiatric explanation—is what Blatty's novel is centrally *about*. Director Friedkin's decision not to render that anguish in voice-over (or monologue prayers) but rather to hint at it in externals (hence all the shots of Karras looking pensive, sad, distressed, exhausted, and the like—and of course his dramatic death) leaves us with a very nearly incoherent cinematic text. But even in that text we glimpse what the novel makes abundantly clear: that for all its spectacle value, Regan's story is finally significant only insofar as it affects the lives of others, above all the tormented spiritual life of Karras. The following passage from the novel suggests the mode (Karras has just listened to a tape recording of Regan's pre-possession voice):

> Karras heard the rest only dimly, from afar, through the roaring of blood in his ears, like the ocean, as up through his chest and his face swelled an overwhelming intuition: *The thing that I saw in that room wasn't Regan!*
>
> He returned to the Jesuit residence hall. Found a cubicle. Said Mass before the rush. As he lifted the Host in consecration, it trembled in his fingers with a hope he dared not hope, that he fought with every particled fiber of his will. " 'For this is My Body . . .' " he whispered tremulously.

No, bread! This is nothing but bread!

He dared not love again and lose. That loss was too great, that pain too keen.[35]

The accessory nature of Regan's story could hardly be clearer; she is the evidence, proof, testimony that the faltering Karras has been yearning for. "Could it be? Could it possibly, conceivably be? Could the only hope for Regan be the ritual of exorcism? Must he open up that locker of aches?" Or: "He felt a moment of elation; saw the door swinging open to fields, to escape from the crushing weight of caring and that meeting each twilight with the ghost of his faith."[36] The text hints at its own priorities when it has the devil say to Merrin during the exorcism, "You care nothing at *all* for the *pig* [the devil's word for Regan's body]. You care *nothing!* You have *made her a contest between us!*" and, somewhat later, Merrin to Karras, "I think the demon's target is not the possessed; it is us . . . the observers . . . every person in this house." Certainly the novelist's (and filmmaker's) target is not the female body, but the transformation that body prompts in the male psyche.

Enmeshed from the outset in Karras's spiritual crisis are issues of intimacy and sexuality. Again, Regan provides the palpable field: she stabs a cross in and out of her vagina, speaks incessantly and crudely of sexual matters, is suspected of desecrating the statue of the Virgin Mary, and so on. As before, however, it appears to be Karras's own anxieties that are at stake. The nature of those anxieties is hinted at in an early scene in which Karras is approached for comfort by a young and lonely priest:

Of all the anxieties that Karras encountered among the community, this one had lately become the most prevalent. Cut off from their families as well as from women, many of the Jesuits were also fearful of expressing affection for fellow priests; of forming deep and loving friendships.

"Like I'd like to put my arm around another guy's shoulder, but right away I'm scared he's going to think I'm queer. I mean, you hear all these theories about so many latents attracted to the priesthood. So I just don't do it. I won't even go to somebody's room just to listen to records; or talk; or smoke. It's not that I'm afraid of *him;* I'm just worried about *him* getting worried about *me.*"

Karras felt the weight easing slowly from the other and onto him. He let it come; let the young priest talk.[37]

[35] Blatty, *The Exorcist*, p. 229.
[36] Ibid., pp. 230 and 278.
[37] Ibid., p. 88.

Or later, when Karras is interrupted in his research on possession by a visit from the flirtatious Father Dyer:

> "She [Regan's actress mother, whom Dyer "adores"] can help us with my plan for when we both quit the priesthood."
>
> "Who's quitting the priesthood?"
>
> "Faggots. In droves. Basic black has gone out. Now I—"
>
> "Joe, I've got a lecture to prepare for tomorrow," said Karras as he set down the books on his desk.[38]

Or in the climactic scene, the exorcism, when the devil taunts Karras:

> "Even *worms* will not eat your corruption, you . . ."
>
> Karras heard the words of the demon and began to tremble with a murderous fury.
>
> *Don't listen!*
>
> ". . . homosexual . . ."
>
> *Don't listen! Don't listen!*

This is not the first of the demon's insults, but it is the last, the one that drives Karras to take the ultimate step:

Father Karras regains his faith (*The Exorcist*).

[38] Ibid., p. 220.

"Come on! Come on, loser! Try *me!* Leave the girl and take me! Take *me!*
Come into . . ."[39]

The devil obliges, and Karras is hurled through the window to his
death on the street below. The novel closes with a tender scene in
which Dyer kneels over the dying Karras and offers last rites.[40]

Our concern here is not with whether Karras is or isn't, or has or
hasn't, or hasn't but could. It is rather with the fact that his spiritual
reawakening is cast in the language and imagery of opening up, of
letting things in; the fact that Regan's body stands as the extreme and
negative example of that idea; and the fact that all Karras's intimate
discussions on the subject are with other men (first and foremost Detective Kinderman, but also Fathers Dyer and Merrin).

As with *The Exorcist*, so with *Witchboard*. Its outer or "spectacle"
story is self-evidently the story of a female body; Linda's progressive
entrapment, though understood to be a psychological transformation, plays itself out corporeally in the form of illness, phantom pregnancy, disheveled appearance, and eventually her assumption of the
form, dress, ax, and voice of Malfeitor. And its inner story is just as
self-evidently the story of a male psyche—that of Linda's boyfriend
Jim, in the beginning an alcoholic and unfeeling medical school drop-
out but at the end a sturdy groom. That the story is really Jim's is
clear from the fact that virtually all of the considerable backstory
turns on his past (we know, by contrast, next to nothing of Linda's
past). His parents were alcoholic; he and Brandon were best friends
as children, and indeed he practically lived at Brandon's when his
own home was unlivable; he was an unusually bright student but
dropped out of medical school; the friendship with Brandon broke
up when Linda left Brandon for Jim. And the man to whom this boy
was father is, predictably enough, a man unable to complete medical
school because he is "not capable of giving a shit about anybody but
himself"; a man unable to say he loves Linda, much less marry her;
a man unable to cry, love, marry, trust, succeed professionally, or
believe in God, Ouija, or anything else; a man, as Brandon sums it
up, with "ice in his veins," scheduled for alcoholic self-destruction.
In the world of satanic or spirit films, the horror of being too open is
matched only by the horror of being too closed.[41]

---

[39] Ibid., p. 328.

[40] See Derry's discussion of *The Exorcist* in *Dark Dreams*, pp. 103–06.

[41] "The body of the 'individual' is very different from women's bodies," Carole Pateman writes. "His body is tightly enclosed within boundaries, but women's are permeable, their contours change shape and they are subject to the cyclical process of
birth. Physical birth symbolizes everything that makes women incapable of entering
the original contract and transforming themselves into the civil individuals who up-

The double project of *Witchboard* is thus to clean and close, at least to a compromise point, the excessively open female (through exorcism) and simultaneously to "open," again to a compromise point, the overly closed male. Taken at face value, the former project is a physical one (Linda is as forcibly de-penetrated as she was penetrated) and the latter a psychological-emotional one (Jim's reservoir of blocked feelings is finally penetrated), and taken together they add up to the grander joint project of heterosexual coupling (the film ends with their wedding). But in rather heavy-handed ways, the film also invites us to look beyond face values. There is first and foremost the backstory, which turns on Jim's life—more particularly on his relationships, and even more particularly on his relationship to Brandon. "I know why you dropped out of med school," Brandon tells Jim at the construction site. His voice rises: "Because you knew you'd make a lousy doctor. Because you're not capable of giving a shit about anybody but yourself. And when you get tired of Linda, you're going to walk away from her, too, just like you did with school, *just like you did with your parents*, JUST LIKE YOU DID WITH M—!" (At which dramatic moment the phone rings.)

Perhaps because it can be only incompletely expressed, the story of male affection is a poignant one. In the film's opening scenes, Brandon and Jim, clearly at odds, exchange insults and very nearly blows as well. Between them stands Linda, Brandon's former and Jim's present lover, at once a barrier and a conduit. Linda's slide into spiritualism, whatever its manifest meaning, also serves to vacate an emotional territory on which the male story will now play itself out. That story culminates in a motel room in Big Bear, where Brandon and Jim have gone to investigate the circumstances of the boy David's death. As they are unpacking, Jim suddenly turns to Brandon: "What happened to us, man? We used to be like brothers." Brandon explains that he cannot bear the sight of Jim and Linda together: "I tell myself, Brandon, stop being an asshole, but then my mouth pops open and out comes another stupid remark." That confession prompts Jim to one of his own: "You know what I'm afraid of more than anything else? That I'll never be able to love anyone and will spend the rest of my life alone." "What have you got that I don't have?" Brandon asks. "I make her laugh," Jim replies, and then continues, in his deadpan style, "The only place you made her laugh was the bedroom." Brandon first bristles, then laughs ruefully. "You really are an asshole, you know that." Jim borrows a toothbrush and the scene cuts.

---

hold its terms" (*The Sexual Contract*, p. 96). It is precisely this civil individuality, in exactly these bodily terms, that the occult film seems bent on escaping.

This scene of male confession is the film's turning point: the narrative has from the outset been leading up to it, and once it takes place, the denouement follows suit. The question is what precisely is being confessed. On the face of it, we have two men butting heads over Linda; but the fact that Linda is virtually short-circuited in the process confirms the impression that this is an essentially male drama with its own history and its own present—a history and a present with their own erotic charge. The confrontation is viewed over beds, in a lexicon in which the words "asshole," "open/ing," and "portal" loom large, and, indeed, in a motel named "Wishing Well." If Jim intends his joke about Brandon's shortcomings in the bedroom to establish their separate and contrasting sexual identities, it in fact works in this loaded context to put them in the same sexual frame, flanking and speaking to one another through Linda. And again, in this context of beds, sentimental recollections, and "asshole" name-calling, Brandon's confession—that he goes crazy when he sees Jim and Linda together—is tellingly ambiguous.

Given the charged exchange of the previous evening, we are not surprised when we see Jim and Brandon, the next day, sitting together over a Ouija board properly used, we have been told, by a heterosexual couple. Nor is it a surprise when, minutes later, Brandon is killed (by Malfeitor); nor that Jim finds and embraces his corpse and—at long last—breaks down and cries wildly; nor that he can now, in the film's next and final scenes, rush back to the city and finally reclaim Linda and fulfill his heterosexual destiny. In that final exchange, between Jim and the Malfeitor-possessed Linda, the implicit themes of the film are finally published. "Time for Linda to close the portal!" Jim shouts, brandishing a gun. "Only you can do that, James," says the voice of Malfeitor; "You're the portal, James, not Linda. You're the one I opened. You're the one I terrorized by torturing Linda and by killing your friends! You want to save Linda? You've got the means right there in your hands." For a moment, Jim follows the suicidal logic and puts the gun to his own temple—until he realizes that in the world of horror, the devil always lies (in the words of *The Exorcist*, "the demon is a liar, but also mixes lies with the truth"), and instead shoots the Ouija board, thus exploding Malfeitor's spirit out of Linda's body.

But if the devil tells a literal lie, he tells a figurative truth. Jim may not be the designated "portal," but he has been, in the film's own language, opened—to the supernatural and to the past and present truths of his own feelings. On the face of it, as I have suggested, Jim's opening is strictly psychological—as opposed to the almost anatomical nature of Linda's. But even as it sets up that opposition, the

Jim unreconstructed (*Witchboard*).

Jim holding Brandon and sobbing (*Witchboard*).

film degrades it. There is above all the brazen fact that Jim is
"opened" in the context of a same-sex relationship. It is not only that
we are presented with two hierarchically arranged love stories—Jim/
Brandon and Jim/Linda—and that the latter cannot proceed without
a resolution of the former; it is that the former story—the story of Jim
and Brandon—lies at the emotional heart of the film. To the scene in
which the weeping Jim embraces the corpse of Brandon, the film's
remainder—the de-possession of Linda and the wedding—stands as
a pale heteroerotic epilogue.[42]

Witchboard, to be sure, is unusually blunt. Most possession films
consign more firmly to the subtext the erotic/sexual dimension of the
male-opening story. This is not to say that the subtext cannot be au-
dacious, however. Poltergeist II, for example, positions the troubled
Steve Freeling (a white male head of household) between two other
men: a satanic emissary posing as a southern preacher (whom all the
women—daughter Carol Anne, wife Diane, and helpful medium
Tangina—fear and hate) and a Native American, Taylor (whom the
women adore and with whom they share spiritual talk). One day the
satanic preacher appears on the doorstep of the household and begins to rant at Steve: "Who do your wife and family turn to with their
problems? They turn to him [Taylor], now don't they? They don't
trust you any more, and what you fear is that you're not man enough
to hold this family together! . . . Now, let me in. Let me in! LET ME
IN!!!" Steve, shaken, barely manages to close the door. In a state of
distress, he turns to Taylor, and that evening the two of them retire
to the tepee together for something like a sauna. Steve at first resists
Taylor's mystical talk of good, evil, and reincarnation ("a lot of
crap!") but slowly yields to his calming ways. Taylor begins to chant,
summoning magic smoke-wisps to swirl about them. Alarmed, Steve
starts to rise—but the smoke-wisps strike him back to his seat, where
he sits holding a large feather upright in his crotch. "The Entity has
revealed his presence to you, his enemy [i.e., a rationalist white
male]," Taylor explains—upon which he inhales the Entity and, lean-
ing over Steve's face, exhales it into his mouth and nostrils, intoning,
"Smoke, make him one with power and knowledge." It is not only
that the pair of scenes are all but labeled "masculine" (the white
preacher's solution) and "feminine" (the Native American solution);
it is that the "feminine" is cast in terms of being opened, entered,
and possessed—by another male and a masculine essence. In the

[42] The "homosociality" of this arrangement, whereby male relationships are chan-
neled through the figure of a woman, has of course been detailed by Eve Kosofsky
Sedgwick in her Between Men, a work of some relevance to the present discussion.

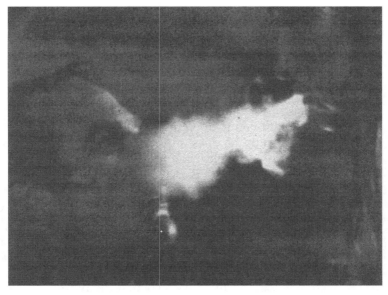

Steve inhales the sacred smoke (*Poltergeist*).

end, Steve—the man who is repeatedly exhorted, in both *Poltergeist I* and *II*, to have (or keep) an "open mind"—proves himself just as able as a woman to gulp things *in*.

Subtext verges on text in *Prince of Darkness*, when, shortly after the "lesbian scene" mentioned above, Kelly (a female research assistant of Dr. Birack's) simultaneously develops a cross-shaped bruise and undergoes something resembling an accelerated pregnancy. Her fellow assistant Walter, who jokes early in the film that he normally "likes to be dominated by women," announces that he too once developed a bruise and that a doctor told him it was a "sign of homosexual panic." He is himself penetrated—orally—shortly thereafter. The classic instance of the device—using a lesbian scene to "homosexualize" subsequent words between men—occurs in *The Haunting* (1963). The handsome Dr. Markway, head of the haunted-house exploration team, warns the scoffer Luke: "A closed mind is the worst defense against the supernatural. . . . If it happens to you, you'll have that shut door in your mind ripped right off its hinges." "Now look, Doc," Luke responds, "We're buddies, okay, but don't try to convert me." The conversation might seem innocent enough were it not for the fact that it is immediately preceded, and hence ambiently invaded, by a startling scene in which the lesbian Theo makes her own move of "conversion" on Nell. The one scene spills over into the other, and the talk of closed doors being forcibly opened, and conversion, slides into a (homo)sexual register.

In Cronenberg's *Videodrome*, a secular cousin of the possession film, a man is opened literally—by the application of a vagina-like gash on his abdomen into which is inserted a videotape (= the malevolent spirit) that will control his behavior (more particularly to activate his masochism, much as his girlfriend's masochism has been activated).[43] "I want you to open up, Max. Open up to me!" says his "penetrator." Open up he does; in the film's final moments, following instructions from the television set, he blows himself to smithereens. Like Father Karras, and perhaps indeed like Brandon, he goes too far.

Christine's peculiar complication of the formula is especially revealing. The car Christine is on one hand the equivalent of the "possessed" house whose ghosts or unclean spirits eventually "possess" its occupants (the houses in, for example, *Witchboard, Poltergeist, The Haunting, Rosemary's Baby, Beyond Evil, Prince of Darkness, Salem's Lot, The Gate, The Shining*). In much the way that the houses are typically invaded from the graves over which they were wrongly built, Christine is entered from the assembly line pit over which she passes. Just how she in turn manages to invade Arnie is not fully explicit, but the name "Cuntingham" and the raft of orifice jokes in the film suggest that he is entered in roughly the same way she was entered. The effect is in any case similar: just as Linda and Regan become aggressively masculine in the course of their possession (as signified by their generally pugnacious behavior and their "male" voices and, in the case of Linda, male clothes), so Christine and Arnie slide into hypermanliness: she by cruising about driverless, smashing her enemies to bits, and "speaking" hostilities (via popular song lyrics on the car radio), and he by the usual set of telltale behaviors (swearing, sarcastic joking, threatening, and physical bullying). Against Arnie's abnormal gender extremes—in the beginning too feminine and hence too open, and thereafter too masculine—stand the rather more moderate qualities of his male and female friends, Dennis and Lee. Arnie at the end of *Christine* is what Jim is at the beginning of *Witchboard*: a crude, sarcastic, abusive, and selfish isolate. The difference is that Jim is "opened up" by his male friend and survives to marry, whereas Arnie (perhaps too recently—and too extremely—"Cuntingham") ignores his friends' efforts to rein in his newly discovered machismo and so dies, leaving Lee to the properly balanced Dennis.

---

[43] See also Cronenberg's *Shivers*, in which a man who has become a host for a parasite develops a vaginal slit in his abdomen, undergoes a "pregnancy" of sorts, and "gives birth" to the monstrous parasite through both his mouth and his abdomen. Cronenberg is generally inclined to put men at very much the same risk as women.

If Arnie dies for going too far, John (*Don't Look Now*) dies for not going far enough. More than his wife, in fact, he "has the gift. That's why the child is trying to talk to him. Even if he doesn't know it. Even if he's rejecting it. It's a curse as well as a gift." So says Heather, the older, blind seeress. But if we are to believe John, the problem is not so much the "curse" of painful knowledge as it is the womanishness of the whole project—the "mumbo jumbo" of "neurotic old women." Given, as he repeatedly is, the choice between reality and imagination, or visible and invisible, or provable and unprovable, John robotically opts for the White Science explanation, closing his eyes and mind to the images from past and future that flash across it. "It's okay, I found the *real* world," he says as he leads Laura back onto a thoroughfare after an eerie interlude in the back alleys of Venice. Over and over he sees but dismisses the supernatural signs that present themselves to him. No indistinct aging woman he ("Age makes women grow to look more like each other. . . . But men, each becomes quite distinct," says the Venetian police officer); but the price of his masculine distinctiveness is death. *Don't Look Now* does not worry homosexuality in the way *Witchboard* and *The Exorcist* do, but it shares the larger proposition and it stands as the negative case: to deny interiority, or the "gift," is to commit spiritual or literal suicide.

SHIFTING GROUND

The world at the opening of the standard occult film is a world governed by White Science—a world in which doctors fix patients, sheriffs catch outlaws, mechanics repair cars, and so on. The intrusion of the supernatural turns that routine world on its head: patients develop inexplicable symptoms, outlaws evaporate, cars are either unfixable or repair and run themselves. Experts are called in, but even the most sophisticated forms of White Science cannot account for the mysterious happenings, which in turn escalate to the point at which the whole community (school, summer camp, family) borders on extinction. Enter Black Magic. Some marginal person (usually a woman, but perhaps a male priest or equivalent) invokes ancient precedent (which in a remarkable number of cases entails bringing forth and reading from an old tome on witchcraft, voodoo, incubi, satanic possession, vampirism, whatever).[44] Her explanation

---

[44] In *The Evil Dead*, The Book is a videotape, in which a deceased man with knowledge of zombiism spells out the necessary incantations. In *Prince of Darkness*, the role of The Book is played by computer.

offers a more complete account of the mysterious happenings than
the White Science explanation. The members of the community take
sides. At first White Science holds the day, but as the terror in-
creases, more and more people begin to entertain and finally embrace
the Black Magic solution. Doctors admit that the semen specimens or
the fetal heartbeats are not human; sheriffs realize that the "outlaw"
has been around for four hundred years; mechanics acknowledge
that the car is something more than a machine. Only when rational
men have accepted the reality of the irrational—that which is unob-
servable, unquantifiable, and inexplicable by normal logic—can the
supernatural menace be reined in and the community returned to a
new state of calm. That state of calm is not, however, the same as the
opening state of calm, which is now designated as a state of ignorance. It is a new, enlightened state in which White Science, humbled
in its failure, works not arrogantly *against* but respectfully *with* Black
Magic. It is an ABC story, the C being a kind of religioscientific syncretism.[45]

So goes the social version. But as I suggested at the outset, the
conflict between White Science and Black Magic is a deeply gendered
one, constitutive of a conflict between male and female and also constitutive, *within* the male story, of a conflict between "masculine" and
"feminine." It is a rare occult film that does not show us a man in
crisis, forced by circumstances to question for the first time the universal claims of White Science and to entertain for the first time the
claims of a world—of religious, spiritual, magical, and mystical feelings and occurrences—that he has until now held in contempt. Parallel to and simultaneous with this spiritual crisis is an interpersonal
one, as the man confronts and accepts the deep feelings he has toward others—wife, girlfriend, children, parents, and male friend.
Whereas the female story traces a circle (she becomes again what she
was when the film began), the excesses of its middle disappearing
without a physical or psychic trace (Regan is explicitly amnesiac,
Linda implicitly so), the male story is linear (he is at the end radically
different from what he was at the beginning), public (he and the
world *know* he has changed), and apparently permanent. In other
words, hers is an ABA story of restoration in which she emerges unaware of what has transpired, whereas his is an ABC story of revision
or conversion in which he emerges a "new man" fully cognizant of

[45] As Wood notes of *I Walked with a Zombie*: "It is built on an elaborate set of apparently clear-cut structural oppositions—Canada–West Indies, white-black, light-dark-
ness, life-death, science-black magic, Christianity-Voodoo, conscious-unconscious,
etc.—and it proceeds systematically to blur all of them" ("Return of the Repressed,"
p. 18).

what has befallen not only himself but her as well. At the same time, his C is very much like her A. The man he becomes is a man who not only accepts the feminine against which he railed at the outset but even, up to a point, shares it. If he does not accept and share it, as in *Don't Look Now*, he dies.

The C of the male story is thus the individual and personal version of the religioscientific syncretism that forms the C of the White Science–Black Magic story. In the same way that arrogant science must yield to an explanatory system that embraces the paranormal, clearly coded feminine, so machismo must yield to a gender mode explicitly tempered by the feminine. (Both C's, it might be added, are arrived at not so much through mystical enlightenment as through a series of professional failures and humiliations.) The business of the occult film at every level is to confront the reigning masculine with the problematic feminine and to arrive at some compromise or syncretic position.

But let us look a little more closely at the split on which the story of male revision is predicated: the split between bad, old masculinity on one hand and new, good masculinity on the other. The man who stands for the former, the unreconstructed masculine, looks more than a little like Rambo. Clearly Rambo (I refer to the general type) has his secure place in popular cinema. That place is not horror, however. If Rambo were to wander out of the action genre into a slasher film, he would end up dead. If he were to wander into an occult film, he would end up reformed—a kinder, gentler man, at last able to marry and communicate openheartedly with his wife, children, parents, and neighbors. Because horror film and action film are both low forms and especially violent, they are commonly linked in the public mind. In many crucial ways, however, they are almost contraries, the former a virtual commentary on the latter. What the action film mystifies, the horror film confesses. If action cinema mourns the passing of the "real man," horror in general urges it along, and occult films go so far as to imagine a new, revised edition.[46]

The idea of the "new man" crops up here and there in modern horror and science fiction—from occult movies to films like *Starman*,

[46] I may be taking Rambo more seriously than he deserves. There is reason to believe that even Rambo fans understand the figure as hyperbolic, bordering on camp. He does not in any case square, in any direct way, with the picture of the "new man" that emerges from studies of men's self-perceptions. See Lynne Segal, *Slow Motion*, esp. pp. 292 and 130–33. Cf. Susan Jeffords, "The Remasculinization of America" (chapter 6 of *The Remasculinization of America*). As Jeffords's analysis and my own indicate (particularly in comparison), different genres can tell different stories about the same culture at the same moment.

Making Mr. Right, and even *Robocop.* Like other "new" ideas of modern horror, it is presumably part and parcel of the social changes from the late sixties on, from feminism to the Vietnam experience and the new family.[47] It is worth noting a small but for our purposes significant linguistic event of that same time period: the installation in the popular lexicon of the loan word *macho (machismo).* It is a term that simultaneously labels something for which the existing lexicon had no simple word—excessive or hyper- or old-style masculinity—and codes it as nonnative. Needless to say, the bad masculine not only lives on but thrives in a variety of cultural forms; I do not mean to suggest that it somehow got expelled. But *some* cultural forms have concerned themselves with the remapping of masculinity, even turned it into a topic; and in those forms, both the concept and the term "macho/machismo" are commonplace.

So far so good. Beyond that, however, the picture grows confused. Especially tangled is the relation of the "new man" to femininity. Why, in a form so maximally concerned with the masculine and so minimally concerned with the feminine (in any precise or exploratory sense), should the female story loom so large? What precisely does the female body have to do with the "new man," and what do we make of the homoerotic dimension of the occult film?

At the risk of redundancy, let me return to horror's low-mythic tendency to materialize abstractions, turn ideas and feelings into things, and represent gender if not by sex then by the figurative apparatus of sex. Teresa de Lauretis has argued that the two "functions" of myth—the mobile heroic function and the immobile obstacle function—are gendered masculine and feminine and hence naturally represented by males and females respectively.[48] So, in horror, the victims of rape and knife-wielding psychokillers are females (regardless of the fact that, in reality, males constitute a certain per-

---

[47] For a useful and detailed survey of changes in the masculine since the fifties in the Anglo-American world, see Segal, *Slow Motion* (and for a bibliographic survey of the "men's movement" in particular, see chapter 8). Sobchack makes some related observations in her "Child/Alien/Father" and "Bringing It All Back Home," in which she distinguishes usefully between patriarchy and paternity. This is not to say that the "changed man" story is an invention of the sixties and seventies. It is, however, to suggest that the recent versions have a distinctive urgency and character (they seem among other things to be responding to certain claims of the women's movement about the nature of the feminine).

[48] De Lauretis, "Desire in Narrative" in *Alice Doesn't,* p. 118–19 and "The Violence of Rhetoric," in *Technologies of Gender,* p. 43, commenting on Jurij M. Lotman's well-known "The Origin of Plot in the Light of Typology," *Poetics Today.* See also Lévi-Strauss, "Structure and Form."

centage of raped and especially knifed persons), while rapists and knife-wielding psychokillers are males.

In the same way that the slasher film codes aggressive behavior as masculine and outfits those who engage in it, females as well as males, with chain saws and power drills (commonly positioned at crotch level), occult films code emotional openness as feminine, and figure those who indulge it, male and female, as physically opened, penetrated. The language and imagery of the occult film is thus necessarily a language and imagery of bodily orifices and insides (or a once-removed but transparently related language of doors, gates, portals, channels, inner rooms). At the level of representation, then, the male story of occult horror is an echo version of the female story: it tells of being opened up by and to something, letting something in. It is only by referring to her body that his story can be told.[49] In short, the operation of the occult film rests on a syllogism: horror's concretizing nature means that gender will be represented by bodily sex; being impressionable or emotionally open is gendered feminine; therefore, emotional openness will be represented as female bodily openness.[50] It is presumably for this reason that Blatty made his pos-

[49] In his essay "Vas," Paul Smith suggests that Freud similarly took recourse to the female body in his analysis of (his own) migraine headaches. "The further his parallel investigations of hysteria and dreams go, the more inclined Freud becomes to allow the puzzle of the migraine headache to begin to give way to a puzzle of what is by now for us a more familiar kind: the puzzle of the feminine symptom and of female sexuality in general." Smith regards as particularly telling Freud's suggestion to Fliess that "hysterical headaches rest upon an analogy in fantasy which equates the top with the bottom parts of the body (hair in both places—cheeks [*Backen*] and buttocks [*Hinterbacken*]—lips [*Lippen*] and labia [*Schamlippen*]—mouth = vagina), so that an attack of migraine can be used to represent a forcible defloration, and yet the entire ailment once again represents a situation of wish-fulfillment. The necessary conditions of the sexual become clearer and clearer." "Perhaps it would be possible," Smith remarks, "to consider the shift that the above passage represents—away from Freud's general 'scientific' and social worries about male symptoms, male neuroses, and male hypochondria, towards the condition of femininity and towards the fuller expression of what will become Freudian metapsychology—as in some ways a loss. This isn't to suggest that the earlier Freudian method is in any sense preferable, but rather to surmise that in the shift from male to female object of investigation something apparently irredeemable occurs. Perhaps what psychoanalysis comes to repress is masculinity, or rather a particular experience of masculinity which is uncomfortably close to hysteria" (pp. 93–94; quotation from *The Complete Letters of Sigmund Freud to Wilhelm Fliess, 1887–1904*, p. 340). See also Alice A. Jardine's remarks on the relation of the male subject to the female body, and the hysterical gap between the two, in psychoanalytic thought (*Gynesis*, pp. 159–77).

[50] Psychoanalyst Elizabeth B. Mayer ("Everyone Must Be Just Like Me") has added to the discussion of primary femininity the claim that girls' awareness of the vaginal opening leads to a more or less formulated realization that something is inside, which realization in turn leads them to worry about the absence in boys of an equivalent

sessed child a girl, despite the fact that the real-life case on which the novel is said to be based is that of a boy—and, moreover, that the real-life case director Friedkin heard on audiotape was also that of a boy.[51]

But at the deepest thickets of the syllogism is the female body. Unlike the male story, which for all its variation is an essentially coherent account of a change of heart, the female story ricochets from extreme to extreme, flailing as narrative and as a system of sympathies in much the same way the woman herself flails as a character. What the films define as women's openness is in its moderate expression, in its correct degree, the subject of awe (so the *Poltergeist* series, for example—the weepies of horror cinema). Especially in possession films, however, moderate slides into excessive; appealingly open becomes monstrously open, emotionally impressionable becomes mentally ill, charmingly pregnant becomes hideously pregnant, and so on. (If the man who stands for the unreconstructed masculine in the occult film looks a lot like Rambo, the woman who stands for the hyperbolic feminine looks a lot like a schizophrenic in rape position—a battered, frightened loony.) To make matters even worse, although some of the stories peak there, others go a step further and have the woman become so completely colonized that she virtually becomes her possessor: hence Linda's sudden emergence dressed in Malfeitor's clothes, brandishing his ax, and speaking in a deep, synthesized voice, and in *The Exorcist*, Regan's more gradual and less explicit but

interiority. Hence the complaint that males are "closed"—a formulation that is, of course, part and parcel of our social language (as in, e.g., the popular title, by Steven Naifeh and Gregory White Smith, *Why Can't Men Open Up?* and its cover note "Closed men—the country is full of them!"). Popular culture would suggest that boys at some point come to share the construction, and the recent collection *The Psychology of Men* (ed. Gerald I. Fogelet et al.) would suggest that it may be more common than the clinical tradition of the last few decades has allowed. See especially the case of "Louis" reported by analyst Frederick M. Lane. According to Lane, but for the emergence into consciousness of a "vulvar" fantasy, Louis's symptoms would have been read as castration anxiety. "His vaginal dream imagery would have remained symbols of castration to my understanding, and his language imagery—'I want to let you in,' 'I want to be open to you'—might not have been connected to envy of female capacities. I suspect that much of such data is missed in the analyses of men, though quickly recognized when there are phallic references in the analyses of women" (Lane, "The Genital Envy Complex," p. 146).

[51] So it was widely reported; see also Kinder and Houston, "Seeing Is Believing," p. 52, and Michael Ryan and Douglas Kellner, *Camera Politica*, p. 58. See also the interview with Friedkin recorded by Derry: "I have a cassette recording of an actual exorcism performed in Rome. It's in Italian. It involves the exorcism of a fourteen-year-old boy. I got the tape through the Jesuit Provincial of New York, and on the tape are the sounds produced by this young man supposedly possessed" (*Dark Dreams*, p. 122). It is worth remembering that many of the biblical examples also involve males.

no less decisive assumption of the voice, aggressive speech, and physical strength of a masculine being.[52]

This "male" outburst of the possessed person is one of the complex's most archaic features. From biblical times on, the invading devil or dybbuk has been construed as a male being, and the possessed woman as hence subject to masculinization from the inside out.[53] At first glance, the story seems an object lesson on what happens to the woman who drifts out of the orbit of male control—a reading supported by the fact that it sometimes requires an act of male agency to bring her back to "normal." Up to a point, the case could be made for *Witchboard* and even for *The Exorcist*: both females are possessed when crucial men are absent (Jim in the case of Linda, her father in the case of Regan), and both are retrieved only by the intervention of men (Jim and Father Karras). One problem with this analysis is that when *men* are possessed, in both the historical tradition and the recent one, they are subject to the same effect (so Arnie Cunningham in *Christine* and Steve Freeling in *Poltergeist*, who, in the fullness of their possession, turn as mean and macho as their occult sisters). Another problem is that the films under consideration in this chapter are not possession narratives pure and simple. Viewed historically, they are hybrids: possession narratives joined with conversion narratives (the "changed man" story). The emphatically secondary status of the possession narrative suggests that, rather than taking the former's "masculine efflorescence" as a political allegory

[52] In fact, Regan's possessed voice is that of a woman, Mercedes McCambridge. Director Friedkin has stated that after listening to audiotapes of an actual exorcism in Rome, he decided on "a woman's voice that would be sharp, abrasive, and slightly neutral . . . neither male nor female. Certainly not a voice that anyone could say: 'Oh, that's just a man's voice' " (as quoted in Derry, *Dark Dreams*, pp. 122–23). On the "depositing" into the female voice of unusual qualities, see Silverman, *The Acoustic Mirror*, esp. p. 61.

[53] *Beyond Evil* is a curious exception. Here the occupying spirit is said to be that of the house's original owner—a woman named Alma Martin. And Barbara (the woman possessed) does indeed develop an *A* on her skin. But the convention will out: Alma Martin was herself occupied by the devil, having sold her soul to him; thus the operative occupant remains male, though an additional female body has been interposed (Barbara is possessed by Alma who is in turn possessed by the devil).

I am told by Naomi Janowitz (private communication) that the early tradition involves the idea that the spirit of an improperly buried person becomes malevolent and seeks a new host. Malevolent spirits appear to be conceived as masculine despite the fact that women figure among the improperly buried. This squares with the more general observation that sexual difference as we know it exists only among living humans in the here and now. Although vampires, zombies, invading spirits, werewolves, and the like may have a sex, they typically lack gender, so that female vampires and female zombies, while quite feminine in life, become in their undead state just as aggressive as their male counterparts.

on its own terms, we might better ask how that moment serves the
dominant story and the project as a whole. Finally, there is the fact
that the masculine outburst appears to be an optional feature, and
the fact that some films have it and others do not would seem to
suggest that whatever politics it intimates are not ingrained in the
genre; it suggests, on the contrary, that the alternative climaxes—
masculine efflorescence on one hand and hyperfemininity on the
other—are functionally equivalent. I will come back to the "one-sex"
reasoning that underlies this construction later. For the moment let
me simply suggest that what is at stake at the peak of the female
story is not masculinity per se and not hyperfemininity or sexual ag-
gressiveness per se; it is gender transgression, crossing over.[54] The
issue is not so much what kind of excess the woman slides into in
the middle part of the story, but *that* she does so, and in such extrav-
agant terms.

It is no accident, given the workings of the syllogism, that the
woman's slide into excess is simultaneous with the "yielding" phase
of the male story and that her complete break is simultaneous with
the male story's crisis point. The stories remain almost rigidly mono-
tonic, ratcheting up together, peaking together, and resolving together. It is in the systematic quality of this parallelism—the fact that
however intense the male story becomes, the female story is always
a few degrees more so—that we glimpse the underlying politics of
the occult film. At the risk of overschematization, I would suggest
that the remapping of the masculine in the occult film entails a kind
of territorial displacement in the world of gender. I am suggesting,
in other words, that the expulsion of the bad masculine—machismo—goes hand in glove with the expansion of the good mascu-

[54] For Tudor, it is the new aggressive female sexuality that drives supernatural horror: "At a very general level, however, it is worth emphasizing the degree to which
aggressive female sexuality has become a prominent element in the supernatural
threat-structure of the seventies and eighties." "Historical factors like the uneven distribution of change in women's social status, the emergence of vocal women's movements in many western societies and the declining credibility of traditional marital
values and their associated gender roles have undoubtedly contributed to confusion
and fluidity in contemporary conceptions of female *and* male sexuality. Such social
stresses, such mismatches between beliefs, actions and institutionalized expectations,
inevitably pervade our cultures where—depending on the forms available—they are
given highly mediated and conventional expression. There is nothing automatic about
the process, but in supernatural horror movies it is to be found in the modern extension of the genre's traditional concern with the threat of female sexuality, as well as in
the emergence of paranoid horror more generally" (*Monsters and Mad Scientists*, p. 183).
Although I do not disagree with this analysis as far as it goes, I note that despite its
remark "*and* male sexuality," it ignores the psychosexual experience of the males of
these films—who are, after all, the protagonists.

line, the redefined masculine or the "new man"; that this expansion encroaches on and appropriates characteristics traditionally located in the feminine; and that the boundaries of the feminine are correspondingly displaced into territories of distaff excess. Crudely put, for a space to be created in which men can weep without being labeled feminine, women must be relocated to a space where they will be made to wail uncontrollably; for men to be able to relinquish emotional rigidity, control, women must be relocated to a space in which they will undergo a flamboyant psychotic break; and so on. Steve Freeling, in *Poltergeist II*, is able to give up his efforts at machismo and accept the Native American Taylor's feather-phallus instead, with its kinder, gentler version of "knowledge and power," only because the feminine has been emphatically relocated in the far reaches of mysticism. Or the reaches of a virtual sex change, in the case of *Witchboard* and *The Exorcist*: here the male story encroaches so vigorously on the terrain of femininity/effeminacy that the only move equivalently transgressive—and sufficiently accommodating—on the female side is a move into flat-out madness/maleness. Behind the image of Linda in Malfeitor's tuxedo lurks the shadow of Jim in drag.

The diegesis (or story-as-it-is-presented) of *Witchboard* would have it that Linda's condition—penetrated, spiritually flaky, possessed, suffering, pregnant, hysterical—is what causes Jim to become emotionally opened. But the real order is surely the other way around: the nature of Jim's story requires Linda to have her condition. Told alone, his story would be (especially given the operations of the syllogism) too nakedly effeminate. But with Linda there to define the category in far more hyperbolic terms, his story seems the very soul of moderation, the essence of good masculinity. The fact that the woman eventually comes back from the crazy fringe may or may not contemplate a split in the feminine (that is, a turn from the bad to the good feminine), but it certainly contemplates the relation of the woman to the "new man." The rules of the genre require that at the end the man and the woman meet each other halfway (usually in order to marry), and in order for the woman to have somewhere to meet the man *from*, she has to be somewhere else; if she has no distance to travel, the cover is blown.

The cultural observer hoping for signs of change in the representation of females and femininity will find little satisfaction in the female story, the spectacular story, of occult horror. If anything, the clichés are more remorseless than ever and the efforts to form and reform the feminine in relation to the definition and redefinition of the masculine depressingly familiar. So remorseless, in fact, and so depressingly familiar that the whole project borders on the ridiculous. In order to accommodate the male's move from machismo to "new man," for example, these films must up the ante on the woman's side in ways that are out of keeping not only with social changes of the last twenty years but often with the individual film's own presentation of its female characters. In order to accommodate Jim's "opening story," *Witchboard* must drive Linda to behaviors that are ridiculously incompatible with her status as a crack law student. No less unconvincing is the kind of spectral coven of fertility and spiritualism to which women are assigned in *Poltergeist II* in order to allow Steve Freeling to give up his last pretense of machismo. It is no wonder that so many occult films are now located in places where women are not imagined to carry briefcases or drive cars—among Caribbean immigrants in New York City, for example, or Cajuns in Louisiana, or in Africa, the Middle East, and Latin America; here normal femininity is imagined to be sufficiently "other" to begin with that the shift to excess does not constitute such a brazen leap. But if recourse to nonwhite "fields" constitutes a political move, it also, like the lapse into camp, constitutes a double admission: the masculine can only be redefined by relocating the feminine, and the relocation of the feminine to the world of hysterical lunacy has something of the quality of a fatuous joke.

Nor, on the other side, is the space traditionally inhabited by the feminine so easily detoxified for masculine occupancy; in the same way that old ghosts inevitably haunt new buyers of irregularly acquired real estate,[55] so the specters of femininity (effeminacy/homosexuality) plague the man who tries to develop as his own a place, like *Poltergeist*'s Cuesta Verde or *Beyond Evil*'s Casa Fortuna, that somewhere along the line was improperly seized from its original owners. Even the relatively coherent male story of occult horror—the opening story—erupts periodically into a kind of gender chaos. Try though he may, Steve Freeling (in *Poltergeist II*) has some trouble accepting the feather as a sufficient phallus, and one evening he relapses, over a bottle of tequila, into the most brutal sort of machismo, brutalizing and indeed raping his wife. The consequence is a pregnancy of sorts—but on *his* part, not hers. For it seems that in his macho fit he swallowed the tequila worm, which caused him to swell to monstrous proportions and give explosive "birth" to a hideous

---

[55] *Poltergeist*, Walter Michaels notes, "centers on what is in effect a title dispute between a real estate development company and the corpses who inhabit the bulldozed cemetery the developer builds on" ("Romance and Real Estate," p. 90). An extraordinary number of horror films center on just such a title dispute, the corpses not infrequently representing Indians.

alien.[56] We could hardly ask for a more telling example of the syllogism's operation in the male-opening story than this, in which the
man bouncing between gender extremes becomes, in effect, the victim of his own rape. If the project of these films is to update the
binaries, the upshot is a sex/gender swamp—of male and female bodies collapsing into one another, of homo- and heterosexual stories
tangled to the point of inextricability. Again, the feminine and what
it stands for are not so easily pushed aside.

It is in comparison with the slasher film that the occult film (above
all the possession film) comes into full focus. Both subgenres have as
their business to reimagine gender. But where the slasher concerns
itself, through the figure of the Final Girl, with the rezoning of the
feminine into territories traditionally occupied by the masculine, the
occult concerns itself, through the figure of the male-in-crisis, with a
shift in the opposite direction: rezoning the masculine into territories
traditionally occupied by the feminine. Jim at the end of *Witchboard*
and Stretch at the end of *Texas Chain Saw Massacre II* are mirror images of one another. They are triumphant survivors of horror precisely because they have transcended their assigned gender: Stretch
by finally ceasing to flee and taking her stand with the chain saw,
and Jim by finally "opening up." It is only fitting that, given its concerns with femininity, the slasher film is a world of phalluses lost and
reclaimed—a world of missing or withered or doubled or inert male
genitals, and a world in which more or less phallically defined
knives, power drills, and chain saws float in free circulation. It is by
the same token only fitting that, given its concern with masculinity,
the occult film is a world of passageways, interiors, conception, pregnancy, childbirth, and breastfeeding, and that even males may find
themselves burdened, or blessed, with something from the list.

The difference, of course, is that masculinizing a woman is a far
more acceptable project than feminizing a man. For at least some
spectators, Stretch's slide from victim to phallically endowed hero
would seem self-evidently a move for the better. The myth might run
into trouble were she to slide too far, into the sort of hypermasculin-
ity that fares so badly in horror, but in the recent versions of the
story, the Final Girl seems to represent some happy medium. Jim's
slide from emotional closedness to emotional openness is quite another story. Coded by the binary as either feminine or effeminate
(that is, receptively homosexual) or both, but in either case fraught

[56] Similarly Tom Lopez's "pregnancy" in the *The Believers*. So frantic does he become
at the realization that something is growing inside him (it turns out to be snakes) that
he stabs himself fatally in his belly.

with taboo, Jim's "new man" is far more problematic and the occult film in general a messier category. What is surprising is that the occult film is as willing as it is to dare the double taboo as far and openly as it does. To be sure, it fiddles with the terms—most obviously by casting female characters at least temporarily out onto a crazy fringe—but on the whole one is impressed by the risks, culturally speaking, these films take. There *is* a line, as the deaths of Father Karras and Brandon show, but it lies remarkably far from the traditional terms of masculinity.

In chapter 4 I will offer some psychoanalytic speculations about the male spectatorial stake in horror, especially those genres which, like the occult and rape-revenge film, are organized around the experience of perceived femaleness. I resist doing so here in part because I want to talk about the two genres in combination and as they relate to the somewhat different construction of the slasher film. In anticipation of that discussion, however, it might be useful to look at the possession story from the perspective of a cultural understanding of sexual difference that produced and cultivated it and continues to inform it.

I am referring to the construction of femaleness in what Thomas Laqueur refers to as the "one sex model."[57] Where two-sex science, focused on the genitalia, has especially since Freud tended to understand sexual difference as first and foremost a matter of the presence or absence of a penis, one-sex reasoning saw and sees it in terms of outside and inside apparatuses. One-sex reasoning may be "wrong" in what it thought/thinks is inside the woman, but it thinks *something* is there. Woman represents many bad things, but lack and castration are not among them. Interiority, not penis-absence, is woman's difference in the one-sex system.[58] And although a woman's bodily experience is in principle and up to a point extrapolatable from that of a male, his visible genitals serving as a kind of map to her invisible ones, there is difference enough to stimulate curiosity—about how it might feel to have it all happening on the inside, and about sensations that might attend the more dramatic effects of interiority (pregnancy, for example).

[57] Laqueur, *Making Sex*. For a fuller account of the one-sex model and its relevance to horror, see the Introduction.

[58] In this respect, the two-sex model which is most relevant is that of Ernest Jones, who argued, contra Freud, that the girl does in fact experience interior sensations, which in turn organize her thinking. See especially his "The Early Development of Female Sexuality" and "Early Female Sexuality." See also Michele Montrelay, "Inquiry into Femininity"; and Silverman, *The Acoustic Mirror*, esp. p. 67. See also Smith's "Vas" for an intriguing reconsideration of the somatics of male sexuality.

Small wonder, given its antiquity and its millennial popularity, that the possession story has such a "one-sex" ring to it even in its most updated forms. The female body at the center of the possession story is the object of concern not because it is missing something, but because it seems to have got, in a sense, something extra. The occult genre in general is remarkably uninterested in castration and remarkably interested in female insides—in the workings of menstruation and pregnancy, in whether and how those functions can be tampered with, and in how those functions, and the female insides in general, might feel.[59] Possession films thus take on the "occult" in its original sense (that which is hidden, derived from Latin *occultus*, past participle of *occulere*, "conceal"), a sense that in turn squares nicely with Freud's notion of uncanny sensations as the effect of the "former *Heim* [home] of all human beings."[60] They are exactly about what cannot be seen—not nonexistent and not even precisely unseeable, but hidden: the inner life. So the occult film's preoccupation with evidence, signs, proof; these attest to the reality of that which is obscured from view. It is tempting to explain the slasher film's relative clarity and the occult film's relative confusion as the result of just this inside/outside problem: because protuberances are easier to see than orifices, and their functions hence more visibly symbolized, the career of the Final Girl of the slasher film lends itself to cinema's "frenzy of the visible" in a way that the career of the occult film's female story—not to speak of its male one—does not. But occult films do their best, in much the way pornography does, to make the female body "speak" its experience.[61] Through moaning, vomiting, fevers, hypnotic revelations, swearing, swaggering, swelling, and the

[59] On the difficulty of disambiguating, in psychoanalytic practice, castration fantasies from other fantasies connected with femaleness, see Lane, "The Genital Envy Complex." Note too that in "Analysis Terminable and Interminable," Freud declares the "bedrock" psychic fear in the male to be not castration per se or in a blanket sense, but the sort feared to result in the adoption of a passive posture with respect to other males. "At no other point in one's analytic work does one suffer more from an oppressive feeling that all one's repeated efforts have been in vain. . . . than when one is seeking to convince a man that a passive attitude to men does not always signify castration and that it is indispensable in many relationships in life" (p. 252).
[60] Freud, "The 'Uncanny,' " p. 245.
[61] The term "frenzy of the visible" is Jean-Louis Comolli's ("Machines of the Visible"); see also, with respect to representations of the female body, Williams (*Hard Core*, pp. 48–51 and passim); Dennis Giles ("Pornographic Space: The Other Place"); Stephen Heath (*Questions of Cinema*, chapters 8 and 9); and Silverman (*The Acoustic Mirror*, esp. chapter 2, "Body Talk"). The discussion issues from the psychoanalytic commonplace that, as Bice Benvenuto and Roger Kennedy sum up the Lacanian paradigm, "the visibility of the phallus predominates over the black hole of the female genitals" (*The Works of Jacques Lacan: An Introduction*, p. 186).

sudden appearance of rashes, bruises, and scars (sometimes spelling out a message), the woman is made to bring forth her occulted self.[62]

The concern with female interiority is by no means confined to the possession film (or indeed to the one-sex model). Kaja Silverman has observed the "astonishing frequency" with which the "talking cure is negotiated" in the psychoanalytically informed women's films of the 1940s; focused on the interaction between a male doctor and a female patient, such films "manifest an intense fascination with a space assumed to be inside the patient's body."[63] If for "talking cure" we read "exorcism" (or some equivalent process), and for "intense fascination" we read "fantastic and obsessive anxiety," we have a fair description of at least the surface story of possession horror. Historically speaking, of course, the horror version of the "affliction/cure" story is prior; that is to say, the "talking cure" film is a realistic and secular calque on a tradition represented in something closer to its archaic form in possession horror.[64] The comparison is a useful one, for the spectacular crudeness of horror's exploration of the "space assumed to be inside the patient's body" reveals, in ways that mainstream versions of the story may work to deny (not least, perhaps, because of the homosexual resonances), the deeply ambivalent relationship of the male to that "inner space." If it is on one hand a site of horror—something to be exposed, denied, fixed, filled, colonized, detoxified—it is also manifestly a site of curiosity and desire. Science fiction, further removed than horror from the realist mode, takes the further step in films like *Alien/Aliens*, in which space travelers actually enter and explore an otherworldly maternal cavity of tubes and eggs, or *Innerspace*, in which a man, reduced to microscopic size, finds himself adrift in the "inner space" of his girlfriend, where he encounters, floating vastly before him, the fetus of his own unborn son.[65]

Distinctly "one-sex" is the way the possession film's male and female stories are figured as one and the same—the one psychological or spiritual and the other physical, but both finally modeled on the architecture and presumed experience of the female body. The con-

[62] "The symptom," as Doane puts it, "makes visible and material invisible forces to which we would otherwise have no access; it is a delegate of the unconcious" (or the possessing spirit, as the case may be) (*The Desire to Desire*, p. 40).

[63] Silverman, *The Acoustic Mirror*, p. 59. On the issue of representing female interiority more generally, see her chapter "Body Talk" and Doane, *The Desire to Desire*, chapter 2, "The Medical Discourse."

[64] This is not to say that horror does not repeatedly gesture toward psychoanalytic explanation; it is to suggest that the gesturing is a secondary influence.

[65] At the same time, and presumably not accidentally, *Innerspace*, the Dante-Spielberg version of *Fantastic Voyage*, plays on homosexual themes (e.g., the fact that the hero is first inserted into the body of a man).

struction of one sex's experience as the echo or mirror of the other is as pure an expression of one-sex reasoning as one can hope to find. What is surprising here is the direction of the reflex—the fact that male experience is cut so brazenly to the bias of the female. The canonical body of medical-scientific discourses is male, which is to say the female body is constructed in reference to and in terms of the male one ("For those that have the strictest searchers been, / Find women are but men turned outside in"),[66] and stories of sexual drift, in both the medical and nonmedical discourses, are mostly in the female-to-male direction.[67] Stories of drift in the male-to-female direction—of men who come to lactate, menstruate, and undergo pregnancy—are also attested, but scantily, and more in "vernacular" (narrative and visual) sources than in scientific ones. I draw attention to the distribution of these imaginative constructions over the types of sources because it so neatly anticipates my impression of the equivalent distribution in our own time. That is, in the "official" discourse of sexual difference known as psychoanalysis, the male body is standard and the female variant, and although psychoanalysis does have some "stories" to tell of male identifications with females qua females (fantasies of receptive intercourse, fantasies of giving birth), its main "story," the drama of castration, is entirely organized around the male body.[68] If "unofficial" or "vernacular" cultural forms share the general bias, they are also more willing to elaborate fantasies of femaleness as such, to judge from horror and science fiction. (Also to judge from literary fiction, if Robert Glück's *Jack the Modernist* is any measure: "Slowly increase the speed. Touch the skin more firmly as it becomes wetter dart press your fingers down on Bob's clit faster put your fingers together, thrust them into Bob two fingers right above the edge of the opening; Bob feels your fingers move into his belly, press against the muscle walls of his clit again.")[69]

The most willing form of all, I suggest, is the possession or occult film. It is not just the centrality of a female body, and the interest in its passages and interiors and its capacity to accommodate alien intrusion, that mark the possession film as somehow "feminine," but

[66] Doggerel quoted by Laqueur, *Making Sex*, p. 4.

[67] Ibid., pp. 122–34 and passim.

[68] A corrective effort, on the clinical side of psychoanalysis, is the recent volume *The Psychology of Men*, edited by Fogel et al. See especially the essays by John Munder Ross, "Beyond the Phallic Illusion," Ethel S. Person, "The Omni-Available Woman and Lesbian Sex," Roy Schafer, "Men Who Struggle against Sentimentality," Cooper, "What Men Fear," and Lane, "The Genital Envy Complex."

[69] Robert Glück, *Jack the Modernist* (New York: Sea Horse Books, 1985), p. 111.

the fact that the male psyche/body is understood in like terms, and its story told with reference to the "internal space" of a woman. For all its confusion, the occult film *does* have a language for the female body, a set of tropes and images that refer not to lack or absence but rather to the presence of things hidden from view but no less there for their invisibility.[70] And for all the ambivalence, manifest anxiety, offensive imaginings, and even overt hostility toward and about that body, the occult film *does* construct the male story around it, *does* measure the hero's success (or indeed survival) by his ability to acknowledge, and within measure even cultivate, his own occulted parts—in the language of the films, his own interior "gift" and his own route of access. The man who equated his antisentimentality with the disavowal of his anus ("It's like denying I have an ass-hole")[71] is exactly the man to whom the occult film is addressed. In the possession film, in short, the usual priority is exactly reversed: *hers* is the standard or canonical body and *his* the variant, the one subject to redefinition. In the possession film, man is consistently and repeatedly construed as a not-woman.

Whatever one thinks of these films, one cannot help appreciating their paradoxical project: to tell, in a two-sex world, a one-sex story in the "wrong" direction. And whatever else one wishes to make of their radical ambivalence toward the feminine and their garbled approach-avoidance relationship to homosexuality, it must also be so that these are effects of the same paradoxical project. Nor is it clear whether the desired freedom in these films is the freedom to acknowledge homosexual feelings or, within the heterosexual realm or perhaps above and beyond any sexual realm, the freedom to indulge a wider range of emotions, or both of the above in some combination.

[70] Doane's "Althusserian" reading of female symptoms in the "woman's films" lends itself to possession horror as well. "But the logic of the symptom might be used to read the film texts differently. Althusserian theory and strategies of interpretation derived from it assume that what is invisible, what the symptom indicates, is not an essence (as in the films) but a structure, a logic—in short, an ideological systematicity which is by definition unconscious. A symptomatic reading in this sense reveals what is excluded as the invisible of a particular discourse, what is unthought or what the discourse wishes very precisely not to think. . . . The symptom gives access to, makes readable, the work of repression and hence indicates the process of transition from one system in the psychical apparatus to another. In a way, the symptom can be seen as manifesting the severity of the repression or the force of the energy attached to the repressed idea which 'breaks through' to the surface" (*The Desire to Desire*, p. 44). This rather precisely describes the relation between the possession film's female bodily symptoms and the story of the male psyche, which "leaks" as a narrative on every level.

[71] See the epigraph to this chapter, from Schafer, "Men Who Struggle against Sentimentality."

(On the contrary, it is so profoundly unclear as to defeat any effort at disambiguation.) Nor is that discrimination particularly relevant to my purpose. What interests me in possession films is not so much the end point of the underlying fantasy (which I assume to vary from film to film and from viewer to viewer) but the fact that they consistently repudiate a kind of masculinity that mainstream commentary imagines to be a cultural ideal, and that in so doing they invoke as a structural standard a specifically female body in ways that critical theory does not fully accommodate.[72]

The vision is hardly an egalitarian one. The garish monstrification of the female in these dramas makes it abundantly clear that the project is one of rezoning, not equality. But to focus solely on the monstrousness of Regan and Linda, as gender-interested commentaries have tended to do, is to fall for the very feint the films throw up, to be taken in by their diversionary tactics—to give them a clean getaway without asking what they stole. That the feint—snarling, hyperpregnant, toxic women—is offensive goes without saying. My concern in this chapter has been to suggest that it is that offensive because it has that much to hide, and more generally to propose that we have as much to learn, in the study of popular culture, from what frightful women are meant to conceal as from what they are meant to represent.

[72] It is worth noting here that psychoanalytically derived critical theory is even more exclusively organized around castration than clinically based psychoanalysis. Freud recorded male fantasies of anal intercourse and birth, and although he went to some lengths to efface the apparent contradiction between such fantasies and the "dread of castration" in order to interpret them as ultimately castration-derived, his accounts nonetheless attest to a very strong concern, on the part of some male patients, with interiority. See, in particular, his "Anal Erotism and the Castration Complex" as well as, to name just a few more modern writings on the clinical side, Cooper, "What Men Fear"; Ralph R. Greenson, "Dis-Identifying from Mother"; Lane, "The Genital Envy Complex"; and Rangell's "The Interchangeability of Phallus and Female Genital." Ross's "Beyond the Phallic Illusion" (with bibliography) repeats the assertion that the interest of early psychoanalysis in male fantasies about femaleness (bearing, breast-feeding, rearing babies) was eclipsed at some point as the field moved into its own phallocentric phase. On Freud's own investment in "anal creativity," see Koestenbaum's remarkable "Privileging the Anus."

Getting
Even

I Spit on Your Grave (1977) has done a brisk business in video rentals, and not only among horror fans.[1] Michael Weldon blames its success on critical condemnation. "Thanks to the PBS Sneak Previews show, which labeled it inhumane and sexist, this revenge exploitation feature has gained a new audience of videocassette buyers. Camille Keaton (Buster's grandniece) stars as a novelist spending the summer alone at an isolated lakeside house. Four locals (one retarded) beat and rape her. She eventually hangs, axes, or castrates the whole group. A humorless and disturbing movie shot in Connecticut."[2] Mick Martin and Marsha Porter are less generous. "After being brutally raped by a gang of thugs (one of whom is retarded), a young woman takes sadistic revenge. An utterly reprehensible motion picture with shockingly misplaced values. It seems to take more joy in presenting its heroine's degradation than her victory. She is repeatedly raped and tortured. When the tables finally turn, she proves to be just as vicious as her attackers. The scene where she robs a man of his offending 'weapon' is one of the most appalling moments in cinema history. This is, beyond a doubt, one of the most tasteless, irresponsible, and disturbing movies ever made. Regardless of how much you may enjoy 'bad' films, you will hate yourself for watching this one."[3]

[1] Although reference works date the film variously between 1977 and 1981, it seems in fact to have been first released in 1977 under the title *Day of the Woman*.

[2] Michael Weldon, *Psychotronic Encyclopedia*, p. 354. The PBS Sneak Preview in question is that of Gene Siskel, "Extreme Violence Directed at Young Women" (23 October 1980). Together with Ebert's essay "Why Movie Audiences Aren't Safe Any More," it set the benchmark for the film's reception. In Britain *I Spit on Your Grave* was the centerpiece of the "video nasty" hearings, and it figures centrally in *The Video Nasties*, ed. Martin Barker.

[3] Mick Martin and Marsha Porter, *Video Move Guide: 1987*, p. 704.

There is no doubt that *I Spit on Your Grave* is an extreme case. But case it is—an almost crystalline example of the double-axis revenge plot so popular in modern horror: the revenge of the woman on her rapist, and the revenge of the city on the country. Although some films of the genre work on the male-female axis only (*Ms. 45*, for example, or *Eyes of a Stranger*), and some concentrate on the city-country axis (*The Hills Have Eyes*), a striking number are hybrids, combining the two in ways which suggest that the connection is more than casual. Those revenge plots, singly and in combination, are the subject of this chapter. Revenge dramas are by no means the sole property of horror; vengeance may very well be the mainspring of American popular culture, from westerns and *Dirty Harry* to teen comedies and courtroom dramas. "Revenge," Dirty Harry says in *Sudden Impact*, a film in fact focused on rape, "is the oldest motivation known to mankind." Nor is the rape-revenge drama exclusive to "low" genres; the success of such mainstream films as *Lipstick*, *The Accused*, *Straw Dogs*, *Extremities*, *Sudden Impact*, and *Deliverance* (a male-only version) suggests that the appeal of rape-revenge stories is in fact broadly based. (There are, as we shall see, some telling differences between high and low treatments of the story.) It would be easier to discuss the category without reference to *I Spit on Your Grave*—it is an extraordinarily difficult film to watch—but given its video popularity, and further given the fact that it reduces the genre to its essence, and finally given the project of this book to offer an account not just of the most but also the least presentable of horror, I have decided, at the risk of compounding the sin of PBS Sneak Previews, to use it as a point of entry into a thriving branch of modern horror.

That having been said, let me add that I do not fully share the critical judgments quoted above. This is not the place to go into the reception of *I Spit on Your Grave*,[4] but I might note that I have talked with several viewers, including feminist critics, who hate themselves more for having seen *Dirty Harry* (which Martin and Porter give a top rating) or *Rambo: First Blood II* (which Martin and Porter judge "exciting, involving, and explosive entertainment") or the rape-murder in Hitchcock's *Frenzy* (a film they give four-and-a-half stars) than *I Spit on Your Grave*, which for all its disturbing qualities at least problematizes the issue of male (sexual) violence. One such viewer (female) went so far as to call it a radical feminist film; another (male) found it such a devastating commentary on male rape fantasies and also on the way male group dynamics engender violence that he thought it

---

[4] Marco Starr gives a brief account in his "J. Hills Is Alive."

should be compulsory viewing for high school boys. In Britain, commentators bent on censoring *I Spit on Your Grave* (in the "video nasty" hearings) claimed that it glorified the act of rape and indeed had inspired "copycat" crimes, whereas commentators bent on defending it claimed that it "wants us to hate the nature of the act of rape and what it calls forth."[5] I mention these responses not in an effort to arrive at the *real* politics of *I Spit on Your Grave*, but to suggest that pinning down politics can be a tricky business even in the most apparently transparent of cases, and that the politics of horror in general and this film in particular are less than self-evident. (Certainly Martin and Porter's assessment of the castration scene as "one of the most appalling moments in cinema history" is itself a pretty appalling testimony to the double standard in matters of sexual violence.) *I Spit on Your Grave* is a shocking film, and one is inclined to suspect its makers of the worst possible motives. But if cash-value shock were grounds for dismissal, our collective film list would be a lot shorter than it is. It would in any case not include *Straw Dogs* and *A Clockwork Orange*—films that, were they less well and expensively made by less famous men, would surely qualify as sensationalist exploitation. My point is not that *I Spit on Your Grave* has particular artistic merit or offers particularly original insights into the nature of sexual violence; it is simply that there are viewers, including myself, who do not find its values more "shockingly misplaced" than those of a great deal of critically acceptable mainstream film and video fare, and who moreover appreciate, however grudgingly, the way in which its brutal simplicity exposes a mainspring of popular culture.

The story goes as follows. Jennifer, a published writer of stories for women's magazines, has rented a riverside summer house in the country in the hopes of finishing a novel. When she arrives at the village gas station, she encounters three of the four men who will later seize and rape her: Johnny, an ex-marine who works at the station and is the group leader, and Stanley and Andy, both unemployed. These three will later be joined by the retarded Matthew, played in exaggeratedly comic terms, who works as a delivery boy for the local grocery and who brings an order to Jennifer that same afternoon. Jennifer settles in, but it quickly becomes plain that she will not get the peace she came for. The four men keep coming by her house and harassing her, either on foot or by speedboat. One day, when she is sunning herself in a canoe, the men motor up, lasso her canoe, and drag her upriver. They put ashore, chase her through the woods, catch her, throw her down, and strip her. At first they

[5] Martin Barker, " 'Nasties,' " p. 105.

offer her to the virginal Matthew, but when he runs away in fear,
Johnny falls on her and rapes her brutally. She staggers to her feet
and runs through the forest but is caught, beaten, and now sodom-
ized by Andy—again after being offered to Matthew. They leave her
bloody and unconscious. When she comes to, she struggles back to
the house, staggering and crawling by turns, but they have preceded
her there, and a third rape ensues. This time Matthew manages to
penetrate her inert body, but his victory is short-lived and he gives
way to Stanley, who tries to force her to fellate him ("Suck it, you
bitch!"), but she falls into unconsciousness. After reading a page of
her novel aloud, laughing uproariously at her references to "love-
making" and tearing the manuscript to bits, they go outdoors.
Johnny gives Matthew a knife and instructs him to go back and kill
her. He goes in but is even less able to stab than he was to rape her,
so he wipes some blood on the knife to satisfy the others and they
leave her for dead.

So the first forty minutes. After a short transition (representing the
passage of two weeks) during which we watch Jennifer shower and
bandage herself, tape together the pieces of her manuscript, begin
typing again, stare fixedly out at the river, and go to church to pray
to the Virgin Mary, the revenge half of the film begins. She calls in a
grocery order. The terrified Matthew (who has in the meantime been
beaten by his comrades when they discover she is still alive) takes a
butcher knife on the delivery, intending to perform the murder once
and for all. When he arrives, however, he is disarmed by Jennifer's
seductive demeanor. Promising him a summer to remember, she en-
tices him outdoors and, as they begin to have intercourse, slips a
noose over his head, trips a switch, and hangs him. She pushes his
body and bicycle into the lake. Next comes Johnny. She drives to the
gas station and wordlessly invites him into the car. Because he is all
too ready to believe that she "really liked it" and wants more, he
goes along. At a secluded spot they get out of the car and she pulls
a pistol on Johnny and tells him to drop his pants—evidently planning to shoot him in the genitals. He slowly registers that this is genuine danger and tries to talk her out of it. She seems to yield, throws
the gun to him, and invites him to her house, an invitation that
quickly throws him back into his earlier conviction that she "really
liked it." We cut to her bathroom, where the two of them are sitting
facing one another in a bathtub, Johnny chatting cheerily. "God bless
your hands," he repeats, as she fondles him underwater. She then
slips a knife into the tub. "God bless your hands," he repeats, and
then, "that's so sweet . . . that's so sweet it's painful"—at which
point he bellows and rises, blood gushing from his now genital-less

crotch.[6] Jennifer locks him in and coolly listens to opera downstairs as he bleeds to death. That body too goes into the river. There remain Andy and Stanley. They come to her place by boat with the intention of killing her. After a struggle, she takes possession of Andy's ax and the motorboat and pushes the two of them into the river. After buzzing them in much the way they earlier buzzed her, she puts the ax into one of them and mangles the other with the boat propeller.[7] With that, the film ends, aftermathless.

I Spit on Your Grave is a roughly made, low-budget production.[8] Like a number of revenge-horror films, it owes a clear debt to *Deliverance* (the retarded country man, the harmonica-playing sequence, and so on). Although there are a couple of men-only sequences, the film is framed from beginning to end as Jennifer's story. Most of the action is registered from her vantage, and there is no doubt whatever that its sympathies lie with her.[9] The film gives equal time and in some sense equal terms to the presentation of the rape and the revenge. The claim that *Spit* shows the woman enjoying the rape is flatly dishonest; not for a moment does she express anything but protest, fear, and pain.[10] And neither I nor those viewers with whom I have spoken found in the rape sequence even a trace of the "joy" of which Martin and Porter speak; the rapes are presented as almost sexless acts of cruelty that the men seem to commit more for each other's edification than for their own physical pleasure.[11] Nor is there

[6] The shower sequence in *Psycho* is probably the most echoed scene in all of film history. The bathtub scene in *I Spit on Your Grave* (not a slasher, though with some affinities) is to my knowledge the only effort to reverse the terms.

[7] The videocassette box cover twice states that the woman kills five men, but the versions I have seen, and the discussions I have read, have her killing only four.

[8] I would not go so far as Starr, who calls it "well made, interestingly written, beautifully photographed and intelligently directed" ("J. Hills Is Alive," p. 49).

[9] See ibid., esp. p. 50; and Phil Hardy, *Encyclopedia of Horror Movies*, p. 329.

[10] See Barker, " 'Nasties,' " p. 114. I refer here as well to the verbal reports of colleagues who have not themselves seen the film but who "have heard" that "she liked it."

[11] It should be noted that Siskel and Ebert's well-known attack on the film is said to have been prompted in part by their observation of live-audience shouting and cheering during the rape sequences. Starr notes much the same response at the New York showing he attended but offers a somewhat different analysis. Noting the infamous tendency of horror audiences to call out to the screen, to cheer and boo apparently indiscriminately, and to get into verbal duels with each other (vide Pauline Kael's appalled reaction, twenty years earlier, to the live-audience response to Franju's *Eyes without a Face*), he cautions against any simple reading of such behavior. (As Levine's history of public performance—opera and drama as well as lower forms—eloquently demonstrates, the silent audience is both a modern phenomenon and a created one, the product of a variety of "taming" strategies. Historically speaking, horror audiences represent the norm and the silent audiences of mainstream cinema the exception.)

any discernible "joy" in the revenge section; Jennifer goes about the business of catching and murdering her assailants almost impassively. It is in fact an oddly external film.[12]

One of the most disturbing things about *I Spit on Your Grave*, I think, is its almost perverse simplicity. The men are not odd specimens but in the normal range of variation; their acts of brutal rape are not traced to dysfunctional upbringing (no Mother Bateses here); Jennifer takes the revenge she does not for deep-seated psychological reasons but because it is the punishment that fits the crime; there are no extenuating circumstances; the law is not involved, nor are legal questions raised; and there is no concern whatever, not even at the level of lip service, with moral and ethical issues. In short, *I Spit on Your Grave* offers no outs; it makes no space for intellectual displace-

---

Starr offers an additional explanation. "Watching a film as personally intense as *I Spit on Your Grave* is, to some degree, an upsetting experience under any circumstances. To watch it in the presence of a large, mostly male audience, however, is to witness the film with some terrified viewers, despite appearances to the contrary. The realisation that one's fellow viewers are potential rapists can be devastating when one is relating to the experience of being raped. No wonder men resort to laughing and joking around—they will do anything to prove that they are *not* upset by all this rape business, so that the real 'vicarious sex criminals' [the film's point of address, according to Siskel and Ebert] in the audience will *not* become aggressive toward *them*, the 'woman-identified' men. Camille Keaton, the actress who played Jennifer Hills, said it all when she commented that the film 'made males in our audiences singularly uncomfortable.' Thus far, the critics have taken the mood of the audience completely for granted, as if it was inseparable from the film itself. (One critic was so influenced by the hecklers that he actually described the rape scenes as 'silly'.) Sometimes, though, the truth will inadvertently find its way into print. It can be found in the wonderful comment of a gore-enthusiast turned reviewer who noted that while *I Spit on Your Grave* may sound 'like great fun . . . unfortunately, [it] has a disturbing quality about it in that it takes itself far too seriously' " ("J. Hills Is Alive," p. 54). Starr and others also argue that one cannot take account of audience reactions during the rape sequence without also taking account of the reactions ("stunned silence") during the revenge.

[12] Hardy (*Encyclopedia of Horror Movies*, pp. 329–30) finds this impassivity problematic. "By allowing her to lapse into an almost catatonic, silent obsessive, the film distances the viewer from her, making her seem like a mere cipher and pushing her dangerously close to that negative female stereotype, the all-destructive femme castratrice (quite literally, as it happens, in this case)." Although Hardy has, I think, put his finger on a question raised by Zarchi's "external" approach, it would take a very tone-deaf viewer to imagine that Jennifer's motives are anything other than situational. It is also worth noting that Zarchi has inserted a scene, during the transitional period between rape and revenge, in which Jennifer is shown going into a church, dressed in black, kneeling at the altar, crossing herself, and asking in advance for forgiveness. The scene is designed, I think, to establish the purity (as it were) of Jennifer's coming actions. But for this quibble, I regard Hardy's discussion of the film as one of the very few sensible ones I have found (Starr's is another).

ment.[13] If higher forms of the rape-revenge story involve us in a variety of ethical, psychological, legal, and social matters—hooks and angles that allow us to look away from the action itself to a system of explanations and solutions—*I Spit on Your Grave* closes all such windows and leaves us staring at the lex talionis or law of retribution for what it is. *I Spit on Your Grave* shocks not because it is alien but because it is too familiar, because we recognize that the emotions it engages are regularly engaged by the big screen but almost never bluntly acknowledged for what they are.

I have overstated the case slightly. Although *I Spit on Your Grave* comes remarkably close to being an explanation-free revenge narrative, it is not absolutely so. The polarities I mentioned before—male/female and city/country—do function, however primitively, as a set of analytic categories, and it is to them I now turn.

Jennifer's urbanity is announced in the film's opening shots, which show her amid city bustle in New York, tipping her doorman, climbing into her car, and threading her way through downtown traffic. She gives the impression of being well-heeled and self-possessed. If her pumps and chic dress are in place in New York, they are very much out of place at Johnny's gas station, where we see her next. Local women, we will later see (in the scene where Johnny's wife comes looking for him), wear jeans, sloppy shirts, and sneakers. Money and city are explicitly linked when Jennifer tips Matthew for bringing her groceries. In reply to Matthew's "You come from an evil place!" she responds lightly, "Here's a tip from an evil New Yorker." "I never got a tip like that before!" he blurts. Jennifer, in short, is not just a woman; she is a woman from the city, and to be from the city is to be, at least in the eyes of the country, rich.

To be from the country is, by the same token, to be poor. Andy and Stanley are unemployed, a point to which the film repeatedly returns ("I despise people who don't work," Johnny will later say; "they just get in trouble"). Matthew and Johnny work at jobs that

---

[13] It is precisely the absence of psychological motivation for the rapists' behavior that seems to bother Ebert. Even films as "apparently disgusting as *The Texas Chain Saw Massacre* somehow redeem themselves, become palatable to large audiences (if not, of course, to the squeamish). These films are *about* heinous villains and contain them as characters. They are studies of human behavior, no matter how disgusting, and the role of the audience is to witness a depraved character at work within his depravities." The killer of *Halloween*, for example, "has been clearly established in the film as a character. We see a traumatic childhood experience that warps him. We learn through his psychiatrist that the unfortunate child has grown up to become the embodiment of evil. As he develops in the film, he takes on a very specific reality, and it's up there on the screen. In the audience, we watch. We are voyeurs. We are not implicated" ("Why Movie Audiences Aren't Safe Any More," p. 56).

have them performing menial tasks for the city rich: Matthew by delivering groceries on his bike, and Johnny by servicing a far better car than he himself could ever hope to own. They are all uneducated (so we judge from their bad grammar). Johnny is an ex-marine. Matthew is of course retarded—which condition locates him in the venerable "degenerate locals" tradition in horror (more on this later). The community in general appears economically depressed.

City, money, and women come together in the conversation the men share during a nighttime fishing expedition early in the film. After some general talk about women as a category ("Sometimes I look at those gorgeous chicks . . . and I wonder, do they take a shit too?" "Sure—women are full of shit."), the discussion turns to their new summer neighbor. To Matthew's report of her generous tip, Johnny says, "The New York broads are all loaded, Matthew." "Yeah, they fuck around a lot," Stanley adds, "I'm going to go to New York and fuck all the broads there." "Yeah, I'm going to do the same in California," Andy chimes in, "Sunset Strip is just swamped with broads looking to get laid." Stanley agrees: "Chicks come from all over the country to places like that for one reason—and that's to get laid." The conversation is punctuated with remarks about Matthew's virginity, his possible homosexuality, and the need to find him a "broad." The next day, they seize Jennifer and the rapes begin.

At this point, the city/country axis yields to gender issues. The nighttime fishing conversation just quoted introduces two features of what the film defines as masculinity that will underwrite the remainder of the story: categorical claims about male and female nature and a group dynamic that drives men to deeds of which they might not be singly capable. The latter, in fact, is what *I Spit on Your Grave* is centrally about. The organizing fiction of the threefold rape (meadow, forest, house) is that it is all for the virginal Matthew. "Here she is, Matthew," they call out when they have her pinned in the meadow (two holding her legs, one her arms). "You want to be a man, don't you? Don't miss your chance, Matthew. . . . you're going to die a virgin," and so on. But Matthew cannot even get near; he is in fact visibly horrified. So Johnny takes her instead. Likewise the forest episode. When they get her pinned on the rock, they begin goading Matthew again: "Come on, Matthew, move your fucking ass!" This time he comes closer and tentatively helps hold her down for a few moments before fleeing into the forest. Andy elects to sodomize Jennifer, a move meant at once to one-up Johnny and to win his approval. It is in the third attack, in the house, that they bear down on Matt in earnest: "Hey Matthew! Come on, Tiger! Don't miss your chance—show us what you can do!" And then, in unison, "Go!

Go! Go! Go!" At first it seems that Matthew will succeed: he strips (at least down to socks and hat), imitates a victory trumpet, and falls on and penetrates Jennifer. Stanley puts his foot on Matthew's rump to help him along: "All right! Come on, killer!" But Matthew's nerve fails ("You're interrupting my concentration") and he again pulls away. After some remarks about Matthew's impotence, virginity, masturbation, and homosexuality, Stanley, who had earlier declared that he likes a woman who is totally submissive, tries to force the near-unconscious Jennifer to fellate him. She faints, a fight starts up ("You wanted total submission, you got it," Matthew says to Stanley), and they leave.

To regard Matthew as a nonparticipant, as do the remarkable number of descriptions that speak of three rapists rather than four, misses an important point. For one thing, it is against his failed performance that the others can define their own as successful. They are what Matthew is *not*; Matthew is what they are better *than*. Once set in motion, the proposition that masculinity is little or nothing more than a function of comparison leads to another series of questions: how *much* better is Stanley than Matthew? Andy than Stanley? and Johnny than Andy than Stanley? and so on. Matthew is not only the one they compare themselves *to*; he is the one they compare themselves *through*. The pretense is that the assault on Jennifer is an act of generosity toward one of their members, a gift from the guys to Matthew. The fact is that it is a sporting competition, the point of which is to test and confirm an existing hierarchy: Johnny the winner, Andy a strong second, Stanley the loser, Matthew on the bench. To all but Matthew, the woman is little more than the playing field—and even Matthew is finally goaded into at least trying to join the game. The goading itself, particularly during the sequence in the house (when Matthew manages to effect penetration), echoes the crowd cheers of a football game ("Go! Go! Go! Go!"—faster and faster, in unison). For *I Spit on Your Grave*, at least, gang rape has first and foremost to do with male sport and male pecking order and only secondarily to do with sex, the implication being that team sport and gang rape are displaced versions of one another, male sorting devices both, and both driven by male spectatorship.

Ironically, the men's individual protestations, when they find themselves at Jennifer's mercy, almost perversely acknowledge the force of the group dynamic. Stanley facing the boat propeller: "I'm sorry, I really am. It was Johnny who talked me into it. It was Johnny made me do it. *I* didn't want to do it." Or Johnny at gunpoint: "Look, you've got the wrong man. Stanley, the guy with dark hair, the guy's a sex maniac." Or Matthew: "I hate you. I've had nothing but bad luck with you. I have no friends now because of you. . . . I'm sorry for what I did to you with them, but it wasn't my idea. I have no friends." In a sense, each of the men is right to feel that he is not individually responsible, for the film keeps insisting that the dynamic of male groups is larger than the sum of its parts. But that does not mean, in this primitive universe of the lex talionis, that the individuals are therefore not responsible for the actions of the group. On the contrary, as under the laws of blood feud, they are corporately liable; any of them—in this case all—are proper targets for retribution, regardless of their own degree of participation. For the viewers with whom I have spoken, the murder of Matthew is the film's most disturbing moment, for he is so clearly drawn as the others' victim. But *I Spit on Your Grave* gives no points for hesitation or reluctance or action under pressure. That Matthew never quite made it off the bench is beside the point; what matters is that he *would* have played if he could. Reviews may speak of "three rapes" and "three rapists," but, as the final body count of four shows, Jennifer knows better.

The "explanation" that *I Spit on Your Grave* presents on the gender axis is thus one having to do not with male sexual nature per se (that is, the individual male's sexual appetite) but with male social nature, or male sexual nature as it is constituted by group dynamics. The only appeal made to male sexual nature is made by Johnny at gunpoint, and only as a gambit for sympathy. "Look, you can't do this to me—I got a family," he begs, when his argument that it was all Stanley's fault falls on deaf ears. "This thing with you is a thing any man would have done. You coax a man into doing it to you and a man gets a message fast. Now look, whether he's married or not, a man's just a man. Hey, first thing, you come into the gas station, you expose your damn sexy legs to me, walking back and forth real slow . . ." But if Johnny thinks this appeal to his uncontainable sex drive will elicit sympathy, he is dead wrong; it is this speech that causes Jennifer to toss away the gun and invite him to the house for the hot bath. If maleness caused the crime, then maleness will suffer the punishment.

When the tables are turned, Martin and Porter remark, Jennifer "proves to be just as vicious as her attackers." That is of course true. It lies in the nature of revenge or self-defense stories (horror makes the point over and over) that the avenger or self-defender will become as directly or indirectly violent as her assailant, and, as we shall later see, these films are in some measure *about* that transformation. They are also about our nervous relationship to third-party dispute settlement, at least as far as rape is concerned. *The Accused* (the 1988 film based on the New Bedford gang-rape case) is an example of a

rape-revenge film in which the woman's quest for retaliation is submitted to the legal system, thereby displacing the conflict into the
verbal arena. Even in this most respectable version of the story, however, there is overt suspicion of and frustration with the legal system,
and the case is won only through a last-minute, long-shot ploy—an
eventuality that hardly inspires confidence in the regular workings of
the law. I shall speculate later on what it is about rape in particular
that seems to justify the syncope of the third party and the lapse into
blood feud. For the moment suffice it to say that as the bottom-line,
"policeless" version of *The Accused, I Spit on Your Grave* reveals a great
deal about our cultural stake not only in low horror but in the long
march of film and television dramas that concern themselves in varying degrees of civility with "getting even."

URBANOIA

The city/country split is by no means confined to the rape-
revenge film—or even the revenge film in general. An enormous pro-
portion of horror takes as its starting point the visit or move of
(sub)urban people to the country.[14] (The eternally popular haunted
house story is typically set, if not in the country, then at the edge of
town, and summer camps set in deep forests are a favorite setting of
slasher films. Stephen King tirelessly exploits the device.) That situation, of course, rests squarely on what may be a universal archetype. Going from city to country in horror film is in any case very
much like going from village to deep, dark forest in traditional fairy
tales. Consider Little Red Riding Hood, who strikes off into the wilderness only to be captured and eaten by a wolf (whom she foolishly
trusts), though she is finally saved by a passing woodsman. Multiply
and humanize the wolf, read "rape" for "eat," skip the woodsman
(let Red save herself), and you have *I Spit on Your Grave*. (Nor is the
woodsman's revenge in the folktale—slashing open the wolf to let
Red back out—all that much prettier than its cinematic counterparts.)
The point is that rural Connecticut (or wherever), like the deep forests of Central Europe, is a place where the rules of civilization do
not obtain. People from the city are people like us. People from the
country (as I shall hereafter refer to those people horror construes as
the threatening rural Other) are people not like us.

---

[14] A filmographic discussion can be found in Kim Newman, *Nightmare Movies*, especially chapter 5, "Deep in the Heart of Texas, Or: The Down-Home, Up-Country,
Multi-Implement Massacre Movie."

Just *how* they are not like us is of some interest. In horror, country dwellers are disproportionately represented by adult males with no ascertainable family attachments (Abner in *The Nesting*, various unnamed men in *Deliverance*, the backwoods poachers in *Hunter's Blood*).[15] These men do no discernible work and are commonly shown lying about the home farm in the middle of a workday—usually singly, sometimes in groups. When we do see country families, something is always terribly wrong with them. One standard problem is a weak or missing father and a correspondingly too-powerful mother (so the parodic *Mother's Day*, in which a ridiculously controlling mom sends her hick sons out on commando raids). More commonly, however, the problem is patriarchy run amok. Such is Mr. Sawyer's tyranny in the womanless family of the *Texas Chain Saw* films that his grown sons are cowering boys. Likewise Papa Jupe's authority over the feral family of *The Hills Have Eyes* (apparently influenced by the *Texas Chain Saw Massacre*): he treats his grown sons like slavish errand boys and for her misdeeds puts his daughter in ball and chain. In *Hunter's Blood* (1986), the primitive backwoods poachers keep women only to "use" them: "They last a mite longer if you give them food and water," one reproaches another. The terrible Hittites of *Deadly Blessing* live under the Law of the Father—a law that infantilizes all the younger men and drives the women to lesbianism. One way or another, in short, country parents produce psychosexually deformed children. The ubiquity of degenerate specimens (the retarded Matthew of *I Spit on Your Grave*, the "genetically deficient" banjo player in *Deliverance*, Henry in *Straw Dogs*) is the material expression of family wrongness (inbreeding being one obvious form of wrongness).

More to the point, country people live beyond the reaches of social law. They do not observe the civilized rules of hygiene or personal habit. If city men are either clean-shaven or wear stylish beards or moustaches, country men sport stubble. Likewise teeth; the country is a world beyond dentistry. The typical country rapist is a toothless or rotten-toothed single man with a four-day growth. (It is remarkable how many cinematic rapists both in and beyond horror—in *Viridiana*, for example, or *Virgin Spring*—are orally deficient.) As with hygiene, so with manners. Country people snort when they breathe,

[15] As Robin Wood notes, the in effect all-male family of *Texas Chain Saw Massacre* "derives from a long American tradition, with notable antecedents in Ford's Westerns (the Clantons of *My Darling Clementine*, the Cleggses of *Wagonmaster*) and in *Man of the West*. The absence of Woman (conceived of as a civilizing, humanizing influence) deprives the family of its social sense and social meaning while leaving its strength of primitive loyalties largely untouched" ("An Introduction to the American Horror Film," pp. 20–21).

snore when they sleep, talk with mouths full, drool when they eat. The hill people of *The Hills Have Eyes* do not even know how to use knives and forks. Country people, in short, are surly, dirty (their fingernails in particular are ragged and grimy), and slow ("This ain't the big city, you know, things take *time*," a local handyman drawls to our city heroine in *The Nesting*, and the city invaders of *Pumpkinhead* refer to the locals as "vegetables"). What is threatening about these little uncivilities is the larger uncivility of which they are surface symptoms. In horror, the man who does not take care of his teeth is obviously a man who can, and by the end of the movie will, plunder, rape, murder, beat his wife and children, kill within his kin, commit incest, and/or eat human flesh (not to speak of dog- and horsemeat, lizards, and insects), and so on and on. No wonder, given their marginal humanity, country people are often nameless or known by cognomina only (Leatherface and Hitchhiker/Chop Top in the *Texas Chain Saw* films, Papa Jupiter and sons Pluto and Mars in *The Hills Have Eyes I*, The Reaper in *Hills II*, Redbeard and Birdie in *Hunter's Blood*, and, in a campy reflex, Ike and Adlai in *Mother's Day*).

Finally, and above all, country people are poor—if not utterly impoverished, at least considerably poorer than their city visitors. They drive old cars, wear old clothes, watch old televisions (if they have any at all), use old phones, eat badly, are uneducated, are either unemployed or work at menial service jobs or subsistence agriculture, and live in squalor (their delapidated houses are surrounded by rusting cars and couches with springs sticking out). The city visitors, by contrast, are well dressed (city youths inevitably wear college T-shirts), drive late-model cars (often foreign), are laden with expensive gear (hunting, fishing, camping), and so on (*Deliverance*, *Hunter's Blood*, *Pet Sematary*, *Cujo*). One of the obvious things at stake in the city/country split of horror films, in short, is social class—the confrontation between haves and have-nots, or even more directly, between exploiters and their victims.

With that in mind, let us turn to the film that stands as the influential granddaddy of the tradition: *Deliverance* (1972). Although *Deliverance* is commonly taken less as horror than as a "literary" rumination on urban masculinity, its particular rendition of the city-country encounter has been obviously and enormously influential in horror—so much so that it is regularly included in cult/horror lists. The homosexual rape of *Deliverance* will of course become a heterosexual one in the films that follow—a point to which I shall return—but the city-country dynamic remains intact.

Four men from Atlanta (Lewis, Drew, Ed, and Bobby) decide to go canoeing in what is said to be the last free-running river in the

South—a river that is itself near extinction, thanks to a dam that is being erected by the "power company." The film proper opens with their arrival in the Appalachian backwoods and their encounter with the local mountain people. While their cars are being filled with gas, Drew pulls his guitar out and begins to play "Dueling Banjos" (also known as "Feuding Banjos") with a retarded local youth ("Talk about genetic deficiencies," Bobby asides to Ed as they look on. "Ain't that pitiful."). After they negotiate to have their cars driven to the end of their river run, they set off. Three of them are visibly inept; only Lewis, their leader and a self-appointed primitive man, seems to know what he is doing. On the second day of their run, Ed and Bobby put ashore and encounter two mountain men who, after a verbal exchange, tie Ed to a tree and force Bobby onto all fours to squeal like a pig ("Is he a hog or is he a sow?") before one of them sodomizes Bobby. The other mountain man then turns to Ed and makes moves to force him to "pray" ("He's got a real pretty mouth, ain't he?") when Lewis silently appears and with bow and arrow shoots one of the rapists in the back. The other flees. The question now is whether they should take the body downriver and turn themselves in or hide the whole matter. Drew argues passionately for the legal solution but he is outvoted by Lewis (whose belief in the primitive inclines him toward the lex talionis), Bobby (who realizes that going to law would make his sodomy public), and Ed (who, having narrowly escaped rape himself, is now identified with Bobby's humiliation). So they bury the body and set off. The feud played out initially at the musical level—guitar and banjo answering each other in an escalating tit-for-tat—now turns flesh and blood. The price of rape (of Bobby) is murder (Lewis shoots the mountain man). The price of that murder will be the death of Drew, which Lewis is quick to interpret not as an accident but as a retaliatory killing,[16] and the price of *that* death will be yet another (Ed shoots one of the mountain men). After a harrowing run down a sequence of rapids (during which they lose a canoe and Lewis is wounded), they arrive, finally, at the village where their cars are waiting. Lewis is hospitalized and the other two try to harmonize a story for the suspicious sheriff. The film closes with Ed's nightmare memories of the rising lake.

The economic context of this story is spelled out during the credit sequence: over scenes of a dam being built and a lake filling, we hear the voices of city men in loose conversation about the "drowning" of

[16] Whether Drew falls into the rapids because he is shot from the cliff (as Lewis claims) or because of a psychotic impulse (as his increasingly erratic behavior might suggest) is not clear.

the "last wild, untamed, unpolluted, unfucked-up river in the South." Why is the dam being built? A voice we will come to recognize as Lewis's tells us: "You push a little more power into Atlanta, a little more air conditioners for your smug little suburb, and you know what's going to happen? We're gonna rape this whole goddamn landscape. We're gonna rape it!" "Oh, Lewis," the others respond, "That's an extreme point of view, Lewis. You're an extremist."

But Lewis is of course right: it is at bottom an issue of class. When the city men drive into the Appalachian backwoods community that will serve as their point of departure, the first question they are asked by the first local they meet is: "Are you from the power company?" The following sequence—the scenes in which the men interact with the locals—is fraught with a tension that devolves, finally, on money. After Drew and the banjo player have finished playing "Dueling Banjos," Drew asks the young man whether he would like to play another tune. When the boy turns away wordlessly, Bobby says sotto voce to Drew, "Give him a couple bucks." This is followed, minutes later, by an analogous "duel" in which Lewis and a mountain man negotiate a fee for the driving downriver of the cars. Lewis offers thirty dollars; the man demands fifty; they agree on forty. Ed, fearing an outburst, keeps begging Lewis to back off, but Lewis, who knows a challenge when he sees it, persists.

The city not only has money; it uses its money to humiliate country people. Uses it, indeed, to commit an economic and environmental version of the act in question ("We're gonna rape this whole goddamn landscape!"). The last section of the film (in which Ed and Bobby are detained in the village) shows us a community in the process of literal dismemberment: the church being dragged up the main street on wheels for relocation on higher ground, the cemetery being exhumed a coffin at a time. This so Bobby on the strength of his career selling insurance can have an air conditioner (the air conditioner that created the need for a power-creating dam), a purchase that in turn, because it causes his electricity bills to rise, disposes him to vote for the bond that would build the dam, a dam that in its turn, because it will destroy the last free-running river for all time, disposes the city men toward a final sentimental canoe trip. We must add another step to our blood feud sequence. The chain does not begin with the mountain men's rape of Bobby in the forest; it begins with the city men's "rape" of the landscape, the visible destruction of the physical habitat of the mountain people. The city approaches the country guilty, and by aligning our sympathies relentlessly with the city people, director Boorman invites us to participate not only in their arrogance ("Give him a couple bucks"), but also in their palpable nervousness at having to face directly those they recognize, at some level of consciousness, as the rural victims of their own city comfort.

The construction of the city as metaphoric rapist of the country is an increasingly common one in horror. The *Hills Have Eyes* films play out their horror in a desert area once alive with silver mines but now, the silver gone, given over to nuclear testing. If in fact the feral family of that set of films came into being as a result of radiation, as the first film suggests (the son born to a displaced silver miner is a mutant who eventually takes to the hills), then we have yet another way that country folk are the direct victims of urban interests (in this case the military-industrial complex). The wilderness to which the city men betake themselves in an annual deer-hunting ritual in *Hunter's Blood* is about to be "ripped up for toothpicks and firewood"—and by the very company that two of the city hunters own and that a third of them, Marty, serves as "big-city lawyer." *Mother's Day* twits the convention when it has one of the city characters remark, as she looks out at a lake, "You know, we could really make this place into something. Six lanes of blacktop right there to the lake, pave that whole area there for a parking lot, maybe a taco stand here, some landfill, shopping centers, casinos." Environmental sentiments in fact thrive not just in city-revenge films but in modern horror in general. In *Prophecy*, for example, a big-city lumber company is releasing mercury into northwoods rivers, thus causing monstrous birth defects among the Native Americans who live there. In *Wolfen*, animal-related Native Americans living and working in Manhattan (in skyscraper construction) bring a halt to the building of a new development on their ancestral land. It is no surprise that a text in the business of defending the environment should expose the depredations of big-city industry; what is rather more surprising is that a text in the business of justifying the anger of particular city folks toward country people should also be so willing to expose and play up those depredations.

Needless to say, not all horror located on the city/country fault line explores the economic tensions with the same degree of sophistication that *Deliverance* does. But it is by the same token the rare example that does *not* appeal, however crudely, to some version of economic resentment. In *I Spit on Your Grave*, that resentment comes up in the attention paid to Jennifer's nice car and clothes and her generous tip, which seems to cause as much resentment in the other men as it does pleasure in Matthew. (The source of Jennifer's income is a particularly sore point; from the perspective of someone who pumps gas for a low wage, writing, like selling insurance, is at best a nonjob and at worst a parasitic scam.) The *Texas Chain Saw Massacre* films take it a step further. Once top workers in the local slaughterhouse, but now displaced by mechanization, the Sawyers have turned their death-dealing expertise onto human subjects; and as a solution to their unemployment, they have in the best entrepreneurial tradition set up their own cottage industry—producing sausages made of special secret ingredients. The irony, of course, is that the sausages, which are much sought after as a specialty item, are made for city people of city people. (The same joke is elaborated at length in the parodic *Motel Hell*.)

Class confrontation is manifest in the opening sequence of *Texas II*, in which two obnoxious Mercedes-driving college boys force the Sawyers' country pickup into a game of highway chicken. Certainly the Cleveland family of *The Hills Have Eyes* that gets stuck in this desert wilderness are folks with all the usual signs of affluence (nice car, large trailer house, Ohio State T-shirt, and the like), whereas the feral family is literally starving and in fact attacks the city people in the first instance to get food. The "profession" of the city youths in the sequel—motorcycle racing—is, relative to the feral family's struggle to subsist, not so different from writing fiction or selling insurance.

Hunter's Blood, spinning off from *Deliverance*, pulls out all the stops. The city men who go on a hunting trip to an Arkansas forest "swarming with whitetails and rednecks" commit every possible offense against local people. From the window of their new Bronco 4x4, one of them, the New Yorker Marty, takes pictures of local "rednecks" barbecuing outside a run-down bar. "It's like something out of *National Geographic!*" he exclaims as he snaps away, utterly unaware of the insult involved and startled when one of the natives comes over to the car and asks, "What do you want with that picture? I ain't done nothing to you." (Picture taking of "natives" figures in *Pumpkinhead*, as well.) In the bar where they later stop for a beer, David, the young man who will emerge as the film's hero, fabricates a long tale intended to humiliate the waitress, at whose gullibility the city men laugh openly in front of a group of local men. "City cocksucker!" she shouts when the trick is revealed. Now offended, the "rednecks" gather around the city men and try to extort fifty dollars to let them go their way, but the city men escape, their Bronco easily outrunning the local men's dilapidated pickup. (That evening, at campfire, the city men play poker for stakes considerably higher than fifty dollars; a close-up shot shows stacks of bills lying on the ground.) In addition to driving a Bronco (understood, in the film, as a vehicle city men buy in order to seem rugged), the urban hunters tote ludicrously overpowered weapons and wear expensive gear of the Banana Republic or Urban Survival sort. They have brought Jack Daniels (in contrast to the backwoodsmen's moonshine), marijuana, a boom box, and all manner of small comforts. More to the point, the wilderness they so visit is not long for this world, for again, three of the city hunters are involved in the business venture that will soon deforest it. The primitive backwoods poachers who will attack the city men kill not for fun but for a living, and not just deer but the occasional human, and not for their own immediate consumption but for city markets (the local Razorback Meat Company is said to provision hamburger chains). The city, in short, could hardly be richer and the country could hardly be poorer; and the job of the narrative is to acknowledge in order to override that fact, to engage the spectator in the project of destroying the country despite—or, rightly, because of—that guilt-inducing difference.[17]

But imbricated in the economic confrontation in these films is another confrontation, equally central and equally brutal: the confrontation, cast in almost Darwinian terms, of the civilized with the primitive. The scenario to which city/country horror obsessively returns is one in which the haves, the civilized urbanites, are separated from the system of supports that silently keep their privilege intact. What would happen—and this is always the underlying question—if the haves had to face the have-nots in a struggle for survival just muscle on muscle, wit on wit, without recourse to the law, or to verbal argument, or to money payoffs, or to sophisticated weaponry, or whatever? Could "we" (the film's "we"—city people) do what is to be done under such conditions—eat raw meat, sleep on the bare ground, betray our comrades, kill someone? Or have city people, like Hegel's master, refined themselves out of the Darwinian game?

"It's true, Lewis, what you said," one of the men remarks at campfire the first evening in *Deliverance*. "There's something in the woods and water we've lost in the city." "We didn't lose it; we sold it," Lewis responds. For Lewis, however, the "it" we sold refers not just to our relationship to the mysteries of the wilderness; it refers to our relationship to the physical realities of life before air conditioning and the social realities of life before insurance. Insured and air-conditioned man is a man unfit for what Lewis calls "the game"—the dog-

---

[17] *Pumpkinhead* offers a rather different solution. Rather than annihilate the country man bent on murdering the city youths who ran down his son with dirt bikes, the plot instead drafts him to their side; when he sees how cruel is the monster he unleashed to take revenge (the "pumpkinhead"), he changes his mind and joins the city folks in hunting it down and killing it. The "good" country assists in its own demolition, in other words.

eat-dog world of survival that lies in our common past, according to
Lewis in our common future, and for the space of a few days in Ap-
palachia (and a couple of hours in a movie theater) in our present.
Certainly the city men (Lewis excepted) are inept at canoeing, and
certainly they are risibly dependent on expensive gear (only Lewis
sleeps under the open sky and on unmattressed ground). Ed has
brought his bow and arrow with the intention of shooting at something other than a straw target, but when he actually draws a bead
on a deer, his nerve fails and his weapon falls. City man may be rich,
but he is also soft; and he is soft *because* he is rich.

So soft that he is rapable. Whether Lewis's unhesitating willingness to put an arrow through the rapist is right or wrong is irrelevant
for present purposes. The point is that civilization sits lightly on even
the best-bred among us; turn push to shove and we will revert to
savagery. When the "shove" is sodomy, savagery seems to come especially easily. Lewis has of course kept his savagery skills honed (as
if waiting for a moment like this), but his friends are novices. At the
moment they bury the mountain man's body, however, they bury
their civilized innocence. From that point on, they are in the "game,"
and they play it with all the energy they can muster. When they realize that bringing Drew's body back for burial might reveal not only
their own crime but their own humiliation, they sink it in the river
with remarkably little ado. Ed, the member of the group initially unable to shoot a deer, finally finds it in himself to shoot and kill a man.
And he and Bobby negotiate the harrowing final run down the river
and engineer the set of lies that will get them off. The journey they
began as good men—honest husbands, fathers, and workers—they
end as killers and liars. Innocence too is an artifact of civilization, a
middle-class luxury the moral equivalent of insurance.

To be in the country, then, is not only to confront the poverty that
one may have colluded in creating and maintaining; it is to confront
poverty without the protection of the judicial system and its coercive
apparatus—to face the victims of one's class comforts without recourse to the police. It is no surprise that the site of city/country horror is always just inches beyond the grasp of the law's long arm (and
that telephones are always absent or broken)—"out there where no
one can hear you scream," as the promotional poster for *Hunter's
Blood* puts it. For the collision between city and country is also a collision between a state mentality (in which citizens can submit their
grievances to the executive function) and statelessness (in which citizens rely on vigilantism). Much of the ambient horror of these films
resides in the fact that statelessness—our collective past—is not dead
and buried but is just a car ride away; what the city limits mark, in

horror, is the boundary between state and no-state. And the question that these stories worry is whether, in their dependence not only on the appurtenances of civilized living (air conditioners) but on the apparatus of the state, city folks have not become unfit.

The Hills Have Eyes I works on the contrast between two families: the civilized family from Cleveland and the primitive family up in the hills.[18] Part of that contrast, as I have suggested, devolves on questions of affluence and social class (the wild family's personal habits are as atrocious as the city family's are proper, the wild family's food is as inadequate as the city family's is abundant, and so on). But the other part has to do with their respective relationship to coercive power. Against the "outlaw" family, beyond the reaches of legal responsibility, is a city family whose father is, significantly, a retired policeman. Aging but tall, tough, and familiar with guns and violence, he ought to be a match for his rural assailants, but he is not; he is quickly killed by them and his family left to their own devices. Those devices are pitifully inadequate in the beginning, and the city people are picked off one by one until they grasp the life-and-death nature of the situation and sink to the occasion. By the end they have not only set out their dead mother as bait; they have burned, shot, and stabbed their way to survival. The final scene of Part One shows us a recently peaceable young man from Cleveland plunging a knife into the back of his rural assailant; the scene fades to red at that moment and the film ends.[19] Like other city-revenge films, *The Hills Have Eyes* both asks and answers the question of hypercivilization. Yes, city people *are* up to the challenge; despite air conditioning and insurance, despite their concentration on mental activities rather than physical ones, and despite reliance on "authorities," they still *can* kill. Even David (in *Hunter's Blood*), who by his own account became a doctor because as a child he was so disturbed at duck hunting, finds it in his heart to murder some backwoods poachers before the day is out, and his girlfriend Melanie unhesitatingly sinks a set of antlers into the back of a would-be rapist.

"He's typically suspicious of city folk," says the urban Lauren of the country handyman in *The Nesting*. Just the reverse is true, of course; Lauren and her city boyfriend are the ones suspicious of

---

[18] D. N. Rodowick pursues the comparison further in his "The Enemy Within."

[19] "Craven's obsessive theme," Newman writes, "is the depiction of antagonistic groups, usually parallel families . . . more or less representing the forces of destructive anarchy and normal repression. The only possible contact between the two is psychopathic violence, and Craven wittily has the carnage stem from each group's desire to emulate its mortal enemy"—the point being, once again, that victims, in the process of combating monsters, become themselves monstrous (*Nightmare Movies*, p. 55).

country folk (though nowhere suspicious *enough*, naturally). The term "urbanoid" is up to a point apt. At least at the archetypal level (the "deep, dark forest" level), the city-revenge film seems built, as a character jokingly puts it in *The Hills Have Eyes II*, on the "typical paranoia of a person alienated from his planetary roots by too much urbanization." But "paranoia" in this general ("planetary") sense does not account for these films' obsessive contrasting of city wealth and country poverty and, more to the point, the notion that the former has *caused* the latter. It is not just that the city men have more money than the country people; it is that their city comforts are costing country people their ancestral home. The real motor of the city-revenge or urbanoia film, I suggest, is economic guilt.

The story is a familiar one in American popular culture. The city approaches the country guilty in much the same way that the capitalist approaches the proletarian guilty (for plundering her labor) or the settler approaches the Indian guilty (for taking his land). In fact, films like *Deliverance*, *Hunter's Blood*, and the *Hills Have Eyes* films resemble nothing so much as thirties and forties westerns of the settlers-versus-Indians variety. The latter genre rests, of course, on a land seizure of fantastic dimensions. Although we all inhabit, as Michael Rogin has put it, a "society built on Indian graves,"[20] the original audiences for those films, as children and grandchildren of the settlers in question, would have had an immediate stake in an account that in one stroke admits the land theft and even the genocide (the Indians in these films being depicted as a decimated, displaced, and ragged band whose sad leader is given to intoning speeches about the white man's treachery) but in the next attributes to the Indians characteristics so vile and deeds so heinous that the white man's crimes pale in comparison. The modern urbanoid film is no less brazen in its admission of urban crimes against the country (dammed rivers, stripped forests, dirt-biked and snowmobiled wilderness, mercury-filled lakes, irradiated rangeland) and by extension against those who have been economically dispossessed in the process. In both cases—urbanoid horror and settler western—it is as

[20] Michael Rogin, "Liberal Society and the Indian Question," p. 137. Note that actual Indian graves figure in horror, as well. In *Poltergeist*, the trouble begins when a real estate developer builds over a local graveyard without translating the burials. Although the dialogue gives us no reason to suppose that the buried are anything but white, the ghastly figures who eventually invade the Freeling house look very much like Indians (and in *Poltergeist II*, present-day Native Americans become part of the story). A remarkable number of horror films turn on "title disputes" between present living owners and past dead ones, and one cannot help suspecting that the past dead ones always, at some level, represent the original ones—that even "haunted house" horror devolves, finally, on the Indian Question. See also chapter 2, n. 55, above.

though the demonizing mechanism must begin by acknowledging that which must be overridden.

But it is not just the demonizing mechanism that the city-revenge films have inherited from the western. It is the redskin himself—now rewritten as a redneck. If "redneck" once denoted a real and particular group, it has achieved the status of a kind of universal blame figure, the "someone else" held responsible for all manner of American social ills. The great success of the redneck in that capacity suggests that anxieties no longer expressible in ethnic or racial terms have become projected onto a safe target—safe not only because it is (nominally) white, but because it is infinitely displaceable onto someone from the deeper South or the higher mountains or the further desert (one man's redneck is another man's neighbor, and so on). In fact, the race and ethnicity of the Other of revenge narratives have always been subject to historical shifts (from Indians and blacks to Vietcong) and there is a sense in which the redneck of the films under consideration here is doing multiple duty for the lot.[21] But I would like to make a case for a special connection between the coun-

[21] Rogin has argued that the history of demonology in American politics comprises three major moments: racial (Native Americans and blacks), class and ethnic, and cold war. Of the first two, which bear most directly on the revenge films under discussion here, he writes: "The expropriation of Indian land and the exploitation of black labor lie at the root not only of America's economic development, but of its political conflicts and cultural identity as well. A distinctive American political tradition, fearful of primitivism, disorder, and conspiracy, developed in response to peoples of color. That tradition draws its energy from alien threats to the American way of life, and sanctions violent and exclusionary responses to them. Class and ethnic divisions define the second demonological moment. The targets of countersubversion moved from the reds and blacks of frontier, agrarian America to the working-class 'savages' and alien 'reds' of urban, industrializing America. The defense of civilization against savagery still derived from repressive conditions of labor on the one hand and from internal, imperial expansion against autonomous communities on the other. But the terms of the struggle shifted from racial conflict to ethnocentric class war" ("Kiss Me Deadly," p. 1). "Ethnocentric class war" is very much alive in recent horror. A number of commentators have noted the tendency of popular culture to understand the Vietnam war in White-Indian or White-Black terms (Harlan Kennedy in "Things That Go Howl in the Id," for example, or Newman in *Nightmare Movies* or Gaylyn Studlar and David Desser in "Never Having to Say You're Sorry"), but the displacement of ethnic otherness onto a class of whites—to my mind far and away the most significant "ethnic" development in popular culture of the last decade—has gone unnoticed. *Southern Comfort* (1981) goes so far as to blame the entire Vietnam experience—from initial involvement to failure— on the "redneck." For a "scapegoat" analysis of *Texas Chain Saw Massacre* (which also gestures in the direction of the Indians), see Christopher Sharrett, "The Idea of Apocalypse in *The Texas Chainsaw Massacre*." The film *Pumpkinhead* gestures toward the blackness as well as the Indianness of the redneck subtext when it has one of the (white) city youths explain to his girlfriend why he has brought a rifle: "Because yo' never know what yo' goin' to find in the jungle—yo!"

try folk of the urbanoia films and the Indians of the settler-versus-Indian western. For in these stories, both redneck and redskin are figured as indigenous peoples on the verge of being deprived of their native lands, and the force of the demonizing mechanism derives, I think, from just this issue of land- and genocide-guilt. Consciously or not, the makers of city-revenge horror fall back on the analogy, to the point that the rednecks of modern horror even look and act like movie Indians. *I Spit on Your Grave* indulges the convention only obliquely, if at all, but the mountain family of the *Hills Have Eyes* films is blatantly based on movie Indians (a tattered band of last survivors, living a subsistence life in the hills, wearing moccasins and head-bands, engaging in pagan rites, and so on), and the "redneck" clans of the *Texas Chain Saw* films, *Hunter's Blood*, and *Deliverance* bear a more-than-passing resemblance. Like the world of the movie Apache, the world of the horror movie's redneck is a world of tribal law, primitive hygiene, tyrannical patriarchs (or matriarchs), canni-balism, incest, genetic failure from inbreeding, enslaved women, drunkenness, poverty, and cognomina in place of Christian names.[22] Between Running Deer and Leatherface (Chop Top, Hitchhiker, Ju-piter, Pluto, Reaper, Redbeard, Birdie) there is not much to choose.

If what he *is* goes a long way in establishing the exterminability of the redneck/redskin, it is what he *does* that makes it happen. In the modern urbanoia film, murder (of one's fellow) and rape (of one's fellow or oneself) have pride of place. To judge from the two thou-sand plot summaries in Brian Garfield's *Western Films: A Complete Guide*, the standard precipitating incidents are murder and abduc-tion, particularly of women and children. In this Hollywood echoes nineteenth-century representations of Indian atrocities. "When we make the case of Mrs. Manly and her family and Mrs. Crawly our own," Andrew Jackson wrote to Willie Blount in 1812, "when we figure to ourselves our beloved wives and little, prattling infants, butchered, mangled, murdered, and torn to pieces by savage blood-hounds [Indians] and wallowing in their gore, you can Judge of our feelings."[23] Outright rape is rare in the western, but it could be ar-gued that the possibility of sexual violation inheres in the abduction situation. It certainly hovers about the abduction of Lucy in *The Searchers*. "They'll raise her as one of their own, until she's of an age to . . ." an experienced frontiersman predicts, his voice discreetly trailing off. When her body is found, her brokenhearted fiancé asks,

---

[22] See Rogin's "Liberal Society and the Indian Question" for an enumeration of the barbarisms attributed to Indians.

[23] *Correspondence of Andrew Jackson*, 1:231; also quoted in ibid., p. 149.

"Did they . . . was she . . . ?" "Don't ask!" comes the brusk answer.[24] What 1940s Hollywood knew is that the implication of rape makes the deed all the more avengeable. And what 1970s horror realized is that one's own rape is the most avengeable deed of all.

RAPE REVENGE

Rape—real, threatened, or implied—has been a staple of American cinema more or less from the beginning. Until the early 1970s, however, rape was typically a side theme: one of several horrors blacks would visit on whites in the case of a Union victory (*Birth of a Nation*), a psychopathic flourish in a suspense plot (*Frenzy*), one assault in an escalating sequence on a man's household (*Straw Dogs*), the starting point for a blackmail plot (*Blackmail*), a datum in the consideration of the nature of violence (*A Clockwork Orange*), and so on. In the 1970s, rape moved to center stage and the rape-revenge story as a drama complete unto itself came into its own. (In folkloric terms, what had been a motif graduated to a tale-type.) An example that achieved a certain underground notoriety was Wes Craven's *Last House on the Left*, a gritty low-budget film from 1972, inspired by Ingmar Bergman's *The Virgin Spring* (1959). Bergman's film (based on a novel by a woman, Ulla Isaksson, the novel in turn based on a medieval ballad) tells of the rape and murder by toothless, unshaven itinerants of a virginal girl on her way to church and of her otherwise gentle father's rise to anger and his grisly revenge. (A central concern here, as in *Straw Dogs* and the distantly related *Hardcore*, is with the provocation of essentially peaceful men to acts of savagery.) *Last House on the Left* also has the raped woman die and the parents take revenge, but it adds a twist that points to the genre's future development: the raped girl's mother participates in the revenge by offering to fellate one of her daughter's rapists and then, in the act, biting off his penis.[25] The rape and murder are conducted with considerable sexual energy, but when they are over, the assailants look at the girl's limp body in a kind of dumbfounded shame; it is a very long take and indeed "the most disturbing moment in this most disturbing of films."[26] *Act of Vengeance* (1974, a.k.a. *Rape Squad*) takes the next step,

[24] According to Rogin, the historical record presents a picture of the Native American as sexually underfunded, in contrast to the plantation black. If that is so, Hollywood has emended the picture.

[25] See Wood's defense of *Last House on the Left* in his "Neglected Nightmares."

[26] Craven's own description is worth quoting. "The killing of Phyllis is very sexual in feeling, and ended with her being stabbed not only by the men but by the woman

dispensing with male help altogether and having the victims take their own revenge. Angry in the first instance at their rapes (a serial rapist forces his victims to sing "Jingle Bells" as he assaults them) and in the second because of their humiliating treatment at the hands of the police (who wonder why women don't just lie back and enjoy it), a group of victims band together to track down and kill their hockey-masked assailant. *Act of Vengeance* is an amateurish and (at least in hindsight) predictable film, but its influence, particularly its critique of a male justice system, has been extraordinary. It is one of the prototypes of *Lipstick* (1976), in which a model named Chris is raped by her kid sister's music teacher and takes the case to court. Because she is unable to prove that she did not consent, she loses the case and the rapist is acquitted. When he then assaults the kid sister, Chris goes into a rage and shoots him in a parking lot. With *Lipstick*, the rape-revenge tradition enters the mainstream; in the spate of rape-revenge films that follow in the late seventies and eighties, rape becomes a problem for women themselves to solve.

In *I Spit on Your Grave*, the parodic *Mother's Day, Act of Vengeance, Eyes of a Stranger, Ms. 45, Ladies' Club, Extremities, Savage Streets, Positive I.D., The Accused*, and even, in its way, *Sudden Impact*, women seek their own revenge—usually on their own behalf, but sometimes on behalf of a sister (literal or figurative) who has been murdered or disabled in an act of sexual violence. The twists and solutions vary (as do the proportions of calculated revenge to self-defense): *The Accused* (based on a real-life case) has the raped woman and her woman lawyer win the case in court; *Sudden Impact* interweaves the rape-revenge story with a Dirty Harry plot; *Extremities* shows us a woman who has the chance and desire to take blood revenge but comes to her senses in the nick of time and submits the case to the law; *Ladies' Club* has victims form a vigilante action group that tracks down and castrates recidivist rapists; *Positive I.D.* puts the rape in the backstory and focuses on the woman's violent revenge; *Eyes of a Stranger*, like *Lipstick*, has sisters kill a serial rapist; and so forth. But they share a set of premises that, while not entirely unprecedented, are conspicuously conditioned by changes in social attitudes of the two decades in question: that rape deserves full-scale revenge; that a rape-and-revenge story constitutes sufficient drama for a feature film and that

---

repeatedly. Then she fell to the ground and Sadie bent down and pulled out a loop of her intestines. They looked at it and that's where it all stopped. That's when they realized what they had done, and they looked at each other and walked away. They were disgusted at what they had done. It was as if they had been playing with a doll, or a prisoner they thought was a doll, and it had broken and come apart and they did not know how to put it back together again" (as quoted by Wood in ibid., p. 28).

having the victim survive to be her own avenger makes that drama even better; and (more directly politically) that we live in a "rape culture" in which *all* males—husbands, boyfriends, lawyers, politicians—are directly or indirectly complicit and that men are thus not just individually but corporately liable.

The representation of rape has undergone a striking evolution since the early seventies. *Frenzy* and *Straw Dogs* are for all practical purposes the last of the "old style" rape films—films in which the rape is construed as itself an act of revenge on the part of a male who has suffered at the hands of the woman in question (to have been sexually teased, or to have a smaller paycheck or lesser job, is to suffer) and in which the viewer is invited by the usual narrative and cinematic conventions to adopt the rapist's point of view. The rape in *Frenzy* (the camera focuses in excruciating detail on the woman's face as she is simultaneously raped and strangled) exudes a kind of lascivious sadism with which the viewer is directly invited to collude. The rape in *Straw Dogs* is a classic in the "asking for it" tradition: Amy goes braless and flaunts her looks in front of the local men, and when they undertake to rape her, her "no, no" turns to a "yes yes" (so during the first man's turn, in any case). Director Peckinpah is quoted as saying that "there are women and there's pussy," and his Amy is pure pussy.[27] On the other side of the divide is *Lipstick* (1976), which rings the old theme of rape as an act of male revenge, but for purposes of exposing it as such, not drawing us into it. The rapist, a music teacher and would-be composer, is given reason enough to resent Chris: she is beautiful but rejecting (the cocktease motif), she is visibly bored with his music tape, she is rich and famous, she has pictures of well-known people all over her house, and so on. There is only one way he has left to prove his maleness, and he uses it. The rape itself—he ties her to her bed and sodomizes her—is brief, brutal, and unerotic. The rapes of *I Spit on Your Grave* are more problematic, focusing as they do at length on Jennifer's tortured body, but there is much truth in Starr's observation that "instead of getting close-ups of a terrified woman staring into a camera (a standard cinematic device equating viewer with attacker), the film features similar shots of the rapists' threatening faces; the viewer is thus forced into the position of victim, not villain" and in Phil Hardy's judgment that "the men are so grossly unattractive and the rapes so harrowing, long-drawn-out and starkly presented that it is hard to imagine most male spectators identifying with the perpetrators, especially as the film's

---

[27] As quoted (from a *Playboy* magazine interview) by Molly Haskell, *From Reverence to Rape*, p. 363.

narrative structure and *mise-en-scene* force the spectator to view the action from [Jennifer's] point of view. Further, there is no suggestion that 'she asked for it' or enjoyed it, except, of course, in the rapists' own perceptions, from which the film is careful to distance itself."[28] Even *Savage Streets*, a film otherwise relentlessly invasive in its relation to female bodies, manages to rein in its voyeuristic impulses during the rape proper. *Ms. 45* marks yet another phase, moving the very brief and very unerotic rape to the front of the film in such a way as to give it the character of a credit-sequence incident.[29] By the mid-1980s, rape moved virtually offscreen. By having no rape, technically speaking, but rather attempted rape, *Extremities* draws attention away from the sex act to the dynamics of force. *Sudden Impact* shows us the actual rapes only in brief and fuzzy flashback. *Positive I.D.* puts the rape entirely in the backstory and devotes itself to the woman's revenge. A striking exception is *The Accused*, which puts rape back on screen in elaborate detail and close to real-life time—though only at the end of the film, after ninety minutes of legal arguments on both sides of the consent issue. Despite considerable individual variation, the general drift is clear: from a more or less justifiable male-centered event to an unjustifiable female-centered one; from the deed of a psychopathic creep to the deed of a "normal" man; from an event construed as an act of sex, in which one or both parties is shown to take some pleasure (if only perverse), to an act of violent humiliation.

To get a better idea of the politics of the double-axis revenge film, let us look at a single-axis example—a rape-revenge story that is set in the city and has nothing to do with city/country tensions but everything to do with male/female ones. The example I have in mind is *Ms. 45*, a low-budget production from 1981, like *I Spit on Your Grave* a film with something of a cult following.

A beautiful young woman named Thana (lest we miss the association, a character remarks that it sounds Greek) has a menial job ironing clothes in a New York garment district firm. Thana is mute—a handicap, her boss says, that means that she will have to try harder, be better—and obviously shy. The boss is male, and his employees (models, seamstresses, secretaries, and ironers) are all females. On

---

[28] Starr, "J. Hills Is Alive," p. 50 (see also pp. 52–54), and Hardy, *Encyclopedia of Horror Movies*, p. 329. See also Barker, " 'Nasties,' " pp. 112–18.

[29] "There was no conscious decision not to have nudity in the film," director Abel Ferrara is quoted as saying. "Zoë Tamerlis [the actress who plays Thana] was willing to do it. It was just a flash decision to not have it. We were aiming at a cold sexuality, a violent tone. Roman Polanski is an influence in all my work" (as quoted in Danny Peary, *Cult Movies 2*, p. 102).

her way home from work one evening, Thana is yanked off the street and raped at gunpoint by a man in a mask. She pulls herself up and gets home only to be assaulted a second time by another man, lying in wait in her living room, who first robs and then rapes her. As he comes to orgasm, he drops his gun, enabling Thana first to stun him with a paperweight and then to grab an iron (the tool of her trade) and bludgeon him to death. After she pulls herself together, she saws the body into pieces, puts them into a number of garbage bags, and stuffs them into her refrigerator. Every day she takes a garbage bag out—this is the film's structuring device—and deposits it somewhere in the city. On one of those forays she is nearly apprehended by a street heckler in a back alley, and she shoots him with a .45-caliber pistol.

At this point, reactive murder turns to proactive murder. For the violence visited on Thana has caused her to notice, as the film has us notice, that in every corner of life, men take it as their due to dominate and abuse women. The remainder of the film shows Thana (increasingly sexily dressed) as a kind of ultimate feminist vigilante gunning down men who traffic in women. She shoots an arrogant photographer ("I'm a gourmet of beauty . . . I mean, when I see beauty, I got to go after it") who offers her a career chance in exchange for sex. She shoots a pimp in the act of beating a whore for low productivity. She shoots an Arab sheik who smugly believes that the huge bill he waves in front of her will buy her for the night. (The morning newscast, noting that the dead man had $2,800 on his person, wonders what the motive for his murder could have been.) She shoots street guys who circle around for a gangbang. She shoots (or tries to shoot—he ends up seizing the gun and shooting himself) a man who picks her up in a bar and pours out a long and self-pitying monologue about his girlfriend's becoming a lesbian and his strangling her cat in revenge. (This man, like those before him, does not notice she is mute but takes her silence for feminine attentiveness.) And in the end, at the Halloween dance party, she goes on a rampage (dressed as a nun) and guns down a string of men: one who brags about buying virgins in Puerto Rico for a mere three hundred dollars; one who reneges on his promise to his wife to have a vasectomy; her boss, who has just referred to the women in his firm as "my little brownies, my little workers" and to Thana as "a protégé of mine"; and others who qualify for elimination by virtue of the simple fact that they are male.[30] ("Thana" indeed.) The slaughter ends only

---

[30] According to Peary, who does not question the male spectator's "identification" with the rapist, "something fascinating happens" in the theater at this point. "Once

Thana takes revenge (*Ms. 45*).

when she is (literally and figuratively) stabbed in the back by a co-worker.

It goes without saying that the notion of women going around New York putting bullets through male chauvinists has everything to do with fantasy and little to do with reality. Just what the male spec-

these men identify with the rapist, the filmmakers have Thana conk him on the head with an iron and kill him. Then she chops him up into little slabs and stores his parts in the refrigerator. Unexpectedly, the men who had whooped all through *Amin* and the obscenely gory previews of *Dr. Butcher* (1982), whimpered worrisomely 'Oh, my God!' and slumped in their seats and shut up. Never has a 42nd Street theater been so quiet and disciplined as when Thana went through her rounds and murdered every offensive male who crossed her path. Had the men in this audience witnessed their own possible fates if they continued to relate to women as they did?" (*Cult Movies 2*, pp. 101–2). The "silenced male audience" phenomenon is widely reported in discussions of rape-revenge films, though no one, to my knowledge, has asked the rather obvious questions it prompts. If the male silence is simply the result of chagrin, why do the silent men sit through the rest of the film (the rapes are over in the first five minutes), and why is this film so abidingly popular with male audiences (surely word would get around if it were a true bummer)? If the male spectator is able to "identify" with the woman on her revenge quest, then is he not equally able to "identify" with her during the rape sequences—is not, in fact, his identification during the revenge *predicated* on some "identification" with her as rape victim? If the male spectator can only identify with male characters, he must get some sort of pleasure in being repeatedly "killed" at the hands of a woman. However you cut it, the male spectator of this film is masochistically implicated.

tator's stake is in that fantasy is not clear, but it must surely be the case that there is some ethical relief in the idea that if women would just toughen up and take karate or buy a gun, the issue of male-on-female violence would evaporate. It is a way of shifting responsibility from the perpetrator to the victim: if a woman fails to get tough, fails to buy a gun or take karate, she is, in an updated sense of the cliché, asking for it. Moreover, if women are as capable as men of acts of humiliating violence, men are off the guilt hook that modern feminism has put them on. At the very least, the male spectator may take some comfort (sadistic delight?) in the idea that his services as protector of his wife or girlfriend are not as obligatory as an earlier era would have them be. That would seem to be the lesson of *Mother's Day*, in which the sons who have been required to devote their lives to the protection of their mother end up as idiotic louts. That would also seem to be the lesson of the stock figure of the would-be savior who is incompetent, unneeded, too late, self-important, and generally useless: don't even try. "*You* save her—she's *your* girlfriend," one young man says to another in *The Evil Dead*. Better yet, let her save herself.

Extremities in particular plays to the "tough woman" notion: Farrah Fawcett is both convincingly athletic in her self-defense and eventual command of the situation and convincingly murderous when the tables are turned (she undertakes to bury her assailant alive). Likewise the parodic *Mother's Day*, in which Trina and Abby do in the two rapist-killers of their girlfriend by putting a television aerial through the neck of one and, once they have poured Drāno down his throat, taking an electric carver to the other. What Jane and Tracy in *Eyes of a Stranger* lack in athletic ability, they make up in resourcefulness: the blind Tracy throws hot coffee in the face of her assailant, putting them at least temporarily on equal terms, and her sister grimly pulls the trigger. Julie, in *Positive I.D.*, proves herself as skillful in mugging one man and shooting another as she is in creating a new legal identity for herself. Jennifer in *I Spit on Your Grave* turns out to be perfectly capable of rigging up a spring-noose, driving a speedboat, slicing off genitalia, and getting rid of bodies. The women of the *Ladies' Club* vigilante squad locate, seduce, sedate, and castrate the rapists on their hit list with perfect efficiency; Julie, the policewoman of the group, is a karate expert. And so on; female self-sufficiency, both physical and mental, is the hallmark of the rape-revenge genre. (Some of these female avengers are more convincing in their role than others; if Farrah Fawcett of *Extremities* stands at the more credible end of the continuum, Linda Blair in *Savage Streets* stands at the other.) It is perhaps no accident that the "masculinization" of the rape victim is accompanied by a "normalization" of the rapist (that is, the decline of the rapist-as-psychopathic-creep and the rise of the rapist-as-standard-guy). It is as though narratives of rape stand in a zero-sum relation to denial mechanisms. If feminism took away one standby denial mechanism (rape is committed by people totally unlike oneself), feminism has also supplied a happy substitute (self-defense and assertiveness training for women). If a fair percentage of males go around feeling even faintly guilty on one hand at their own complicity in creating and maintaining a world in which women cannot walk alone after dark and/or, on the other, at their reluctance to play the role of protector in a world that has grown unsafe for them as well, then it is clear how these films might afford relief.

But there must be more to the story than that. For revenge fantasies to work, there must be something worth avenging—something egregious enough to justify hideous retaliation. In the case of rape-revenge films, that something has to do not only with rape, but with the power dynamic between men and women that makes rape happen in the first place and, in the second, that makes it so eminently avengeable. We might expect that an unadorned attack on the part of a savage psychopath would be cause enough, but for whatever reason, the isolated-act explanation is not sufficient in the modern examples. As if in deference to the feminist discussion of rape in the last two decades, rape is virtually always seen not just as an individual act but as a social and political act as well. Ironically, then, the fantasy of female revenge, which may serve less than savory purposes for the male viewer, brings with it, is indeed predicated on, detailed and sometimes trenchant analyses of quotidian patriarchy.

In *I Spit on Your Grave*, that analysis turns on the dynamic of males in groups—how they egg each other on to increasingly abhorrent behavior, and then, when they are brought to account, how they disavow individual responsibility. *Ms. 45* plays in a rather different key. Except for a few moments in the Halloween party sequence, male buddyism per se is not an issue. The interest here lies rather in the way individual acts of domination add up to pervasive structural misogyny. The two rapes that open *Ms. 45* state the basic proposition: men use their superior strength to victimize women, and women for that reason live in constant threat. What follows is the social generalization of that physical fact: men plunder women not only sexually, but economically and socially as well. Thana kills not only for her own literal rape, but for the figurative rape of all women. *Ms. 45* is a virtual checklist of masculine privilege. *Ladies' Club* concerns itself not with the reasons men rape (that is a given), but rather with the variety of ways that "good" men (boyfriends, husbands) fail to comprehend the nature and significance of the crime—a failure that inheres in the law itself. *Hunter's Blood*, one of the few hybrid forms to pursue an analysis of masculinity, considers rape and hunting ("that male ritual") part and parcel of the same masculinist ideology. *Positive I.D.* focuses on the way rapes and rape trials are publicized—what several of these films call the "second rape." *Lipstick*'s analysis is multilayered. The immediate reason for the rape is male backlash: men rape when rape is the only way they have left of asserting their domination over women.[31] But *Lipstick*'s trial defense also exposes the cultural context for rape. Because Chris, in her capacity as a world-famous model, sells an image of herself as a woman "asking for it," she is construed, by the court and by the culture, as party to the rape; and to the extent that women everywhere admire and imitate her, and buy the products she is advertising, they too are "asking for it," and they too are construed to be party to whatever rapes might come their way.

But the real concern of *Lipstick*, and of the other mainstream versions of the rape-revenge drama, is with the law and the legal system. We see the rape in *Lipstick* with our own eyes; we watch the man overpower the woman against her objections, tie her to the bed, and sodomize her. Chris decides to pursue the case legally despite the warning that to do so constitutes "its own form of rape" and also despite the fact that her boyfriend Steve, initially eager to have her press charges, changes his tune when he finds out that it will become public (tune changing on the part of the boyfriend is another cliché of the tradition). What emerges in court is quite another story: a "rough sex" narrative in which Chris is claimed to have been a consenting partner with masochistic tastes. The jury buys the lie and the rapist is acquitted. When the rapist later assaults her younger sister, Chris takes the law into her own hands and murders him in a parking lot. The law fails in *Eyes of a Stranger*, too, but in a rather different way. A rapist/killer ("phone freak") is on the loose, but when a woman calls the police to report suspicious phone calls, an officer responds in some irritation that they don't have time to deal with all the inquiries the television reports are generating and that they'll try to get out in the morning; the caller is of course attacked and killed that night. And when the hero of the piece, Jane, begins to suspect one of her neighbors of being the killer and to submit bits of evidence

---

[31] "When other expressions of manhood such as gainful employment and economic success are blocked," writes Robert Staples, "those men will express their frustration and masculinity against women" ("Commentary," p. 363). Menachim Amir has argued that such men are the ones most likely to commit gang-rape as they compete for status with one another" (*Patterns in Forcible Rape*).

to her criminal lawyer boyfriend Steve, he is dismissive: "Before you start taking the law into your own hands, think for a minute . . ." The evidence is circumstantial, he explains; if he were to take it to court, he would lose and his reputation as an up-and-coming criminal lawyer would be ruined. When Jane ends up indeed taking the law into her own hands (she shoots the killer in the act of assaulting her sister), it is because the proper authorities refused to take it into theirs. *Ladies' Club*, a poorly made but ideologically energetic film based on the novel *Sisterhood* by Betty Black and Casey Bishop, is precisely *about* the failure of rape law ("Where rape is concerned, the system stinks"). Angry in the first instance at how few rapists are actually convicted (this film too turns on a successful "rough sex" defense) and in the second instance at the fact that even those who are convicted and sentenced are soon released to rape again or to kill the women who turned them in, a group of rape victims and relatives of rape victims form a self-help group in which they locate, capture, and castrate recidivist offenders (in the interest of reducing their testosterone levels).

Extremities too takes sharp aim at the law—at the distinction it draws between rape and attempted rape, at the issue of consent, and, again, at its failure to acknowledge the fact that the men who are released can freely return and punish the women who put them away. Joe never quite rapes Marjorie. He is on the verge in the car when she escapes (she goes directly to the police but quickly realizes there is no point in even filing a charge under the circumstances), and he is again on the verge when, having traced her home address, he captures her in her house. But as he shouts when the tables are turned, "Go ahead! Go ahead and call the cops! You can't prove a fucking thing! You got no witnesses, you got no come up your snatch, you got nothing, pussy. It's my word against yours!" And even if she *does* win the case, he says, he'll come right back and get her as soon as he's free. Marjorie gets the point and sets about digging a grave in the yard to bury him alive. Her roommates, when they come home, are shocked at her fury and touched by Joe's bid for pity. But Marjorie is implacable. He'll come back, she says, and kill them all: "Choose: him or us." Only when she has extracted a full confession in front of the others (holding a knife to his genitals) is she willing to turn him over to the police.

With *The Accused*, the rape-revenge drama hits Oscar level. It is perhaps no coincidence that the most highly produced version of the story to date should also be the one not only most focused on third-party intervention but also the one in which the third party succeeds in meting out justice, thereby proving the judicial system woman-

friendly after all. It is of course true that the story is constrained by
the facts of the real-life case on which it is based, but it is also true
that there have been a fair number of cases in the last decade, some
of them just as highly publicized, in which the outcomes are less
happy: cases in which men plead "rough sex" and are acquitted,
cases in which men are convicted and sentenced but come back to
kill the women who turned them in, and so on.[32] But for reasons at
which we can only guess, it is *The Accused*'s happy-ending, "feel-
good" version of the rape-revenge story that made it through the
Hollywood gauntlet and that proved one of the biggest box-office
movies of the year.

The Accused has its considerable virtues, one of which is the broad-
side way it engages the issue of consent and another of which is the
way it highlights the legal difficulties in prosecuting rape. And like
other films of the tradition, it is informed by an analysis of sorts.
Rape, in *The Accused*, is male sport. The college boys who turn up at
the bar that night and end up party to the rape have just come from
"the game"; the television set there keeps blaring out sports events;
for her job waitressing at "The Dugout," Sarah (the victim) dresses
as a baseball playerette; a framed newspaper on the wall in the DA's
office bears the headline "Plowing Match"; the rape takes place on a
pinball machine featuring the game "Slam Dunk"; and during the
rape itself, the male spectators cheer and clap and chant in unison
"One, two, three, four—poke that pussy till it's sore" and the rapists
in turn undertake their task as if it were the World Series (one spits
on his hands as he steps into the batter's box). The rape-sport analogy is hardly new—*I Spit on Your Grave* made the same point a decade earlier, right down to the recognition that they also serve who
cheer from the sidelines—but with *The Accused* it enters the mainstream, and the status of those who serve by cheering from the sidelines is established as criminal.

If something gets gained in this most civilized version of the rape-
revenge story, something also gets lost. There is a sense in which the
third party, the legal system, becomes the hero of the piece; focus
has in any case shifted from the victim to her lawyer, from questions
of why men rape and how victims feel to questions of what constitutes evidence, from bedroom (or wherever) as the site of confrontation to courthouse. (Compare the final shot of *I Spit on Your Grave*,
which shows us a triumphant Jennifer speeding along in a motorboat, with *The Accused*'s helicopter shot of the courthouse.) Sarah is

[32] Katha Pollitt enumerates a variety of recent examples in "Violence in a Man's
World."

The final shot of *I Spit on Your Grave*.

vehement enough in her wish for revenge ("I want those mother-
fuckers put away forever!"), and when the law fails her on the first
round, she even engages in an act of vigilante justice (ramming her
car into the pickup of one of the men who cheered her rapists on),
but for the most part, the retaliatory urge is displaced onto the
woman assistant district attorney assigned the case. And in our increasing engagement with that assistant DA's uphill struggle (to plea-
bargain effectively in the first trial, to hit upon the right charge for
the second, to gain the support of her cynical colleagues, to triumph
over the warning that she will ruin her career, to talk a reluctant witness into testifying, and so on), we lose sight of what the lower forms
of the rape drama unfailingly keep at center stage: the raped woman
herself. And the fact that justice finally is served not through the
straightforward prosecution of rape but through the unorthodox de-
ployment of a statute concerning criminal solicitation—presented, in
the film, as a stroke of luck—does little to dispel suspicion about the
law's efficacy in such cases.

No less undermining is the fact that the film ends where many
women's fear begins, at the moment the jury delivers the "guilty"
verdict. As I have suggested, a more or less explicit complaint about
the justice system in the rape-revenge tradition is the understanding
that even when the law succeeds in the short run, it may fail in the
the long run. A recent *New York Times Magazine* essay offers the case

The final shot of *The Accused*.

of Lisa Bianco, the "battered Indiana woman who finally, after hundreds of attacks, succeeded in having her ex-husband put in prison, only to be murdered by him on a brief furlough"—of which a friend said, "What did she expect? There's only so much the system can do. She should have gotten a gun and blasted him."[33] *Extremities* turns on just this point; as the assailant himself points out, even in the unlikely event that he's convicted and sentenced, he'll be out soon enough and back to kill the women who turned him in. Their choice is exactly what Marjorie says it is: to kill or be killed ("Choose: him or us"). And *Ladies' Club* is a wall-to-wall indictment of the system that either fails to convict rapists or convicts and sentences them only to release them so they can rape (and/or murder) again: "Where rape is concerned, the system stinks." From the perspective of the rape-revenge tradition, and indeed from the perspective of those involved in real-life male-on-female violence, *The Accused*, in its implication that the story is over when the men are sentenced, is pure Pollyannaism.

Finally, there is the fact that although *The Accused* seems to bring male gazing to account (by bringing to bear on the cheering onlookers a charge of criminal solicitation), the authority for that conviction, and indeed for the status of the incident as a whole, rests finally and

[33] Ibid., p. 16.

solely on the authority of a male spectator: Ken, the college boy who witnessed the event, called the police, and finally, after some equivocating, provided the testimony that convicted his fellows. The importance of his vision is established in the first shots of the film, and it is remarkable how often and at what length the film has us look at his eyes looking at something—or nothing, as in the case of two intercut shots of him staring pensively out of his fraternity house window, shots whose only purpose can be to remind us that amid all the conflicting accounts there *is* a truth and *this* is where it resides. Likewise the rendition of the rape itself, during which the camera seems as interested in watching Ken's face watching Sarah being raped as it is in watching the rape itself. But the real giveaway is the fact that the rape itself can be shown directly—the flashback can happen—only when Ken takes the stand and narrates his eyewitness account. Sarah, the victim, testified to precisely the same events shortly before, but whereas her testimony remained her own version, his testimony becomes our version, *the* version. After a few sentences, his voice-over ceases and the rape unfolds before us as visible, omniscient history takes over. Seldom has a set of male eyes been more privileged; without their witness, there would be no case—there would in fact, as the defense attorney notes, be no rape.[34] Those male eyes point up a fundamental difference between *The Accused* and the lower forms of the rape-revenge story, in which there is a rape because a woman knows she has been raped. The features of *The Accused* that make it such a welcome contribution to the ongoing consciousness-raising regarding the workings of rape law are the very features that make one understand just why the self-help versions of the story not only exist but flourish. As the public reaction to the Bernard Goetz subway incident makes clear, even respectable citizens can sink to the vigilante mentality when they feel inadequately acknowledged by the justice system. *The Accused* shows the system working—but only barely (only by loophole, actually), and only slowly, and only because a man of goodwill and a very smart, sympathetic, and stubborn female lawyer happen to be in the right place at the right time.

Although *The Accused* may at first glance seem a world apart from *I Spit on Your Grave*, the two films are, in fact, high and low (and pretty and ugly) versions of one and the same story, right down to the sports metaphor. I have included *The Accused* in this survey not only for that reason, but also because it owes its conception, its

[34] This is perhaps the answer to Leonard Maltin's "only quibble: Was the climactic reenactment really necessary?" (*TV Movies and Video Guide: 1990*, s.v. "The Accused").

terms, and much of its success to a lowlife ancestry that has been neatly erased in its migration from the category of horror to the category of courtroom drama. But take away *The Accused*'s elaborate displacement machinery—its legal, psychological, ethical, and social ruminations—and relocate it beyond the reach of the law ("out there where no one can hear you scream") and you have *I Spit on Your Grave*: the story of a gang-raped woman hell-bent on revenge. One cannot quarrel with civilization, but it is sometimes useful to look past its comforts to see the stories we tell ourselves, as a culture, for what they really are. I suggested earlier that what disturbs about *I Spit on Your Grave* is its perverse simplicity, the way it closes all the intellectual doors and windows and leaves us staring at the lex talionis unadorned. Let me now be more explicit: what disturbs about *I Spit on Your Grave* is the way it exposes the inner workings of *The Accused* and films like it—the way it reminds us that lots and lots of the movies and television dramas that we prefer to think of in higher terms are in fact funded by impulses we would rather deny. *I Spit on Your Grave*, in short, is the repressed of *The Accused*, and I suspect that it is for this reason as much as any other that it has met with the punitive response it has.[35]

The rape-revenge genre deserves fuller treatment than I have been able to give it here. Not only is it a premier processing site for the modern debate on sexual violence in life and law, as I have suggested, but it presents us with the same contradictions as the slasher film—and even more starkly. With few exceptions (e.g., *Ladies' Club*), these films, in which women are heroized and men vilified, are written, produced, and directed by males; and although the mainstream versions (e.g., *Lipstick*, *Extremities*, *The Accused*) are presumably aimed at and consumed by mixed audiences, the examples at the lower end of the scale appear, perhaps even more than the slasher film, to be disproportionately if not overwhelmingly consumed by young males.[36] Actually, the rape-revenge film goes the slasher one better, for rape-revenge films not only have female heroes and male villains, they repeatedly and explicitly articulate feminist politics. So trenchant is the critique of masculine attitudes and behavior in such films as *I Spit on Your Grave*, *Ms. 45*, *Eyes of a Stranger*, *Positive I.D.* (up to a point), and moments in *Mother's Day* (the scene on the pitcher's mound) that, were they made by women, they would be derided as male-bashing. (Were they mainly consumed by women, they

[35] On *Thelma and Louise*, a rape-revenge film of sorts that appeared as this book was going to press, see the Afterword, below.
[36] On audiences, see the Introduction.

would by the same token be derided as a sop to feminism.) I have suggested some ways in which the rape-revenge plot may not be as inimical to male interests as it might at first seem (ways having to do with the abnegation of male responsibility in matters of sexual violence), but these "advantages" hardly seem sufficient explanation for the market success of the genre among male viewers, nor do they reasonably account for the intense engagement of the spectator in the revenge drive on which the drama is inevitably predicated.

The only way to account for the spectator's engagement in the revenge drive is to assume his engagement with the rape-avenging woman. I argued in chapter 1 that the slasher film draws the male spectator into identification with the Final Girl, and that the slasher genre is predicated on spectatorial identification with females in fear and pain. So too the rape-revenge film, even more unambiguously and even more passionately. The female victim-hero is the one with a backstory and the one whose experience structures the action from beginning to end. Every narrative and cinematic device is deployed to draw us into her perceptions—her pain and humiliation at the rape, her revenge calculations, her grim satisfaction when she annihilates her assailant. Although earlier cinematic rapes allow for a large measure of spectator identification with the rapist (I am thinking of *Frenzy* and *Straw Dogs* in particular), films from the mid-1970s go to increasing lengths, both cinematic and narrative, to dissociate us from that position. Even when the rapes are shown, they are shown in ways that align us with the victim. And often the rapes are not shown at all but are only reported or suggested in flashback (in which case we may not even see the rapist). It may be impossible to depict a rape in a way that forecloses on any possibility of sadistic participation, but it is certainly the case that the array of cinematic and narrative devices traditionally employed to that end are not in evidence in the films discussed here.

In distancing oneself from the rapist, one also distances oneself from the rape, however. There is an odd sense in which the rape-revenge film simultaneously declares and denies the sexual nature of the crime. The fact that explicit rape is just one of several precipitating crimes, and a recent one at that, in the larger revenge tradition (it fills a structural slot that can also be filled by theft, murder of a family member, land dispossession, and the like) reminds us that this subject is as historically overdetermined as the next. Ironically, it may be the feminist account of rape in the last two decades that has both authorized a film like *I Spit on Your Grave* and shaped its politics. The redefinition of rape as an offense on a par with murder, together with the well-publicized testimonials on the part of terrified and angry victims, must be centrally responsible for lodging rape as a crime deserving of the level of punishment on which revenge narratives are predicated. (After all, *I Spit on Your Grave* is nothing more or less than a dramatization of the "castrate rapists" slogan of the seventies.) No less welcome to popular cinema has been the redefinition of rape as less an act of sex than an act of power—"not a crime of irrational, impulsive, uncontrollable lust," in Susan Brownmiller's formulation, but a "deliberate, hostile, violent act of degradation and possession on the part of a would-be conqueror, designed to intimidate and inspire fear."[37]

Whatever else they may be, these are terms that men can "identify with."[38] Whereas rapes of the *Straw Dogs* (1971) sort, in which the woman is up to a point complicit and even sexually welcoming, must complicate the male viewer's relation to the victim position, rapes of the *Ms. 45* or even *I Spit on Your Grave* variety, largely desexualized acts of humiliating force, slide easily into the popular-culture lexicon of heinous crime and sweet revenge. It is no coincidence that the emergence of rape as a full-fledged cinematic subject is simultaneous with its being yoked to a retaliation plot and coded as an action film.[39] And for the action plot, resting as it does on an aesthetic of suffering and retribution, and hungry as it is for more and worse humiliations, the "new rape" is a natural. Tania Modleski has defined "post-feminism" as the appropriation of feminist thought for nonfeminist purposes, and despite the fact that the politics of the rape-revenge film are not readily classifiable as non- or antifeminist (and also despite the fact that feminists themselves have on other grounds begun to question the desexualization of rape),[40] it is certainly the case that these movies constitute an unsettling unintended consequence.

Still, however desexualized, minimalized, and distanced, the crime *is* a rape, and the question is why—what, in other words, the male

[37] Susan Brownmiller, *Against Our Will*, p. 439.

[38] Of *Ms. 45*, Zoë Tamerlis (the actress who played Thana) is reported to have said, "It's truly, in my more elaborate view, about anyone who's been raped or screwed in any way. The real villain is Thana's boss, who wants to keep his women for forty years in his service. He's the one person she sets out to kill" (as quoted by John McCarty, *Psychos*, p. 129).

[39] A number of the rape-revenge films I viewed in connection with this chapter are categorized in video rental stores under "action" or "suspense." Production values, not just subject matter, play a role in the perception of genre. High-budget forms are likely to be categorized as drama, suspense, or action and low-budget forms as horror or cult—even when the plots are virtually identical.

[40] See, in particular, Monique Plaza's critique of Foucault's wish to "desexualize" rape law ("Our Costs and Their Benefits").

viewer's stake might be in imagining himself reacting to that most quintessentially feminine of experiences. The answer lies, perhaps, in the question: it is precisely *because* rape is the most quintessentially feminine of experiences—the limit case of powerlessness and degradation—that it is such a powerful motivation, such a clean ticket, for revenge. I have argued that the center of gravity of these films lies more in the reaction (the revenge) than the act (the rape), but to the extent that the revenge fantasy derives its force from *some* degree of imaginary participation in the act itself, in the victim position, these films are predicated on cross-gender identification of the most extreme, corporeal sort.

THE BODY IN QUESTION

But how do we square the male-on-male rape of *Deliverance* with the female standard in the tradition before and since? We might be inclined to dismiss it as a singular, "literary" variant were it not for the obvious influence it has had on low-horror versions—including, in fact, on *I Spit on Your Grave*. Thus although the heterosexual rape of *Spit* is very much in line with the tradition at large (including the pre-*Deliverance* tradition), it is also the case that one of its immediate models was a homosexual one. That fact alone suggests that the sexual politics of the rape-revenge tradition, at least in its recent phase, are not as straightforward as they may at first seem. Certainly *Hunter's Blood* (1986), another *Deliverance*-based text, mixes homo- and hetero- in ways that unsettle the apparent categories.

I have mentioned *Hunter's Blood* in passing, and it is now time to give a fuller account. Even in the horror world of promiscuous borrowing, *Hunter's Blood* (from 1986) is a highly derivative piece of work, referring not only to *Deliverance* but also to *The Hills Have Eyes* and the "human meat" films (e.g., *Texas Chain Saw Massacre*). It tells the story of five men (two are brothers, two are father and son, and one, Marty, is the New York lawyer) who go on a deer-hunting expedition in the northern Arkansas wilderness. The wilderness, as I mentioned earlier, is doomed, for two of the big-city hunters, the brothers Al and Ralph, work for a company that, with the legal help of Marty, is about to timber the forest into oblivion. The city men could hardly be more obnoxious about and toward the country folk they encounter at the "redneck bar" where they stop for beer. (This is the site of the barbecuing incident and the female bartender incident.) After a car chase in which they eventually leave their "redneck" pursuers in the dust, our city heroes turn their Bronco off the road and tear cross-country to their destination. There they set up camp. Two game wardens on horseback come by and warn them that the woods are full of poachers—dangerous, primitive folk. The poachers show up that very evening and are threatening to rape three of the city men (who are both drunk and stoned) when David and his father, Mason, return from a walk and drive the poachers off at gunpoint. (Although the poachers and the "rednecks" are different sets of folks, they stand in an economic relationship, the former supplying the latter with meat—meat that is of course city-bound.)

The remainder of the film charts the efforts of the country poachers to rape/kill the city hunters and the efforts of the hunters to escape with their lives. The chief difference between poachers and hunters, the film observes, is that the latter own the law. The hunters realize the extent of their danger only when they find the bodies of the two game wardens strung up on trees. The hunters find it in themselves to wound and kill as many of the poachers as possible, and the poachers in turn kill Ralph and wound Mason. This chase or "feud" sequence is crosscut with a sequence showing David's girlfriend Melanie driving to the country to join him as they earlier agreed. When she arrives at the bar, the "redneck" there offers to drive her into the woods, but he of course drives her straight into the arms of the poachers. She too is strung up and David, who has been captured and brought to the same place, is invited to watch her be raped. Just as Redbeard is on the verge of penetrating Melanie, David breaks loose and frees her; the two of them vanquish their captors (Melanie stabbing Redbeard in the back with antlers) and, after a chase through the woods, jump onto a passing train.[41]

"I wouldn't dream of joining your male ritual," Melanie says in the film's opening scene when David suggests she might meet him in the country. And male ritual—ceremonialized deer hunting—is precisely what *Hunter's Blood* is all about. The men themselves speculate on the meaning of hunting in a campfire conversation the first evening. For Mason, it is not the hunting but the stalking. The fatuous Marty suggests that "the act of hunting brings out a rapport with a certain forgotten part of you"—to which Ralph retorts, "Yeah, the killer part." For Al, the crudest but most on-point member of the group, it is somehow sexual: the appeal of hunting for him lies in facing "whatever's out there" with "just your brains and your balls." "A man's got to *feel* his balls," he exclaims. "I mean, when a man gets old enough for his pecker to stand up, he's got to go hunting."

What distinguishes *Hunter's Blood*'s otherwise predictable working

[41] The closing shot of the film shows us the back of the train—which features an advertisement for Razorback Meats. Just where the train is going, on a city delivery or back to the country source, is not clear, but the sign is ominous; the horror, we are to assume, is not over.

out of the rifle = penis equation is its interest in the object: what or whom exactly the standing pecker is aimed *at*. There are no actual rapes in *Hunter's Blood*. There are repeated threats and attempts, though—and with the exception of the Melanie episode, they are all threats and attempts traded between men. If the "male" of "male ritual" is a standard genital trope, the "ritual" has to do with enacting a barely disguised buggery drama. At the level of hunting, that means preferring a buck—"a *big* buck"—to a doe as the object of one's bullet.[42] But what our heroes encounter in the woods is not unarmed deer but armed men—other bearers of standing peckers, and other seekers of "male ritual."

"I'm going to ream your butt in a minute, Ralph," Al responds to one of his brother's remarks during the drive to the country. "These road trips bore me," Ralph responds. "I'm just trying to amuse myself." "*I'll* 'bore' you," says Al, with emphasis. Later, during the car chase following the encounter in Tobe's Bar,[43] the locals shout out remarks like "We're gonna run right up their ass!" and "We're gonna run right up their butts!" Word nearly becomes flesh when, in the woods that night, the poachers start unzipping their pants and choosing up the city men ("He's a pretty one, ain't he?"); the scene breaks off when Mason and David return and scatter the poachers. The rather ambitious standing-pecker theory of *Hunter's Blood* thus links the stalking and shooting of (preferably male) deer with the stalking and raping of (preferably male) humans—all of which is further linked to ingestion. When David has been caught and strung up from a tree (in the same way that deer are strung up for gutting and that Melanie is later strung up for raping), the poachers remark that he "looks tasty": "You know what we do to bucks, don't you?" But after all these exchanges between males, the person who comes closest to being explicitly raped is Melanie. It is as though she is imported for the purpose; her role in the film as a whole consists of little more than a brief appearance in the opening scene (when she sees David off) and then, midway through the film, a few brief and sketchy glances at her drive to the country, her capture, and (with David looking on) near-rape, and (with David) escape.[44]

We could hardly ask for a more paradigmatic case of the confusion,

[42] Ironically, the one deer they stalk and attempt to shoot, and call a buck, is clearly a doe. Whether the misidentification is intended or accidental is not clear, but given the thematics of the film, it is in either case marvelously telling.

[43] Presumably a reference to director Tobe Hooper, whose *Texas Chain Saw Massacre* is a benchmark in the urbanoia tradition.

[44] The near-rape of Melanie answers the humiliation of the "redneck" barmaid in the early beer-drinking scene.

or confusability, of male and female bodies. Not even in the rape-revenge film, it seems, is gender clear-cut. One reason the slasher film can go as far as it does in playing with gender is that it deals with genital behavior only indirectly, through the metaphor of violence; thus women as well as men can come by knives or power drills, and men as well as women can have holes drilled or bored into them. The slasher film is in this respect rather like the vampire film, which, through its symbolic displacement of "real" or genital sex onto mouths and necks, with which women and men are equally well endowed, allows for a full set of transgressive gender exchanges.[45] The rape-revenge film, however, would seem to require the use of a real penis and a real orifice.[46] Anchored in the literal, it cannot engage in the obvious kinds of gender play that characterize the more symbolic or fantastic forms of modern horror. And yet even this most body-based of genres manages to complicate the sex/gender system—especially on the side of the victim-hero, whose gender is clearly coded feminine (at least in the first phase of the story) but whose sex, it seems, is up for grabs. *I Spit on Your Grave*, *Deliverance*, and *Hunter's Blood* all tell the same story; but where one puts a vagina, the second puts a male anus, and the third equivocates. The equivocation of *Hunter's Blood* is particularly telling, for it suggests that the (male) anus and the vagina are, in certain social matters, one and the same thing. Nor is the gender of the rapist as secure as it might seem. At least in the rape-revenge films that operate on the city/country axis, the rapist's masculinity is typically compromised by his economic victimization. In *Deliverance*, that victimization is specifically figured as itself a "rape," and equivalent notions of cultural or economic emasculation sound loudly throughout the tradition.[47] Paradoxically enough—and the generalization extends beyond the rape-revenge film—it is the man who is deprived of the phallus who must live by the penis.

But let us stick to the status of the raped person, the victim-hero

---

[45] See especially Christopher Craft, " 'Kiss Me with Those Red Lips.' "

[46] Although several of the rape scenes also involve at least the threat of forced fellatio, that act is typically presented as following on, and secondary to, vaginal/anal rape. The standard hierarchy is: vagina, then anus, then mouth in the case of a woman (e.g., *I Spit on Your Grave*, *Rape of Love*) and, in the case of *Deliverance*, anus and then mouth. For this reason I have focused on vaginal and anal rape. On the symbolic relation between vagina and mouth, see chapter 2, above.

[47] *Demon Seed*, a rape narrative with practically no revenge, makes much of the tit-for-tat logic. "I refuse to assist you in the rape of the earth," Proteus (the all-powerful computer-camera) tells the scientist who designed him for precisely an earth-raping project. Instead, Proteus rapes and impregnates the scientist's wife.

whose experience the rape-revenge film is all about. In the previous
two chapters, I have discussed "one-sex" logic as it has been elaborated by Thomas Laqueur—the notion, dominant in medical literature until the late eighteenth century (and recurrent in popular forms
since then), that male and female are merely inside versus outside
versions of a single genital system, differing in degree of warmth or
coolness but essentially the same in form and function. One-sex reasoning thus rests on "systems of analogues" whereby male parts are
thought to have their counterparts in the female and (to a lesser extent) vice versa. The "system of analogues" that underwrites the possession film, I suggested, is one that repeatedly associates vagina
with (male) anus, and the question now is whether the same "system" underwrites the rape-revenge films as well. It clearly underwrites *Hunter's Blood*, and it provides a ready explanation for the relation between the heterosexual rape of *I Spit on Your Grave* and the
homosexual rape of the film—*Deliverance*—that stood as its immediate model. Viewed as a group, these three films present a universe
in which men are sodomizable in much the same way that women
are rapable and with much the same meaning and consequences.
They suggest a universe, that is, in which vagina and anus are indeed for all practical purposes the same thing and a universe in
which that thing has no specific relation to male or female bodies. [48]

Again, the world of one-sex reasoning is one in which gender is
primary and sex secondary—a world, that is, in which gender pre-
cedes and determines sex. It is not that the abject terror of the slasher
film—screaming, pleading, sobbing—proceeds from the femaleness
of the victim, but that the femaleness of the victim proceeds from the
fact that abject terror, the slasher film's raison d'être, is gendered
feminine (though not so completely so that *all* victims are female).
Likewise the rape-revenge film, of course, the femaleness of whose
rape victim proceeds from the quintessential femininity of being
raped (though again not so quintessentially feminine that *all* victims
are female). [49] In both cases, the gender of the "victim" part of the

[48] *Vagina*, meaning "sword sheath," could also refer to the anus in Latin sources.
The female sheath had no separate name (construed, as it was, as an inverted penis)
until relatively late—according to Laqueur, around 1700 in the European vernaculars
(*Making Sex*, pp. 159 and 270 n. 60).

[49] In fact, in their focus on a girl victim-hero who survives near-death to rise and kill
her assailant, the rape-revenge and slasher films share the same general plot. The difference (apart from the fact that one inhabits a world of violence including sex and the
other a world without sex) is one of proportions: in the slasher film, the girl defeats
the killer only at the end and almost in spite of herself, whereas in the rape-revenge
film, the girl spends at least half the film calculating and taking revenge.

story (the rape sequence in the rape-revenge film, the flight-and-pursuit sequence in the slasher) overrides the gender of the "hero" part of the story as far as the fixing of the main character's sex is concerned. In chapter 1, I proposed that the willingness of the slasher film to re-represent the traditionally male hero as an anatomical female suggests that at least one traditionally heroic act, triumphant self-rescue, is no longer strictly gendered masculine. The rape-revenge film is a similar case, only more so; it is not just triumphant self-rescue in the final moments of the film that the woman achieves, but calculated, lengthy, and violent revenge of a sort that would do Rambo proud.[50] (Paradoxically, it is the experience of being brutally raped that makes a "man" of a woman.) What I am suggesting, once again, is that rape-revenge films too operate on the basis of a one-sex body, the maleness or femaleness of which is performatively determined by the social gendering of the acts it undergoes or undertakes.[51]

The advantage of thinking about the rape-revenge genre in terms of the one-sex model is that it obviates the two-sex question of which body, male or female, is *really* at stake, and which of the films in question, therefore, tells the truth and which lies. If the body in question is experienced as neither strictly male nor strictly female, but as a common body with a penetrable "sheath" figurable variously as anus and vagina, then *Deliverance* is telling one part of the truth, *I Spit on Your Grave* another, and *Hunter's Blood* both. This is not to say that the male spectator will have identical reactions to Bobby's and Jennifer's rapes. Representation does matter, and the rape of Bobby, because he is figured as a male, is accorded a level of dishonor that the rape of Jennifer is not, and hers, because she is female, is accorded a level of danger that his is not—differences in code that must affect the spectator's unconscious response as well. What I am proposing is that the position of rape victim *in general* knows no sex, and that a film like *I Spit on Your Grave* is literally predicated on the assumption that *all* viewers, male and female alike, will take Jennifer's part, and via whatever set of psychosexual translations, "feel" her violation. Without that identification, the revenge phase of the drama can make no sense.

---

[50] It is worth remembering, however, that the weapon-wielding female avenger of modern popular culture does have her antecedents in Greek myth and, in Germanic heroic legend, in such figures as Brynhild and Kriemhild/Gudrun and the Norse women of, for example, *Laxdaela Saga*. Historically speaking, it is the splitting of the functions of suffering and revenge (especially between female and male) that is the innovation, and the all-in-one form that is prior.

[51] The formulation is Judith Butler's (*Gender Trouble*).

CITY GIRLS AND   YOU KNOW I LOVE WESTERNS BECAUSE I

REDNECK RAPISTS   DISGUISE A LOT OF MY FILMS. THEY'RE

                               REALLY WESTERNS UNDERNEATH.

                               —*Horror director John Carpenter*

In what I have called the hybrid film—
the rape-revenge film staged on the city/country axis—two sets of
politics come into play and are played off against one another: the
politics of gender and the politics of urban/rural social class.

I Spit on Your Grave (1977) is one of the first films to stage the female
self-revenge drama in city/country terms. On one hand a film like
Ms. 45, Positive I.D., or *Lipstick*, in which a woman virtually annihilated by a rape mends and rises to annihilate her attackers, *Spit* sets
a woman against men and makes overt gestures toward feminism.
On the other, it draws on the venerable urbanoid themes of B movies, working to justify the annihilation of country people by their
guilty city cousins. It is to the politics of this combination, which associates the city with the woman and the country with the man, that
I now turn.

If Jennifer is raped because she is a woman, she is also, according
to the logic of popular culture, a woman because she is raped. Although sex need not always follow gender (as *Deliverance* demonstrates), rape stories traditionally want female victims. She is likewise
a woman because she is from the city. There has always been a
strong hint of the unmasculine in the attributes ascribed to urban folk
in a country setting. Even when they are tall and healthy, city men
are seen as appearance-concerned, trinket-laden, physically weak
and incompetent, queasy about the hard facts of rural life (animal
slaughter, for example), unfamiliar with weapons and fearful of
them, overly dependent on the buyable services of others, and even,
under duress, given to tears (so Marty in *Hunter's Blood*). Certainly
the city men of *Deliverance*, with the exception of Lewis, are less than
masculine specimens. From such a man to an actual woman—from
Bobby in *Deliverance* to Jennifer in *I Spit on Your Grave*—is but a short
step. Add high heels and you have the hypercivilized urbanite incar-
nate. The sense of effeminacy that has always attended the worry
about hypercivilization is now manifest in a "naturally" rapable female body.

Although their function as rapists would in itself seem sufficient to
guarantee the maleness of Johnny and his fellows in *I Spit on Your*

Grave,[52] it is worth remembering that even in the larger city-revenge tradition, country folks are conspicuously male even when they are not rapists and even when the targets of their aggression are not women. There are, in other words, reasons beyond the simple possession of the "offending weapon" that country folk are, by virtual definition, menfolk. Their maleness also proceeds from their command of the manly skills (fixing cars, loading guns, skinning animals) whereby they intimidate their city visitors, and it must also proceed from the narrative need for a worthy opponent. The demonizing impulse that underwrites these films depends on the fiction that country folk always pose an immediate threat of brute force, and for that threat to be sufficiently credible to justify their annihilation, it must be male. The maleness of the country, in other words, is even more overdetermined than the femaleness of the city.

But the picture is, of course, not so simple. Jennifer's transformation from passive victim to aggressive avenger, from mutilatee to mutilator, can be construed as a regendering not unlike the one undergone by the Final Girl of slasher films. The difference is that whereas the Final Girl answers a stabbing with a stabbing in a narrative that explicitly equates the knife with the penis, Jennifer answers an explicit rape with a castration, a hanging, an ax blow, and a propeller mutilation, and although we may wish to understand those acts as symbolic rapes, the closest a penis-less person can get to the real thing, the film itself draws the equation only vaguely if at all. Nor do other rape-revenge films play up the potential analogy. It is an available meaning, but the fact that it is not particularly exploited suggests that it is not particularly central.

What *is* exploited, and what *is* central, is the gender snarl around the figure of the "redneck" rapist. I remarked earlier on the lengths to which these films go to establish right from the outset the disenfranchisement, recent or imminent, of rural folk; even before we meet them, we know that they have been (or are about to be) driven off their land, have been (or are about to be) deprived of their traditional livelihood, and so on. And although fixing cars, loading guns, and skinning animals are indeed coded as masculine behaviors that will be put to threatening use in the film's present, they are also understood to be short-run and last-ditch skills employed in an equally short-run and last-ditch act of resistance against what the locals of *Deliverance* call—and the term has some allegorical force—the "power

[52] A counterexample of sorts, though not from a rape-revenge film proper, is the supernatural rapist in *The Incubus* who turns out to be a beautiful woman transformed into a monstrous incubus and whose "ejaculate" is hence part semen and part menstrual blood.

company." This is an economic story, but it is one that is repeatedly told as a gender story and even, indirectly or directly, as a "rape" story. *Deliverance* may not be the first film to figure land seizure and economic exploitation in explicitly sexual terms ("We're gonna rape this whole goddamn landscape"), and it is certainly not the last. In one urbanoid film after another, the local people are presented as "fucked" by city interests even before real city people arrive on the scene. Country men may be male, in other words, but they are symbolically feminized, and as any viewer of horror knows, where feminized males are, violent trouble is soon to follow.

Despite their differences, particularly where the characteristics of the female victim-hero are concerned, the rape-revenge film and the slasher film tell similar gender stories. In both a feminine/feminized male or males (the slasher killer, it should be remembered, is typically figured as a mama's boy, a transvestite, or genitally defective) squares off against and is finally overpowered by a strong, young woman. As in the slasher film, the losing combination is the feminine male (he who is deprived of the phallus must live by the penis) and the winning combination is the masculine female. If the city raped the country metaphorically (raping the landscape, fucking up the only "unfucked-up" river in the South), the country responds in literal, carnal kind. Thus in the double-axis film, the (metaphorically) raped are pitted against the (literally) raped. And the question is no longer whether the city can sink to the barbarous levels of the country, but whether the urban female can sink to the barbarous standards set by the rural male. I have speculated in chapter 1 on the current appeal of this configuration and will not rehearse the arguments here beyond noting again that the figure of the self-saving Final Girl and the self-avenging rape victim may, for better or worse, be the main contribution to popular culture of the women's movement and the "new family." In either case, urbanoia is well served by its female victim-hero.

In the effort to account for the double-axis film's success, it might be useful to take it one axis at a time—to see, that is, what advantages accrue to the "class" story by its being told in connection with a gender story, and then to see what advantages accrue to the gender story by its attachment to a "class" story.

The first scenario assumes that the real story, the prior and primary story, is the economic and racial drama that looms so large in our national consciousness. The urbanoia films of the sixties and seventies and the settler-versus-Indian films of the thirties and forties bear an astonishing resemblance to one another—not only in plot structure and in political and economic sensibility, but in fine details of appearance, character, and behavior. The difference, of course, is that the redskins have become rednecks, the white settlers city vacationers, and the cavalry the corporation—the "power company." The new story of land plunder is a story of dam building, lumbering, mining, oil drilling, nuclear testing, toxic dumping—all of which work, in the same way that frontier settlement earlier worked, to enrich the haves at the expense of the have-nots. The justification for that process—how to acknowledge the guilt so as to allow ourselves (the films' "ourselves": city people) to get on with business—lies ready at hand in the traditional story of an Indian atrocity repaid with genocide and a land grab. I do not mean to suggest that urbanoia films are retelling the Indian story for its original purpose only (although I suspect that there remains some of that original purpose in the retelling); I am suggesting, rather, that in telling a new story, essentially a class story, about real estate plunder, we fall back on the terms of the older, originary story that haunts our national consciousness.

That older story, of course, is no longer tellable in its original terms. What makes it tellable in modern terms is precisely its hybridization. The updating is perversely brilliant: by making the representative of urban interests (what would normally be taken as the white male elite) a woman, and the representatives of the country (what would in the western have been Native Americans) white males, these films exactly reverse the usual system of victim sympathies. That is, with a member of the gender underclass (a woman) representing the economic overclass (the urban rich) and members of the gender overclass (males) representing the economic underclass (the rural poor), a feminist politics of rape has been deployed in the service of class and racial guilt. Raped and battered, the haves can rise to annihilate the have-nots—all in the name of feminism.[53]

Let us now reverse the terms and give priority to the rape story. To assume that the rape drama is primary is to assume that the real work of these films is psychosexual and turns on the deep excitement generated by the vicarious living-through of violation, humiliation, and sadistic redemption—feelings that must be carefully concealed in their conscious expression—and that the class or economic/ethnic dimension plays a supporting role. The success among young male audiences of single-axis films like *Ms. 45* makes it clear that narrative and cinematic positioning can in themselves go a long way in insur-

---

[53] A woman, in other words, has been inserted into the "regeneration through violence" myth that Richard Slotkin finds characteristic of the frontier (Slotkin, *Regeneration through Violence*).

ing sympathy with the humiliation and rage of a raped person. But by coding the raped person as a "white settler" and the rapists "Indians," the hybrid film seals the guarantee. For the "white settler" role is an immediately familiar one in our cultural unconscious; it is one we have inhabited repeatedly, and one whose terms and outcome are secure. At some level, when we hear Johnny and his friends (in *I Spit on Your Grave*) whooping in the forest outside Jennifer's house at night, we must recognize the trope of the restless natives, and when we see Matthew deliver groceries and rush back to report to his companions, we must recognize the trope of the Indian who comes to trade and reconnoiter. To the psychosexual story of sweet victimization and sweet revenge, the "white settler" resonances add a kind of surplus mechanism, designed to suture us even more firmly into the underdog position.

The "white settler" resonances suture us into a familiar guilt-revenge dynamic as well. I suggested earlier that the city approaches the country guilty in the same way that the whites approach Indians guilty, and that the urbanoia plot works to resolve that guilt by justifying the annihilation of the guilt-inducing party. At first glance, the formula would seem not to apply to the rape-revenge films, for women hardly approach men bearing the same kind of exploitation- or abuse-guilt with which whites approach Indians or city approaches country. But if we understand the story in psychosexual terms, even the guilt dynamic may make a kind of sense. In chapter 4 I shall consider in some psychoanalytic detail the male viewer's stake in the kind of masochistic scenario—the adoption of the "feminine" position—that the rape-revenge film offers. (The centrality of *Deliverance* in the tradition guarantees that the "feminine" position knows no sex.) For the moment suffice it to say that, as a psychosexual document, *I Spit On Your Grave* may play on two powerful moments of the male oedipal drama: the fantasy of being "beaten" (sexually penetrated) by the father (a fantasy well accommodated and at the same time well distanced by its enactment in female form) and the fantasy of killing the father. Although the fantasy of parricide is not normally so tightly joined with the "child is being beaten" fantasy, it seems to me plausible that the circumstances of the rape-revenge plot may work to bring them together.[54] In either case, the revenge phase must be funded by punitive desires; in much the way the Greeks are said to have killed the bearer of bad news, the guilty masochist may be prompted to expunge, in the course of disavowal,

[54] For an extended analysis, adapted from the Freudian paradigm, of the patricidal tendencies of horror, see Twitchell, *Dreadful Pleasures*, pp. 93–104.

the agent of his unacceptable pleasure. If the agent of his pleasure happens to be his father, so much the better. And if that paternal agent can be coded in such a way as to make him necessarily or deservingly killed, as the Indian is necessarily or deservingly killed in order to clear the way for the subject to establish his own claim (to the land, to the mother), better yet. Raped and battered, the boy rises to exterminate his paternal aggressor—all in the name of justice.

There is indeed, as John Carpenter suggests in the remark that heads this section, a remarkable fit between horror and the western (or at least a certain kind of horror and a certain kind of western). And although his language suggests that he gives priority to the western ("I disguise a lot of my films. They're really westerns underneath"), the case could also be made that westerns are really horror "underneath," for the terms of violation and revenge in the western seem often to slide beyond an economic analysis into a psychosexual register.[55] In fact, of course, if the two genres really do stand in the kind of reciprocal relationship that I have suggested, then it must be that both things are true—that each is the other "underneath," that the terms of the one are inherent, if not manifest, in the terms of the other, and that each enables the other to be told. *Deliverance* is an object lesson on just how the demonizing mechanism of the urbanoia or white settler plot enables the telling of a rape-revenge story, and at the same time how a rape-revenge story enables the rehearsal of the old story whereby the have-nots are exterminated with impunity by the haves.

To that combination, *I Spit on Your Grave* added a sex change and feminism. In retrospect, there is something inevitable about *Spit*'s revision. Both of its stories have turned from the outset on "femininity"—of city folks, of rape victims—and once the social changes of the sixties and seventies made credible the image of a self-avenging female, Jennifer had to happen. And with her appearance, the syncretism was complete. Her femaleness allowed the "body" story to be told with far greater relish, and her feminist rage pumped new energy into the "social" story. Horror is built on exploitation and appropriation, and *I Spit on Your Grave*'s exploitation and appropriation of feminism are no cause for surprise. What interests me here is what this particular instance reveals about the male viewer's investment in the tormented female body that appears before him on-screen, and how that relation in turn invites us to read with new eyes backward and outward in the literature of suffering and revenge.

[55] John Carpenter, as quoted by Cumbow, *Order in the Universe*, p. 191. Carpenter's psychoanalytic speculations elsewhere indicate that he has a more complex notion of "underneath" than his remark about westerns suggests.

CHAPTER 4

The Eye of Horror

WE ALL UNDERSTAND THAT EYES ARE THE MOST VULNERABLE OF OUR SENSORY ORGANS, THE MOST VULNERABLE OF OUR FACIAL ACCESSORIES, AND THEY ARE (ICK!) *SOFT.* MAYBE THAT'S THE WORST . . .

—Stephen King, Danse Macabre

EYES ARE EVERYWHERE in horror cinema. In titles: *The Eyes of Laura Mars, Eyes of a Stranger, The Hills Have Eyes, The Eye Creatures, Terrorvision, Scanners, White of the Eye, Don't Look Now, Crawling Eye, Eyes of Hell, Headless Eyes,* and so forth. Or on posters, videocassette box covers, and other promotional materials, where wide-open eyes staring up in terror (for example) at a poised knife or a naked face or something off-box or off-poster are part of the standard iconography. (The fact that many of these "eye" scenes do not in fact occur in the films they advertise suggests their super-textual nature.) Or the extreme close-up of an eye in the film's opening moments or credit sequence (e.g., *Vertigo, The Eyes of Laura Mars, White of the Eye, Black Widow, Dream Lover, Incubus, Repulsion*). Only after the credits have run their course does the camera draw back to let us see whose eye it is (often a dead person's) and what the sequence is about.

At one level, this "screen eye" is simply another in a long row of examples of the traditional call for attention: just as the first sounds of medieval romance—"Herkneth" or "Escoutez"—apostrophize the collective ear of the audience, so the ocular opening images of cinematic horror apostrophize its collective eye. But insofar as it introduces a narrative that necessarily turns on problems of vision—seeing too little (to the point of blindness) or seeing too much (to the point of insanity)—and insofar as its scary project is to tease, confuse, block, and threaten the spectator's own vision, the opening eye of horror also announces a concern "with the way we see ourselves and others and the consequences that often attend our usual manner of perception."[1] Horror privileges eyes because, more crucially than any other kind of cinema, it is about eyes.

More particularly, it is about eyes watching horror. Certainly the act of watching horror films or horror television also looms large in horror films. Horror film characters are forever watching horror movies, either in theaters (e.g., *Demons*) or on television at home (e.g., *Halloween*), and not a few horror plots turn on the horrifying consequences of looking at horror (e.g., *Demons, Terrorvision, Videodrome*). Noël Carroll rightly observes that responses of horror movie characters—shuddering, nausea, shrinking, paralysis, screaming, and revulsion—serve as a kind of instructive mirror to horror movie audiences and that this mirroring effect is one of the defining features of the genre:[2]

> In the classic film *King Kong*, for example, there is a scene on the ship during the journey to Skull Island in which the fictional director, Carl Denham, stages a screen test for Ann Darrow, the heroine of the film within the film. The offscreen motivations that Denham supplies his starlet can be taken as a set of instructions for the way both Ann Darrow and the audience are to react to the first apparition of Kong. Denham says to Darrow: "Now you look higher. You're amazed. Your eyes open wider. It's horrible, Ann, but you can't look away. There's no chance for you, Ann— no escape. You're helpless, Ann, helpless. There's just one chance. If you can scream—but your throat's paralyzed. Scream, Ann, cry. Perhaps if you didn't see it you could scream. Throw your arms across your face and scream, scream for your life."[3]

Note the emphasis on *looking* as the avenue of horror ("Now you look higher. . . . Your eyes open wider. . . . you can't look away. . . . Perhaps if you didn't see it you could scream"). Note too that Ann is not looking at an actual monster at this point; she is being asked to see on her "mindscreen" the monster that we will soon see on the film screen.[4] Likewise modern horror, which repeatedly aligns us not just

---

[1] J. P. Telotte, "Through a Pumpkin's Eye," p. 16. See also his "Faith and Idolatry in the Horror Film," Bruce F. Kawin's "*The Funhouse* and *The Howling*," and Dennis Giles's "Conditions of Pleasure in Horror Cinema."

[2] Carroll, *The Philosophy of Horror*, esp. chapter 1, "The Nature of Horror," pp. 12–58. Carroll thus brings to bear on film the line of reasoning developed by Michael Fried in his *Absorption and Theatricality* and David Marshall in *The Surprising Effects of Sympathy*, works to which this chapter is also indirectly indebted.

[3] As quoted in Carroll, *The Philosophy of Horror*, p. 18. Audience reactions to *The Exorcist* are a case in point: seeing Regan vomit apparently caused viewers to vomit.

[4] I refer to Bruce Kawin's argument (in *Mindscreen*), particularly appropriate to horror cinema, that the visual fields of dream and film are analogous, both reflecting a

with victims facing monsters, but with audiences of horror movies in which victims face monsters, or with audiences of horror movies who are watching horror movies in which victims face monsters, and so on. It is not only the look-at-the-monster that is at issue here, but the look-at-the-movie. The horror movie is somehow more than the sum of its monsters; it is itself monstrous.

A strong prima facie case could be made for horror's being, intentionally or unintentionally, the most self-reflexive of cinematic genres.[5] From titles and posters to images of eyes, and from tales of blindness or paravision to plots involving audiences looking at (audiences looking at) horror movies, horror talks about itself. What it has to say, in particular what it has to say about the psychology of its own production and consumption, is the subject of this chapter. Horror's metacinematic dimension has been oddly underexploited both in the critical literature on horror and in film theory, despite (or, as I shall later suggest, because of) its obvious relevance to the "official" discussion. The distinction I am drawing between horror's self-commentary and the commentary of critics and theorists is roughly akin to the distinction folklorists draw between "ethnic" categories (those designated by the text or the culture itself) and "analytic" ones (those deduced by outside observers).[6] For although mass media can scarcely be characterized as in any sense less self-conscious or analytic than criticism and theory about them, the fact that the discourse *within* horror cinema and the discourse *about* it diverge on some crucial points would seem to suggest that the folks who make horror movies and the folks who write about them are, if not hearing different drummers, then reading different passages of Freud. What follows is an effort to pin down what horror movies themselves have to say about why people see them at all, much less keep coming back at six dollars a pop, again and again.

BULL'S-EYE: *PEEPING TOM*

I take as my point of departure Michael Powell's *Peeping Tom*—a film that sets out with astonishing candor and clarity a psychosexual theory of cinematic spectatorship. Released in 1960, the same year as *Psycho*, *Peeping Tom* met with an "outraged press re-

mediated form of the unconscious. See also his essay "The Mummy's Pool," and Gaylyn Studlar, *In the Realm of Pleasure*, chapter 8.

[5] See, in particular, Telotte, "Through a Pumpkin's Eye," and Philip Brophy, "Horrality."

[6] Dan Ben-Amos, "Analytic Categories and Ethnic Genres."

sponse" which "virtually ended Michael Powell's career as a major director in Britain."[7] Powell especially objected to the reception of *Peeping Tom* as a horror film akin to the gory "Hammers" that flooded the British market during those years.[8] "It's not a horror film," he insisted. "It's a film of compassion, of observation and of memory, yes! It's a film about the cinema from 1900 to 1960."[9] It is in any case the self-reflexive dimension of *Peeping Tom* that has led to its revaluation, over the decades, as first and foremost a sustained reflection on the nature of cinematic vision—in the opinion of many the finest metafilm ever made.[10]

More particularly, however, it is a *horror* metafilm: a film that has as its task to expose the psychodynamics of specularity and *fear*. The early critics were not entirely wrong to spot a connection between *Peeping Tom* and the Hammer productions of the period (*Horrors of the Black Museum*, from the previous year, featured a set of binoculars that snapped daggers into the eyes of the would-be user), and Powell was not entirely ingenuous in his denial of the connection. For insofar as *Peeping Tom* is the theory of a cinematic undertaking of which the Hammer productions and *Psycho* are the practice, it necessarily plays in the register of horror. At the same time, the definition of horror that *Peeping Tom* implicitly proposes is one that includes itself in the category only as the most marginal of examples.

Peeping Tom tells the story of a professional cinematographer, Mark, who moonlights as a photographer for pornographic magazines. Mark, it turns out, is also given to killing the (female) objects of his gaze. Precisely how he does so is not immediately clear, for our vision is limited to what we can see through his movie-camera's eye as we move in for a close-up of the woman's face registering first bewilderment as light flashes into her eyes and then terror at something, unseen by us, in the vicinity of the camera—at which point the narrative cuts. Why the sudden expression of fear, and what the blinding light, are questions fully answered only in the film's final moments, when Mark demonstrates his cinematographic method to Helen, the young woman neighbor toward whom he feels his first stirrings of nonmurderous friendship. The tripod is equipped with a hidden, extendable spike and the movie camera with a mirror, nei-

---

[7] Ian Christie, "The Scandal of *Peeping Tom*," p. 53.

[8] See ibid., p. 54.

[9] As quoted in Elliott Stein, "A Very Tender Film," p. 59.

[10] As Christie puts it, "Powell is the principle of cinematic specificity at work in British cinema; and the 'scandal' of *Peeping Tom* is the denial of that specificity, the refusal to acknowledge the illicit pleasure principle of cinema" ("The Scandal of *Peeping Tom*," p. 59).

ther of which appears in the visual frame of the murder scenes; when
Mark moves in for a close-up, the spike pierces the victim's throat
and she sees her own terrified face in the mirror. "Do you know what
the most frightening thing in the world is? It's fear," Mark tells
Helen. "So I did something very simple. *Very* simple. When they felt
this spike touching their throats, and knew I was going to kill them,
I made them watch their own deaths. I made them see their own
terror as the spike went in. And if death has a face, they saw that,
too."

But if the revelation of the "killer camera" explains the past murders of the prostitute and the actress, it simultaneously explains the
film's other past: Mark's own childhood, filmed in excruciating detail
by his scientist father. (We glimpse the father's achievement in a
bookshelf close-up of multivolume works entitled *Fear and the Nervous
System*, *The Physiology of Fear*, and so forth.) As Mark explains to
Helen, he was his father's first and best subject. "He watched me
grow up," he says, in his quiet, halting voice. "He wanted a record
of a growing child. Complete in every detail. If such a thing were
possible. And he tried to make it possible—by training a camera on
me at all times. I never knew, in the whole of my childhood, one
moment of privacy." We are shown passages of those childhood
films, grainy black-and-white home movies, in which Mark as a child
is filmed asleep, at play, viewing his mother's corpse, stealing a look
at a couple embracing on a park bench, and, above all, in situations
of fear—fear induced by the tortures the father inflicts on him. The
"magic camera," as it comes to be called in the film, has passed from
father to son, and indeed, the son has made it his life's work to carry
on his father's life's work—not only by extending it to other subjects
(the prostitute and the actress) but by continuing his own story
where his father left it off. The film *Peeping Tom* is about the making
of another film: the documentary record of Mark's life, begun by his
father and continued by Mark himself (through the filming of his
murders and of the public reaction that attends them) and finally
completed by him as well, as he films his own suicide with and by
the same "magic camera."

"I hope to be a director, very soon," Mark declares to Helen—an
ambition also visible on the director's chair bearing his name, Mark
Lewis, in his upstairs workroom. Lest we suppose that directors are
less sadistic than cinematographers, we are shown a long sequence
on the movie set in which a director requires an actress to do fifty-
odd takes of a fainting scene on grounds that she is unconvincing.
The episode is played for comedy, and we are invited to laugh when
the vain and incompetent actress finally pleases the director by faint-

ing in fact, out of sheer exhaustion from her earlier efforts.[11] There is an edge to the joke, however. The actress's tumble into unconsciousness recalls the film's earlier photographic session, in which one of Mark's pornographic models asks him to obscure the bruises that mar her body, and the other to obscure her grotesquely scarred lip ("He said you needn't get my face"). Where the bruises and the damaged face come from we do not know, but the point is clear: to be on the object side of the camera is to be hurt. The only difference between Mark and the director he aspires to be is that the latter has, in the terms of the film, internalized the "magic camera." It is the cinematic apparatus itself, not just its mechanical representative the camera, that is in question. Just because the sadism of that apparatus is less overt on the movie set than it is in Mark's individual photographic sessions does not mean that it is less brutal. For Powell, clearly, the difference between Mark's direct sadisms and the institutionalized sadisms of the movie set—all the more chilling because they can be made funny—is merely one of degree. The point is driven home by the fact that the role of Mark's sadistic father, in the childhood footage, is played by director Powell himself, and the boy Mark by his son.

One day a psychoanalyst appears on the movie set—a jovial older man with a German accent.[12] When Mark approaches, the psychoanalyst asks him what his job on the set is. "Focus puller," Mark replies. "So am I, in a way," the analyst replies. Mark introduces himself as the son of the famous Dr. Lewis and, after listening to the expected encomia, moves to his real concern: does the psychoanalyst know of his father's final, unpublished research? "What was the subject?" the analyst asks. "I don't remember what he called it," Mark responds, "but it has something to do with what causes people to be Peeping Toms." "Scoptophilia!" the analyst pronounces emphatically, "the morbid urge to gaze!"—the cure for which, Mark is crestfallen to learn, is a couple of years in analysis.

The exchange is a heavily coded one, of course, not only because of the conventional understanding, in films of that era, that psychiatrists and their ilk speak the truth, but also because of the utterance of the term "Peeping Tom" and the equation between focus pulling

[11] The moment brings to mind the incident reported of Hitchcock during the filming of *The Birds*, in which Tippi Hedron was required to do so many takes of the attic-attack sequence that she ended up in the hospital. See Spoto, *The Dark Side of Genius*, pp. 480–86.

[12] As Doane notes, psychoanalysts were employed by the film industry in the 1940s as technical advisers. At least two films, *Dark Mirror* and *Sleep My Love*, advertised that fact (*The Desire to Desire*, p. 45).

(reversing the relationship of foreground and background in an image, or, more generally, cinematography) and psychoanalysis. It has all the earmarks, in short, of a classic narrative-film "explanation." Still, there is reason to wonder whether this particular psychoanalytic pronunciamento is as sterling as it seems. The fact that the analyst is after all an admiring colleague of Mark's father would seem to compromise his judgment on the face of it. The film's strong implication is that the field of psychiatric research is itself built on sadistic inquiry, and if that is so, then the psychoanalyst stands as morally condemned as the father. Too, there is under the circumstances something unsettling about the "focus-pulling" joke. When Mark, in response to the psychoanalyst's question, identifies himself as a "focus puller," we understand the term in both its workaday sense (cinematographer) and in our privileged sense (camera murderer); and when the psychoanalyst then replies "So am I, in a way," he plays to that double possibility, again inviting us to link the practice of psychoanalysis with violence. (Mark's father, after all, was a "focus puller" in both senses.) It is in any case clear from his persistent questioning that the psychoanalyst is far more interested in getting his hands on Dr. Lewis's unpublished papers on "scoptophilia" than he is in Mark. And, of course, there is the simple fact that the psychoanalyst is apparently in the employ of the studio and hence part of a cinematic apparatus that the film defines as assaultive.

Finally, there is the obvious inadequacy, relative to the film's own workings, of the psychoanalyst's snap label "scoptophilia" and its definition as the "morbid urge to gaze." It is no small part of the brilliance of *Peeping Tom* that it splits this unitary formulation into two gazes and two varieties of morbidity—gazes and morbidities that co-exist in one and the same person (here Mark) and gazes that, by extension, are claimed to coexist in the cinematic spectator. The two gazes are neatly formulated—share double billing, as it were—in the opening doubled sequence. The sequence presents us with two viewings of the same event (the assault on the prostitute) by the same person (Mark) from precisely the same perspective. The "present" half of the sequence is preceded by a shot of a whirring camera (held close to the chest between jacket lapels), which we then move behind and look through. Our vision from this point on is through the viewfinder, which, like a rifle-sight, is marked by cross hairs. We approach and tacitly solicit a prostitute, follow her upstairs, watch her begin to undress, then bear down on her as light flashes on her face and she reacts in terror—all this through the cross hairs.[13] This is the

---

[13] The device is also popular in thrillers and action movies; see, for example, the opening sequence of *Dirty Harry*.

narrative's present and causal gaze, its "doing" gaze. It is also, of course, a predatory, assaultive gaze—in the story's own terms, a phallic gaze. Mark has his movie camera with him always, slung over his shoulder. "You have it *in* you, boy," Vivian says of it; according to Helen, it is "growing into an extra limb." When in the wake of his second murder he hands it over to a police officer for inspection, he is visibly nervous and keeps half-reaching to get it back. It is no surprise, as Mark himself ironically notes, that he got it as a gift from his father—though even at this "moment of seeming phallic transition," Kaja Silverman remarks, "the father's camera remains fixed on the son's," thus underscoring the "father's punishing power and . . . the son's lack."[14] At the end of the film, when the police rush to Mark's apartment, Mark quickly sets up to capture their arrival on film. As they jump from their car, they hear the sound of a second-story window shattering and look up, fearing a gun. "It's only a camera," says one cop. "*Only!*" replies the other. "Only" is precisely what *Peeping Tom's* cameras are *not.*

The second or "past" half of the sequence simply duplicates the first half—but without the hairline cross, for, as the opening shot of a whirring projector announces, we are now watching, through Mark's eyes, a screening of the earlier film. It is over this replay that the screen credits roll. At the climactic moment, Mark at last (and for the first time) enters our vision as he half-rises in a state of agitation and faces his screen. If the "present" or "doing" gaze was predatory, penetrating, murderous, at once brutalizing the woman and recording that brutalization, *causing* the event to happen, the second or "past" gaze is after the fact, at some contemplative distance—a distance underwritten by the relocation of the image further back in our screen (in such a way as to show us a screen in a screen) and by the superimposition of screen credits. What was action is now speculation. What was present is now pluperfect. What was real life is now movie—now *our* movie, too. What was active cinematographer is now passive spectator. We never saw the cinematographer of the opening sequence; but at the end of the screening, we see the spectator as he interposes himself between the screen and the images he earlier created, now projected on his own body. (We will later see the same gesture in a more exaggerated form as Mark rises fully and, arms outstretched, presses himself against the screen so that the projected image, the close-up face of one of his terrified female victims, falls directly on his back.)

But what does this gesture of Mark's—rising to face the screen—

14 Silverman, *The Acoustic Mirror*, p. 33.

mean? Contrary to Elliott Stein, who states matter-of-factly that it de-
notes sexual climax,[15] I would suggest that it is deliberately ambiguous—a tease, an invitation to stay tuned for the explanation. It is actually the second tease of the film, the first being the light and
expression of fear in the prostitute's face. That is, each of the two
gazes that opens *Peeping Tom* poses a distinct question, one having to
do with Mark's stake as a photographer (what is he *doing* to that
woman?) and one having to do with his stake as a spectator (why is
he rising toward the screen?). I emphasize the "twiceness" of the
opening sequence—the doubled representation of the prostitute's
murder and the "tease" embedded in each—because it is so frequently ignored in discussions of the film, with the result that the
binary it proposes, and that underwrites the film proper, has not
been done critical justice.[16]

Mark, we come to understand, has survived in adulthood the spectatorial cruelties of his childhood by splitting and reenacting them—
on one hand through the assumption of his father's role, using the
camera to "kill and fuck" (as Stein puts it)[17] and on the other through
the obsessive re-viewing of his own boyhood experience of having
been on the *receiving* end of his father's cinematic "killing and fucking." If the emotional project of the first gaze is to assault, the emotional project of the second is to be oneself assaulted—vicariously,
through the process of projection in both senses. In that re-view of
unpleasure there lies perverse pleasure, for the sight of pain inflicted
on others is "enjoyed masochistically by the subject through his identification of himself with the suffering object."[18] *Peeping Tom's* light-
geometry underscores Mark's identification, in his "spectatorial"

[15] Stein, "A Very Tender Film," p. 59.

[16] One of the few critics to distinguish between the gaze of Mark the cinematographer and that of Mark the spectator is Peary. "In Mark's peculiar case," he writes, "the
murder of a woman does not by itself give him sexual satisfaction. The insertion of the
blade into her is a necessary step, but his onanistic 'climax' takes place in the back
room when he projects her dying expression on his wall. And only when his camera
has captured in her face the absolute expression of fear (he is always disappointed/
frustrated) can he truly be sexually satisfied." Immediately upon suggesting that there
are two "pleasures" involved here, however, Peary backs off and proposes that it is
really a question of two perspectives, two distances, on one and the same pleasure—
a voyeuristic, sadistic pleasure. "By having Mark's 'sexual act' take place in two
stages—the murder and the screening of the murder—Powell makes the distinction
between participation (count us out) and voyeurism (count us in). Both have their own
erotic appeal: for instance, one can enjoy active sex and still derive a different pleasure
from watching sexual acts at a distance" (*Cult Movies*, p. 254).

[17] Stein, "A Very Tender Film," p. 59.

[18] Jean Laplanche and J.-B. Pontalis (quoting Freud) in *The Language of Psycho-Analysis*, s.v. "Sadism/Masochism," p. 402.

mode, with the women facing the fear-mirror: just as they are shown blinded by the mirror light, so the boy Mark is shown blinded by his father's flashlight; just as the adult Mark is pinned to the screen by the light when he finishes watching his prostitute film, Helen is likewise pinned at the end of the film. This second gaze—the horrified gaze of the victim, or more complexly, one's gaze at surrogates for one's own past victimized self—I shall for want of a better term call "reactive."

The two gazes of *Peeping Tom* divide straightforwardly along sexual lines. Those who photograph are males (Mark as an adult; his father, Dr. Lewis; the film director), and the act of photographing is plainly figured as an act of phallic cruelty.[19] Those who are photographed are, with the sole exception of Mark as a child, females (prostitute, actress, models), and the experience of being photographed—of gazing reactively—is figured as an experience of being bruised, scarred, terrified, made to faint, and stabbed to death. Mark thus occupies both categories: as an adult on the side of the masculine and as a child on the side of the feminine. Preadolescent boys are frequently figured as premasculine in traditional cultures (and in our own popular culture), but Mark's is a more complicated case, for he has carried his "femininity" with him into adulthood, and it is a living part of his psyche. He is the bearer of both gazes, and it is the relation and distinction between them that Powell's film is all about.

Assaultive and reactive gazing are, in the case of Mark, housed in one and the same person, and they are, at least in the initial sequence, structurally identical: the "present" half of the prostitute sequence (the assaultive view) is in all phenomenal aspects (with the exception of the cross hairs) identical to the "past" half (the reactive view). The same footage does for both. The point of this homology is not, however, to demonstrate the one-and-the-sameness of the two gazes. They are marked as experientially different by a whole range of signs: pace, present/past, camera/projector, and above all Mark's dialogue lines and acting (facial gestures in particular, but also tone of voice). Rather, the homology points up the causal relationship between the two. In the same way that child abusers in the present were abused children in the past, assaultive gazing, for Powell, proceeds from and is predicated on reactive gazing (in my meaning of that term). Inside every Peeping Tom is a peeped-at child, trying incessantly to master his own pain by re-viewing it in the person of

---

[19] Just before Mark murders her, the actress Vivian steps behind Mark's camera and attempts to see through it. Helen, who is notably uninterested in Mark's camera, survives it.

another. Mark's "feminine" look is not at odds with his "masculine" one, but constitutive of it, its necessary condition.

The reactive gaze of *Peeping Tom* is doubly marked as masochistic: in its drive to pleasure-in-pain and in its characteristic need to revisit, over and over again, an originary story in hopes of getting it right so as to put it to rest. "Every night you turn on this film machine," Helen's mother complains, and Mark himself observes that although he plans for every murder to be his last, none quite satisfies: the "light" is somehow always wrong. So the circle: the compulsion to repeat "what is unpleasant or even painful" inherent in the "reactive" gaze needs a steady supply of projected images that only the direct application of an "assaultive" camera can satisfy.[20] (The relation between masochism and repetition compulsion is a topic to which I will return.) With the exception of the (significantly) blind Mrs. Lewis, virtually every character in *Peeping Tom*—from the big-time movie producer (whose telephone conversations are all about "box office") to the old man who furtively buys "views" in the cigar shop, and even to Helen, whose children's book *The Magic Camera* romanticizes photography—is implicated in some such circle. To suppose that *Peeping Tom* is about one psychopath is very much to miss the point; in one way or another, the traffic in pictures involves us all.

I would go so far as to argue that Powell is interested in Mark the assaultive gazer only inasmuch as he represents the *outcome* of Mark the assaulted gazer. Certainly the evolving love story with Helen, the "domestic" passage, turns on Mark's damaged character and the pathos of his efforts to behave normally. The fact that he commits suicide rather than be killed or taken marks him as a tragic figure. And if the film opened with a scene of pure aggression, it closes on a note of pure helplessness, with the sound, as Mark dies, of a tape-recorded dialogue from his childhood. "Don't be a silly boy," says a stern voice we understand to be the father's, "there's nothing to be *afraid* of." And then the film's final words, spoken in the frightened voice of a small boy, after the screen has darkened: "Good night, Daddy—hold my hand." *Peeping Tom*, in short, is shaped around the experience of fear and pain. It would be going too far to say that the sadistic sequences (in which Mark "photographs" the women) are nothing more than staging moments for the exploration of Mark's masochism, but it is nonetheless the case that, after the "unmarked" assault on the prostitute that opens the film, there is no assault of Mark's that is not obviously animated by his own historical pain.

---

[20] Laplanche and Pontalis, *The Language of Psycho-Analysis*, s.v. "Compulsion to Repeat," p. 79.

And as is indicated by Powell's insistence that his film is "not a horror film" but "a film of compassion, of observation, and of memory
. . . a very tender film, a nice one" his interest is not in the assaultive
but the reactive side of the equation.[21]

Susan Sontag found in *Peeping Tom* a perfect vindication of her
view that the act of photography is an act of power, aggression, pred-
atoriness, and sexual voyeurism. "To photograph people is to violate
them. . . . to photograph someone is a sublimated murder. . . . The
act of taking pictures is a semblance of rape."[22] To Jonathan Rosen-
baum's designation of *Peeping Tom* as "the *only* English New Wave
film," Elliott Stein added that "it *is* the only movie that equates
watching movies with killing and fucking—something Godard might
well have thought up."[23] Note the slide here from Sontag's claim that
making movies is a form of transitive sexual violence to Stein's that
watching them is such an act. This elision of making films and watching them (most succinctly expressed in the film's Italian title *L'Occhio
che Uccide* [The eye that kills]) is part and parcel of the familiar theoretical claim that the spectator's perspective is constituted by the perspective of an assaultive camera. To which feminist film theory
added that the perspective in question is paradigmatically male: that
the first-person positions which the camera repeatedly has us adopt
are positions occupied by male characters (as in the cross-hair sequence of *Peeping Tom*), and that whatever the technical "person" of
the gaze, it has us looking at women in ways men do. The cinematic
apparatus, in the influential formulation of Laura Mulvey, is characterized by the fixing of the female body as the quintessential and
deeply problematic object of sight.[24] The reason for that fixing, in
Mulvey's view, has to do with the male spectator's unease at the
spectacle of female lack, an unease he resolves either through denial-
driven looking (fetishistic scopophilia) or punishment-driven looking
(sadistic voyeurism). Although Mulvey refers to *Peeping Tom* only
obliquely,[25] her scenario of sadistic voyeurism, whereby spectator
and camera, both presumed "male," collude in an act of phallic violence toward women, is obviously appropriate to that film and has in
turn conditioned discussion of it.

But feminist film theory's emphasis on the union of spectator and

[21] As quoted in Stein, "A Very Tender Film," p. 59.

[22] Susan Sontag, *On Photography*, pp. 14–15, 24.

[23] Stein, "A Very Tender Film," p. 59.

[24] Mulvey, "Visual Pleasure and Narrative Cinema," pp. 6–18.

[25] "At the extreme," Mulvey writes, "it [scopophilia] can become fixated into a perversion, producing obsessive voyeurs and Peeping Toms, whose only sexual satisfaction can come from watching, in an active controlling sense, an objectified other"
(ibid., p. 9).

assaultive camera, Elliot Stein's equation of *watching* movies with "killing and fucking," and *Peeping Tom*'s Italian title obliterate the very distinction on which Powell's metacinematic proposition rests: the proposition that assaultive gazing, associated with the camera, is one thing and reactive gazing, associated with the projected screenings, quite another. Phil Hardy recaptures the distinction when he writes that *Peeping Tom*'s "chinese-box structure allows us to watch the image of a film-maker filmically penetrating the object of his desire while he, and we, watch her looking at her own image, unsettlingly splitting the audience's identification process as we—and he—are both in the position of aggressor and victim, at both ends of the sado-masochistic spectrum,"[26] but he pursues neither the larger metacinematic point nor the dimension of gender.

Silverman, on the other hand, pursues both.[27] "*Peeping Tom* gives new emphasis to the concept of reflexivity," she writes. "Not only does it foreground the workings of the apparatus, and the place given there to voyeurism and sadism, but its remarkable structure suggests that dominant cinema is indeed a mirror with a delayed reflection." Mark's mirror "functions to disavow male lack even further by suggesting that the female subject reflects only herself, and so denying the place of the male subject within the mimetic circuit." *Peeping Tom* thus "exposes the machinery whereby Hollywood promotes the imaginary coherence of the male subject by displacing onto women all signs of lack."[28] For Silverman, Mark-the-spectator's "inability to project the projections necessary to disburden himself of lack" exposes voyeurism for what it is: an exercise not in phallic mastery, but in the *fantasy*—by nature unachievable—of phallic mastery. The moments in which Mark-the-spectator "slips" or "slides" or "tips" into identification with the woman are thus moments when his resistance fails, moments that prove his inability to keep his distance and his difference.[29] For Silverman, in other words, Mark-the-spectator and Mark-the-filmmaker are versions of one another—the one a conflicted purveyor of the fantasy and the other its conflicted consumer, but both engaged in the same cover-up project.

[26] Hardy, *Encyclopedia of Horror Movies*, p. 135.

[27] See Silverman, *The Acoustic Mirror*, pp. 32–41.

[28] Ibid., pp. 32–36.

[29] One such "tipping" moment is when Mark presses himself against the screen during one of his projections in such a way that the image which covers his back is the close-up face of Vivian recoiling in fear. Another is when he demonstrates his killing method to Helen: the sound we hear is that of his own voice as a five-year-old, screaming in terror. A third, which Silverman mentions, is Mark's "mirroring" hand movements on his own chest as Helen adjusts, on her own chest, the dragonfly brooch he has just given her.

The question I want to raise here has to do not with Silverman's larger point, which seems indisputable, but with her failure to take account of *Peeping Tom*'s early, long, and obvious association with horror film and hence of the possibility that its metacinematics, while generalizable to "dominant" or "Hollywood" cinema up to a point, refer specifically to the cinema of terror. I would suggest, from the perspective of horror, that *Peeping Tom* is proposing a rather more radical division of labor than the one outlined by Silverman (a division of labor, I repeat, that is urged at the outset in the visual repetition of the same story event from first the camera's and then the spectator's point of view). As a *horror* spectator, Mark is more than a failed voyeur; he is a positively successful masochist. If, in his capacity as horror filmmaker, Mark is fighting for voyeuristic distance from the victim, he is in his capacity as horror spectator not only failing to resist her embrace, but hurling himself into it. Uniting with the victim position seems to be the point of his spectatorial enterprise, the shameful fantasy his home-studio has been constructed to fulfill. When Mrs. Stephens accuses Mark of running his projector so incessantly, it is not clear which footage is in question, the childhood footage figuring himself as victim or the adult footage figuring women as victims. Nor does it matter; as projections, they are functionally speaking one and the same movie.

Peeping Tom, in short, should also be taken at face value as a commentary not only on the symbiotic interplay of sadistic and masochistic impulses in the individual viewer but equally as a commentary, within the context of horror filmmaking, on the symbiotic interplay of the sadistic work of the filmmaker and the masochistic stake of the spectator, an arrangement on which horror cinema insists.[30] There may be no such thing as purely masochistic spectatorship (or even, perhaps, purely sadistic moviemaking), but the job of horror—the job of movies people see *in order to be scared*—is to give the viewer as pure a dose as possible. ("The pleasure of the text," Philip Brophy writes of horror, "is, in fact, getting the shit scared out

---

[30] Williams appreciates the distinction: "In making his films (the *mise-en-scène* of which is murder), Mark assumes the role of his sadistic father, mastering his own terror by becoming the victimizer himself. Then in watching his films he can relive his original experience of terror at a safe distance, identify with his own victims and repossess his own look of terror from a safer aesthetic distance." She does not, however, take her logic to its end point—that the second look is driven by masochism, that Mark is at that moment in the position the film otherwise assigns to the feminine, and that even when the *man* looks, he "recognizes" himself. On the contrary, she reverts to the male-sadistic model: "*Peeping Tom* thus lays bare the voyeuristic structure of cinema and that structure's dependence on the woman's acceptance of her role as narcissist" ("When the Woman Looks," esp. p. 92).

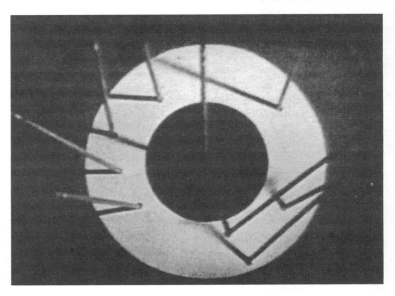

The first and second shots of *Peeping Tom*.

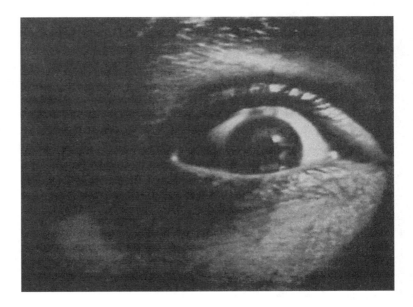

of you—and loving it; an exchange mediated by adrenalin.")[31] The victim's femaleness is a subject to which I shall later return; for the moment let me briefly suggest that it is overdetermined not only by her classic deflective function, but also by her equally classic role in male masochistic fantasies (on which more below). I suspect that horror is not as concerned as "dominant" cinema with disavowing male lack; on the contrary, as I have suggested in earlier chapters, it seems almost to indulge it, to the point of reveling in it. This too *Peeping Tom* acknowledges, most explicitly when, at the climax, Mark commits ecstatic suicide—on camera, amid a burst of flashbulbs, "drowned out" by prerecorded sound.[32]

Actually, what I, like others before me, have referred to as the opening sequence of *Peeping Tom*, the prostitute sequence, is not the film's first moment. The prostitute sequence is preceded by two close-up images. The first is a brief and startling close-up image of an archery target, which, after a static second or two, is suddenly punctured at the center—in the bull's-eye—by an arrow hurtling from some source off-frame. (It is the Powell-Pressburger logo, but used here for particular effect.) The moment has no "story"—no archer, no setting, no context—and immediately upon the penetration of the bull's-eye, the film cuts abruptly to the second prenarrative image: the super close-up of a human eye, first closed, then opening as if in alarm. The fact that this "eye doublet" bears no narrative relation to the remainder of the film—and is the *only* narratively disembodied moment in the entire film—fairly shouts out its supertextual status. In case we doubted which of the eye's two operations *Peeping Tom* wishes to privilege in its analysis of horror cinema, this opening minute spells it out: not the eye that kills, but the eye that is "killed."

LOOKING IN AND AT HORROR

The question is whether *Peeping Tom*'s analysis of horror is borne out by horror itself—whether horror movies too draw a distinction between the assaultive gaze, figured as masculine, of the camera (or some stand-in) and the reactive gaze, figured as feminine, of the spectator, and at which pole they locate the horror experience. It is to other horror, mostly of recent vintage, that I now turn.

[31] Brophy, "Horrality," p. 5.

[32] "In a stunning reprise of all the many textual references to light," Silverman notes, "Mark times numerous flashbulbs to shine on him at half-second intervals as he levels the psychic barrier separating himself from the female subject, and embraces his own castration" (*The Acoustic Mirror*, p. 37).

The Assaultive Gaze

For obvious reasons, it is on the assaultive gaze of modern horror—on its sexual trappings and flamboyant depredations—that critical attention has by and large been trained. To judge from the commentaries, assaultive gazing, more or less phallically figured, is the
sine qua non of the modern horror movie: its cause, its effect, its
point. To argue (as I mean to) that this judgment is defective—that it
fails to take account of the larger system of looking to which assaultive gazing is inevitably subordinated—is not to deny the existence
and at least temporary power of the "male gaze" in modern horror.
On the contrary, as the following examples suggest, horror movies
are obsessively interested in the thought that the simple act of staring
can terrify, maim, or kill its object—that a hard look and a hard penis
(chain saw, knife, power drill) amount to one and the same thing.

The most phallic camera on record is undoubtedly the one that im-
prisons, rapes, and impregnates Susan in *Demon Seed* (1977). Susan's
home security system is invaded by an advanced intelligence system
named "Proteus" (both systems are the handiwork of her scientist-
husband) who, once installed, proceeds to lock her in, train his lens
on her, and force her, by a variety of household tortures (including
electrical shock) to do his will—all of which she watches on video
monitors. Although we never see "Proteus" (as pure intelligence, he
has no being), we assume his masculinity from his name, low (digi-
talized) voice, and telescopic metal penis. "What do you want?" Susan finally screams in desperation. "A child," answers the camera
and after some preliminaries extrudes a lens-like appendage with
which he rapes and impregnates her—the only rape I know of that is
"filmed" from the ostensible point of view of the penis.[33] Although
Demon Seed's manifest concern is with technology gone wild, its con-
stellation of lenses, monitors, and camera-penis is only an update of
Peeping Tom's mirror and spike. The difference is that Mark's camera
fucked symbolically and killed literally, whereas *Demon Seed*'s reverses the priority.

In *From Beyond*, the phallic gaze is materially (and presumably ironically) realized in the representation of an externalized pineal gland
as a third, sexual eye or seeing genital. In his mad and (what in horror amounts to the same thing) impotent desire to stimulate the pineal, Dr. Pretorius invents a "resonator," to which he himself, his
assistant Crawford, and Dr. Katherine McMichaels are all serially

---

[33] The fact that realistic photography gives way, at the moment of penetration, to a
sequence of startling psychedelics speaks volumes on the issue of representation and
female sexuality.

subjected. In the first phase, the resonator effect entails a heightening of sexual appetite in its more sadomasochistic forms. In the second phase, the pineal bursts through the forehead, dangling and waving in the air like a small penis-camera, seeking on one hand to "see" (we briefly share its vision of the world in the psychedelic forms and colors of a Peter Max poster) and on the other to attack and penetrate others' brains—mindfucking in the most literal sense. "She will go into my mind, and I will go into hers," declares Pretorious at his pineal, and sadomasochistic, mightiest. "It's the greatest sensual pleasure there is." For this genital eye, rape and vision are one and the same thing. Only when his dangling pineal is bitten off by Katherine can Crawford resume his normal life.[34]

Predatory gazing through the agency of the first-person camera is part of the stock-in-trade of horror. The mechanics are laboriously spelled out by Laura Mars in her effort to explain the nature of her proleptic "visions" of women being stalked and stabbed in the eyes (*The Eyes of Laura Mars*, 1978).[35] "Look through that," she tells the investigating officer, handing him a camera. "Now if you think of that camera as the eyes of the killer, what you're seeing through that lens is what the killer sees. It's on the monitor, there. When it happens to me [that is, when she has a "vision" that allows her to see what the unknown killer sees when he stalks a victim], I can't see what's in front of me. What I see is that [the scene on the monitor]. Do you understand?" Like Mark in *Peeping Tom*, Laura Mars is not only a photographer, but a photographer of women—of beautiful women surrounded and threatened by violence—and on the set we see her as we saw Mark, camera poised.[36] At first glance, *The Eyes of Laura Mars* seems something of a gender-bender in its positioning of a female behind an assaultive camera that bears down on women only (and one gay man). But it turns out that she is not, in fact, the subject of the assaultive gaze as much as the unwitting conduit or medium of the *real* assaultive gazer—the killer-cop whose vision she has tapped into—and in the end, she becomes his object as well. As a photographer who objectifies women, Laura aids and abets phallic gazing, but the act itself remains emphatically male.[37]

[34] The pineal eye of *From Beyond* is remarkably like the one adumbrated by Georges Bataille, *Visions of Excess*, esp. p. 82.

[35] Though directed by Irvin Kershner, *The Eyes of Laura Mars* was scripted by John Carpenter and David Zelag Goodman, based on a story written by John Carpenter (and Jon Peters, uncredited) before *Halloween*. Despite directorial changes, the Carpenterian concern with vision remains intact.

[36] For an exploration of specularity in *The Eyes of Laura Mars*, see Lucy Fischer and Marcia Landy, "*Eyes of Laura Mars*."

[37] "Thus Laura Mars has what we might term 'male vision'—a way of seeing that

One of the most popular assaultive gazing stories of the past two decades is the telekinesis or telepathy film. David Cronenberg's *Scanners* (1980) features certain "gifted" individuals able, by looking, to link themselves into the nervous system of others, thus causing headaches or nosebleeds or, in the extreme case, exploded brains or incinerated bodies.[38] What is striking about the telekinesis film is that it is the one subset of horror which regularly features females as assaultive gazers.[39] Merely by casting a concentrated glance, the girl-heroes of *Carrie, Firestarter, The Fury,* and *Friday the 13th VII* can respectively demolish an entire high school, spark a firestorm, bloody the noses of bystanders, and move heavy objects.[40] It is worth noting that the damaging power of these girls' looks stems not from their natural selves—not even their natural selves equipped with cameras or chain saws—but rather from the supernatural apparatus of telekinesis.

That apparatus does not sit easily on the female, however. The plots of these films turn on the girls' ambivalent relationship to their power (they alternate between abuse and renunciation) and, more to the point, on institutional efforts to contain or correct it. The prepubescent Charlie (Charlotte) McGee (girl-hero of *Firestarter*) comes by her blaze-starting glance in the same way that Mark came by his camera and Leatherface his chain saw: her father, to whom she is unusually close (her mother, like the mothers of Mark and Leatherface, be-

reflects the dominant sexist ideology," write Fischer and Landy . "What is intriguing about this narrative configuration is not Laura's status as a psychic, which seems a mere narrative ploy. Rather, what stands out is the connection implied between Laura's work as a photographer and the act of homicide, her artistic vision and the murderer's point of view (ibid., p. 65). It is worth noting that the character whose eyes are punctured when the binoculars "backfire" in *Horrors of the Black Museum* is a woman, and recalling that the only time the image of *Peeping Tom* grows fuzzy is when a woman is at the cinematographic helm (when Mark's stepmother attempts to film Mark and his father).

[38] Scientist Ruth's explanation of "scanning" has a particularly meta-horror-cinematic ring: "Telepathy is not mind reading. It is the direct linking of two nervous systems separated by space. I want you to make a link from your brain to his heart. I want your brain to make his heart beat faster."

[39] The theme owes much of its popularity to the imagination of Stephen King. His novel *Carrie* (brought out as a film in 1976) expressed the idea tentatively, Brian De Palma exploited it more fully in *The Fury* (1978), and King's *Firestarter* (brought out as a film in 1984) is the story full-blown.

[40] The appearance of the telekinesis theme in *Friday the Thirteenth VII* is yet another indication that the slasher formula pure and simple was exhausted by the late eighties. That film's rewriting of the Final Girl as a telekinetic heroine in the Carrie mode bespeaks not only the conceptual affinity between the two character types but also the way in which subgenres (and genres) are constantly cannibalizing one another.

ing dead), "gave" it to her. When her father dies and Charlie flees to safety—to the home of a kindly farm couple, who will now stand in for the proper parents she never had—she renounces the "gaze" that has brought her so much grief. It is at this moment, at the very end of the film, that we hear her for the first time referred to by her "real" name, Charlotte. To this extent the story is a virtual calque, one suspects intentional, on Freud's account of the young girl's march toward femininity, which entails a renunciation of her own phallic strivings (in this case her powerful gaze). But the film's dramatic conflict—what it is *about*—complicates and undermines a strictly internal reading. For when government agents become aware of Charlie's psychic powers, they capture her and in a "controlled environment" try to harness her "gift" for good (anti-Soviet) purposes. Failing that, they decide simply to annihilate her. "My God," says the agent in charge of the mission, "one of these days she'll grow up to be a beautiful woman. Can you imagine what kind of destruction she'll be able to cause then? She must be stopped!" But she escapes, pursued by men armed with flamethrowers and grenades, and flees to the couple who greet her as "Charlotte" and who promise, by virtue of their own sturdy normality, to make a regular girl of her. The march toward femininity is indeed inevitable in this account, not because it is in the psychosexual scheme of things, but because society—indeed, the very survival of the state—rests on disempowering half its citizens. If Charlie's gaze is phallic, in other words, then the message of the film, is simply, better castrated than dead.

But far and away the most conspicuous sort of "assaultive gazing" follows the 1978 lead of John Carpenter's *Halloween*, in which we adopt the vision of an entity that stalks a house, peers in windows, enters and goes to the kitchen for a carving knife, then proceeds upstairs, opens a door, and stabs a young woman to death—all without knowing who "we" are, and all without direct reference to the mediation of a camera.[41] There is a camera, of course, and presumably in the interests of realism, it is in Carpenter's use unmounted, yielding an image that wavers and trembles much the way a mad killer might. But no camera, no photographer, is shown. If *Peeping Tom* clearly established the camera as the machine between us and it, *Halloween* seeks to efface the intervention of the photographer, to try for

---

[41] Even the infamous *Halloween*, however, complicates the gaze. See the suggestive analysis of Steve Neale, who concludes, on the basis of a close analysis of that film, that "the identifications of the spectator are thus split between the polarities of a sadistic, aggressive and controlling position and a masochistic, suffering, and controlled position" ("*Halloween*" pp. 341–42).

the direct connection: we are invited to look not through a murderous camera, but with our own murderous eyes, listening to the beat of our heart and the breathing of our lungs. "The subjective camera makes killers—albeit shocked, unwilling ones—of us all, the heavy breathing of Michael becoming our own as we wonder what he/we will do next."[42] The device is probably the most widely imitated—and widely parodied—cliché of modern horror.[43] That this first-person, assaultive gaze is a gendered gaze, figured explicitly or inexplicitly in phallic terms, is also clear. Slasher films draw the equation repeatedly and unequivocally: when men cannot perform sexually, they stare and kill instead. The first-person sequence that opens the standard slasher duplicates, without the cross hairs, the opening sequence of *Peeping Tom*: the I-camera stalks and stabs an attractive woman. The woman we see through the I-camera is thus, according to the code, scheduled for death. And the reason she must be killed, rather than fucked, is that slasher killers are by generic definition sexually inadequate—men who kill precisely because they *cannot* fuck.[44]

Mick Martin and Marsha Porter echo the common response to such first-person camera horror movies of the *Halloween* or *Friday the Thirteenth* sort when they write that the director "uses a subjective camera in the stabbing scenes, which, essentially, makes the viewer the killer. The camera moves in on the screaming, pleading victim, 'looks down' at the knife, and then plunges it into chest, ear, or eyeball. Now that's sick."[45] What Martin and Porter and others like them fail

[42] Cumbow, *Order in the Universe*, p. 49.

[43] See, for example, the opening sequence of Brian De Palma's *Blow-Out*, in which a panting, heart-beating, lurching first-person camera approaches a house and peers in the window.

[44] The idea is neatly formulated in the notorious "crotch episode" of *Texas Chain Saw Massacre II*, in which the female victim-hero Stretch is cornered by Leatherface—chief of the deadly gazers in a series famous for its deadly gazing. Power fails Leatherface's chain saw at just the moment he is about to do her in, and in a state of apparent confusion, he instead slides the now-quiet saw up her leg to her crotch, where he moves it back and forth. Despite her terror, Stretch immediately senses the issue: "You're really good, you really are good, you're the best," she murmurs—at which point Leatherface achieves his first orgasm. Although a chain saw is not a camera in the normal scheme of things, Leatherface's particular chain saw and Mark's particular camera have a great deal in common. Both are specifically figured as not simply phallic but as ersatz substitutes for the real thing. Both are used to bear down on and do violence to female victims—though both also lose their "power" in the presence of a "special" woman. Both are the products of phallic transmission—gifts from punishing, all-powerful fathers. Although we do not "see" the action through Leatherface's chain saw in the way we see it through Mark's camera, we do see it mainly through Leatherface's eyes—in a way that suggests a classic "displacement upwards."

[45] Martin and Porter, *Video Movie Guide: 1987*, p. 690.

to note, however, are the shortcomings and ultimate failure of that gaze. For one thing, it does not see well—at least not since 1978, when John Carpenter popularized the use of the unmounted first-person camera to represent the killer's point of view.[46] Although critics tend to assign a kind of binding power to marked first-person cinematography, the fact is that the "view" of the first-person killer is typically cloudy, unsteady, and punctuated by dizzying swish-pans. Insofar as an unstable gaze suggests an unstable gazer, the credibility of the first-person killer-camera's omnipotence is undermined from the outset. One could go further and say that the assignment of "real" vision to "normal" characters draws attention, in the hand-held or Steadicam sequences, to the very item the filmmaker ostensibly seeks to efface: the camera. To the extent that its "jiggle will remind the audience that they are indeed looking at a movie," William Earle writes, it is an ironic device that works against, not for, "acquiescence to the real."[47] Or John Carpenter himself of the hand-held cameras in Grizzly and The Eyes of Laura Mars: "There's nothing that gets you, because you know it's this jiggling camera. . . . there's nothing scary about it."[48] Moreover, inasmuch as the vision of the subjective camera calls attention to what it cannot see—to dark corners and recesses of its vision, and above all to the space, and what might be in it, just off-frame—it gives rise to the sense not of mastery but of vulnerability.

More to the point, assaultive gazing never prevails, and mean lookers do not survive as such (if at all). A remarkably durable theme of horror involves turning the assaultive gaze back on itself. *The Incredibly Strange Creatures Who Stopped Living and Became Crazy Mixed-Up Zombies*, a cult-horror classic from 1964, offers a paradigmatic example. A group of three teenagers go to the carnival. After sampling the rides, Jerry proposes to his companions, a boy and a girl, that they go to the girlie show. Offended by Jerry's leering attitude, the girl refuses, and the other boy takes her home. Jerry enters the tent

[46] Carpenter and others draw a distinction between the hand-held camera and the Panaglide or Steadicam, which produces an effect midway between hand-held and dolly-mounted. Says Carpenter of the Panaglide: "So it doesn't have the rock-steadiness of a dolly, but it also doesn't have the human jerky movements of a hand-held—it's somewhere in between" (as quoted by Cumbow, *Order in the Universe*, p. 51). My own sense is that insofar as any shot is marked as different from "normal," it is marked as deviant and untrustworthy.

[47] William Earle, "Revolt against Realism in the Films," p. 40. I would also argue that the use of unattributed point-of-view shots adds to the sense of instability. See Vera Dika for the opposite view ("The Stalker Film") and Neale on assigned and unassigned looking in *Halloween* ("Halloween").

[48] As quoted by Cumbow, *Order in the Universe*, p. 51. See also Prawer, *Caligari's Children*, p. 66 and Tudor, *Monsters and Mad Scientists*, pp. 201–2.

and joins a crowd of hundreds of men whistling and shouting at the exotic dancers. He becomes visibly entranced by the stripper Carmelita. When a note is passed to him inviting him to a back room to meet her, he goes eagerly. At the appointed place sits a gypsy woman, ostensibly the go-between; but as he waits, she induces him to look into a whirligig, which "pulls" his gaze hypnotically into its "eye."[49] If the assaultive gaze here could hardly be more phallic, its object could hardly be more vaginal. The swaggering male imagines his gaze potent until faced with the "insatiable organ hole" of the feminine; in that war of "visions," he cannot but lose.[50] ("Black holes in the universe—if that's not feminine, I don't know what is," raves the killer of *White of the Eye.* Another critic has noted the ubiquity of the "vortex of a ventilation fan" as "the image that, for some reason, became the standard symbol for menace in horror films of the '80s.")[51] Similarly the scene in *Gothic* in which Claire realizes a long-standing fantasy of Shelley's by baring her breast and entreating him to look into her eyes—at which point her nipples become lids that slowly open to reveal monstrous eyes, causing him to look away. This relocation of the eyes to the nipples reconfigures the torso as a face of sorts—with the mouth now occupying the position of "insatiable organ hole." The idea takes its most elaborate form in *Poltergeist,* a film structured around the sucking of first the gaze and then the gazer into a series of vacuums: the vacuum tube of the television that Carol Anne watches with such emotional intensity; the vacuum of the storm that nearly pulls Robbie out the window; the vacuum of the red and fleshy sucking hole that opens and tries to pull the whole family in. The vaginal nature of this series of vortices becomes more or less explicit when Diane, with the help of Dr. Lesh and the medium (spiritual midwives, as it were) finally lets herself be drawn into

[49] The moment is quoted in *Hairspray* in a scene in which John Waters appears as the whirligig-equipped hypnotist charged with keeping Tracy immured in her bedroom. *Bringing Up Baby* offers a comic turn on the idea when David says to Susan, "The only way you'll get me to do what you want is to hold a bright object in front of my eyes and twirl it."

[50] Montrelay, "Inquiry into Femininity," p. 91. Creed also speaks of the "voracious maw, the mysterious black hole which signifies female genitalia as the monstrous sign which threatens to give birth to equally horrific offspring as well as threatening to incorporate everything in its path. This is the generative archaic mother, constructed within patriarchal ideology as the primeval 'black hole.' " Although that "black hole" can be the sign of castration, it is not so in the horror texts she studies. There, emphasis is on the "gestating, all-devouring womb of the archaic mother," which, unlike the female genitalia, "cannot be constructed as a 'lack' in relation to the penis. The womb is not the site of castration anxiety. Rather, the womb signifies 'fullness' or 'emptiness' but always is its own point of reference" ("Horror and the Monstrous Feminine," p. 63).

[51] Cumbow, *Order in the Universe,* p. 125.

the last "hole" (the red cavern) in order to extract her daughter from the first "hole" (the television) and allow themselves to be reborn, complete with blood and amniotic slime, into the world.

Life Force, an s/f-horror version of the femme fatale story, is also an extended reverie on just how the assaultive gaze can backfire. On a strange planet, space travelers from earth find a sleeping beauty in a glass capsule and, after looking at her at lustful length, decide to bring her back to earth. The link between staring and sexual possession is clearly drawn. "I'd say she looks perfect. I've been in space six months now, and she looks perfect to me," says one, staring through the glass. On earth, however, those perfect looks prove vampiric; the girl attracts the desiring gaze of males only to destroy them by draining them of their "life force." She has no problem getting her fill; human males prove themselves only too willing to leer and, when she responds, to believe themselves fine figures of men, about to be rewarded for their bold stares. One by one the phallic gazers are depleted by the feminine. "She's looking for a man, any man, a healthy man; she wants to draw some energy from him," one near-victim explains. "She was draining me!" exclaims another who escaped. *Life Force* is at one level a standard femme fatale story; but on another, like others of its kind, it is an object lesson along Medusan lines on the danger of would-be-phallic looking. It is striking how many femme fatale stories begin with overzealous male gazing. At best, it seems, assaultive gazing is risky business.

At worst, it is fatal. If the jerky vision of the first-person murderer is a cliché of horror, it is an inexorable law of horror that this vision must be extinguished, that its bearer be punished and incapacitated—typically blinded or killed or both. If jerky vision signals a force ready to be unleashed, it also signals its own imminent demolition; the gaze is unstable because its bearer is doomed. Mark in *Peeping Tom* dies by his own camera, but most assaultive gazers exit less gracefully. Crawford in *From Beyond* has his pineal eye bitten off. "Proteus" (the intelligent computer-video apparatus in *Demon Seed*) is blown to smithereens (although "he" does leave behind him a human-appearing child). Michael in *Halloween* has his eyes stabbed out. The drunken farmer who tries to rape Rose in Cronenberg's *Rabid* is stabbed in the eye. *Every* slasher killer whose gaze the audience was invited to share at the beginning of the film is disabled, evacuated, or dead by film's end. Paradoxically enough, the unmounted camera originally intended to make it scarier ends up, at least for the competent spectator, as a reassurance: the wielder of this knife or this chain saw, it announces, is dead meat.[52]

---

[52] Earle has argued that the hand-held camera is an ironic device. "In ironic films we

It is no wonder, given the phallic associations of assaultive gazing, that rape-revenge films are so conspicuously concerned with vision and (hence) so frequently end with the blinding of the (would-be) rapist. So the victim-hero of *Extremities* saves herself by spraying insect repellent into the eyes of her assailant-eyes through which we watched her stalked in the early parts of the film. *Eyes of a Stranger* doubles the idea. The killer's chief target is Tracy, the heroine's blind, deaf, and mute younger sister. Now in her apartment, the killer observes and approaches the oblivious girl as she taps her way to the kitchen to make coffee. He makes his presence known and begins to torment her, but she suddenly dashes coffee in his face, temporarily blinding him, and kicks him in the groin. She flees and hides, and as he gropes after her, she regains her vision (we experience the dawning through her eyes), grabs a gun, and shoots him. The equation between sight and (phallic) power, traded back and forth between male and female, is thus relentlessly played out. It turns out that Tracy's disabilities stem from her rape as a child. Faced with the same threat in the here and now, she reverses the terms: by blinding her present assailant (and harming his genitals), she "renounces the passivity into which she had withdrawn" (as Robin Wood put it) and, equipped with both vision and pistol, does him in.

In his appreciative discussion of *Eyes of a Stranger* (one of the few notices of any kind the film received), Wood remarked the ways it complicates any simple understanding of sadistic gazing. For one thing, he notes, the film ends with the murderer "definitively dead, slumped ignominiously in the bathtub, his eyes closed, his glasses still perched incongruously on his nose: an unflattering reflection for any male who relished the sadistic assaults."[53] *Eyes of a Stranger* is indeed a departure from the rule—but one of degree, not kind. Not all gazer-killers are as definitively and ignominiously done away with as the "overweight creep" of *Eyes of a Stranger*, but many are, and even those who get off easier do not get off altogether.[54] What is exceptional about *Eyes of a Stranger*, I would argue, is the directness and intelligence with which it exposes the phallic gaze for what it is—but

---

have the double awareness of seeing some action as it is refracted through an artificial medium. Now the camera will be hand held, so its jiggle will remind the audience that they are indeed looking at a movie; sometimes processing perforations are shown, and the trailers and leaders of the film as they come back from the developer; sometimes the actors ham it up so we are aware they are acting" ("Revolt against Realism in the Films," p. 40).

[53] Wood, "Beauty Bests the Beast," p. 65; cf. Maltin, *TV Movies and Video Guide: 1990*, s.v. *Eyes of a Stranger*.

[54] Maltin, *TV Movies and Video Guide: 1990*, s.v. *Eyes of a Stranger*.

not the *fact* of that exposure, which is par for the course in horror. In other words, the kind of looking that Martin and Porter call "sick"—looking in which camera and male gazer make common cause in some act of aggression toward women—is also denoted as "sick" by the films themselves and treated accordingly: ridiculed, punished, annihilated. At the very least, it is ironized or played for comic effect—used to stage its own annihilation. So obviously insufficient and/or silly is "killer-camera" gazing in these films that one cannot help wondering how and why critics have taken it seriously. (One of my teen consultants on this project theorizes that the purpose of the first-person killer gaze, and the reason for its prominence at the beginning of the film, is to drive parents away so kids can watch the remainder in peace. It clearly works that way for most reviewers.) My suspicion, as I shall suggest in some detail below, is that our cultural stake in male sadism in all its forms is such that we cannot afford to see otherwise, even when, as in horror, the "otherwise" is the main point.

The Reactive Gaze

For, as *Peeping Tom* insists, the eye of horror works both ways. It may penetrate, but it is also penetrated: so the plethora of images of eyeballs gouged out or pierced with knives, ice picks, and hypodermic needles, and so the scenes of persons suddenly blinded by hot coffee, acid, insect spray, or simply—and significantly—bright light.[55] The opening eye of horror is far more often an eye on the defense than an eye on the offense. The eyes on promotional posters and videocassette boxes are in the great majority of cases threatened,

[55] The eye in *Un Chien andalou*, slit in close-up by a razor, is perhaps the grandfather of the tradition, and the Salvador Dali eye in *Spellbound*, cut by scissors, the father. Both point up the relation between surrealist notions of shock and the larger project of horror. Consider too Bataille's "pineal eye": "The eye, at the summit of the skull, opening on the incandescent sun in order to contemplate it in a sinister solitude, is not a product of the understanding but is instead an immediate existence; it opens and blinds itself like a conflagration, or like a fever that eats the being, or more exactly, the head . . . the head has received the *electric power of points*" (*Visions of Excess*, p. 82). Prawer too notes the special emphasis on the eye in horror: "Within the face it is of course the eye which leads most directly to where we live—and the human eye has, indeed, played an especially important part in the terror-film. The photographed eye may be that of a sinister watcher, as in some frightening close-ups of Robert Siodmak's *The Spiral Staircase* (1946), which also shows the distorted way in which the watcher's mind interprets what his eye sees; or it may be the eye of a sad victim, the mirror of a tortured soul, as at the opening and close of Polanski's *Repulsion*. It hardly needs saying that the vulnerability of the eye is also played on by sequences enlisting our fear of physical injury, in films that range from *An Andalusian Dog* to *The Flesh and the Fiends* (1959)" (*Caligari's Children*, pp. 75–76).

frightened eyes—commonly a woman's eyes reacting in horror at a poised, bloody knife, an advancing shape, or something off-poster or off-box. "One of the most frequent and compelling images in the horror film repertoire," writes J. P. Telotte, "is that of the wide, staring eyes of some victim, expressing stark terror or disbelief and attesting to an ultimate threat to the human proposition."[56] A standard moment in horror is one in which a person is caught by surprise—her vision assaulted—by the sight of things she does not want to see: Laurie in *Halloween*, for example, who looks into a closet only to see the dead body of her friend staring her in the face. And as Telotte points out, the effect is maximized by the reversal of the normal sequence in such a way that the reaction comes first.[57] Over and over, horror presents us with scenarios in which assaultive gazing is not just thwarted and punished, but actually reversed in such a way that those who thought to penetrate end up themselves penetrated. The multi-eyed aliens of *The Eye Creatures* (1965) threaten, by virtue of their superior vision, to take over the world—until the army turns spotlights on them and, piercing them with light, causes them to explode. And when the two chief "scanners" in Cronenberg's *Scanners* face off, the loser ends up incinerated and the "winner," Daryl Revok, completely inhabited by the persona of his opponent. Scanning, it seems, gets as good as it gives—a point clarified by Revok himself, whose head is populated by all the "people" who have gotten in during his scanning career. He drills a small hole in his forehead, just at the bridge of his nose, to let the "people" out, and then covers it over with a bandage on which he paints an eye. "A door," he explains to Dr. Ruth, "[I] put an eye on the door so they won't know it's a door, and they can't get back in because they see the eye."[58] What appears to be an eye, in other words, is in fact a mask—and not only a mask, but a secondary, counterdefective mask, designed and installed after

[56] Telotte, "Faith and Idolatry in the Horror Film," p. 151.

[57] "Normally an action is presented and then commented upon by reaction shots; the cause is shown and then its effect. The horror film, however, tends to reverse the process, offering the reaction shot first and thus fostering a chilling suspense by holding the terrors in abeyance for a moment; furthermore, such an arrangement upsets our ordinary cause-effect orientation" (ibid., p. 152).

[58] For William Beard, "the idea of an almost physical invasion of the mind and of the seeing eye as a barrier to intrusion and the guardian of privacy and self is a nice symbol of the related ideas of control, awareness and aggression. The people in Revok's head are trampling him, stripping him of control. To keep them out, he must establish an appearance of awareness and vigilance (the 'eye'). Thus is established the notion of seeing as a weapon—awareness as an aggressive tool. Revok the monster scanner, using the 'eye' in his head to control and destroy others, is born in this act of his younger self" ("The Visceral Mind," p. 42; more generally, pp. 39–50).

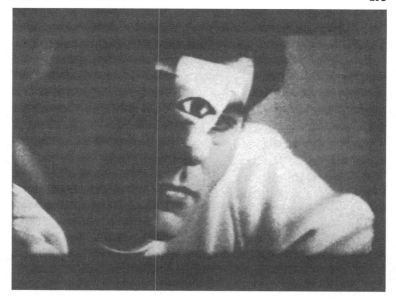

Daryl Revok's "eye" and what it protects (*Scanners*).

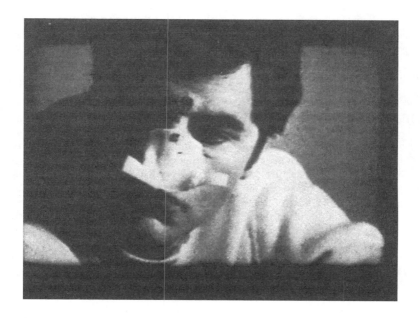

the fact to protect a natural and original vulnerability.[59] Whatever
else they may be, eyes are also (ick!) *soft*.[60]

Looking at screens is particularly perilous and perilous in particular ways. As a film manifestly *about* the perils of horror spectatorship, Lamberto Bava's *Demons* (1986) is worth considering in some detail. A number of people are lured to a new movie theater to see a free "mystery" movie as part of the opening celebrations. A character hopes aloud that it won't be horror, but it of course turns out to be just that ("Oh, shit, it *is* a horror movie"). As suspense mounts, members of the audience become sexually aroused, especially at the sight of a woman being stabbed repeatedly in close-up by an off-frame killer (all we see of him is his knife-holding hand). One audience member, a black prostitute, senses something on her cheek and reaches up to feel a strange boil emerging from a lesion—a development that precisely mirrors what is happening to the cheek of one of the film-within-the-film characters. (Crosscutting establishes the connection between the black female in the audience and the white male on the screen.) The hooker goes off to the lavatory to investigate her face (in yet another mirror), but she is within minutes transformed into a crazed zombie and begins to roam the back corridors of the theater building. Meanwhile, in the auditorium, the audience is raptly watching a second woman, the film-within-a-film's heroine, about to fall to the killer's knife. She is pleading and screaming, and the knife is on the verge of sinking in, when the screen onto which those images are projected is suddenly slashed and ripped from behind, and the zombie lunges through it out onto the proscenium and down into the frantic audience.[61] That zombie attacks and transforms others, who in turn attack and transform still others. As more audi-

---

[59] As even this short survey should make clear, the standard equation eyes = testicles, although much in evidence, does not begin to do justice to the ways eyes work in horror film, particularly in their "reactive" mode.

[60] It is important to remember that Freud's main treatment of horror, "The 'Uncanny,' " turns not on the phallic, mastering eye, but the vulnerable, threatened one. Of E.T.A. Hoffman's "The Sand-Man," a story that is precisely about eye-fear, he notes (p. 231): "We know from psycho-analytic experience . . . that the fear of damaging or losing one's eyes is a terrible one in children. Many adults retain their apprehensiveness in this respect, and no physical injury is so much dreaded by them as an injury to the eye. . . . A study of dreams, phantasies and myths has taught us that anxiety about one's eyes, the fear of going blind, is often enough a substitute for the dread of being castrated." That fear may be associated with female genitalia—not so much as a site of castration but as the site of intrauterine or birth memory (see esp. pp. 244–45).

[61] The setup is reminiscent of the scene in *The Blob* (1958) in which "goo came dripping down from the projection booth and onto our surrogate selves watching a horror movie at the downtown theater" (as Twitchell puts it in *Dreadful Pleasures*, p. 15).

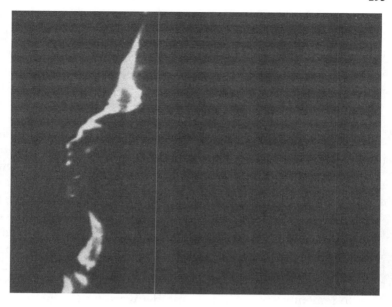

A crazed zombie slashes through the movie screen from behind out toward the audience (*Demons*).

ence members are infected, and those trying to escape discover that all exits are locked, mayhem reigns.[62] "The movie is to blame for this!" someone shouts. In an effort to halt the unfolding horror, other members of the audience break into the projection room and, once they register the fact that there is no projectionist (the system is automatic), they smash the projector itself to bits. "Now the movie is not going to hurt us any more," says one of the attackers. "It's not the movie, it's the theater," someone answers. Bava's point (to which I shall return) seems to be that the foul impulses of horror lie not in the movie but in the spectator. But in either case, his scenario admits the power and the aim of the movie to excite such foul impulses, and in this sense, his movie-within-the-movie is indeed invasive and does indeed "hurt."

Likewise television. *Demons II* tells of a woman, Sally, who watches a television horror film in which a vicious zombie is raised from the dead. As Sally stares at the tube, the vicious zombie, in close-up, seems to stare back for a moment before "pouring" itself, the tube

[62] The scene recalls the passage in *King Kong* (1933) in which an audience is similarly invited to a mystery spectacle. They expect a movie only to be confronted with reality: Kong himself. And Kong too breaks out of the spectacle position, rampaging into the viewing audience and causing pandemonium.

reformed around it, through the screen, and lunging out after Sally. In *Terrorvision*, space invaders step into a human living room from a television screen, into which they have been conveyed via a satellite dish, and kill the American viewing family one at a time. A special broadcast warns that "its appetite is insatiable, its curiosity is boundless, its strength knows no limits—it will continue to absorb all life forms." Similarly *Looker*, which turns on an advertising scheme to "use computer animation to put an electronic light impulse in the eyes of the commercial"—an impulse that is beamed out into the receptive eyes of the home viewer. The hero, Larry, is literally slugged in the eyes from the screen—until he dons protective glasses that enable him to go around slugging others in *their* eyes. And *Max Headroom*'s "blipvert" program causes certain television spectators—overweight and inactive ones—to become neurally overheated and explode. Even telekinetic vision can work the other way. In *The Fury* (1978), a nurse at the Paragon Institute explains to her telekinesis students that, in effect, the power of invading rests on being invadable: "Try to remember that Alpha is another word for passive. . . . Visualize sitting in an empty theater in front of a blank screen—and let that screen fill your mind." Theory becomes practice in *Scanners* when the man who wins the "scanning" duel does so only by allowing his own psyche to be invaded and replaced by that of his now-dead adversary.

In *Poltergeist*, the "fatal television" story enters the mainstream. Carol Anne perceives "people" in a blank, static-filled television screen and is eventually drawn in to join them. The film turns on the Freeling family's efforts to retrieve her. (It turns out that the "friendly child" whom Carol Anne followed into the television was the devil in disguise.) In the final scene, Steve Freeling is shown ejecting the television set from the motel room to which the family has finally escaped.[63] What distinguishes *Poltergeist*'s television set from others in the tradition is that it does not strike out and penetrate its viewers but instead sucks them in and swallows them up—in images and language that could hardly be more vaginal. Its "viewers," however, remain female (Carol Anne and her mother).

The most elaborate expression of "snuff television" is undoubtedly David Cronenberg's *Videodrome* (1982)—a film whose message William Beard sums up as: "Look not too deeply into the television

---

[63] For all its garishness, the female body imagery of *Poltergeist* has been little mentioned in the commentaries, which focus for the most part on the role of the father and the haunted house.

screen, lest it begin to look into you."[64] "The battle for the mind of North America will be fought in the video arena—the videodrome," Professor Brian O'Blivion declares. "The television screen is the retina of the mind's eye. Therefore the television screen is part of the physical structure of the brain. Therefore whatever appears on the television screen emerges as pure experience for those who watch it. Therefore television is reality and reality is—less than television." The front organization for O'Blivion's videodrome is an optical company whose new line of eyeglasses is being promoted by the slogans "Love comes in at the eye" and "The eye is window of the soul." The eyes/screens in question here are those of Max Renn, a producer of hardcore pornography whose fascination with the outlaw video signal leads to his eventual fusion with it. Evidently because as a woman she is "open," his girlfriend Nicki gives herself over to extreme forms of masochism without further ado. The horrified Max, however, resists. One evening, while Max is watching a videodrome-produced tape that includes footage of his girlfriend Nicki, the television itself begins to swell and writhe and the screen (displaying an extreme-close-up image of Nicki's lips) comes bulging out toward him. He kneels and buries his face in it. Shortly thereafter his abdomen develops a huge gash—into which a videodrome goon will later shove a videocassette tape. "What do you want with me?" the invaginated Max asks. "I want you to open up, Max. Open up to me," comes the answer. And Max does open up, is implanted, and is doomed. "*Videodrome* demonstrates that, if thoughts can escape from the brain, new thoughts can be just as easily crammed back in," notes one critic. "TV is lethal because it quite literally penetrates your brain and fucks with it."[65]

[64] Beard, "The Visceral Mind," p. 70.
[65] Geoff Pevere, "Cronenberg Tackles Dominant Videology," in *The Shape of Rage*, p. 142. In an interview, Cronenberg himself responded to a question about "interchangeability happening between the sexes" in his films as follows: "Yes. You realize how important sexuality is to the human race, in terms of art, culture, society, psychology, everything. My instinct tells me that an enormous amount of sexuality, and everything that springs from that in our society, is a very physical thing. Human beings could swap sexual organs, or do without sexual organs as sexual organs per se, for procreation. We're free to develop different kinds of organs that would give pleasure, and that would have nothing to do with sex. The distinction between male and female would diminish, and perhaps we would become less polarized and more integrated creatures to the extent that there is, generally speaking, a male sensibility and a female sensibility. . . . I'm not talking about transsexual operations [in *Crimes of the Future* in particular]. I'm talking about the possibility that human beings would be able to physically mutate at will, even if it took five years to finish that mutation. Sheer force of will would allow you to change your physical self. I think that there would be a dimin-

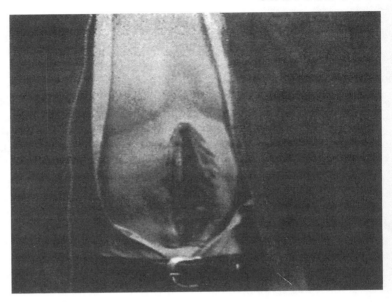

Max opens up (*Videodrome*).

To the extent that Michael Powell meant *Peeping Tom* to be a commentary on the production and consumption of horror cinema, it is brilliantly on point. Mark's alternation between assaultive and reactive gazing is commonly taken to suggest the interdependence of sadistic and masochistic impulses. But a survey of modern horror confirms that it is equally a function of the fact that Mark happens, in a way that most folks do not, to be both producer and consumer of his own movies; separate those functions the way they are separated in the real world and you have an arrangement whereby—at least in its horror film codification—assaultive gazing is associated with those who hold the camera and reactive gazing with those who stare at the screen after the fact. When Bava (*Demons*) has a character say "Now the movie can't hurt us any more" as he smashes the projector and another respond "It's not the movie, it's the theater," his less than ingenuous point seems to be that no one—not the theater, not the projectionist, not the movie, and by extension not the filmmaker—is ultimately responsible for the "hurt" but the viewer himself; the screen does nothing more than provide a mirror reflection of the spectator's own preexisting "hurt."[66] Powell too understands the "hurt" to preexist the movie, but he regards it as the cruel business of the horror industry to locate such "hurts" and mine them for their masochistic possibilities. *Peeping Tom*, in other words, locates accountability, if not for the "hurt" per se then for the masochistic exploitation of "hurt," squarely in the persons of the mirror wielder, the image maker: all the focus pullers, directors, and possibly consulting psychoanalysts, who together construct the mirror and brandish the spike.

Over and over, and in a remarkable variety of ways, modern horror plays out the same adversarial scenario. Film after film presents us with stories in which audiences are assaulted by cameras, invaded by video signals or film images, attacked from screens. The implication, of course, is that the audience in question is meant to represent *us* in relation to the screen *we* are watching, and now and then the equation is drawn directly. I refer again to Hitchcock's marginal note in the shooting instructions for the shower scene of *Psycho*: "The slashing. An impression of a knife slashing, as if tearing at the very screen, ripping the film." We could hardly ask for a clearer set of equivalents: as Norman is to Marion, Hitchcock is to the audience of *Psycho*; or, more generally, as slasher is to slashed, horror filmmakers

---

ishing of sexual polarity, and there would be a reintegration of human beings in a very different way" ("The Interview," in *The Shape of Rage*, pp. 190–91).

[66] According to Beard, *Videodrome* leaves the question of accountability deliberately unresolved ("The Visceral Mind," p. 52).

are to horror audiences.[67] Hitchcock's "impression" becomes Bava's diegetic reality when, in *Demons*, the screen of the movie-within-the-movie (also a horror film, also featuring a knife-wielding killer) is suddenly slashed and ripped from behind by raging zombies who flood through it into the theater. The equation is overt: as the diegetic audience is to the diegetic movie, so we are to Bava's *Demons*; as the screen of the diegetic horror movie "attacked" its audience, so the screen of *Demons* means to attack *us*.[68]

Certainly horror plays repeatedly and overtly on the equation between the plight of the victim and the plight of the audience. Whatever else it may be, the ploy of showing us an about-to-be-attacked woman watching a horror film depicting an about-to-be-attacked woman is also a clear metacinematic declaration of our common spectatorial plight. But the screen-within-the-screen arrangement only makes explicit what is perhaps universally implicit in horror: the alignment of the audience with screen victims in general, regardless of how directly or indirectly they are figured as themselves spectators. The point is wittily made in the climactic sequence of *Texas Chain Saw Massacre II*. Dripping with sweat and gore and searching desperately for a way out of the horrible underground labyrinth, Stretch is on the verge of being seized by mad killers when she glances up and sees, in the dim, bloody, cobwebbed recesses, a glowing EXIT sign. It is a moment that audiences greet with shouting and laughter, partly

[67] William Rothman argues that Hitchcock in this sequence "divides our identification. We identify with Marion, who must now confront the vision that was ours. But we are also implicated in this visitation and cannot separate ourselves from the whose sudden intrusion frightens Marion. We view Marion through this creature's eyes, as she turns to possess it in her gaze" (*Hitchcock*, p. 301). Rothman elsewhere (p. 296) admonishes that "our pleasure in viewing Marion [shortly before the attack] cannot be separated from our fantasy that we are about to possess her sexually. (If this is a male fantasy, it is not one that only the men in Hitchcock's audience may indulge. For men and women among the film's viewers, the act of viewing possesses both active and passive aspects, call them 'masculine' and 'feminine.')" I note that Rothman invokes "active and passive" and the possibility of cross-gender identification only to secure the possibility that women participate in aggressive male fantasies. The case could further be made that even when Rothman claims to be in Marion's position, he constructs it as a function of male desire (esp. p. 296). One of the aims of my own chapter is to hold critics like Rothman to the lip service they pay to cross-gender identification.

[68] The trope crops up in the "woman's film" as well. "The image and voice in these films act as the 'third persons' of the paranoid delusion (the agents of persecution), and ultimately it is the cinema itself, through its organization of image and sound, which attacks the woman, becoming the machine of her torment. This operation is literalized in a significant number of films which explicitly activate the materials of the cinematic signifier, or even the cinema itself, in an assault on the female protagonist" (Doane, *The Desire to Desire*, pp. 152–53).

because of the analogy it admits (labyrinth = moviehouse, chain saw-wielding sons = camera-wielding filmmakers, terrified victim = audience) but partly because the "clue," the EXIT sign, is so obviously excessive, such a breach of third-person protocol—such a naked disclosure of the cinematic signifier.[69]

It is in promotional materials that this architecture is most explicit—not least because promotional materials, unlike the movies they promote, stand outside cinema's third-person law. The poster for *The Maniacs Are Loose!* (1965) promises maniacs "not only on screen, but maniacs in audience! All over theater looking for victims! Believe it or not, as *you* watch this movie you become *part* of the picture—*you* are put in the *middle* of it—with bloodthirsty maniacs all around *you*—not only on screen, but LIVE MANIACS IN AUDIENCE! All over theater looking for victims!" The tone and gimmicks may be dated, but the promise, in the second person, that audiences will share the victim's fate remains current: "We'll tear your soul apart—again!" promises the trailer for *Hellbound: Hellraiser II*. Or "They'll get you in the end!" (*Ghoulies*), "First it destroys your mind, then it destroys your body!" (*Videodrome*), "Are you eating it or is it eating you?" (*The Stuff*), "The first kiss could be your last" (*Vamp*), "At dawn they hide. At dusk they wake. At night they search for blood. Pray for daylight" (*Near Dark*), or "High seas. Deep terror. Try to stay calm" (*Dead Calm*), and "So you think you're lucky to be alive . . ." (*The Hills Have Eyes II*). The fifties and sixties also saw the rise of what Stephen King calls the "in-theater gimmick." The classic example is William Castle's *The Tingler* (1959), in which a monster given to attaching itself to people's spines and "tingling" them to death is said to have just gotten loose in a movie theater, killed the projectionist, and shorted the electricity—at which moment the actual theater lights go off, the screen goes blank, and a soundtrack voice advises audience members to scream for their lives; in some theaters, certain seats were wired for effect.[70] Theaters showing *Wait until Dark* turned off every house light but the EXIT signs during the "blind" sequence at the end.[71] Charles Derry speculates that the "consistent reports of

---

[69] See Silverman, *The Acoustic Mirror*, p. 27: "Cinema challenges the imaginary plenitude of the viewing subject whenever it reveals the fantasmatic basis of its objects—whenever it reenacts the foreclosure of the real from representation. . . . Even more threatening to the subject's coherence is the disclosure of the cinematic signifier, since that disclosure not only finalizes the rupture with the phenomenal realm, but draws attention to the invisible enunciator—to the fact, that is, that films and their spectators are spoken by an unseen Other."

[70] For more examples, see King, *Danse Macabre*, pp. 184ff.

[71] "I never realized until the last ten minutes of *Wait Until Dark* how much light there is in most theaters, even when the movie's playing. . . . In a pinch, you can always

vomiting and fainting in the theaters where *The Exorcist* was playing"
may have been "planted at first by publicity departments," thus in
effect daring the viewer, evidently with great success, to match the
terms.[72] And, of course, there is the simple fact that the darkness in
which the vast majority of horror action transpires matches the darkness in which we sit—an equation Stephen King makes much of in
his *Danse Macabre*. "The horror movie is planning to get us, all right,"
he concludes, "and that is exactly why it is lurking here in the very
darkest part of the forest. At this most basic level, the horror film
isn't fooling around: it wants to get you."[73]

No one who has attended a matinee or midnight showing of a horror film with a youth audience can doubt the essentially adversarial
nature of the enterprise. The performance has the quality of a cat-
and-mouse game: a "good" moment (or film) is one that "beats" the
audience, and a "bad" moment (or film) is one in which, in effect,
the audience "wins." Judged by plot alone, the patterns of cheering
and booing seem indiscriminate or unmotivated or both. It is when
they are judged by the success or failure of the film to catch the audience by surprise (or gross it out) that the patterns of cheering and
booing fall into place. At such moments, the diegesis is all but short-
circuited, and the horror filmmaker and the competent horror viewer
come remarkably close to addressing one another directly—the
viewer by shouting out his approval or disapproval not to the on-
screen characters but to the people who put them there, and the people who put them there, in their turn, by marking the moment with
either a tongue-in-cheek gesture (the EXIT sign in *Texas Chain Saw
Massacre II*) or an actual pause to accommodate the reaction—both
amounting to a silent form of second-person address.

And, of course, horror films *do* attack their audiences. The attack
is palpable; we take it in the eye. For just as the audience eye can be
invited by the camera to assault, so it can be physically assaulted by

---

find your way back to your seat after using the bathroom by the light being thrown
from the screen itself. Except that the climactic few minutes of *Wait Until Dark* are set
entirely in that black apartment" (King, *Danse Macabre*, p. 184).

[72] "In some strange way, the possibility that a viewer might faint or vomit was an
attractive one; seeing *The Exorcist* was a rite of passage, and only those that fainted
and vomited were the winners. In an era where death—in the form of Vietnam killing,
live riots, and assassinations—is watched daily over a long period of time on the evening news, and our responses to death have become complacent and anesthetized,
going to *The Exorcist* and throwing up reaffirms man's ability to be revolted, his ability
to feel; thus the viewer's vomit almost becomes a valid artistic response to the world
around him" (Derry, *Dark Dreams*, p. 104). The viewer who vomits is also mirroring
the on-screen reactions of Regan.

[73] King, *Danse Macabre*, p. 178.

the projected image—by sudden flashes of light, violent movement (of images plunging outward, for example), fast-cut or exploded images. These are the stock-in-trade of horror. Film after film blinds us with a flash of lightning or spotlight, or points a gun or camera at us and shoots, or has a snake-like alien or rat burst toward us. It is no surprise that 3-D should at more or less the moment of its invention seize on such moments and include at least one in every film as a matter of course.[74] It is also no surprise that the narrative flow of images should burst into fragments at the most gruesome or shocking moments. The locus classicus, of course, is the shower scene of *Psycho*, which lasts for forty seconds and is composed of as many shots: a rapid-fire concatenation of images of the knife-wielding hand, parts of Marion, parts of the shower, and finally the bloody water as it swirls down the drain.[75] It is a breathtaking piece of cinematic violence—and as much at the editorial as at the diegetic level. (The extinction of the protagonist midway through the story is an act of violence at the narrative level.)[76] The fact that such sudden visual attacks are typically preceded by a protracted sequence of calm underscores their violent intent. These are calculated assaults on the part of the film; they are aimed at the audience, and they hurt in the most literal, physiological sense.[77] "Cruel cinema" indeed.[78] Shutting or covering the eyes protects the viewer not only from taboo images but from the literally painful "visuals" that can accompany them. Much of the art of horror lies in catching the spectatorial eye unawares—penetrating it before it has a chance to close its lid. Only when the house curtain drops can our own "curtains" relax.[79] And

[74] Maxim Gorky has written of the shock he experienced at the moment, in the Lumière film *L'Asseur arrosé* (*Teasing the Gardener*), that the gardener squirted the hose: "You think the spray is going to hit you too, and shrink back." As quoted by Siegfried Kracauer, *Theory of Film*, p. 31.

[75] Rothman, *Hitchcock*, pp. 296–309.

[76] As Greenberg notes, "it is incomprehensible that Janet Leigh should simply cease to be. Never before had a star of such magnitude, a female sex goddess, been so utterly expunged in midstream. Thus Hitchcock drives home the incontrovertibility, the awesome finality of death. Our yen for sanctioned sex and sadism has been dreadfully surfeited by Marion's crucifixion. With Leigh gone, the comfortable conventions of the Hollywood suspense vehicle have been totally violated" (*The Movies on Your Mind*, p. 126).

[77] Carroll notes the physical pain inflicted by horror movie effects, but it is insufficient to account for horror's total effect (*The Philosophy of Horror*, p. 36).

[78] The term is Greenberg's (*The Movies on Your Mind*) though he uses it to refer to horror's underlying ideologies, not its immediate effects.

[79] It is remarkable how resilient a feature of movie theaters the curtain is and how many of even the most functional "plexes," stripped of nearly all the other traditional accoutrements, retain it.

indeed, horror cinema repeatedly equates the film screen and the dream screen, guarded by the eye, as sites for invasion.[80] For Daryl Revok in Cronenberg's *Scanners*, the eye is really just a mask, intended to frighten would-be intruders (because eyes are in theory frightening), over a hole, an open doorway, that leads directly to the brain.

(We also take it in the ear, of course. Although my interest here and throughout is with the ocular, it would be remiss not to mention sound in connection with horror's directly assaultive effects. The shower sequence of *Psycho* shocks at the auditory as well as the visual level; preceded by an ominous silence [the unadorned natural sounds of Marion's preparations], the attack triggers the sound of "shrieking violins" whose hammering thrusts duplicate both the stabbing action of the diegesis and the editorial shattering of the image.[81] Some viewers claim that they are more disturbed by the "music" of horror movies than the images, and that they cover not their eyes but their ears in the "scary parts." Sound in cinema in general has been undertheorized, and horror sound scarcely theorized at all.)

Horror movies themselves, in short, bear out in both letter and spirit the double gaze of *Peeping Tom*. On one side is the killer's (or monster's) predatory or assaultive gaze, with which, as in *Peeping Tom*, the audience is directly invited to collude—at least formally and at least temporarily. Such gazing is repeatedly associated with the camera (either as theme or device), and it is resolutely figured as male (when the assaultive gazer is a woman, she is either not really the gazer, as in *The Eyes of Laura Mars*, or not really a woman, as in the "telekinetic girl" films). What is striking about this male gaze, however, is how often it remains at the level of wish or threat—how seldom it carries through with its depredations, and, even when it does succeed, how emphatically it is then brought to ruin. It has, in horror, the status of a fiction straining to be a fact, and not a few plots precisely turn on exposing its posturings for what they are. On the other side is the reactive gaze. It too is associated with the cinematic or televisual apparatus—but as its object, not its subject. The fre-

---

[80] For a more general consideration of film screen and mind or eye screen, see Kawin, *Mindscreen*, especially chapter 1, "The Mind's Eye."

[81] Rothman, *Hitchcock*, p. 100. Further: "Much of the shattering impact of this moment derives from Bernard Herrmann's score. Hitchcock's original intention was to release the shower-murder sequence with no musical accompaniment at all, but Herrmann prevailed on him to try it out with music. . . . It is above all the sudden high-pitched shriek of violins, so compellingly suggestive of an attacking birdlike creature, that creates the shock that constitutes *Psycho's* best-known effect" (p. 298). See also Heath, "Body, Voice" in *Questions of Cinema* (pp. 176–93).

quency, in horror, of images of victim-eyes under attack—punctured, burned, gouged out, and blinded by light, by everything from hypodermic needles and hot coffee to "blipverts"—underlines the interest of horror in hurtable vision, vision on the defense. The reactive gaze too invites our collusion—if not through a hand-held camera, then through the steady accumulation of "normal" first-person shots and, on the narrative level, through a marshaling of all the usual empathic devices. And the reactive gaze too is resolutely gendered—but as feminine, not masculine. The movie-within-the-movie that is playing in *Demons* when the zombies break through the screen and attack the audience is a horror movie in which, at that very moment, a woman is shown being slowly stabbed in close-up. The person in threat when the EXIT sign flashes (in *Texas Chain Saw Massacre II*) is a woman. The body through whose slashing Hitchcock wanted to sensationalize the "body" of the audience is that of a woman. In *Peeping Tom*, to be on the receiving end of the camera is to be feminine by definition. In a representational system in which cinematic or televisual apparatuses "kill and fuck," in other words, *Videodrome*'s Max is as inevitably invaginated and implanted as *Demon Seed*'s Susan is raped and impregnated. When the reactive gazer is male, he is either too young to count, like Robbie in *Poltergeist*,[82] or, like Max in *Videodrome*, literally regendered by the experience. It is the reactive gaze that has pride of place in the scopic regime of horror—both within the diegesis, as the look that sees the truth, and outside it, in the theater, as the look that is assaulted from the screen.[83]

CRUEL CINEMA

Let me return now to the tendency, in both criticism and theory, to regard camera and spectator in a collusive relation intended to generate a sense of mastery, more or less sadistic, over the

[82] Again, young boys, like women and old men, are regarded as "unsubjects." See chapter 2, especially n. 20.

[83] In an interview with Derry, director William Friedkin makes much of the "expectancy set" that operates among horror audiences. "The cinema takes advantage of this factor. Alfred Hitchcock takes advantage of the fact that an audience comes into the theatre expecting to be scared. When they are standing in line they are afraid. So he takes them for about an hour and dangles them and lets them do it for themselves until he hits them with something. . . . The same is true for *The Exorcist*. People are afraid while they're standing in line. And for the first hour of the film, while there is little more than exposition and some of that very hard to follow unless you've read the book, people are working themselves into an emotional state that is inducive to becoming terrified" (*Dark Dreams*, pp. 123–24).

object of their common vision. At the theoretical level, the idea that cinematic pleasure is funded by the desire for voyeuristic command derives chiefly from the work of Laura Mulvey, as I mentioned earlier, and Christian Metz.

Again, Mulvey identifies two ways cinema looks at women, both of which presuppose a male (or masculine) gazer: a sadistic-voyeuristic look, whereby the gazer salves his unpleasure at female lack by seeing the woman punished, and a fetishistic-scopophilic look, whereby the gazer salves his unpleasure by fetishizing the female body in whole or part. Mulvey's work has been rightly appreciated, but in recent years it has also come in for criticism, including Mulvey's own.[84] The chief complaint has to do with the place (no place) of the female spectator in the model, but the question I would like to raise here is a rather different one—namely, whether cinematic looking always and inevitably implies mastery over its object, even when the looker is male and his object female. D. N. Rodowick has suggested that Mulvey's concern to construct a sadistic male subject led her to overlook the masochistic potential of fetishistic scopophilia. Given her assumption that active voyeurism is sadistic, her failure to consider the possibility that passive fetishistic scopophilia may point to masochism constitutes a blind spot. Mulvey, Rodowick writes, "defines fetishistic scopophilia as an overvaluation of the object, a point which Freud would support. But he would also add that this phenomenon is one of the fundamental sources of *authority* defined as passive submission to the object: in sum, *masochism*."[85]

For Metz, too, the viewer necessarily identifies with the camera in an operation that is essentially assaultive. In the often-cited passage from "The Imaginary Signifier" entitled "The Passion for Perceiving," Metz argues that because cinema is predicated on a distance between the spectator and the object of vision (a distance in time as well as space), the cinematic spectator is necessarily a voyeur, and voyeurism, with its drive to mastery, is by nature sadistic.[86] That con-

---

[84] As has often been noted, Mulvey's model, in its original formulation, allows for female spectatorial pleasure only as a male-identified or "transvestite" activity. In her later "Afterthoughts on 'Visual Pleasure,' " she suggests a psychosexual model for the cross-gender "visual pleasure" of the female spectator. See also the issue of *Camera Obscura* devoted to "The Spectatrix" ([1989]: 20–21).

[85] D. N. Rodowick, "The Difficulty of Difference," p. 7. Studlar (*In the Realm of Pleasure*, especially chapters 2 and 8) suggests that the relocation of fetishism to the preoedipal period (relating it to the loss of the mother rather than phallic loss) provides a model for a masochistic relation to the screen. Although it is my impression that horror scenarios bear out Freud's view that masochistic fears can stem from any period of development, I would argue emphatically that oedipal conflicts occupy pride of place.

[86] Metz, *The Imaginary Signifier*, esp. pp. 58–65.

struction has been queried by Silverman, who, following Jean Laplanche, argues that in the scenario of the primal scene (for Metz and
others the Ur-movie),[87] the seeing child is, at the level of identification, not master but victim of the situation. "Far from controlling the
sounds and images of parental sexuality, the child held captive
within the crib is controlled—indeed, overwhelmed—by them. Adult
sexuality invades him or her through the eyes and ears, puncturing,
as it were, those vital organs. The mastering, sadistic variety of voyeurism discussed by Metz can perhaps best be understood as a psychic formation calculated to reverse the power relations of the primal
scene—as a compensatory drama whereby passivity yields to activity
through an instinctual 'turning around' and reversal."[88]

Metz himself, in fact, gestures in the direction of reactive or "punctured" vision in an earlier passage ("Identification, Mirror") from the
same essay. Because the passage in question has been underappre-
ciated by critics, I quote it here in toto:

> All vision consists of a double movement: projective (the "sweeping"
> searchlight) and introjective: consciousness as a sensitive recording surface
> (as a screen). I have the impression at once that, to use a common expres-
> sion, I am "casting" my eyes on things, and that the latter, thus illumi-
> nated, come to be deposited within me (we then declare that it is these
> things that have been "projected," on to my retina, say). A sort of stream
> called the look, and explaining all the myths of magnetism, must be sent
> out over the world, so that objects can come back up this stream in the
> opposite direction (but using it to find their way), arriving at last at our
> perception, which is now soft wax and no longer an emitting source.
>
> The technology of photography carefully conforms to this (banal) phan-
> tasy accompanying perception. . . . During the performance the spectator
> is the searchlight I have described, duplicating the projector, which itself
> duplicates the camera, and he is also the sensitive surface duplicating the
> screen, which itself duplicates the filmstrip. There are two cones in the

[87] "For the spectator," Metz writes, "the film unfolds in that simultaneously very
close and definitively inaccessible 'elsewhere' in which the child sees the amorous play
of the parental couple, who are similarly ignorant of it and leave it alone, a pure on-
looker whose participation is inconceivable. In this respect the cinematic signifier is
not only 'psychoanalytic'; it is more precisely Oedipal in type. . . . The cinema retains
something of the prohibited character peculiar to the vision of the primal scene . . .
but also, in a kind of inverse movement which is simply the 'reprise' of the imaginary
by the symbolic, the cinema is based on the legislation and generalisation of the prohibited practice" (*The Imaginary Signifier*, pp. 64–65). See also Patrick Brantlinger,
"What Is 'Sensational' about the 'Sensation Novel'?" esp. pp. 25–26.

[88] Kaja Silverman, "Too Early/Too Late," pp. 156–57. See also her "Masochism and
Male Subjectivity," p. 50, and Jean Laplanche, *Life and Death in Psychoanalysis*, esp. p.
102.

auditorium: one ending on the screen and starting both in the projection box and in the spectator's vision insofar as it is projective, and one starting from the screen and "deposited" in the spectator's perception insofar as it is introjective (on the retina, a second screen).[89]

The oscillation between these two gazes, Metz adds, is crucial to the apparatus: "In the cinema, as elsewhere, the constitution of the symbolic is only achieved through and above the play of the imaginary: projection-introjection, presence-absence, phantasies accompanying perception, etc."[90]

It is hardly surprising that Metz's introjective gaze has been shunned by subsequent commentaries, for after putting it forward, Metz himself quickly subordinates it to the figure of the camera,[91] which in turn quickly resumes its status as the quintessential tool of projective and voyeuristic gazing. As it is formulated above, however, the distinction between projective and introjective looking, the latter described as a "receiving, recording, sensitive surface" onto which "things are deposited" or "projected" onto the "retina," corresponds more or less exactly to the distinction that I have argued horror itself draws between assaultive and reactive gazing. (I cannot help noting how close Metz's characterization of the retina as a "second screen" comes to Professor O'Blivion's definition, in *Videodrome*, of the television screen as the "retina of the mind's eye.") At first glance, horror's tendency to locate the reactive gaze outside and "against" the camera, not inside and "with" it, would seem to stand in direct contradiction to Metz's model of two gazes internal to the camera. A psychoanalytic perspective explains horror's scenario as a secondary formation of fiction, one that hypostasizes the gazes as both mechanical and imaginary opposites. A narrative form that materializes a split psyche as Jekyll and Hyde, in other words, will also materialize a split "viewer" as filmmaker and film spectator. Perhaps the introjective gaze is the one most frequently externalized from the

[89] Metz, *The Imaginary Signifier*, pp. 50–51. The passage is noted by Silverman in *The Acoustic Mirror*, p. 23.

[90] Metz, *The Imaginary Signifier*, p. 51. Studlar also stresses the double movement of the apparatus, and she too wants to correct the usual bias by stressing the passive and receptive side of the equation; see especially her "Masochism and the Perverse Pleasures of the Cinematic Apparatus" (chapter 8 of *In the Realm of Pleasure*). For a provocative discussion of two-way vision in relation to transvestite pornography, see Kaite, "The Pornographic Body Double."

[91] "When I say that I 'see' the film, I mean thereby a unique mixture of two contrary currents: the film is what I receive, and it is also what I release, since it does not preexist my entering the auditorium and I only need close my eyes to suppress it. Releasing it, I am the projector, receiving it, I am the screen; in both these figures together, I am the camera, which points and yet records" (Metz, *The Imaginary Signifier*, p. 51).

camera because the projective gaze seems intrinsic to it; or perhaps
the introjective or reactive gaze is the one externalized because that
arrangement harmonizes with the audience's real sense of victimization at the hands of the "movie" in the viewing situation ("the movie
is hurting us!"). In either case, it is to be expected, given the low-
mythic terms of horror, that what are experienced as competing visual experiences should be animated as competing figures in the diegesis.[92]

Where is masochism in all of this? Its absence in Metz's text
screams for attention, for while he emphatically identifies projective
looking as sadistic, he does not, for reasons on which we can only
speculate, proffer an equivalent analysis of introjective looking. His
blind spot thus corresponds exactly to Mulvey's. His language is suggestive enough (the receiving spectator is a "sensitive surface," "our
perception . . . is now soft wax," "things . . . come to be deposited
within me," and so on), but there the matter drops. It is in horror, I
suggest, that Metz's (and Mulvey's) blank is filled in. For even more
variously than it imagines ways that projective looking (to use Metz's
terms) can be sadistic, horror imagines ways that our "sensitive surface" can be intruded upon, that "things" can come to be deposited
within us—that our eyes are "soft."

Before I turn to the matter of masochism per se, however, let me
revert to an aspect of horror gazing that stands as a corollary to the
opposition between assaultive/reactive or projective/introjective gazing as it has been articulated in film theory. I am referring to the
extraordinarily popular theme of assaultive gazing that is foiled—
thwarted, swallowed up, turned back on itself—and of assaultive
gazers who end up blinded or dead or both. Within the classical psychoanalytic paradigm, needless to say, the notion of fallible phallic
gazing is something of an oxymoron, and the question is how to
make sense of its ubiquity in horror. A solution is suggested in a distinction proposed by Lacan between the gaze and the "eye" (look),
the former, in Silverman's elaboration, occupying much the same position in relation to the latter as the phallus does to the penis. The
gaze, in other words, is the transcendental ideal—omniscient, om-

[92] Cronenberg's work is something of an exception. Like Mark, *Videodrome*'s Max is
both filmmaker (aggressive, intrusive) and video viewer (intruded into). Likewise the
"scanners," in the film of that name, are simultaneously assaultive and "admissive"
in their gazing. In this respect, Cronenberg's work is closer to the intellectual or
metacinematic mode of *Peeping Tom* than straight horror. But insofar as it nonetheless
concretizes the dynamic (in bodies slit, heads exploded, and the like), it is very much
in the tradition of real horror. As Beard suggests, somatizing ideas is what Cronenberg's art is all about ("The Visceral Mind").

nipotent—which the look can never achieve but to which it ceaselessly aspires. The best the look can hope for is to pose and pass itself off as the gaze, and to judge from film theory's concern with the "male gaze," Silverman argues, it sometimes succeeds.[93]

It is just this distinction, I suggest, that horror repeatedly elaborates—in remarkably similar terms and in remarkably theatrical forms. Of the many examples enumerated above of wanna-be gazers who are blown out of the water, one stands out as particularly apt: the passage in *The Incredibly Strange Creatures Who Stopped Living and Became Crazy Mixed-Up Zombies* in which Jerry, having leered possessively at a stripper-dancer named Carmelita, and having imagined that the power of his gaze earned him an invitation to a rendezvous after the show, ends up having his "look," and his consciousness, sucked right out of him into the gypsy woman's whirligig (he awakes to find himself not only not in possession of Carmelita, but incarcerated). What is striking about this example is not just the fact that the male looker fails to "fix" the female object, but the fact that she ends up fixing him, and in a way that is as vaginal in its figuration as his would-be gaze is phallic.[94] Shelley is differently but equivalently "fixed" (in *Gothic*) when he stares at Claire's bare breasts only to see that they are staring back, their nipples having become large, wide-open eyes. So common is the theme of failed gazing in horror that I would venture as a rule of the genre that *whenever* a man imagines himself as a controlling voyeur—imagines, in Lacanian terms, that his "look" at women constitutes a gaze—some sort of humiliation is soon to follow, typically in the form of his being overwhelmed, in one form or another, by the sexuality of the very female he meant to master. In *Scanners*, theme assumes the proportions of theory when Revok explains that his gazing eye is in fact a front designed and installed to mask the invadable hole leading to his brain (he "put an

[93] "Although the gaze might be said to be 'the presence of others as such,' it is by no means coterminous with any individual viewer, or group of viewers. It issues 'from all sides,' whereas the eye '[sees] only from one point.' The gaze, moreover, is 'unapprehensible,' i.e., impossible to seize or get hold of. The relationship between eye and gaze is thus analogous in certain ways to that which links penis and phallus; the former can stand in for the latter, but can never approximate it. Lacan makes this point with particular force when he situates the gaze outside the voyeuristic transaction, a transaction within which the eye would seem most to aspire to a transcendental status, and which has consequently provided the basis, within feminist film theory, for an equation of the male voyeur with the gaze" (Kaja Silverman, "Fassbinder and Lacan," pp. 71–73).

[94] See Karen Horney's remarks on the male fear of the vagina not as a signifier of mutilation, but as a distinct, and for some men uniquely frightening, genital ("The Dread of Women").

eye on the door so they won't know it's a door, and they can't get back in because they see the eye").[95] Again, like Mark's murderous gaze in *Peeping Tom*, Revok's monstrous look in *Scanners* is not a primary or natural feature, but a secondary and counterdefective one, a construction "born in this act [the act of covering over his vulnerability] of his younger self."[96]

The question is whether this pattern of "looks" in horror's diegesis represents or misrepresents the terms of its extradiegetic scopic regime. As I suggested earlier, there is some variation on this point. There are horror passages that would seem to position the spectator at least temporarily as an assaultive gazer. But the most decried of these passages, the first-person killer-camera of slasher films, is also the one that calls the most blatant attention to its own insufficiency and instability. And although many horror films provide other, more "normal" opportunities for assaultive gazing (looking, that is, that more or less successfully passes itself off as the gaze), I would argue that it is generally speaking the case that such passages are fewer, more attenuated, and more pro forma in horror than they are in the most mainstream Hollywood cinema. (Few horror films approach *The Unbearable Lightness of Being* in the unembarrassed empowerment of male looking.) I repeat that I do not mean to suggest that horror utterly forecloses the possibility of voyeuristic pleasure. There are viewers and there are viewers, some of whom are more sadistically inclined than others, just as there are movies and movies, some of which make more space than others for engagement with the assaultive part. What I am proposing, however, is that assaultive gazing in horror is by and large the minority position and that the real invest-

[95] Revok's formulation is remarkably like the formulation of the woman analysand who worried, in terms that her analyst regarded as genitally based, as follows: "I used to feel I had never learned how *not* to be open all the time. I always felt open and couldn't ever shut myself off. But actually what I do is *look like* I'm open on the outside so I take people in, they think I'm really open. But sometimes I'm so frightened I can't really let them in at all, in fact I don't even want to. I stay shut off inside so people can't invade my space. If people can't see where my space is, they can't invade it. I hide it. Like having a hole in a wall and I scurry around patching the whole wall so no one knows where it is and they can't get in" (Mayer, "Everybody Must Be Just Like Me," p. 336).

[96] As Beard notes, "this idea of an almost physical invasion of the mind and of the seeing eye as a barrier to intrusion and the guardian of privacy and self is a nice symbol of the related ideas of control, awareness and aggression. The people in Revok's head are trampling him, tripping him out of control. To keep them out he must establish an appearance of awareness and vigilance (the 'eye'). Thus is established the notion of gazing as a weapon—awareness as an aggressive tool. Revok the monster scanner, using the 'eye' in his head to control and destroy others, is born in this act of his younger self" ("The Visceral Mind," p. 44).

ment of the genre is in the reactive or introjective position, figured as both painful and feminine.

Masochism has only belatedly been taken up in connection with the study of film.[97] One reason for the delay must have to do with the long-standing emphasis on voyeurism's presumed sadism, which has the virtue of rhyming with the aggressive sexuality attributed to conventional heterosexual masculinity—a virtue that has put feminist film theorists from Mulvey on (who view it as deplorable) in an unholy alliance with most male critics (who view it as inevitable).[98] Another reason must have to do with the complexities of the topic. Freud's changes of mind on the subject, as well as Theodor Reik's views and Gilles Deleuze's revision, have been usefully read by Silverman, who also pursues the political implications of exposing the masochistic dimension of particularly those texts produced by and primarily addressed to men.[99]

One of the most obvious features of horror is the way it retells the same stories decade after decade, sequel after sequel—stories that are often age-old and close to worldwide to begin with.[100] As I have suggested in earlier chapters, it is perhaps at the subgeneric level (possession, slasher, vampire) that the "yet again" nature of the enterprise is most evident; but in either case, it is surely fair to say that horror is probably the most convention-bound of all popular genres,

[97] In particular, by Studlar (*In the Realm of Pleasure*); Silverman (especially "Too Early/ Too Late," "White Skin, Brown Masks," "Masochism and Male Subjectivity," and "Fassbinder and Lacan"); Rodowick, "The Difficulty of Difference"; Neale, "Halloween"; Doane, *The Desire to Desire* and "Misrecognition and Identity"); Jacqueline Rose, "Paranoia and the Film System" (via a consideration of paranoia); Smith, "Action Movie Hysteria"; and Linda Williams, "Power, Pleasure, and Perversion" (an expanded version of chapter 7 of her *Hard Core*. Lynne Kirby's remarks on male hysteria also bear on the subject of masochism ("Male Hysteria and Early Cinema"). Leo Bersani's work, while only occasionally about film, suggests ways of theorizing masochistic representations; see especially *The Freudian Body* and "Is the Rectum a Grave?" and, with Ulysse Dutoit, *The Forms of Violence*. More generally, see Gayle Rubin, "Thinking Sex," and Gilles Deleuze, *Masochism: Coldness and Cruelty*.

[98] The point has been underscored by Silverman ("Masochism and Male Subjectivity"), who also quotes Freud in *Three Essays* to the effect that sadism "would correspond to an aggressive component of the sexual instinct," the biological significance of which "seems to lie in the need for overcoming the resistance of the sexual object by means other than the process of wooing" ("Masochism and Male Subjectivity," pp. 33–34).

[99] Silverman, especially "Masochism and Male Subjectivity." For a critical summary of Freud's views, see Laplanche, *Life and Death in Psychoanalysis*, pp. 85–102.

[100] For recent discussions of the archetypal nature of horror, see especially Schechter, *The Bosom Serpent*, and Twitchell, *Dreadful Pleasures*. King's "once-upon-a-time" synopses of twenty especially popular horror films are also telling (*Danse Macabre*, pp. 179–81).

that its conventions are organized around the experience of fear, and that this conjunction—scary stories endlessly repeated—stands as a narrative manifestation of the syndrome of repetition compulsion (*Wiederholungszwang*). Defined as an "ungovernable process originating in the unconscious" whereby a person "deliberately places himself in distressing situations, thereby repeating an old [but unremembered] experience," repetition compulsion thus has its roots in unpleasure.[101] The function and effects of repetition compulsion are not clear. (It is conspicuously driven, however, by the wish to "get it right," one of the oft-noted dynamics of horror films.)[102] What *is* clear is that where there is *Wiederholungszwang* there is historical suffering—suffering that has been more or less sexualized as "erotogenic masochism."[103] At the risk of circularity, I would argue that the very repetitiousness of fear-inducing scenarios in horror cinema is prima facie evidence of horror's central investment in pain.

It is in the nature of repetition compulsion that the repeater "does not recall [the] prototype" of the repetition scenario; "on the contrary, he has the strong impression that the situation is fully determined by the circumstances of the moment."[104] The "prototype" need not be a traumatic event. It may in Freud's formulation inhere in any and all of the developmental phases:

> Erotogenic masochism accompanies the libido through all its developmental phases and derives from them its changing psychical coatings. The fear of being eaten up by the totem animal (the father) originates from the primitive oral organization; the wish to be beaten by the father comes from the sadistic-anal phase which follows it; castration, although it is later disavowed, enters into the content of masochistic phantasies as a precipitate of the phallic stage of organization; and from the final genital organization

[101] Laplanche and Pontalis, *The Language of Psycho-Analysis*, s.v. "Compulsion to Repeat," p. 78.

[102] Recall Mark's anguish (in *Peeping Tom*) when he sees, on watching the projected film of the murder of Vivian, that the lighting was off (the implication being that he must try yet again, with yet another woman, as he has been trying all his adult life, to get it right). See also Greenberg's brief remarks in *The Movies on Your Mind*, pp. 196–97, and, on repetition in film in general, Heath, *Questions of Cinema* ("Repetition Time"), pp. 165–75.

[103] Laplanche and Pontalis, *The Language of Psycho-Analysis*, s.v. "Compulsion to Repeat," p. 78; Edward Bibring, "The Conception of the Repetition Compulsion"; Laplanche, *Life and Death in Psychoanalysis*, pp. 85–102; Sigmund Freud, *Beyond the Pleasure Principle* and "The Economic Problem of Masochism."

[104] Laplanche and Pontalis, *The Language of Psycho-Analysis*, s.v. "Compulsion to Repeat," p. 78. The degree to which, and the precise mechanisms whereby unpleasant experiences are converted to pleasant rehearsals is much disputed. See Bibring, "The Conception of the Repetition Compulsion."

there arise, of course, the situations of being copulated with and of giving birth, which are characteristic of femaleness.[105]

One could hardly ask for a neater roster of the threats in which horror trades: of being eaten (especially by "animals"), beaten, castrated, sexually penetrated, and impregnated. Although some horror stories seem fixed on one particular fear or phase, others seem to play the field. Traditional werewolf stories appear to be generally organized around the fear of being eaten by an animal, for example, and possession films around fears of "being copulated with and giving birth." Slasher films, on the other hand, are organized around thoughts of beating (in the Freudian scheme a residue of the sadistic-anal phase) and castration (phallic), with louder or softer overtones of sexual penetration (genital).

Although Freud was to undergo a radical change of mind between 1919 and 1924 (between the essays " 'A Child Is Being Beaten' " and "The Economic Problem of Masochism") as to the place of masochism in the psychic economy (in particular its role vis-à-vis the pleasure principle and the death instinct), he retained his observation that the perversion took as its programmatic form the assumption of the "feminine" position. In "The Economic Problem of Masochism," he spoke of male masturbatory fantasies of which

> the manifest content is of being gagged, bound, painfully beaten, whipped, in some way maltreated, forced into unconditional obedience, dirtied, and debased. . . . [I]f one has an opportunity of studying cases in which the masochistic phantasies have been especially richly elaborated, one quickly discovers that they place the subject in a characteristically female situation; they signify, that is, being castrated, or copulated with, or giving birth to a baby. For this reason I have called this form of masochism, a potiori as it were [i.e., on the basis of its extreme examples], the feminine form, although so many of its features point to infantile life.[106]

It is frequently noted that although the condition of being bound, painfully beaten, and so on, is regarded by Freud as essentially feminine, all of the cases he lists in this essay are male, the implication being that, although masochism "is a centrally structuring element in both male and female subjectivity," it is only in the female that it is accepted as natural and thus only in the male that it is considered perverse or pathological.[107] One stumbles over the asymmetry, but it

[105] Freud, "The Economic Problem of Masochism," pp. 164–65.
[106] Ibid., p. 162.
[107] Silverman, "Masochism and Male Subjectivity," p. 36. See also Parveen Adams, "Per Os(cillation)."

makes sense if one accepts the argument Freud sets forth (on the basis of mainly female cases) in " 'A Child Is Being Beaten' " to the effect that all children, male and female, are subject to the unconscious fantasy that they are being beaten—that is, "loved"—by the *father*. Whereas the girl's fantasy is "straight" (at least in Freud's reading),[108] the boy's involves a gender complication: to be beaten/ loved by his father requires the adoption of a position coded as "feminine" or receptively homosexual. Thus "feminine masochism" refers not to masochism in women, but to the essence of masochistic perversion in *men*,[109] and it is in this sense that I use the term here. Although Freud's designation of such fantasies as "feminine" has been assailed, it has the advantage of highlighting Freud's abiding interest in a kind of bedrock bisexuality. If bisexuality, in his account, seems to rest on and naturalize a masculine/feminine binary in ways modern critics find uncomfortable, it is a notion that opened the gate to more current formulations, including the idea that one's sex/gender/ sexuality has no existence outside the acts or performances that con-

[108] Silverman argues that the girl's fantasy may in fact be more "perverse" than Freud recognized. See her "Masochism and Male Subjectivity," esp. pp. 48–50.

[109] Laplanche and Pontalis, *The Language of Psycho-Analysis*, s.v. "Masochism," p. 245. Several commentators have objected to the locution "feminine masochism," not least because of the implication that it corresponds to masochism in women. Theodor Reik suggests dropping the term altogether or, failing that, reserving its use for "the perverted inclination of the man" and making clear its distinctness "from the masochism of the woman" (*Masochism in Modern Man*, p. 212). As I shall suggest in the remarks that follow, I have retained it here because of its obvious appropriateness to the sort of male-to-female transvestite or transsexual imaginings that are so central to modern horror cinema.

It is crucial, in parsing Freud on masochism, to distinguish between "femininity" as it manifests itself in female sexuality (a vexed and interesting topic, but not one on the table here) and "femininity" as it manifests itself in male fantasy. For Freud, male fantasies of being "gagged, bound, painfully beaten, whipped, in some way maltreated, forced into unconditional obedience, dirtied, and debased" place the subject "in a characteristically female situation" insofar as they "signify . . . being castrated, or copulated with, or giving birth to a baby." The word "signify" may give pause here as suggesting a natural relation between Set A and Set B (between debasement and being sexually penetrated, for example), but if we keep in mind the conventional homosexual taboo that hovers about such fantasies in the male, a taboo that may moreover understand the vagina in anal terms, feelings of degradation or debasement come into focus as a form of psychic camouflage. That taboo may also help to account for what is claimed by Reik and Freud to be the flamboyant and "self-shattering" character of male masochistic fantasies and practices in comparison with the rather more restrained ones of the female. In either case, the very fact that "feminine" masochism is a male affliction attests to its artifactual status. Also worth remembering in this connection is the fact that, according to psychoanalytic testimony, men fantasize about receptive copulation, being pregnant, and giving birth in pleasant as well as unpleasant terms.

stitute it.[110] Another advantage of the designation "feminine masochism" is simply that it may tell the truth about the way men who
have such fantasies might understand them. And if that understanding is on one hand mixed up with a sense of degradation, it on the
other contemplates the female body—a *specifically* female body—as a
site of intense sexual feeling.[111] It is worth remembering in this connection Freud's declaration, in "Analysis Terminable and Interminable," that the most deeply embedded male anxiety has not to do with
castration in any blanket or straightforward sense, but the fear of
standing in a passive or "feminine" relation to another man and the
particular sort of "castration" that might proceed from that.[112]

The relevance of "feminine masochism" in this technical sense to
a body of cinema addressed to male viewers and featuring female
characters in some form of distress, more or less sexual, is self-evident. Indeed, "feminine masochism" as it is articulated by Freud
suggests a distinctive psychosexual profile or experience-base for
each of the genres in question: the possession film, as I suggested
earlier, seems organized around the thought of being "copulated
with" and impregnated; the slasher around thoughts of being

[110] The possibility of "bisexual" spectatorship has been widely entertained. See especially Mulvey, "Afterthoughts on 'Visual Pleasure,' " Wood, "Repression, the
Other, the Monster" in "An Introduction to the American Horror Film," and de Lauretis, esp. "The Technology of Gender" in *Technologies of Gender*. On "performative"
gender, see Butler, *Gender Trouble*.

[111] As Beard suggests, the female body is virtually the *only* site of sexual feeling for
David Cronenberg. "It is notable that none of Cronenberg's male protagonists before
Videodrome is at all sexual. . . . Sex in these films is in fact vested in the female for the
most part" ("The Visceral Mind," p. 75). The case could be made that the sexuality of
even *Videodrome*'s protagonist is contingent on his "feminization," and that powerful
or transformative sexual feeling is, for Cronenberg, very much associated with masochistic experience and very little with sadism. Beard hints at the homoerotic implications in his discussion of *Videodrome* ("The Visceral Mind," pp. 60–62). Mention should
also be made of Rose's analysis of paranoia in the "film system," in particular her
remarks on the complex paranoia/femininity. "The woman is centered in the clinical
manifestation of paranoia as position. Paranoia is characterized by a passive homosexual current, and hence a 'feminine' position in both man and woman. In the case of
Schreber, the attack actually transforms his body into that of a woman; this is necessary because the 'state of voluptuousness,' which in his delusion is demanded of
Schreber by God, is not restricted for the woman to the genitals but is dispersed over
the whole body . . . and is constant (extension in time and space as a reference to
woman's relation to a non-genital, i.e., un-normativised sexuality). The attack itself is
sexually ambivalent—apparition of the foreclosed phallus in the real (Schreber is to be
inseminated by God) but also the penetration of the body by feminine tissue" ("Paranoia and the Film System," p. 102). See also Doane, *The Desire to Desire*, esp. pp. 129–
34; and Craft, "'Kiss Me with Those Red Lips,' " pp. 114–15). See also chapter 1, n.
55.

[112] Freud, "Analysis Terminable and Interminable," esp. p. 252.

beaten, castrated, and penetrated (the proportions varying with the film); and the rape-revenge film, obviously, around thoughts of being or having been humiliatingly and violently penetrated (this plot more fully than the others allowing for the process of sadistic reversal). "Feminine masochism" also makes remarkably good sense of the figuring, for a predominantly male audience, of horror spectatorship itself as a feminine or feminizing experience.[113]

The "feminine masochism" model also makes sense of the "whose body" problem—if only by suggesting that the muddle is intrinsic, unresolvable by definition. In the preceding chapters I have noted how each of the horror genres in its own way collapses male and female to the point of inextricability: the slasher through the figure of an androgyne, the possession film through the assimilation of male psychic experience to female bodily experience, and the rape-revenge film by obvious implication and through a system of intertextual references (above all to *Deliverance*). In each case I have argued against the temptation to read the body in question as "really" male (masquerading as female) or "really" female (masquerading as male), suggesting instead that the excitement is precisely predicated on the undecidability or both-andness or one-sexness of the construction.[114] Much the same ambiguity, and a similar tension, attends Freud's reading of the male version of the "beating fantasy." For Freud, the male masochist's wish to be beaten by his father "stands very close to the other wish, to have a passive (feminine) sexual relation to him, and is only a regressive distortion of it."[115] In this phase, then, the fantasy is straightforwardly homosexual. Its author will come to

[113] Twitchell has argued that the organizing fear of horror is incest, by which he means that horror texts play out a version of the patricidal scenario outlined by Freud in *Totem and Taboo*. For Twitchell, the "horror of incest" comes down to this: "We humans have developed a code . . . to inform the prepotent males of the consequences *before* they can choose. This information is embedded into both the brain matter and the rites and myths of initiation with one simple message: have intercourse with a 'taken' woman and you will be cast out. It is as simple as that—make a mistake and you will not breed for a while" (*Dreadful Pleasures*, pp. 103–4; see also his *Forbidden Partners*). Although Twitchell must be right that horror trades in incest, I fail to see how his selective and "vanilla" version of the Freudian scenario works as a universal key (it seems inapplicable, or subsidiary, to most horror plots), or how it might work for the female viewer (of whose presence in the audience Twitchell otherwise makes much), or how, stripped of any essentially taboo desire (for Twitchell insists that the woman in question is to be understood not as a mother or a sister but as any woman in another man's possession), and thus reduced, as Twitchell himself acknowledges, to a lesson in social history, it accounts for the play of transgressive desire that manifestly animates most horror texts.

[114] Neale arrives at much the same conclusion about *Halloween* ("*Halloween*").

[115] Freud, "The Economic Problem of Masochism," 169.

"evade" that dimension, however, by "remodeling" the sex of the beating figure to that of a woman, albeit one whose mannish characteristics reveal her paternal origins: "The boy, who has tried to escape from a homosexual object-choice, and who has not changed his sex, nevertheless feels like a woman in his conscious phantasies, and endows the women who are beating him with masculine attributes and characteristics."[116] Freud himself remarked that the remodeled beating fantasy "has for its content a feminine attitude without a homosexual object-choice,"[117] and Silverman spells out the implication: the fantasy in its final form thus "constitutes a 'feminine' yet heterosexual male subject."[118] The beating fantasy, in short, works both sides of the passivity street: the homosexual side *and* the heterosexual side. "Passive" in both phases or dimensions means, for Freud, that the fantast "feels like a woman," a feeling that may entail an identification of his own body with that of his mother in the act of intercourse and perhaps in the condition of pregnancy and childbirth as well.[119] To ask, at this level of enmeshment, where male ends and female begins is somewhat beside the point. Even if one holds that the male can never escape the sensations of his own body, the fact remains that in narrative and cinematic imagery, it is the female body that structures the male drama, and to which he assimilates, in his imagination, his own corporeal experience.

Finally, there is the issue of suspense.[120] Masochism (in both its sexualized and desexualized forms) is unusually generative of vivid fantasies—fantasies, according to Reik, characterized by "the demonstrative factor" (whereby the masochist imagines himself on display) and "the suspense factor" (whereby the masochist imagines himself facing a pain-pleasure fate that is inevitable but also, up to a point, delayable). Consider, for example, the following fantasy, reported to Reik by a male patient:

[116] Freud, " 'A Child Is Being Beaten,' " p. 200. I cannot help noting here the correspondence between the "bisexual" beating figure in the Freudian fantasy and the similarly "bisexual" killer of slasher films.

[117] Ibid., p. 199.

[118] Silverman, "Masochism and Male Subjectivity," p. 57.

[119] See also "Anal Erotism and the Castration Complex." For an analysis of Freud's own investment in anal erotism, see Koestenbaum's "Privileging the Anus."

[120] Although not all horror films are equally suspenseful, and although the suspense may take different forms (including the hesitation between natural and supernatural explanations of horror that Todorov takes as the defining feature of the fantastic), I take suspense to be a hallmark of horror. Carroll writes that "although suspense and horror are distinct—there may be suspense stories without horror and horror stories without suspense—they also have a natural, though contingent, affinity" (*The Philosophy of Horror*, p. 144).

The cruel and nymphomaniac queen of a legendary realm uses explorers
who are lost in her domain for her sexual satisfaction. When she loses
interest in them the queen has the prisoners impaled, flayed or castrated.
The patient now imagines a young man as the next aspirant to the queen's
cruel favor. He witnesses the horrible execution of one of his predecessors
and feels the terror of him whom a similar destiny awaits in the near future. He identifies himself with this victim—a brother-figure—and experiences with him the fettering, torture, and death.[121]

Here—as is, or with sexes switched—is an embryonic horror movie
if ever there was one. What interest me in it are not the actual cinematic analogues, of which dozens come to mind, but its anticipatory
and seriatim structure: the way, person by person, the terrorizer approaches the fantast's surrogate, whose mounting anxiety is the
scenario's organizing experience. That, of course, is the standard
structure of multiple-victim horror, of which the slasher film is only
the most obvious example. Moreover, in both the "execution" fantasy described above and multiple-victim horror cinema, the protagonist *sees* his or her fate in advance as it is visited on the person or
persons ahead in line—impalement, flaying, and castration in the
"execution" fantasy, and all manner of stabbing, drilling, and slicing
in the slasher film. Single-victim horror is equally suspenseful, the
difference being that the advancing terror is not directly theatrical-
ized but left to the mind's eye—and even single-victim horror has its
way of inserting "prior" scenarios (through radio or television reports of atrocities committed by an unknown psychopath, through
the film-within-the-film device, through another person's account of
a dreadful event, or, above all, through analogy and intertextual references to other horror films). In either case, the protagonist is
poised between the absolute desire to escape his turn and the equally
absolute knowledge that it is inevitable; and as the threat draws
nearer, the tension achieves explosive proportions. Reik stressed the
sexual use of such fantasies and his patients' concern with synchro-
nizing the two climaxes.[122]

[121] Reik, *Masochism in Modern Man*, p. 184. In his close analysis of *Halloween*, Neale
notes the imbrication of suspense in the sadomasochistic aesthetic, which he in turn
relates to the traffic in looks: "In moments of suspense . . . the spectator's loss of a
position of control is translated either into an acute anxiety or eventually into an act of
extreme diegetic violence" (p. 342).

[122] The ending of *Peeping Tom*, in which Mark turns his murderous camera on himself
as the police rush in, comes to mind here. "In a stunning reprise of all the many
textual references to light," Silverman writes, "Mark times numerous flashbulbs to
shine on him at half-second intervals as he levels the psychic barrier separating himself
from the female subject, and embraces his own castration" (*The Acoustic Mirror*, p. 37).

Note the lines of identification here. Reik's patient is not himself "in" the story in the first person. Rather, he operates through a third-person surrogate. As Silverman notes of another of Reik's cases, the fantast is "bound to the scenario through a complex imaginary network. His immediate point of insertion occurs via the young man who will be next to fall victim . . . but that figure himself identifies closely with the victim presently suffering that mutilation."[123] The fantasy's imaginary protagonist, in other words, stands in the same relation to the person ahead of him in line that the fantast stands to his imaginary protagonist. Likewise the Final Girl of slasher films stands in the same relation to her teen friends who are ahead of her in line as the viewer of slasher films stands to the Final Girl.[124] "It is certain that the daydreamer identifies with one of the victims," Reik writes of such a fantasy, "usually not the one who is just being castrated but with the next, who is compelled to look on at the execution of his companion. The patient shares every intensive affect of this victim, feels his terror and anxiety with all the physical sensations since he imagines that he will himself experience the same fate in a few moments."[125] I repeat here John Ellis's observation that the crucial dynamic of the war or male action film is the "notion of survival through a series of threats of physical mutilation, to which many characters succumb. It is a phantasy that is characteristic of the male."[126]

The staging here squares with the staging identified in laboratory

---

[123] Silverman, "Masochism and Male Subjectivity," p. 52. For a summary of Freud's views on "subjectivization" in conscious and unconscious fantasy, see Laplanche and Pontalis, "Fantasy and the Origins of Sexuality," esp. p. 22. On the relation of dreams to folktales, see Bruno Bettelheim's brief but to-the-point remarks in The Uses of Enchantment, esp. p. 36.

[124] Of Halloween's episodic stalk-and-kill structure, Tudor writes: "The essence of our involvement, then, is of the 'where is he?', 'when will he strike next?', 'will she get away?' type, and the movie works as a series of tension-building sequences culminating in moments of intense shock and economically portrayed violence. . . . All the films [that follow the Halloween formula] climax with the pursuit of the solitary surviving female" (Monsters and Mad Scientists, pp. 68–69).

[125] Reik, Masochism in Modern Man, p. 42. For an exploration of the psychosexual dynamics of story at the mythic level, see de Lauretis, "Desire in Narrative" in Alice Doesn't.

[126] Ellis, Visible Fictions, p. 44 (italics mine); see also Studlar and Desser, "Never Having to Say You're Sorry." Carroll also reminds us that it is not so much the scary images per se of horror that frighten us, but the narratives in which those images are embedded. "Indeed, I think it is fair to say that in our culture, horror thrives above all as a narrative form. Thus, in order to account for the interest we take in and the pleasure we take from horror, we may hypothesize that, in the main, the locus of our gratification is not the monster as such but the whole narrative structure in which the presentation of the monster is staged" (The Philosophy of Horror, p. 181).

experiments as requisite to the sensation of suspense: "The more convinced audience members are that the protagonist is in genuine peril and is about to succumb to the opposing forces with which he/she is in conflict, up to the point of total subjective certainty of defeat, the more suspenseful is the presentation," write Paul Comisky and Jennings Bryant. Moreoever, "it is clear that the characteristics of the protagonist matter a great deal. The audience evidently 'gets involved with' and anxious about a hero whom it can like."[127] Beyond "goodness," what makes a figure likable is vulnerability, helplessness, a situation of powerlessness[128]—characteristics, one cannot help noting (though Comisky and Bryant make no mention of gender), traditionally coded as feminine and, in horror, conventionally embodied in female characters. The staging also squares with Noël Carroll's observation, from an entirely different standpoint, that horror is virtually defined by the particular relationship it presumes between the "positive, human characters" of the diegesis and the audience, the former serving as a set of visual and aural instructions to the latter *in the bodily response to fear*: "The work of art-horror has built into it, so to speak, a set of instructions about the appropriate way the audience is supposed to respond to it. These instructions are manifested, by example, in the responses of the positive, human characters to the monsters in horror fiction."[129] Carroll notes in detail the correspondence between the screen victim's situation and that of the viewer, but his presumption that the former causes the latter—that the screen image "programs" the viewer's responses—begs the question. I would suggest that the correspondence is a function of masochistic fantasy: that people who make movies sense the iterative "my-turn-is-coming-soon" quality of victimization fantasies; that they consciously exploit the proved willingness of the viewer (proved because he keeps paying for it) to imagine himself as a "next victim"; and that the screen functions as a kind of anticipatory mirror intended not so much to instruct as to heighten the effect. I suspect too that the first fact of film narration—that, unlike written narrative, it imposes its own pace on the viewer—may work to ratchet up the intensity even further.[130]

---

[127] Comisky and Bryant, "Factors Involved in Generating Suspense," pp. 57–58. See also Noël Carroll, "Toward a Theory of Film Suspense."

[128] Comisky and Bryant, "Factors Involved in Generating Suspense," esp. p. 54.

[129] Carroll, *The Philosophy of Horror*, p. 31. I have taken the liberty of yoking Carroll's observation to a psychoanalytic construction—a move he himself resists.

[130] Worth remembering here is director William Friedkin's conviction that horror audiences bring the conditions for fear with them into the theater, and that the business of the movie is to deliver the final slam. "Fear is generally something that is behind

Horror in any case bears a startling resemblance to the masochistic fantasies recounted by both Freud and Reik. It tells the same sort of stories (over and over), creates the same sort of protagonists who stand in the same sort of relation to the "viewer," represents those protagonists as "feminine" (in the sense outlined by Freud), is predicated on a peculiar kind of turn-taking suspense, privileges vision in the creation of that suspense, and openly trades in fear and pain.[131] The similarities, I have suggested, are more than casual. I suspect that the masochistic aesthetic is and has always been the dominant one in horror cinema and is in fact one of that genre's defining characteristics; that the experience horror moviegoers seek is likewise rooted in a pain/pleasure sensibility; that the fantasies in which horror cinema trades are particularly (though not exclusively) tailored to male forms of masochistic experience (accounting for the disproportionate maleness of the audience); and that the willingness of horror moviegoers to return for sequel on sequel, imitation on imitation, and remake on remake bespeaks a degree of *Wiederholungszwang* that in turn stands as proof of the pudding. Although the odd horror movie does follow a masochistic scenario to its annihilatory end point (*The Incredible Shrinking Man*, for example), most undo the dream or fantasy through an eleventh-hour reversal, longer or shorter and more or less sadistic, and thus deliver the spectator back into the status quo. If one focuses (as critics tend to) on the endings of horror films, one sees sadism. But if one takes it as a point of fact, as I have argued throughout this book, that endings (as well as beginnings) are generically overdetermined and that it is in narrative middles that crucial matters are contested, and if one accordingly focuses on those parts of horror films—their middles, especially their "late" middles— in which the tension is greatest and the audience body most engaged, one sees masochism, and in remarkably blatant forms.[132]

---

you, speaking in psychological terms. It's generally something behind you that you cannot see but that you can feel, like a loud sound or someone touching you suddenly." As quoted in Derry, *Dark Dreams*, p. 124. See also n. 83 above.

[131] Carroll dismisses the masochistic motivation of horror spectatorship on grounds that it presupposes an "illusion theory," whereby "theatrical, or alternatively, cinematic techniques of verisimilitude so overwhelm us that we are deceived into believing that a monster really looms before us. . . . Were the illusion theory true, horror would be too unnerving for all save heroes, consummate masochists, and professional vampire killers" (*The Philosophy of Horror*, pp. 63–64).

[132] My view here is conditioned by folklore studies and the textual and narratological study of medieval texts. Laura Mulvey has moved in the same direction in her "Changes: Thoughts on Myth, Narrative and Historical Experience" (1985). See also Bettelheim, *The Uses of Enchantment*, introduction. Smith, however, wants to reprivilege endings; see his "Action Movie Hysteria." Linda Williams sums up the issue

I do not mean to propose that horror movies have nothing to offer but an s/m bang. Nor am I claiming that horror is alone among cinematic genres in its exploitation of the pleasure/pain response; action movies and thrillers are obvious candidates, and the suggestion has been made of sentimental genres, and even early train-wreck movies, as well.[133] (If vision is always both projective and introjective, then *all* visual forms are presumably amenable to a "two-way" analysis, though they may differ in their proportions and intensity.) Nor, finally, do I doubt that female spectators too may engage at some level with the masochistic scenarios in which horror trades; if the particulars of those scenarios are by the lights of psychoanalysis typically male, the general masochistic fantasy of passivity or imprisonment ("pleasure without responsibility") knows no sex, and women, practiced as they are at wresting their own pleasure from forms made by and addressed to men, can presumably translate from horror, too. It is also possible that the surface stories of certain horror subgenres—slashers and rape-revenge films, for example—may offer satisfactions of their own to women viewers, including, perhaps, satisfactions of a more sadistic nature.[134] (Again, however, the fact of horror's dis-

nicely when she remarks of *Stella Dallas* that "although the final moment of the film 'resolves' the contradiction of Stella's attempt to be a woman *and* a mother by eradicating both, the 108 minutes leading up to this moment present the heroic attempt to live out the contradiction" (" 'Something Else besides a Mother,' " p. 24). Although endings are obviously important (enough for studios to present alternative ones to test audiences), their importance is just as obviously contingent on what came before—what it is that needs resolving and sealing off. Because endings are generically overdetermined (one reason they are so often misremembered), it is to middles one should look for the meanings that are being contested in the text.

[133] Doane (*The Desire to Desire*, pp. 94–95 and passim) has suggested that "weepies" offer an essentially masochistic experience to their audiences. She takes the fact that the object of the "weepie" address is female to suggest that women viewers are more susceptible to masochistic spectatorship than males. It seems to me equally possible that, in the same way horror exploits male masochistic fantasies, "weepies" exploit female ones. In either case, the makers of these films go about "jerking tears" in ways manipulative enough to be compared with the sadistic tactics of horror. For a literary perspective, Kirby's summary remarks about the positioning of the spectator of early train films are worth quoting here: "In theoretical terms, the assaulted spectator is the hysterical spectator. The fantasies of being run over and assaulted, penetrated, produce a certain pleasure of pain—beyond the pleasure principle and in the realm of repetition compulsion—which is as much about will-to-submission, to loss-of-mastery, as it is about will-to-mastery/control" ("Male Hysteria and Early Cinema," p. 128).

[134] I assume this is what Raymond Bellour has in mind when he opines that a woman "can love, accept and give a positive value to these films [American cinema] only from her own masochism, and from a certain sadism that she can exercise in return on the masculine subject, within a system loaded with traps" (As quoted in Janet Bergstrom, "Alternation, Segmentation, Hypnosis," p. 84). Judith Butler's suggestion that "it may well be more frightening to acknowledge an identification with

proportionate success among males suggests that its masochistic recipe is indeed one more closely tailored to male than female tastes.)[135] What I *am* saying is that "feminine masochism" as it has been outlined in psychoanalysis finally offers the best answer to the question that modern horror repeatedly raises: just why it is that male viewers would choose to "feel" fear and pain through the figure of a female—a female, in fact, whose very bodily femaleness is at center stage.[136]

My interest at this point, however, is not so much in what this construction makes of the female body (which has been richly noted elsewhere) as in what it makes of the male one. It has been argued, most cogently by Silverman and Leo Bersani, that insofar as masochism swerves away from or "shatters" the male subject's relation to the phallic order, it is subversive of that order and of what Bersani sarcastically calls the "proud subjectivity" that props it up.[137] The

---

the one who debases than with the one who is debased" ("The Force of Fantasy," p. 114) may be true for female spectators (for whom sadistic desire is more severely repressed), but it is hardly true of male ones.

[135] See Williams, "When the Woman Looks."

[136] This is not to deny the displacement value of a female figure in a male-homerotic drama—a possibility I have discussed at length in the previous chapters. It is, however, to suggest that displacement value is an insufficient explanation for the phenomenon.

[137] Of Silverman's several pronouncements on the subject, I quote only one here—one that proceeds from her reading of Deleuze's reading of Freud on masochism: "In inviting the mother to beat and/or dominate him, he [the male who fantasizes himself in the "feminine masochistic" position] transfers power and authority from the father to her, remakes the symbolic order, and 'ruins' his own paternal legacy. And that is not all. As Freud remarks of those two [male] patients in ' "A Child Is Being Beaten" ' the conscious phantasy of being disciplined by the mother 'has for its content a feminine attitude without a homosexual object-choice.' It thereby effects another revolution of sorts, and one whose consequences may be even more socially transforming than eroticism between men—it constitutes a 'feminine' yet heterosexual male subject" ("Masochism and Male Subjectivity," p. 57). See, more generally, her *Male Subjectivity at the Margins* (forthcoming). In his remarkable essay "Is the Rectum a Grave?" Bersani suggests that rather than denying the association, in the public mind and in private fantasy, of the (gay male) anus with the vagina, gay men accept it and embrace its implications. " 'AIDS,' [Simon] Watney writes, 'offers a new sign for the symbolic machinery of repression, making the rectum a grave.' But if the rectum is the grave in which the masculine ideal (an ideal shared—differently—by men *and* women) of proud subjectivity is buried, then it should be celebrated for its very potential for death. Tragically, AIDS has literalized that potential as the certainty of biological death, and has therefore reinforced the heterosexual association of anal sex with a self-annihilation originally and primarily identified with the fantasmatic mystery of an insatiable, unstoppable female sexuality. It may, finally, be in the gay man's rectum that he demolishes his own perhaps otherwise uncontrollable identification with a murderous judgment against him." Bersani continues, "That judgment, as I have been suggesting, is grounded in the sacrosanct value of selfhood, a value that accounts for human beings' extraordinary willingness to kill in order to protect the seriousness of their statements.

psychoanalytic validity of these claims I leave to others. Nor am I prepared to comment on cultural practices over the broad range. My concern is with film theory and horror film criticism and practice—and with the extent to which those discourses may denaturalize, for some people, the received categories of sexual difference.

At the critical/theoretical level the strongest argument for the possibility that there is something subversive about the masochistic experience-base of cinematic spectatorship may be an argument *e silentio*. I am referring to the repeated denial or avoidance of that possibility in both critical and theoretical writings—in contrast to the wealth of attention lavished on male sadism.[138] Mulvey's blind spot (her designation of voyeurism as active and scopophilia as passive—but the both of them as phallic and sadistic) has been argued by Rodowick to be politically motivated (to acknowledge the masochistic potential in scopophilic gazing would undo her feminist project), but to my knowledge Metz's even more glaring blind spot (his designation of projective gazing as phallic/sadistic and his failure to provide an equivalent experiential base for introjective gazing—a lacuna all the more glaring in light of the fact that the distinction between projective and introjective is his own) has not been equivalently explained. And *that* failure—the failure of gender-interested critics/theorists to come to grips with Metz's blind spot—constitutes yet *another* blind spot. Such lapses might seem accidental were they not so consonant with the larger prejudice that the lower cinematic forms play

The self is a practical convenience; promoted to the status of an ethical ideal, it is a sanction for violence. . . . Gay men's 'obsession' with sex, far from being denied, should be celebrated—not because of its communal virtues, not because of its subversive potential for parodies of machismo, not because it offers a model of genuine pluralism to a society that at once celebrates and punishes pluralism, but rather because it never stops re-presenting the internalized phallic male as an infinitely loved object of sacrifice. Male homosexuality advertises the risk of the sexual itself as the risk of self-dismissal, of *losing sight* of the self, and in so doing it proposes and dangerously represents *jouissance* as a mode of ascesis" (p. 222). See also Bersani's *Baudelaire and Freud* (in which, however, he does not pursue the feminine dimension), esp. pp. 67–89, and his and Dutoit's *The Forms of Violence*, esp. pp. 110–25 ("The Restlessness of Desire"); Christopher Newfield, "The Politics of Male Suffering"; Adams, "Per Os(cillation)"; and Tania Modleski, "Three Men and Baby M," esp. pp. 73–74. It is also important to consider the possibility that masochistic fantasy (or masochistic acting-out in a sexual relationship) may work to enable the man to take command in other parts of his life; consider, for example, the phenomenon, repeatedly attested by prostitutes, of the captain of industry (say) with a taste for being beaten. See also Segal, *Slow Motion*, esp. chapter 8.

[138] As Deleuze notes, the work of Leopold von Sacher-Masoch "has suffered from unfair neglect, when we consider that Sade has been the object of such penetrating studies both in the field of literary criticism and in that of psychoanalytic interpretation, to the benefit of both" (*Masochism*, p. 133).

by definition to male sadistic tastes. Of the many such judgments I
have mentioned in previous chapters, the one I will repeat here (not
because it is egregious, but because it is tellingly typical) is Elliott
Stein's characterization of *Peeping Tom* as a "movie that equates
watching movies with killing and fucking," a remark that willfully
misreads most of the film's action and certainly effaces its main point
(not to speak of its ending).[139] I cannot help suspecting that Stein
neglected the masochistic dimension of *Peeping Tom* for the same reason that Metz and Mulvey neglected to fill out the fourth space in
their fourfold charts and that so many subsequent commentators
have turned a blind eye on those empty fourth spaces: because to do
otherwise would be to take on one of the most entrenched, politically
useful (in its time), and status-quo-supportive clichés of modern cultural criticism.

Identifying male sadism, especially toward women, and holding
men at least theoretically culpable for such acts as rape, wife beating,
and child abuse are major achievements of modern feminism. Texts
like Susan Brownmiller's *Against Our Will*, which accumulates case
on case of male brutality until the evidence seems crushing, have
been instrumental in those achievements. Recent years have seen the
production of similar texts by men (texts like Klaus Theweleit's *Male
Fantasies* and Anthony Wilden's *Man and Woman, War and Peace*), and
Tania Modleski has wondered about the politics that underlie such
extended iterations of male sadism.[140] On the basis of my own reading of horror film criticism, which speaks volumes on sadism and
only the occasional sentence on masochism, I second Modleski's nervousness (about any such text, regardless of the author's sex), for
although the practice of remarking male sadism in a film (like the
practice of *showing* male sadism in a film) may be intended to align
the remarker with feminism, it also works to naturalize sadistic violence as a fixture of masculinity—one of the few fixtures of masculinity remaining in a world that has seen the steady erosion of such. It
is a gesture, in other words, that ends up confirming what it de-
plores. Appalling though it may be (the unstated logic goes), the capacity for sadistic violence is what finally distinguishes male from
female. (I take this to be one reason for the current popularity of

---

[139] Likewise Beard, whose repeated observation that *Videodrome*'s Max is "opened"
and "invaginated" by the videodrome experience (and even homoerotically opened to
Harlan) does not prevent his categorization of Max as sadistic and Nicki as the masochist ("The Visceral Mind," esp. pp. 51–52, 56–57, 60, and 63). And likewise Peary,
who observes the separateness of the two gazes in *Peeping Tom* only to recollapse them
into a unitary sadistic-voyeuristic model (see n. 16 above).

[140] Tania Modleski, "A Father Is Being Beaten," esp. pp. 66–67.

"war" movies, whether set in Vietnam, Latin America, or American city ghettos: *this* turf men own.)[141] The reason, then, for the critical eloquence on the subject of male sadism is that it holds the gender bottom line. And the reason for the virtual silence in horror film criticism and for the blank spot in film theory on the possibility of male masochism is that to broach it is not only to bring homosexuality into the picture, but also to unsettle what is apparently our ultimate gender story.

The argument *e silentio* goes another step. As I have noted with respect to both slasher and rape-revenge films, the striking tendency of modern horror to collapse the figure of the savior-hero (formerly male) into the figure of the victim (eternally female) leaves us with an arrangement whereby a largely male audience is in the hands of a female protagonist—an arrangement that self-evidently exposes the ability of male viewers to identify across sexual lines. It is probably safe to assume that the male viewers of horror are in this respect not fundamentally different from male viewers in general, past and present; although horror may exploit the mechanism of cross-gender identification more intensely than other sorts of cinema, the mechanism itself surely knows no genre. Again, however, it is a mechanism that has scarcely been mentioned in film theory and criticism. The silence on male-with-female identification (in contrast to the common assumption of female-with-male identification) thus matches the silence on male masochism (in contrast to the lavish acknowledgment of male sadism), and it seems reasonable to suppose that the coincidence is not accidental.[142]

I take this double silence—silence about masochism and silence about identification with the female—as evidence that something crucial to the system of cultural representation is at stake.[143] That

[141] Modleski makes the related point, apropos Anthony Wilden's argument in *Man and Woman, War and Peace* to the effect that women can never challenge male supremacy by standing outside war culture: "Feminism has now paradoxically become the last alibi for the liberal male's fascination with war" (ibid., p. 67).

[142] These instances of one-way vision are, of course, part and parcel of the long-standing and wholesale assumption, in cultural thought, that people in general identify "upward," toward power and prestige. Thus blacks identify with whites, poor with rich, women with men—and either not the reverse, or the reverse only for purposes of appropriation. A psychoanalytically informed analysis of such territories as horror and pornography (to name just two obvious cases) suggests not only the existence of a "downward" movement, but a more nuanced understanding of it. See Silverman's remarks on the correspondence in chapter 1 of *The Acoustic Mirror*, "Lost Objects and Mistaken Subjects."

[143] I note that although Silverman and Bersani claim to be making their case on strictly psychoanalytic grounds, both of them are acutely conscious of, and seem to an

something, as I have emphasized throughout this book, must be the operation whereby female figures are made to stand for, and act out, a psychosexual posture that in fact knows no sex, but which for a variety of reasons that add up to male dominance, is routinely dissociated from the male.[144] It is, in short, an operation which insures that men can eat their psychosexual cake and have it too: experience the pain/pleasure of (say) a rape fantasy by identifying with the victim, and then disavow their personal stake on grounds that the visible victim was, after all, a woman, and that they as spectators are "naturally" represented by the visible male figures: male saviors or sadistic rapists, but *manly* men however you cut it.[145]

The critical reaction to *I Spit on Your Grave* is a superbly crude case in point. A film that employs every narrative and cinematic device to position us with the victim during both her violation and her acts of revenge, and a film whose second half is precisely predicated on our feeling horribly violated (the ghastliness of the revenge standing in direct relation to the ghastliness of our violation), *I Spit on Your Grave* provides, for many long stretches of its hour-and-a-half narration, as pure a feminine-masochistic jolt as the movies have to offer. No such possibility is even hinted at in the reviews that led to its condemnation and censorship, however. On the contrary, the film was characterized, in tones of outrage and in the name of feminism, as the ultimate incitement to male sadism, a "vile film for vicarious sex criminals," a "sleazy exploitation movie" that "makes rapists of us all." But there is something off here: something too shrill and too totalizing in the claim of misogyny, something dishonest in the critical rewritings and outright misrepresentations of the plot required to sustain that claim, something suspicious about the refusal to entertain even in passing the possibility of involvement with the victim's part, something perverse about the unwillingness to engage with the manifestly feminist dimensions of the script, and something dubious in the refusal to note its debt to *Deliverance* and the critical implications of that debt. *I Spit on Your Grave* is a problematic case for feminism, but the Siskel-Ebert position (if the protest may be summed up

---

extent driven by, the "cultural secret" aspect of male masochism. Both of them, that is, take the silence surrounding the subject as evidence of its importance.

[144] Greenson's "Dis-Identifying from Mother" makes the intriguing suggestion that the boy can "dis-identify" with his mother only by first enjoying the phase of identification with her—a phase of which the generations after Freud have become particularly intolerant. If that is so, horror comes into focus as the site of the repressed "femininity."

[145] In Silverman's formulation, woman is made to bear "double lack." See chapter 1 of *The Acoustic Mirror*.

as such) should not be allowed the last word. Whatever else the Siskel-Ebert position may be, it is also the critical equivalent of Revok's
eye: its insistence that *I Spit on Your Grave* makes rapists of us all
works, in fact, to deflect attention from the possibility that it just as
well makes Jennifers of us all, and that the powerful feelings the film
evokes may have less to do with a sense of mastery than with the
sense that one has just been shafted.

It is no surprise that this feint is reenacted endlessly in movies
themselves; that must be one main thing movies are *for*. What is
rather more surprising is the extent to which film criticism and theory
have fallen for it—indeed, in the name of feminism, embraced it.
And what is most surprising of all (at least to those who believe par-
adigms can be subverted only from above) is the fact that it is in modern horror that the feint is most obviously exposed for what it is, and
that the dominant fiction which generates it is most clearly laid bare.
The disappearance of male heroes (often males of any kind) from
genres like the rape-revenge and slasher, a disappearance that leaves
us alone in the company of a first victimized and then heroic woman,
is a remarkable cultural admission.[146] It admits the pleasure/pain nature of the core experience of certain kinds of narrative (certain parts
of all kinds of narrative, perhaps), and it admits the ways that literal
representations, "images," are conventionally deployed to cover over
the male investment in that experience in such a way as to make it
seem specific to the female. Horror, in short, "tells on" the movies to
an unprecedented and revelatory degree.

Let me draw this together. The "ethnic" evidence suggests that the
first and central aim of horror cinema is to play to masochistic fears
and desires in its audiences—fears and desires that are repeatedly
figured as "feminine." It may play on other fears and desires too, but
dealing out pain is its defining characteristic; sadism, by definition,
plays at best a supporting role. To the extent that a movie succeeds
in "hurting" its viewers in this way, it is good horror; to the extent
that it fails, it is bad horror; to the extent that it does not try, it is not
horror, but something else.[147] This self-portrait of horror is not dis-

[146] I am referring especially to the slasher and the rape-revenge film here. The possession film does not evacuate the male in the same way, but as I suggested at some
length in chapter 2, "Opening Up," it has its own, only slightly less obvious, ways of
"admitting" male engagement with the feminine position.

[147] Thus a film like *Henry: Portrait of a Serial Killer*, which plays definitively on sadistic impulses, does not in my view qualify as horror. The reviews I saw simultaneously
classified it as and distinguished it from horror. ("This low-budget film is gory and
chilling, but not exploitative in the way of most slasher movies. Unrated" [*San Francisco Examiner*, Pink Section, 13 May 1989], and so on.)

guised; it is right on the surface, in a variety of concrete forms, plain for all to see. Its very plainness makes all the more puzzling the insistence of critical commentaries on the primacy of the sadistic dimension. The failure of those commentaries to see beyond sadism, I have suggested, has everything to do with their stake in the dominant fiction.

It may be objected that horror is qualitatively different from other genres (it is certainly one of the most insistently marked and segregated categories) and that its sensibility is sui generis. I would argue, however, both on the basis of the "two-way" eye/camera implicit in the accounts of Mulvey and Metz (despite their attempts to keep it "one way") and on the basis of the psychoanalytic theory of "two-way" aggression (sadism/masochism) that underpins it, that horror merely takes to an overt extreme an operation that is surely as endemic to the act of cinematic spectatorship as aggressive voyeurism is, even if it is less exploited, and/or less admitted, in higher forms. To exaggerate somewhat for purposes of clarity: I am suggesting that, rather than exposing the cultural lie on which higher forms of cinema are based, film theory has wittingly or unwittingly colluded with it, and that it has done so because it is itself deduced from higher forms, in which the dimension of introjective or masochistic gazing is either less important or more muted or both.[148] It is true that when Mulvey and Metz were theorizing sadistic spectatorship in the early seventies, horror was considerably less brazen and less sustained in its exploitation of "feminine masochism" than it has been in the last decade. It is also true, however, that themes and images of painful looking and pierced eyes have long been a staple of the tradition, and that it is not possible to look at many horror movies from any era without confronting the idea; and there was *Peeping Tom*, a film that from its first image (the pierced bull's-eye) to its last (the darkened screen, as Mark's own vision is extinguished by suicide, and the voice-over of a frightened boy saying "Good night, Daddy—hold my hand") insists that the pleasure of looking at others in fear and pain has its origins in one's own past-but-not-finished fear and pain.

[148] This is not to say that all higher or mainstream cinema is so muted or minimally masochistic. See Studlar's analyses of von Sternberg's films (*In the Realm of Pleasure*) and Doane's of woman's films of the 1940s (*The Desire to Desire*). I should also acknowledge some useful discussions with Richard Hutson on a (significantly) "unremembered" genre of forties' films he refers to as "male melodramas."

AFTERWORD

To the questions of why it should be horror—of all genres—that blows the cover, as it were, and why now, I offer this list (distilled from earlier chapters) of tentative and overlapping propositions. Because the popularity of gender-bending scenarios has enabled horror to go up front with its own brand of gender transgression. Because horror operates in an allegorical or expressionist or folkloric/mythic mode, whereby characters are understood to concretize essences; and because, accordingly, that mode allows for the representation of "feminine masochism" in female form, with no male cover, in ways not suitable to more realistic traditions. (Because horror is by definition more brazen, in other words.) Because horror is a marginal genre that appeals to marginal people (not, by and large, middle-aged, middle-class whites) who may not have quite the same investment in the status quo. Because horror plays to youth audiences made up of the sons (and daughters) of the "new family" of the sixties and seventies (woman-headed families, families with working mothers), for whom "sufficient" female figures are more plausible than they might have been to an earlier generation. Because those same audiences, by the same token and for the same reasons, may not have experienced adult male authority in the same form or degree as earlier generations. Because of a splintering of the notion of the masculine under the pressure of Vietnam, the women's movement, the gay rights movement, the sixties in general—in ways that make it psychologically possible for a male viewer to accommodate Arnold Schwarzenegger on Wednesday and Linda Blair on Thursday. Because for at least two decades, the readiest supplier of the scenarios and rhetoric of self-righteous victimization in which horror trades has been neither the labor movement nor the civil rights movement, but the women's movement (I am here thinking especially of the scenarios and rhetoric of the rape-revenge film).[1] Because the venerable American plot in which urban people manage to kill rural savages in the nick of time could likewise be restocked from, and revitalized by, the women's movement. Because, perhaps, of an increased openness, among young people, to a bisexual aesthetic, if not bisexual practices. Because horror is at the same time extraordi-

[1] I recall here Stephen King's remarks about the ways the women's movement underwrote the horror of a film like *Carrie*. See the Introduction, above.

narily imitative, so that once the female victim-hero was introduced, she underwent immediate fission. Because some especially influential horror movies were independent, low-budget productions that reflect the interest of their "authors," people like Romero and Craven, in stretching the generic terms. Because, to judge from their interviews, people like Romero and Craven are acutely aware that they are trafficking in the "repressed" and by their own account have plumbed their best movies from their own worst nightmares and fantasies. Because at least some horror filmmakers read Freud.[2]

Since I began this book in 1986, horror's history has forked rather dramatically. On the one side is a remarkable success story, in which themes and formulas that had emerged and flourished in the exploitation underbrush migrated into higher forms—including the glossiest blockbusters of 1990–1991. Films like *Sleeping with the Enemy* (in which a woman is tracked by a psycho husband), *Blue Steel* (in which a woman detective, played by Jamie Lee Curtis,[3] becomes enmeshed with a psycho lover), *Pacific Heights* (in which a landlady is tormented by a psycho tenant), and *Silence of the Lambs* (in which a woman FBI agent solicits help from one psychokiller in tracking down another) come awfully close to being slasher movies for yuppies—well made, well-acted, and well-conceived versions of the familiar story of a female victim-hero who squares off against, and finally blows away, without male help, a monstrous oppressor. Although *Mortal Thoughts* and *Thelma and Louise* lie further from the horror genre, I suspect that they too have been enabled, if only indirectly, by seventies' and eighties' horror's proof that, as far as identification goes, sex is no object if you write the function right and play the part with conviction.

Of these films, *Silence of the Lambs* (which one reviewer called "a *Nightmare on Elm Street* for grad students")[4] is the most nakedly horrific. The Frankensteinian scheme of killing women for their parts (in this case pieces of skin, like pieces of fabric in dressmaking) is in the best tradition of low horror, from the 1963 *Blood Feast* (in which an Egyptian caterer collects female bodily parts, one female per part, for sacrifice to the goddess Ishtar) to the 1990 *Frankenhooker* (in which a

---

[2] And also, for that matter, because they read film criticism and theory. I am told of three instances in which the directors of slasher films made adjustments in their work in response to reading the separately published version of chapter 1 of this book. The one who has allowed her name to be used is Catherine Cyran, director of *Slumber Party Massacre III*, produced by New Line.

[3] Jamie Lee Curtis being the original Final Girl (*Halloween*).

[4] Ian Shoales, "Virtual Banality," p. 6.

bereaved boyfriend collects bodily parts from other women in an effort to rebuild his mangled girlfriend). And, of course, in both its
conception of Clarice Starling (masculine in both manner and career,
uninterested in sex or men, and dead serious about her career) and
its conception of Buffalo Bill (sexually dysfunctional and effeminate),
Silence of the Lambs is high slasher. Although Bill is played for gay
effect (a point on which the film has been faulted), it is worth remembering that in the long and rich tradition of which he is a member,
the issue would appear to be not homosexuality and not heterosexuality but the failure to achieve functional sexuality of any kind.[5]
Whatever else he may be, Bill is the clear brother of Norman Bates,
Leatherface, Jason, Mark (of *Peeping Tom*), and the rest: a male who
is a physical adult but a spiritual child, locked in the embrace of his
mother. And just as in the slasher film, over that stunted male the
female striving for sexual selfhood will prevail. It goes without saying
that the trope of cannibalism, whether for parts (Bill) or for fun (Hannibal Lecter), is a particularly apt metaphor for a film that has helped
itself as liberally as this one has to the wares of its downscale relatives.[6]

Nor is *Silence of the Lambs* shy about its intentions. As much as any
film I know, it is "in our face," aiming knife-stabs, gunshots, Lecter's
lunges and indeed Lecter's insinuating stares straight into the camera
and straight at us. Although the moments of actual violence are few
and far between, their direction—at us—packs a tremendous wallop.
Lest we wonder at the point, it is spelled out for us in the opening
sequence on a sign nailed to a tree in the vicinity of the training
course, a sign to which the camera very deliberately pans: HURT,
AGONY, PAIN—LOVE IT. Through that sign (as through the flashing
EXIT sign in *Texas Chain Saw Massacre II*) the "apparatus" for a brief
moment short-circuits the diegesis and addresses the spectator directly in the second person, acknowledging in a flash the nature of
the bargain that has brought spectator and movie together in this
dark auditorium. Pain: you paid for it.

On the face of it, *Thelma and Louise* would seem to have nothing to
do with horror and everything to do with the outlaw-buddy tradition
of *Butch Cassidy and the Sundance Kid* and *Bonnie and Clyde*. In fact,

---

[5] Bill's counterpart in *Manhunter* (also based on a Thomas Harris novel and also featuring Hannibal Lecter) is similarly driven to stare at and kill women (the "coveting"
theme), but here the pathology is clearly a matter of incomplete or thwarted sexuality.

[6] *Silence of the Lambs'* innovation is the Lecter-Bill duet, which can be regarded either
as a splitting of the monster function into its acting-out side and its contemplative side
or as the collapse of two roles traditionally held separate—the monster and the psychiatrist (Norman Bates and the doctor, or, in *Halloween*, Michael and Dr. Loomis).

however, Thelma and Louise are not outlaws in the first instance for economic or larger social or political reasons. They are outlaws because the one has killed the other's would-be rapist—in a fit of anger stemming, we later learn from the backstory, not just from the present rape, but from the memory of a rape that took place once upon a time in Texas. And the subsequent havoc these two rape victims wreak on men who swagger (incarcerating a highway patrolman in the trunk of his car, exploding a truckdriver's eighteen-wheeler) is reminiscent of nothing so much as the havoc Thana wreaks on the men who swagger in *Ms. 45* (the pimp, the self-pitying man at the fashion photographer, her boss, and so on). These other men may not themselves be actual rapists, but in the finest tradition of the revenge tale, they are, as men complicit with rape culture (or just as men), held corporately liable, subject to punishment for the actions of their fellows. Holding women corporately liable for male discomfort is a venerable trope of the movies (consider the thousands of women who have been killed on-screen because killers hate their mothers), and although the discourse of feminism is predicated on the like incorporation of men ("patriarchy"), it is rare indeed to see popular culture play out that fantasy in any extended way. It is the idea that drives the rape-revenge film of the 1970s and 1980s, however, and it is the idea that drives *Thelma and Louise*. In its focus on rape, its construction of males as corporately liable, its overt mistrust of the legal system to prosecute rape, and its interest in self-help (= direct revenge) and sisterhood, *Thelma and Louise* is at dead center of a tradition that emerged and throve in the lowest sectors of filmmaking for years before it trickled into major studio respectability.

But in much the way that *The Accused* hedged the bet of *I Spit on Your Grave* by introducing the figure of the lawyer and locating ultimate authority in the testimony of a male, so *Thelma and Louise* hedges the bet of its horror forebears by inserting the figure of a good cop who speaks the social truth of the story: Hal Slocumbe, the Harvey Keitel character, who alone among men discerns that these women have emerged as criminals not because they are bad, but because they have been "fucked over," and who alone among men tries to save them. Although Callie Khouri, the script author, evidently devised the character as a point of insertion for the male viewer,[7] it is not clear that the male viewer in fact needed him. Male viewers of *Bonnie and Clyde* and *Butch Cassidy and the Sundance Kid* needed no such figure. More to the point, male viewers of *I Spit on Your Grave* needed no such figure, and although the audiences for that film and

---

[7] As reported by Larry Rohter, "The Third Woman of 'Thelma and Louise,' " p. C4.

for *Thelma and Louise* may be worlds apart in some ways, I doubt that
their unconscious relation to the positions of oppressor and op-
pressed differ that radically. The good cop may offer the male viewer
an out at the conscious level—at the level of postmovie discussion—
but that viewer's deeper satisfaction must surely derive from the
usual investment in the victim-hero position, just as his sense of dis-
satisfaction must derive from the failure to engage with that position.
"Most guys don't relate to the truck driver or the rapist," scriptwriter
Khouri notes, "and if they do, their problems are bigger than this
movie."[8] Or Geena Davis, who played Thelma: "If you're threatened
by this movie, you're identifying with the wrong person."[9] Khouri
and Davis are right to emphasize "identifying" or "relating," for that
is the larger significance of female-hero movies: they reveal in unmistakable terms that men are quite capable of feeling not only *at* but
through female figures, the implication being that they have always
done so, although the traditional disposition of sex roles on-screen
has allowed the male spectator simultaneously to steal and deny the
theft, as it were. *Thelma and Louise* is being hailed as a turning point
on this score, and although one cannot quarrel with mainstream
breakthroughs, the fact is that horror broke through on the point
over a decade ago and, not least because it does not bother with
"front" figures, admitted much more completely just how far and
deeply the male spectator can go in this feeling-through-the-woman
process. *Thelma and Louise*, in short, has its wonderful virtues, but
relative to the rape-revenge tradition on which it so squarely sits, it
is a very, very safe movie.

The other side of horror's recent history is a less happy one. As
mainstream adaptations of horror thrive, low-budget production has
dwindled as independent studios, in response to profound economic
changes in the industry, fold or change direction. The generation of
filmmakers that energized the low or border tradition in the seventies
and early eighties—conspicuously Hooper, Carpenter, Romero, Craven, Cohen, Lynch, Cronenberg—have moved on to slicker things,
and it is not clear who will replace them or if they will be replaced at
all. Nor is it my impression that there is a new subgenre taking
shape. The slasher film proper has died down (even the sequel activity has subsided), not least because (as I have suggested) its salient
contributions have been absorbed into the mainstream. Frank Henenlotter's amusing *Frankenhooker* is a true low-budget product, but it
is a campy, throwback movie (throwing back all the way to the

[8] As quoted in *Time* magazine, 24 June 1991, p. 55.
[9] As quoted by Rohter in "The Third Woman of 'Thelma and Louise,' " p. C4.

sixties), not horror. Revenge movies thrive in the action genre, but rape-revenge movies have all but disappeared—again, absorbed into the mainstream. Possession movies seem to have run their course, although there may be life left in religious themes more generally. There may also be life in the amazingly durable and adaptable vampire movie, although its mainstream and art-film monumentalization in the seventies and eighties may be hard to come down from. Likewise the mass zombie movie, which Romero himself escalated into high production and which Michael Jackson's "Thriller" has now bracketed as camp. Contagion horror and family horror would seem likely candidates for low budget, but there has been little action in either category in the past couple of years (*Parents* and the *Stepfather* pictures are probably the strongest family-horror contributions since *Eraserhead*). And there remains, of course, the critical question of demographics: is it only the economics of the industry that have changed, or has there been a generational shift in taste and values, as well?

Whatever the cause, the effect is clear: the independent or off-Hollywood horror industry has fallen on hard times. And the effect of that effect seems inevitable. Deprived of the creative wellspring of the low tradition, I suspect, larger studios are more likely than before to imitate their own tried-and-true formulas, and less likely to take a flier on the kind of bizarre and brilliant themes that can bubble up from the bottom. Films like *Arachnophobia* (billed as a "thrillomedy"), *Ghost*, *Dark Man*, *Sleeping with the Enemy*, *Pacific Heights*, *Silence of the Lambs*, and the like have their charms, but they are low-risk films. They are in any case not films that take the kind of brazen tack into the psychosexual wilderness that made horror in the seventies and eighties such a marvelously transparent object of study. Unless and until the direction changes again, I suspect we will soon be back to the dominant fiction in its dominant forms, out of which we must dig meanings rather than have them displayed so obviously and so spectacularly before us.

FILMS CITED

Accused, The.	1988. Jonathan Kaplan.
Act of Vengeance. (a.k.a. *Rape Squad*).	1974. Bob Kelljan.
Alien.	1979. Ridley Scott.
Aliens.	1986. James Cameron.
All of Me.	1984. Carl Reiner.
American Werewolf in London, An.	1981. John Landis.
Amityville Horror, The.	1979. Stuart Rosenberg.
Angel Heart.	1987. Alan Parker.
Arachnophobia.	1990. Frank Marshall.
Attack of the 50-Foot Woman.	1958. Nathan Juran (Hertz).
Audrey Rose.	1977. Robert Wise.
Behind the Green Door.	1972. Mitchell Brothers.
Believers, The.	1987. John Schlesinger.
Beyond Evil.	1980. Herb Freed.
Birds, The.	1963. Alfred Hitchcock.
Birth of a Nation, The.	1915. D. W. Griffith.
Blackmail.	1929. Alfred Hitchcock.
Blade Runner.	1982. Ridley Scott.
Blob, The.	1958. Irwin S. Yeaworth, Jr.
Blood Diner.	1987. Jackie Kong.
Blood Feast.	1963. Herschell Gordon Lewis.
Blow-Out.	1981. Brian De Palma.
Body Double.	1984. Brian De Palma.
Brood, The.	1979. David Cronenberg.
Burning, The.	1981. Tony Maylam.
Carrie.	1976. Brian De Palma.
Chien andalou, Un.	1928. Luis Bunuel.
Christine.	1983. John Carpenter.
Clockwork Orange, A.	1971. Stanley Kubrick.
Crawling Eye, A.	1958. Quentin Lawrence.
Cries and Whispers (Viskningar och rop).	1972. Ingmar Bergman.
Cruising.	1980. William Friedkin.
Cujo.	1983. Lewis Teague.

Dark Mirror, The.	1946. Robert Siodmak.
Dead Calm.	1989. Phillip Noyce.
Deadly Blessing.	1981. Wes Craven.
Deliverance.	1972. John Boorman.
Demon Seed.	1977. Donald Cammell.
Demons.	1986. Lamberto Bava.
Demons II.	1987. Dario Argento.
Dirty Harry.	1971. Don Siegel.
Don't Look Now.	1973. Nicolas Roeg.
Dracula.	1931. Tod Browning.
Dream Lover.	1986. Alan J. Pakula.
Dressed to Kill.	1980. Brian De Palma.
Duel in the Sun.	1946. King Vidor.
E.T. The Extra-Terrestrial.	1982. Steven Spielberg.
Entity, The.	1983. Sidney J. Furie.
Eraserhead.	1978. David Lynch.
Every Woman Has a Fantasy.	1984. Edwin Brown.
Evil Dead, The.	1983 (prod. 1980). Sam M. Reimi.
Exorcist, The.	1973. William Friedkin.
Exorcist II: The Heretic, The.	1977. John Boorman.
Extremities.	1986. Robert M. Young.
Eye Creatures, The.	1965. Larry Buchanan.
Eyes of a Stranger.	1981. Ken Wiederhorn.
Eyes of Hell (a.k.a. *The Mask* and *The Spooky Movie Show*).	1961. Julian Roffman.
Eyes of Laura Mars, The.	1978. Irvin Kershner.
Eyes without a Face (Les Yeux sans visage; a.k.a. *The Horror Chamber of Dr. Faustus).*	1959. George Franju.
Fantastic Voyage.	1966. Richard Fleischer.
Firestarter.	1984. Mark L. Lester.
Fog, The.	1979. John Carpenter.
Frankenhooker.	1990. Frank Henenlotter.
Frankenstein.	1931. James Whale.
Frenzy.	1972. Alfred Hitchcock.
Friday the Thirteenth.	1980. Sean S. Cunningham.
Friday the Thirteenth, Part II.	1981. Steve Miner.
Friday the Thirteenth, Part III.	1982. Steve Miner.
Friday the Thirteenth: The Final Chapter.	1984. Joseph Zito.
Friday the Thirteenth, Part V: A New Beginning.	1985. Danny Steinmann.

I Walked with a Zombie.	1943. Jacques Tourneur.
Incredible Shrinking Man, The.	1957. Jack Arnold.
Incredibly Strange Creatures Who Stopped Living and Became Crazy Mixed-Up Zombies, The (a.k.a. *The Teenage Psycho Meets Bloody Mary*).	1964. Ray Dennis Steckler.
Incubus, The.	1982. John Hough.
Innerspace.	1987. Joe Dante.
It's Alive.	1974. Larry Cohen.
Jaws.	1975. Steven Spielberg.
Kindred, The.	1987. Stephen Carpenter.
King Kong.	1933. Merian C. Cooper, Ernest B. Schoedsack.
Ladies' Club, The.	1986 (prod. 1984). A. K. Allen.
Last House on the Left.	1972. Wes Craven.
Life Force.	1985. Tobe Hooper.
Lipstick.	1976. Lamont Johnson.
Little Shop of Horrors, The.	1960. Roger Corman.
Little Shop of Horrors, The.	1986. Frank Oz.
Looker.	1981. Michael Crichton.
Macabre.	1958. William Castle.
Making Contact.	1986. Roland Emmerich.
Making Mr. Right.	1987. Susan Seidelman.
Man of the West.	1958. Anthony Mann.
Maniacs Are Loose, The (a.k.a. *The Thrill Killers* and *The Monsters Are Loose*).	1965. Dennis Ray Steckler.
Max Headroom.	1986. Rocky Morton and Annabel Janekl.
Motel Hell.	1980. Kevin Connor.
Mother's Day.	1980. Charles Kaufman.
Ms. 45 (a.k.a. *Angel of Vengeance*).	1981. Abel Ferrara.
My Darling Clementine.	1945. John Ford.
Near Dark.	1987. Kathryn Bigelow.
Nesting, The.	1981. Armand Weston.
Night of the Creeps.	1986. Thom Eberhardt.
Nightmare on Elm Street, A.	1984. Wes Craven.
Nightmare on Elm Street, Part 2: Freddy's Revenge, A.	1985. Jack Sholder.

Nightmare on Elm Street III: Dream Warriors, A.	1987. Chuck Russell.
Nosferatu.	1921. F. W. Murnau.
Not a Love Story.	1981. Bonnie Klein.
Omen, The.	1976. Richard Donner.
Ordinary People.	1980. Robert Redford.
Parents.	1989. Bob Balaban.
Peeping Tom (a.k.a. *Face of Fear*).	1960. Michael Powell.
Perils of Pauline.	1914. (Eclectic Film Company)
Pet Sematary.	1989. Mary Lambert.
Pink Flamingos.	1973. John Waters.
Play Misty for Me.	1971. Clint Eastwood.
Poltergeist.	1982. Tobe Hooper.
Poltergeist II.	1986. Brian Gibson.
Positive I.D.	1987. Andy Anderson.
Prince of Darkness.	1987. John Carpenter.
Prophecy.	1979. John Frankenheimer.
Psycho.	1960. Alfred Hitchcock.
Psycho II.	1983. Richard Franklin.
Pumpkinhead.	1988. Stan Winston.
Rabid (a.k.a. *Rage*).	1977. David Cronenberg.
Rambo: First Blood II.	1985. George P. Cosmatos.
Rape of Love (L'Amour violé).	1979. Yannick Bellon.
Repulsion.	1965. Roman Polanski.
Robocop.	1987. Paul Verhoeven.
Rocky Horror Picture Show, The.	1975. Jim Sharman.
Rosemary's Baby.	1968. Roman Polanski.
Salem's Lot.	1979. Tobe Hooper.
Savage Streets.	1984. Danny Steinmann.
Scanners.	1980. David Cronenberg.
Searchers, The.	1956. John Ford.
Serpent and the Rainbow, The.	1988. Wes Craven.
Shining, The.	1980. Stanley Kubrick.
Shivers (a.k.a. *They Came from Within*).	1975. David Cronenberg.
Silence of the Lambs.	1991. Jonathan Demme.
Sleep My Love.	1948. Douglas Sirk.
Sleepaway Camp.	1984. Robert Hiltzik.
Sleeping with the Enemy.	1991. Joseph Ruben.

Slumber Party Massacre.	1982. Amy Jones.
Slumber Party Massacre 3.	1990. Catherine Cyran.
Southern Comfort.	1981. Walter Hill.
Spellbound.	1945. Alfred Hitchcock.
Spiral Staircase, The.	1946. Robert Siodmak.
Splatter University.	1984. Richard W. Harris.
Starman.	1984. John Carpenter.
Stepfather, The.	1987. Joseph Ruben.
Stepford Wives, The.	1975. Bryan Forbes.
Strait-Jacket.	1964. William Castle.
Straw Dogs.	1971. Sam Peckinpah.
Stuff, The.	1985. Larry Cohen.
Sudden Impact.	1983. Clint Eastwood.
Switch.	1991. Blake Edwards.
Taboo.	1980. Kirdy Stevens.
Teasing the Gardener (L'Asseur arrosé).	1895. Lumière Bros.
Terrorvision.	1986. Ted Nicolaou.
Texas Chain Saw Massacre, The.	1974. Tobe Hooper.
Texas Chain Saw Massacre II, The.	1986. Tobe Hooper.
Thelma and Louise.	1991. Ridley Scott.
They Came from Within.	See *Shivers.*
Tingler, The.	1959. William Castle.
Tootsie.	1982. Sydney Pollack.
Unbearable Lightness of Being, The.	1988. Philip Kaufman.
Unholy, The.	1988. Camilo Vila.
Vamp.	1986. Richard Wenk.
Vampyr (a.k.a. Castle of Doom and The Strange Adventure of David Gray).	1931. Carl Dreyer.
Vertigo.	1958. Alfred Hitchcock.
Videodrome.	1982. David Cronenberg.
Virgin Spring, The (Jungfrukällaren).	1959. Ingmar Bergman.
Viridiana.	1961. Luis Buñuel.
Visitor, The (Il Visitatore).	1979. Giulio Paradisi.
Wait until Dark.	1967. Terence Young.
What Ever Happened to Baby Jane?	1962. Robert Aldrich.
White of the Eye.	1988. Donald Cammell.
Witchboard.	1987. Kevin S. Tenney.
Wolfen.	1981. Michael Wadleigh.

WORKS CITED

Adams, Parveen. "Per Os(cillation)." *Camera Obscura* 17 (1988): 7–29.

Amir, Menachim. *Patterns in Forcible Rape.* Chicago: University of Chicago Press, 1971.

Andrews, Nigel. "Nightmares and Nasties." In *The Video Nasties*, edited by Martin Barker.

Austin, Bruce A. *The Film Audience: An International Bibliography of Research.* Metuchen, N.J.: Scarecrow Press, 1983.

———. "Portrait of a Cult Film Audience: *The Rocky Horror Picture Show.*" *Journal of Popular Film and Television* 8 (1981): 43–54.

Barker, Martin. " 'Nasties': A Problem of Identification." In *The Video Nasties*, edited by Martin Barker.

———. "Nasty Politics or Video Nasties?" In *The Video Nasties*, edited by Martin Barker.

———, ed. *The Video Nasties: Freedom and Censorship in the Media.* London: Pluto, 1984.

Barrowclough, Susan. Review of *Not a Love Story. Screen* 23 (1982): 26–36.

Bataille, Georges. *Visions of Excess: Selected Writings, 1927–1939.* Minneapolis: University of Minnesota Press, 1985.

Beard, William. "The Visceral Mind: The Major Films of David Cronenberg." In *The Shape of Rage*, edited by Canada Council.

Ben-Amos, Dan. "Analytic Categories and Ethnic Genres." *Genre* 2 (1969): 275–301.

Benvenuto, Bice, and Roger Kennedy. *The Works of Jacques Lacan: An Introduction.* London: Free Association Books, 1987.

Bergstrom, Janet. "Alternation, Segmentation, Hypnosis: Interview with Raymond Bellour. *Camera Obscura* 3–4 (1979): 66–91.

Bersani, Leo. *Baudelaire and Freud.* Berkeley and Los Angeles: University of California Press, 1977.

———. *The Freudian Body.* New York: Columbia University Press, 1986.

———. "Is the Rectum a Grave?" *October* 43 (1989): 194–222.

Bersani, Leo, and Ulysse Dutoit. *The Forms of Violence: Narrative in Assyrian Art and Modern Culture.* New York: Schocken, 1985.

Bettelheim, Bruno. *The Uses of Enchantment: The Meaning and Importance of Fairy Tales.* New York: Random House, 1989.

Bibring, Edward. "The Conception of the Repetition Compulsion." *The Psychoanalytic Quarterly* 12 (1943): 486–519.

Biskind, Peter. *Seeing Is Believing.* London: Pluto, 1984.

Blatty, William Peter. *The Exorcist.* New York: Harper and Row, 1971.

Boehm, Felix. "Femininity Complex in Men." *International Journal of Psycho-Analysis* 11 (1930): 444–69. Reprinted in *Psychoanalysis and Male Sexuality,* edited by Hendrik M. Ruitenbeek. New Haven: College and University Presses, 1966.

Boss, Pete. "Vile Bodies and Bad Medicine." *Screen* 27 (1986): 14–24.

Bovenschen, Silvia. "Is There a Feminine Aesthetic?" *New German Critique* 10 (1977): 444–69.

Brantlinger, Patrick. "What Is 'Sensational' about the 'Sensation Novel'?" *Nineteenth-Century Fiction* 37 (1982): 2–28.

Brighton, Lew. "Saturn in Retrograde; or, The Texas Jump Cut." *The Film Journal* 7 (1975): 24–27.

Brissenden, R. F. *Virtue in Distress: Studies in the Novel of Sentiment from Richardson to Sade*. New York: Barnes & Noble, 1974.

Britton, Andrew. "Blissing Out: The Politics of Reaganite Entertainment." *Movie* 31/32 (1986): 1–7.

Britton, Andrew, et al., eds. *American Nightmare: Essays on the Horror Film*. Toronto: Festival of Festivals, 1979.

Brophy, Phil. "Horrality—The Textuality of Contemporary Horror Films." *Screen* 27 (1986): 2–13.

Brownmiller, Susan. *Against Our Will: Men, Women, and Rape*. New York: Simon & Schuster, 1975.

Burgin, Victor, James Donald, and Cora Kaplan. *Formations of Fantasy*. London: Methuen, 1986.

Butler, Ivan. *The Horror Film*. London: Zwemmer; New York: A. S. Barnes, 1967.

Butler, Judith. "The Force of Fantasy: Feminism, Mapplethorpe, and Discursive Excess." *Differences* 2 (1990): 105–25.

———. *Gender Trouble: Feminism and the Subversion of Identity*. New York: Routledge, 1990.

Canada Council. *The Shape of Rage*. Don Mills, Ontario: Academy of Canadian Cinema; New York: New York Zoetrope, 1983.

Carroll, Noël. *The Philosophy of Horror: Or, Paradoxes of the Heart*. New York: Routledge, 1990.

———. "Toward a Theory of Film Suspense." *Persistence of Vision* 1 (1984): 65–89.

Castle, William. *Step Right Up! I'm Gonna Scare the Pants Off America*. New York: Putnam, 1978.

Christie, Ian. "The Scandal of *Peeping Tom*." In *Powell, Pressburger, and Others*, edited by Ian Christie.

———, ed. *Powell, Pressburger, and Others*. London: British Film Institute, 1978.

Clarens, Carlos. *An Illustrated History of the Horror Film*. New York: Putnam, 1967.

Clover, Carol J. "Her Body, Himself: Gender in the Slasher Film." *Representations* 20 (1987): 187–228.

Comisky, Paul, and Jennings Bryant. "Factors Involved in Generating Suspense." *Human Communication Research* 9 (1982): 49–58.

Comolli, Jean Louis. "Machines of the Visible." In *The Cinematic Apparatus*, edited by Teresa de Lauretis and Stephen Heath.

Cooper, Arnold M. "What Men Fear: The Facade of Castration Anxiety." In *The Psychology of Men*, edited by Gerald I. Fogel et al.

Craft, Christopher. " 'Kiss Me with Those Red Lips': Gender and Inversion in Bram Stoker's *Dracula.*" *Representations* 8 (1984): 107–33.

Creed, Barbara. "Horror and the Monstrous Feminine: An Imaginary Abjection." *Screen* 27 (1986): 44–70. Reprinted in *Fantasy and the Cinema*, edited by James Donald.

Cumbow, Robert C. *Order in the Universe: The Films of John Carpenter.* Metuchen, N.J.: Scarecrow Press, 1990.

de Lauretis, Teresa. *Alice Doesn't: Feminism, Semiotics, Cinema.* Bloomington: Indiana University Press, 1984.

———. *Technologies of Gender: Theories of Theory, Film, and Fiction.* Bloomington: Indiana University Press, 1987.

de Lauretis, Teresa, and Stephen Heath, eds. *The Cinematic Apparatus.* New York: St. Martin's Press, 1980.

Deleuze, Gilles. *Masochism: Coldness and Cruelty.* New York: Zone Books, 1989.

Derry, Charles. *Dark Dreams: A Psychological History of the Modern Horror Film.* London: Thomas Yoseloff, 1977.

Dickstein, Morris. "The Aesthetics of Fright." In *Planks of Reason*, edited Barry Keith Grant.

Dika, Vera. *Games of Terror: Halloween, Friday the 13th, and the Films of the Stalker Cycle.* Rutherford, N.J.: Fairleigh Dickinson University Press, 1990.

———. "The Stalker Film, 1978–81." In *American Horrors*, edited by Gregory A. Waller.

Dittmar, Linda, and Gene Michaud. *From Hanoi to Hollywood: The Vietnam War in American Film.* New Brunswick: Rutgers University Press, 1990.

Dillard, R.H.W. *Horror Films.* New York: Monarch Press, 1976.

Doane, Mary Ann. *The Desire to Desire: The Woman's Film of the 1940s.* Bloomington: Indiana University Press, 1987.

———. "Misrecognition and Identity." *Ciné-Tracts* 11 (1980): 25–32.

Doane, Mary Ann, Patricia Mellencamp, and Linda Williams, eds. In *Re-Vision: Essays in Feminist Film Criticism.* American Film Institute Monograph Series, 3. Frederick, Md.: University Publications of America, 1984.

Donald, James, ed. *Fantasy and the Cinema.* London: British Film Institute, 1989.

Douglas, Mary. *Purity and Danger: An Analysis of the Concepts of Pollution and Taboo.* 1966. London: Routledge & Kegan Paul, 1989.

Durgnat, Raymond. *Films and Feelings.* Cambridge: Massachusetts Institute of Technology Press, 1967.

Earle, William. "Revolt against Realism in the Films." *The Journal of Aesthetics and Art Criticism* 27 (1970). Reprinted in *Film Theory and Criticism*, edited by Gerald Mast and Marshall Cohen.

Ebert, Roger. "Why Movie Audiences Aren't Safe Any More." *American Film*, March 1981, pp. 54–56.

Ellis, John. *Visible Fictions: Cinema, Television, Radio.* London: Routledge and Kegan Paul, 1982.

Erens, Patricia. "The Stepfather." *Film Quarterly* 41 (1987–1988): 48–54.

———, ed. *Sexual Stratagems: The World of Women in Film.* New York: Horizon Press, 1980.

Everson, William K. *Classics of the Horror Film.* Secaucus, N.J.: Citadel Press, 1974.

Ferenczi, Sandor. "An 'Anal Hollow-Penis' in Woman." In *Further Contributions to the Theory and Technique of Psycho-Analysis,* p. 317. London: Hogarth, 1950.

Fetterley, Judith. *The Resisting Reader: A Feminist Approach to American Fiction.* Bloomington: University of Indiana Press, 1978.

Fischer, Lucy, and Marcia Landy. "*Eyes of Laura Mars*: A Binocular Critique." In *American Horrors,* edited by Gregory A. Waller.

Fogel, Gerald I. "Being a Man." In *The Psychology of Men,* edited by Gerald I. Fogel et al.

Fogel, Gerald I., Frederick M. Lane, and Robert S. Liebert, eds. *The Psychology of Men: New Psychoanalytic Perspectives.* New York: Basic Books, 1986.

Freud, Sigmund. "Anal Erotism and the Castration Complex," in "From the History of an Infantile Neurosis" (1918). *Standard Edition,* 17:1–122.

———. "Analysis of a Phobia in a Five-Year-Old Boy" (1919). *Standard Edition,* 10:1–150.

———. "Analysis Terminable and Interminable" (1937). *Standard Edition,* 23:216–53.

———. *Beyond the Pleasure Principle* (1920). *Standard Edition,* 18:1–64.

———. " 'A Child Is Being Beaten' " (1919). *Standard Edition,* 17:79–204.

———. *The Complete Letters of Sigmund Freud to Wilhelm Fliess, 1887–1904.* Edited and translated by J. Moussaieff Masson. Cambridge: Harvard University Press, 1985.

———. "The Economic Problem of Masochism" (1924). *Standard Edition,* 19:157–70.

———. *The Standard Edition of the Complete Psychological Works of Sigmund Freud.* Translated by James Strachey. London: Hogarth Press, 1986.

———. "The 'Uncanny' " (1919). *Standard Edition,* 17:219–52.

Fried, Michael. *Absorption and Theatricality: Painting and Beholding in the Age of Diderot.* Berkeley and Los Angeles: University of California Press, 1980.

Friedberg, Anne. "A Denial of Difference: Theories of Cinematic Identifications." In *Psychoanalysis and Cinema,* edited by E. Ann Kaplan.

Gabbard, Krin, and Glen O. Gabbard. *Psychiatry and the Cinema.* Chicago: University of Chicago Press, 1987.

Garber, Marjorie. "Spare Parts: The Surgical Construction of Gender." *Differences* 1 (1989): 137–59.

Garfield, Brian. *Western Films: A Complete Guide.* New York: Da Capo, 1982.

Geraghty, Christine, "Three Women's Films." *Movie* 27–28. N.d., n.p.

Giles, Dennis. "Conditions of Pleasure in Horror Cinema." In *Planks of Reason,* edited by Barry Keith Grant.

———. "Pornographic Space: The Other Place." *The 1977 Film Studies Annual: Part 2* (1977): 52–65.

Gilman, Sander, ed. *Introducing Psychoanalytic Theory*. New York: Brunner/ Mazel, 1982.

Gledhill, Christine, ed. *Home Is Where the Heart Is: Studies in Melodrama and the Woman's Film*. London: British Film Institute, 1987.

———. "Recent Developments in Feminist Criticism. *Quarterly Review of Film Studies* 3 (1978): 457–93. Reprinted in *Film Theory and Criticism*, edited by Gerald Mast and Marshall Cohen.

Gould, Stephen Jay. "The Birth of the Two-Sex World." Review of Thomas Laqueur, *Making Sex*. *The New York Review of Books* 38 (13 June 1991): 1.

Grant, Barry Keith, ed. *Planks of Reason: Essays on the Horror Film*. Metuchen, N.J.: Scarecrow Press, 1984.

Greenberg, Harvey. R. *The Movies on Your Mind*. New York: Dutton, 1975.

Greenson, Ralph R. "Dis-Identifying from Mother: Its Special Importance for the Boy." *International Journal of Psycho-Analysis* 49 (1968): 370–74.

Grosz, Elizabeth. *Sexual Subversions: Three French Feminists*. Sydney: Allen & Unwin, 1989.

Hardy, Phil. *The Encyclopedia of Horror Movies*. New York: Harper & Row, 1986.

Haskell, Molly. *From Reverence to Rape: The Treatment of Women in the Movies*. Harmondsworth, Middlesex: Penguin, 1973.

Heath, Stephen. "Difference." *Screen* 19 (1978): 59–112.

———. *Questions of Cinema*. Bloomington: Indiana University Press, 1981.

———. *The Sexual Fix*. London: Macmillan, 1982.

Hillier, Jim, and Aaron Lipstadt. *BFI Dossier No. 7: Roger Corman's New World*. London: British Film Institute, 1981.

Holland, Norman N. "I-ing Film." *Critical Inquiry* 12 (1986): 654–71.

Horkheimer, Max, and Theodor W. Adorno. *Dialectic of Enlightenment*. 1955. Translated by John Cumming. New York: Continuum, 1988.

Horney, Karen. "The Dread of Woman." In her *Feminine Psychology*, pp. 133–46. New York: Norton, 1976.

Jackson, Andrew. *Correspondence of Andrew Jackson*. Vol. 1. Edited by John Spencer Bassett. Washington, D.C.: Carnegie Institution, 1926.

Jackson, Rosemary. *Fantasy: The Literature of Subversion*. London: Methuen, 1981.

Jardine, Alice A. *Gynesis: Configurations of Woman and Modernity*. Ithaca: Cornell University Press, 1985.

Jardine, Alice, and Paul Smith, eds. *Men in Feminism*. New York: Methuen, 1987.

Jeffords, Susan. *The Remasculinization of America: Gender and the Vietnam War*. Bloomington: Indiana University Press, 1989.

Jones, Ernest. "The Early Development of Female Sexuality." *International Journal of Psycho-Analysis* 8 (1927): 459–72.

———. "Early Female Sexuality." *International Journal of Psycho-Analysis* 16 (1935): 263–73.

———. *On the Nightmare*. London: Liveright, 1971.

Kaite, Berkeley. "The Pornographic Body Double: Transgression Is the Law." In *Body Invaders: Panic Sex in America*, edited by Arthur and Marilouise Kroker.

Kaminsky, Stuart M. *American Film Genres: Approaches to a Critical Theory of Popular Film*. New York: Dell, 1977.

Kaplan, E. Ann. *Women and Film: Both Sides of the Camera*. London: Methuen, 1983.

———, ed. *Psychoanalysis and Cinema*. New York: Routledge, 1990.

Kawin, Bruce F. "*The Funhouse* and *The Howling*." In *American Horrors*, edited by Gregory A. Waller.

———. *Mindscreen: Bergman, Godard, and First-Person Film*. Princeton: Princeton University Press, 1978.

———. "The Mummy's Pool." *Dreamworks* 1 (1981): 291–301. Reprinted in *Planks of Reason*, edited by Barry Keith Grant, and *Film Theory and Criticism*, edited by Gerald Mast and Marshall Cohen.

Kennedy, Harlan. "Things That Go Howl in the Id." *Film Comment* 18 (1982): 37–39.

Kinder, Marcia, and Beverle Houston. "Seeing Is Believing: *The Exorcist* and *Don't Look Now*." In *American Horrors*, edited by Gregory A. Waller.

King, Stephen. *Danse Macabre*. New York: Berkley, 1981.

Kirby, Lynne. "Male Hysteria and Early Cinema." *Camera Obscura* 17 (1988): 112–31.

Koch, Stephen. "Fashions in Pornography: Murder as Cinematic Chic." *Harper's*, November 1976.

Koestenbaum, Wayne. *Double Talk: The Erotics of Male Literary Collaboration*. New York: Routledge, 1989.

———. "Privileging the Anus: Anna O. and the Collaborative Origin of Psychoanalysis." *Genders* 3 (1988): 57–81. Reprinted in his *Double Talk*.

Kracauer, Siegfried. *Theory of Film: Redemption of Physical Reality*. London: Oxford University Press, 1960.

Kroker, Arthur, and Marilouise Kroker, eds. *Body Invaders: Panic Sex in America*. New York: St. Martin's Press, 1987.

Lane, Frederick M. "The Genital Envy Complex: A Case of a Man with a Fantasied Vulva." In *The Psychology of Men*, edited by Gerald I. Fogel et al.

Laplanche, Jean. *Life and Death in Psychoanalysis*. Translated by Jeffrey Mehlman. Baltimore: The Johns Hopkins University Press, 1976.

Laplanche, Jean, and J.-B. Pontalis. "Fantasy and the Origins of Sexuality." *International Journal of Psycho-Analysis* 49 (1968):1–18. Reprinted in *Formations of Fantasy*, edited by Victor Burgin et al.

———. *The Language of Psycho-Analysis*. Translated by Donald Nicholson-Smith. New York: Norton, 1973.

Laqueur, Thomas. *Making Sex: Body and Gender from the Greeks to Freud*. Cambridge: Harvard University Press, 1990.

Laxdaela Saga. Translated by Magnus Magnusson and Hermann Palsson. Harmondsworth, Middlesex: Penguin, 1969.

Lenne, Gérard. "Monster and Victim: Women in the Horror Film." In *Sexual Stratagems*, edited by Patricia Erens.

Levine, Lawrence W. *Highbrow/Lowbrow: The Emergence of Cultural Hierarchy in America*. Cambridge: Harvard University Press, 1988.

Lévi-Strauss, Claude. "Structure and Form: Reflections of a Work by Vladimir Propp." In Vladimir Propp, *Theory and History of Folklore*.

Loraux, Nicole. *Tragic Ways of Killing a Woman*. Cambridge: Harvard University Press, 1987.

Lotman, Jurij. "The Origin of Plot in the Light of Typology." 1973. *Poetics Today* 1 (1979): 161–84.

McCarthy, Todd. "Trick or Treat." *Film Comment* 16 (1980): 17–24.

McCarty, John. *Psychos: Eighty Years of Mad Movies, Maniacs, and Murderous Deeds*. New York: St. Martin's, 1986.

———. *Splatter Movies*. New York: St. Martin's, 1981.

Maclean, Ian. *The Renaissance Notion of Woman*. Cambridge: Cambridge University Press, 1980.

Maltin, Leonard. *TV Movies and Video Guide: 1990 Edition*. New York: Signet, 1990.

Marcus, Steven. *The Other Victorians: A Study of Sexuality and Pornography in Mid-Nineteenth-Century England*. New York: Basic Books, 1964.

Martin, Mick, and Marsha Porter. *Video Movie Guide: 1987*. New York: Ballantine, 1986.

Marshall, David. *The Surprising Effects of Sympathy: Marivaux, Diderot, Rousseau, and Mary Shelley*. Chicago: University of Chicago Press, 1988.

Mast, Gerald, and Marshall Cohen, eds. *Film Theory and Criticism: Introductory Readings*. 3d ed. New York: Oxford University Press, 1985.

Mayer, Elizabeth B. "Everybody Must Be Just Like Me: Observations on Female Castration Anxiety." *International Journal of Psychoanalysis* 66 (1985): 331–47.

Meltzer, Françoise. "The Uncanny Rendered Canny: Freud's Blind Spot in Reading Hoffman's 'Sandman.' " In *Introducing Psychoanalytic Theory*, edited by Sander L. Gilman.

Metz, Christian. *The Imaginary Signifier: Psychoanalysis and the Cinema*. Bloomington: Indiana University Press, 1982.

Michaels, Walter. "Romance and Real Estate." *Raritan* 2 (1983). Reprinted in his *The Gold Standard and the Logic of Naturalism: American Literature at the Turn of the Century*, pp. 86–112. Berkeley and Los Angeles: University of California Press, 1987.

Modleski, Tania. "A Father Is Being Beaten: Male Feminism and the War Film." *Discourse* 10 (1988): 62–77.

———. "The Terror of Pleasure: The Contemporary Horror Film and Postmodern Theory." In *Studies in Entertainment*, edited by Tania Modleski.

———. "Three Men and Baby M." *Camera Obscura* 17 (1988): 69–81.

———. *The Women Who Knew Too Much: Hitchcock and Feminist Film Theory*. New York: Methuen, 1988.

———, ed. *Studies in Entertainment: Critical Approaches to Mass Culture*. Bloomington: Indiana University Press, 1986.

Montrelay, Michele. "Inquiry into Femininity." *m/f* 1 (1978): 83–101. Translated from "Recherches sur la fémininité," in *L'Ombre et le nom*. Paris: Éditions de Minuit, 1977.

Moretti, Franco. "The Dialectic of Fear." *New Left Review* 136 (1982): 67–85.

Mulvey, Laura. "Afterthoughts on 'Visual Pleasure and Narrative Cinema' Inspired by King Vidor's *Duel in the Sun* (1946)." *Framework* 15–17 (1981): 12–15. Reprinted in her *Visual and Other Pleasures.*

———. "Changes: Thoughts on Myth, Narrative and Historical Experience." 1985. *History Workshop Journal* 23 (1987): 3–19. Reprinted in her *Visual and Other Pleasures.*

———. *Visual and Other Pleasures.* Bloomington: Indiana University Press, 1981.

———. "Visual Pleasure and Narrative Cinema. *Screen* 16 (1975): 6–18. Reprinted (among other places) in her *Visual and Other Pleasures* and in *Film Theory and Criticism,* edited by Gerald Mast and Marshall Cohen.

Naifeh, Steven, and Gregory White Smith. *Why Can't Men Open Up?* New York: Warner, 1984.

Nash, Mark. "*Vampyr* and the Fantastic." *Screen* 17 (1976): 29–67.

Neale, Steve. "*Halloween*: Suspense, Aggression, and the Look." *Framework* 14 (1981): 25–29. Reprinted in *Planks of Reason,* edited by Barry Keith Grant.

Newfield, Christopher. "The Politics of Male Suffering: Masochism and Hegemony in the American Renaissance." *Differences* 1 (1989): 55–87.

Newman, Kim. *Nightmare Movies.* New York: Harmony Books, 1989.

Nichols, Bill, ed. *Movies and Methods.* Vol. 2. Berkeley and Los Angeles: University of California Press, 1985.

Orgel, Stephen. "Nobody's Perfect: Or Why Did the English Stage Take Boys for Women?" *South Atlantic Quarterly* 88 (1989): 7–29.

Pateman, Carole. *The Sexual Contract.* Stanford: Stanford University Press, 1988.

Peary, Danny. *Cult Movies: The Classics, the Sleepers, the Weird, and the Wonderful.* New York: Dell, 1981.

———. *Cult Movies 2.* New York: Dell, 1983.

Perkins, William. *Film as Film.* Harmondsworth, Middlesex: Penguin, 1972.

Person, Ethel S. "The Omni-Available Woman and Lesbian Sex: Two Fantasy Themes and Their Relationship to the Male Developmental Experience." In *The Psychology of Men,* edited by Gerald I. Fogel et al.

Pevere, Geoff. "Cronenberg Tackles Dominant Videology." In *The Shape of Rage,* edited by Canada Council.

Plaza, Monique. "Our Costs and Their Benefits." *m/f* 4 (1980): 28–39.

Poe, Edgar Allan. "The Philosophy of Composition." In *Great Short Works of Edgar Allan Poe,* edited by G. R. Thompson. New York: Literary Classics of the United States, 1970.

Pollitt, Katha. "Violence in a Man's World." *New York Times Magazine,* 17 June 1989, pp. 16–18.

Prawer, S. S. *Caligari's Children: The Film as Tale of Terror.* Oxford: Oxford University Press, 1980.

Propp, Vladimir. *Theory and History of Folklore.* Edited by Anatoly Liberman. Translated by Ariadna Y. Martin and Richard P. Martin. Minneapolis: University of Minnesota Press, 1984.

Rangell, Leo. "The Interchangeability of Phallus and Female Genital." *Journal of the American Psychoanalytic Association* 1 (1953): 504–9.

Reik, Theodor. *Masochism in Modern Man.* New York: Grove Press, 1981.

Rodowick, D. N. "The Difficulty of Difference." *Wide Angle* 15 (1982): 4–15.

———. "The Enemy Within: The Economy of Violence in *The Hills Have Eyes.*" In *Planks of Reason,* edited by Barry Keith Grant.

Rogin, Michael. "Kiss Me Deadly: Communism, Motherhood, and Cold War Memories." *Representations* 6 (1984): 1–36. Reprinted in his *Ronald Reagan, The Movie.*

———. "Liberal Society and the Indian Question." *Politics and Society* 1 (1971). Reprinted in his *Ronald Reagan, The Movie.*

———. *Ronald Reagan, The Movie; And Other Episodes in Political Demonology.* Berkeley and Los Angeles: University of California Press, 1987.

Rohter, Larry. "The Third Woman of 'Thelma and Louise.' " *New York Times,* 5 June 1991, C21–24.

Rose, Jacqueline. "Paranoia and the Film System." *Screen* 17 (1976–1977): 85–104.

Ross, John Munder. "Beyond the Phallic Illusion: Notes on Man's Heterosexuality." In *The Psychology of Men,* edited by Gerald I. Fogel et al.

Rothman, William. *Hitchcock: The Murderous Gaze.* Cambridge: Harvard University Press, 1982.

Rubin, Gayle. "Thinking Sex: Notes for a Radical Theory of the Politics of Sexuality." In *Pleasure and Danger,* edited by Carole S. Vance.

Ryan, Michael, and Douglas Kellner. *Camera Politica: The Politics and Ideology of Contemporary Hollywood Film.* Bloomington: Indiana University Press, 1988.

Schafer, Roy. "Men Who Struggle against Sentimentality." In *The Psychology of Men,* edited by Gerald I. Fogel et al.

Schechter, Harold. *The Bosom Serpent: Folklore and Popular Art.* Iowa City: University of Iowa Press, 1988.

Schoell, William. *Stay Out of the Shower: Twenty-five Years of Shocker Films Beginning with Psycho.* New York: Dembner, 1985.

Sedgwick, Eve Kosofsky. *Between Men: English Literature and Homosocial Desire.* New York: Columbia University Press, 1985.

Segal, Lynne. *Slow Motion: Changing Masculinities, Changing Men.* New Brunswick, N.J.: Rutgers University Press, 1990.

Sharrett, Christopher. "The Idea of Apocalypse in *The Texas Chainsaw Massacre.*" In *Planks of Reason,* edited by Barry Keith Grant.

Shoales, Ian. "Virtual Banality." *Image. Sunday Examiner,* 28 April 1991.

Showalter, Elaine. "Critical Cross-Dressing: Male Feminists and the Woman of the Year." *Raritan* 3 (1983): 130–49. Reprinted in *Men in Feminism,* edited by Alice Jardine and Paul Smith.

Silverman, Kaja. *The Acoustic Mirror: The Female Voice in Psychoanalysis and Cinema.* Bloomington: Indiana University Press, 1988.

———. "Fassbinder and Lacan: A Reconsideration of Gaze, Look, and Image." *Camera Obscura* 19 (1989): 54–85.

Silverman, Kaja. "Fragments of a Fashionable Discourse." In *Studies in Entertainment*, edited by Tania Modleski.

———. "Masochism and Male Subjectivity." *Camera Obscura* 17 (1988): 30–67.

———. "Masochism and Subjectivity." *Framework* 12 (1980): 2–9.

———. *The Subject of Semiotics*. New York and London: Oxford University Press, 1983.

———. "Too Early/Too Late: Subjectivity and the Primal Scene in Henry James." *Novel* 21 (1988): 147–73.

———. "White Skin, Brown Masks: The Double Mimesis, or With Lawrence in Arabia." *Differences* 1 (1989): 3–54.

Slotkin, Richard. *Regeneration through Violence: The Mythology of the American Frontier, 1600–1860*. Middletown, Conn.: Wesleyan University Press, 1973.

Smith, Paul. "Action Movie Hysteria, or Eastwood Bound." *Differences* 1 (1989): 88–107.

———. "Vas." *Camera Obscura* 17 (1988): 89–111.

Sobchack, Vivian. "Bringing It All Back Home: Family Economy and Generic Exchange." In *American Horrors*, edited by Gregory A. Waller.

———. "Child/Alien/Father: Patriarchal Crisis and Generic Exchange." *Camera Obscura* 15 (1986): 7–34.

Soble, Alan. *Pornography: Marxism, Feminism, and the Future of Sexuality*. New Haven: Yale University Press, 1986.

Sontag, Susan. *On Photography*. New York: Farrar, Straus and Giroux, 1977.

Soren, David. *The Rise and Fall of the Horror Film: An Art Historical Approach to Fantasy Cinema*. Columbia, Mo.: Lucas, 1977.

Spoto, Donald. *The Dark Side of Genius: The Life of Alfred Hitchcock*. New York: Ballantine, 1983.

Stade, George. "Dracula's Women, and Why Men Love to Hate Them." In *The Psychology of Men*, edited by Gerald I. Fogel et al.

Staples, Robert. "Commentary." In *United States of America vs. Sex*, edited by Philip Nobile and Eric Nadler. New York: Minotaur Press, 1985.

Starr, Marco. "J. Hills Is Alive: A Defence of *I Spit on Your Grave*." In *The Video Nasties*, edited by Martin Barker.

Stein, Elliott. "A Very Tender Film, A Very Nice One." *Film Comment* 15 (1979): 57–59.

Stern, Lesley. "Point of View: The Blind Spot." *Film Reader* 4 (1979): 214–36.

Studlar, Gaylyn. *In the Realm of Pleasure: Von Sternberg, Dietrich, and the Masochistic Aesthetic*. Urbana: University of Illinois Press, 1988.

Studlar, Gaylyn, and David Desser. "Never Having to Say You're Sorry: Rambo's Rewriting of the Vietnam War." In *From Hanoi to Hollywood*, edited by Linda Dittmar and Gene Michaud.

Telotte, J. P. "Faith and Idolatry in the Horror Film." *Literature/Film Quarterly* 8 (1980): 143–55. Reprinted in *Planks of Reason*, edited by Barry Keith Grant.

———. "Through a Pumpkin's Eye: The Reflexive Nature of Horror." In *American Horrors*, edited by Gregory A. Waller.

Todorov, Tzvetan. *The Fantastic: A Structural Approach to a Literary Genre*. Translated by R. Howard. Ithaca: Cornell University Press, 1973.

Trillin, Calvin. "American Chronicles: The Life and Times of Joe Bob Briggs, So Far." *New Yorker*, 22 December 1986, pp. 73–88.

Tudor, Andrew. *Monsters and Mad Scientists: A Cultural History of the Horror Movie.* Oxford: Blackwell, 1989.

Twitchell, James B. *Dreadful Pleasures: An Anatomy of Modern Horror.* New York and Oxford: Oxford University Press, 1985.

———. *Forbidden Partners: The Incest Taboo in Modern Culture.* New York: Columbia University Press, 1987.

———. *Preposterous Violence: Fables of Aggression in Modern Culture.* Oxford and New York: Oxford University Press, 1989.

Vale, V., and Andrea Juno, eds. *Incredibly Strange Films. Re/Search* 10 (1986).

Vance, Carole S., ed. *Pleasure and Danger: Exploring Female Sexuality.* Boston: Routledge and Kegan Paul.

Waller, Gregory A., ed. *American Horrors: Essays on the Modern American Horror Film.* Urbana: University of Illinois Press, 1987.

Watney, Simon. *Policing Desire: Pornography, AIDS, and the Media.* Minneapolis: University of Minnesota Press, 1987.

Weldon, Michael. *The Psychotronic Encyclopedia of Film.* New York: Ballantine, 1983.

White, Dennis L. "The Poetics of Horror." *Cinema Journal* 10 (1971): 1–18.

Williams, Linda. *Hard Core: Power, Pleasure, and the "Frenzy of the Visible."* Berkeley and Los Angeles: University of California Press, 1989.

———. "Power, Pleasure, and Perversion: Sadomasochistic Film Pornography." *Representations* 27 (1989): 37–65. Expanded version of chapter 7 of her *Hard Core*.

———. " 'Something Else besides a Mother': *Stella Dallas* and the Maternal Melodrama." *Cinema Journal* 24 (1984): 2–27. Reprinted in *Home Is Where the Heart Is*, edited by Christine Gledhill.

———. "When the Woman Looks." In *Re-Vision: Essays in Feminist Film Criticism*, edited by Mary Ann Doane, Patricia Mellencamp, and Linda Williams.

Wood, Robin. "Beauty Bests the Beast." *American Film* 8 (1983): 63–65.

———. "Gods and Monsters." *Film Comment* 14 (1978): 19–25.

———. "An Introduction to the American Horror Film." In *American Nightmare: Essays on the Horror Film*, edited by Andrew Britton et al. Reprinted in *Movies and Methods*, vol. 2, edited by Bill Nichols.

———. "Neglected Nightmares." *Film Comment* 16 (1980): 25–28.

———. "Return of the Repressed." *Film Comment* 14 (1978): 25–32.

INDEX